MyMaths

for Key Stage 3

1A

Powered by MyMaths.co.uk

OXFORD
UNIVERSITY PRESS

Great Clarendon Street, Oxford, OX2 6DP, United Kingdom

Oxford University Press is a department of the University of Oxford. It furthers the University's objective of excellence in research, scholarship, and education by publishing worldwide. Oxford is a registered trade mark of Oxford University Press in the UK and in certain other countries

First published in 2014

British Library Cataloguing in Publication Data
Data available

978-0-19-830447-0

10 9 8 7 6 5 4 3 2 1

Paper used in the production of this book is a natural, recyclable product made from wood grown in sustainable forests. The manufacturing process conforms to the environmental regulations of the country of origin.

Printed in Great Britain

MIX
Paper from responsible sources
FSC
www.fsc.org   FSC® C007785

Acknowledgements

Although we have made every effort to trace and contact copyright holders before publication this has not been possible in all cases. If notified, the publisher will rectify any errors or omissions at the earliest opportunity.

p2-3: Simon Balson/Alamy; **p9**: Getty Images; **p13**: (r) LiliGraphie/Shutterstock; **p24–25**: Frank Ramspot/ Getty Images; **p32**: (b) Sergieiev/Shutterstock; **p34**: mrmichaelangelo/Shutterstock; **p36**: elgol/iStockphoto; **p44–45**: The Art Archive/Alamy; **p56**: (tl) iordani/ Shutterstock; **p57**: (b) eyedear/Shutterstock; **p68**: Andreykuzmin/Dreamstime; **p75**: (b) vita khorzhevska/ Shutterstock; **p88–89**: Thinkstock/OUP; **p90**: Vladitto/ Shutterstock; **p97**: Debu55y/Shutterstock; **p101**: Sergioboccardo/Dreamstime; **p103**: LVV/Shutterstock; **p105**: Pavel Ilyukhin/Shutterstock; **p110–111**: Carol & Mike Werner/Visuals Unlimited, Inc/Science Photo Library; **p114**: CBW/Alamy; **p128–129**: Ian McKinnell/Taxi/Getty Images; **p135**: Ti Santi/Shutterstock; **p142–143**: Iain Sarjeant/Alamy; **p145**: Dhoxax/Shutterstock; **p148**: (t) Thomas Fredriksen/Shutterstock, (b) HandmadePictures/ Shutterstock; **p153**: Monkey Business Images/Shutterstock; **p158**: (t) ValeStock/Shutterstock; **p161**: (t) Toronto Star via Getty Images; **p170–171**: Bettina Strenske/Glow Images; **p172**: Niserin/Dreamstime; **p179**: Aleksandar Mijatovic/ Shutterstock; **p180**: ilbusca/iStockphoto; **p188–189**: Fotomatador/Alamy; **p192**: (t) Mmaxer/Shutterstock; **p197**: British Museum; **p198**: Narmi81/Dreamstime; **p199**: (l) Olivier Meerson/Dreamstime, (r) dotshock/Shutterstock; **p204–205**: PC Plus Magazine/Future/Getty Images; **p213**: Snr/Dreamstime; **p218–219**: Mira/Imagebroker/Glow Images; **p220**: (l) WendellandCarolyn/iStockphoto, (r) Dan Breckwoldt/Shutterstock; **p225**: Le Do/Shutterstock; **p230**: JERRY LODRIGUSS/SCIENCE PHOTO LIBRARY; **p233**: Mario7/ Shutterstock; **p242–243**: European Space Agency/Science Photo Library; **p245**: Domofon/iStockphoto; **p249**: ANGEL FITOR/SCIENCE PHOTO LIBRARY; **p256–257**: Gallo Images/ Alamy; **p259**: James Boardman/iStockphoto; **p267**: OUP; **p272**: (t) Karen Roach/Shutterstock; **p277**: Marcio Jose Bastos Silva/Shutterstock; **p280–281**: homydesign/Bigstock; **p282**: oksix/Shutterstock; **p287**: (b) Bikeworldtravel/ Shutterstock.com; **p288**: (tr) cjp/iStockphoto, (tl) Luigi Roscia/Dreamstime, (tl) Brad Calkins/Dreamstime, (tl) epicurean/iStockphoto, (tl) Redchanka/Shutterstock, (tl) Olivier Le Queinec/Shutterstock; **p294–295**: Leafedge/ Istockphoto; **p296**: (b) NASA; **p301**: mattjeacock/ iStockphoto

Case Studies:
Eddie Brady/Getty Images; Fernando Soares/Dreamstime; Sarah Van DerHeijden/Dreamstime; Anatoliy Samara/ Dreamstime; Carl Coffman/Dreamstime; Jon Helgason/ Dreamstime.

Artwork by; Phil Hackett, Erwin Haya, Paul Hostetler, Dusan Pavlic, Giulia Rivolta, Katri Valkamo & QBS.

Contents

MyMaths.co.uk

About this book

MyMaths for Key Stage 3 is an exciting new series designed for schools following the new National Curriculum for mathematics. This book has been written to help you to grow your mathematical knowledge and skills during Key Stage 3.

Each topic starts with an Introduction that shows why it is relevant to real life and includes a short *Check in* exercise to see if you are ready to start the topic.

Inside each chapter, you will find lots of worked examples and questions for you to try along with interesting facts. There's basic practice to build your confidence, as well as problem solving. You might also notice the **4-digit codes** at the bottom of the page, which you can type into the search bar on the *MyMaths* site to take you straight to the relevant *MyMaths* lesson for more help in understanding and extra practice.

At the end of each chapter you will find *MySummary*, which tests what you've learned and suggests what you could try next to improve your skills even further. The *What next?* box details further resources available in the supporting online products.

Maths is a vitally important subject, not just for you while you are at school but also for when you grow up. We hope that this book will lead to a greater enjoyment of the subject and that it will help you to realise how useful maths is to your everyday life.

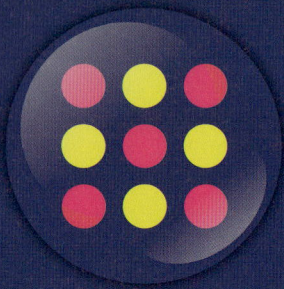

1 Whole numbers and decimals

Introduction

How do you write nothing? With a zero of course, but the idea of using zero as a number didn't always exist. Indian mathematicians in the 9th century were the first to use zero both as a number and a placeholder. From India the idea travelled to Arabic and Chinese mathematicians, finally reaching Europe in the 13th century.

Nowadays we use zero everywhere, for example the Prime Meridian in geography, which allows the eastern and western hemispheres to be defined.

What's the point?

Using a zero as a placeholder allows you to write any number, however large or small, using just the digits 0 to 9.

Objectives

By the end of this chapter, you will have learned how to …

- Use place value and decimal notation in different contexts, including money.
- Compare and order whole numbers.
- Add decimals using mental and written methods.
- Understand and order negative numbers in the context of temperature.
- Round a number to the nearest 10, 100 or 1000.
- Use an estimate to check a result.
- Use the order of operations.

Check in

1 Write these numbers in order from smallest to largest.

    a 6, 8, 4, 7, 5   **b** 12, 10, 14, 13, 11

2 Copy and complete these sums without using a calculator.

    a $7 + 3 = \square$ **b** $5 + 9 = \square$

    c $8 + \square = 12$ **d** $\square + 6 = 10$

3 To the right is a plan of an underground car park.

Each 'level' is given a number.

What level is marked by the letter '**a**'?

Level 1
Level *a*
Level -1

Starter problem

At Notatall School the maths teacher Mr Ceero chooses a secret number and writes it down on a piece of paper. He tells the class that his number lies between 0 and 1000. The class have to guess his number and after each guess Mr Ceero tells them if their guess was too high or too low.

He tells them they can find the answer in just 10 guesses.

Investigate.

1a Place value

The number **235** can be split into

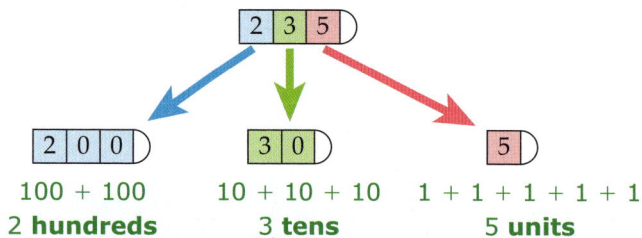

p.130 >

2	3	5

2	0	0		3	0		5

100 + 100   10 + 10 + 10   1 + 1 + 1 + 1 + 1

2 hundreds   **3 tens**   **5 units**

The number **2435** can be split into

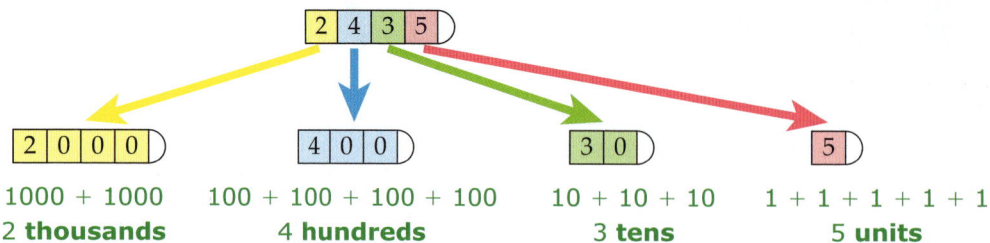

2	4	3	5

p.262, 266 >

2	0	0	0

4	0	0

3	0

5

1000 + 1000   100 + 100 + 100 + 100   10 + 10 + 10   1 + 1 + 1 + 1 + 1

2 thousands   **4 hundreds**   **3 tens**   **5 units**

> Any number can be split into hundreds, tens, units and so on.

⬤ The value of each **digit** in a number is called its **place value**.

If you write the digits in a different order, you get different values.

Thousands 1000s	Hundreds 100s	Tens 10s	Units 1s
5	4	3	2
4	3	2	5
3	2	5	4
2	5	4	3

Five thousand, four hundred and thirty-**two** ⟶

Four thousand, three hundred and **twenty**-five ⟶

Three thousand, **two hundred** and fifty-four ⟶

Two thousand, five hundred and forty-three ⟶

Example

What does the digit 8 stand for in each of these numbers?

a   148   **b**   8305   **c**   80

a   8 units
b   8 thousands
c   8 tens

Thousands	Hundreds	Tens	Units
	1	4	⑧
⑧	3	0	5
		⑧	0

Exercise 1a

1 Split these numbers into hundreds, tens, and units. Part **a** is done for you.

a 347

| 3 | 4 | 7 |

→ 1 + 1 + 1 + 1 + 1 + 1 + 1
→ 10 + 10 + 10 + 10
→ 100 + 100 + 100

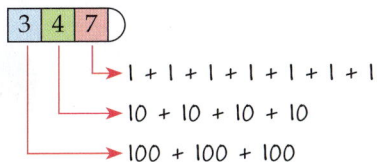

b 123   **c** 852   **d** 234   **e** 727

2 Split these numbers into thousands, hundreds, tens, and units.

a 2324

| 2 | 3 | 2 | 4 |

→ 1 + 1 + 1 + 1
→ 10 + 10
→ 100 + 100 + 100
→ 1000 + 1000

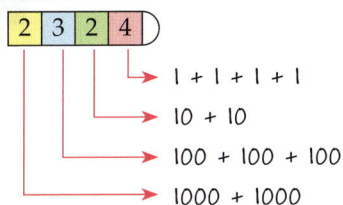

b 1354   **c** 3246   **d** 2515   **e** 2408

3 What does the red digit stand for in each number?

a 164   **b** 4927   **c** 3587   **d** 605
e 5288   **f** 1110   **g** 3621   **h** 2243

4 What does each digit stand for in these numbers?

a 72   **b** 123   **c** 7206   **d** 4642

5 Jez has three number cards.

| 4 | 8 | 2 |

Using all three cards make
a the smallest number you can
b the largest number you can
c a number that is between the largest and smallest.

Problem solving

6 Here are the targets from a paintball competition.
   a Work out the score of the
      i red team
      ii yellow team
      iii purple team
      iv green team.

   b Kirsty had six shots. She says:
      'I scored a ten, then a hundred, a one, another hundred, and a ten.'
      What was Kirsty's total score?
   c How many of Kirsty's shots missed the target?

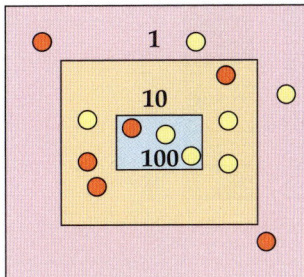

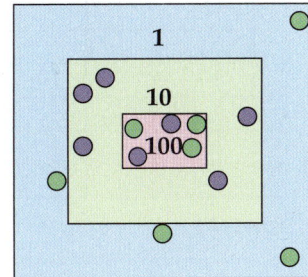

7 Using all three cards make as many different numbers as you can.

| 7 | 3 | 8 |

Write out the numbers you make in order, smallest to largest.

8 How many different 3-digit numbers can you make from these four digits: 5, 2, 0 and 7?

1b Ordering whole numbers

Tyler is **sorting** these numbered cards.

He is putting the cards into **order**.

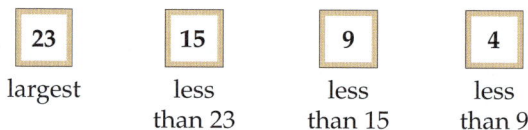

23	15	9	4
largest	less than 23	less than 15	less than 9

I start with the largest number.

⬤ > means **greater than**.

9 is greater than 4.
9 > 4

⬤ < means **less than**.

15 is less than 23.
15 < 23

Example

Which is bigger, 124 or 82?

Here is `1 2 4`   Here is `8 2`

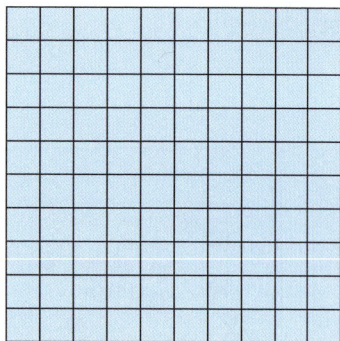
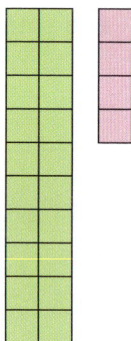
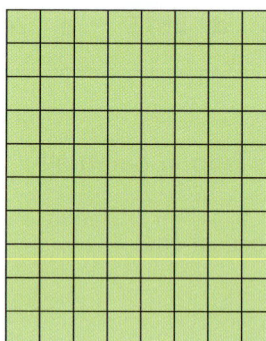

124 > 82.

Example

Sort the family in order by height
a   starting with the shortest
b   starting with the tallest.

135 cm   172 cm   158 cm   148 cm   183 cm   155 cm

a   135 cm is the shortest, so start with 135.
    135   148   155   158   172   183
b   183 cm is the tallest, so start with 183.
    183   172   158   155   148   135

Exercise 1b

1 Use the greater than (>) and less than
  (<) symbols to complete these statements.
  a 9 ☐ 5   **b** 8 ☐ 14
  c 16 ☐ 25   **d** 38 ☐ 83
  e 101 ☐ 98   **f** 210 ☐ 187

2 Copy and complete the sentence using
  each set of numbers.
  _____ is greater than _____ but less
  than _____.
  a 9 2 5   **b** 28 31 16
  c 103 86 102   **d** 17 0 9

3 **a** Write these numbers in order.
      Start with the smallest number.
      i 7, 5, 8 , 4 , 6
      ii 9, 12, 10, 8, 11
      iii 34, 31, 33, 32, 35
      iv 22, 19, 20, 18, 21
      v 91, 90, 88, 92, 89
      vi 101, 99, 98, 102, 100
      vii 237, 235, 234, 238, 236
      viii 998, 1000, 996, 999, 997
  b Now write out the numbers in part **a**
      starting with the largest number.

Problem solving

4 Jim the postman sorts letters by house
  number before he delivers them.
  Write these numbers out in order,
  starting with the smallest.

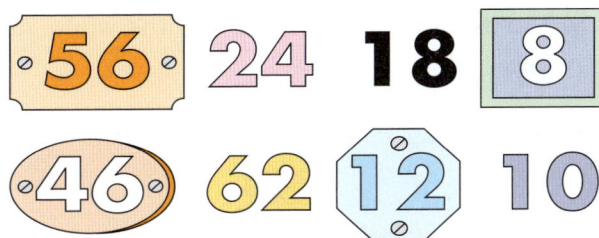

  56 24 18 8
  46 62 12 10

5 Jim the postman sorts these
  parcels by weight.
  Write the weights out in order,
  starting with the largest.

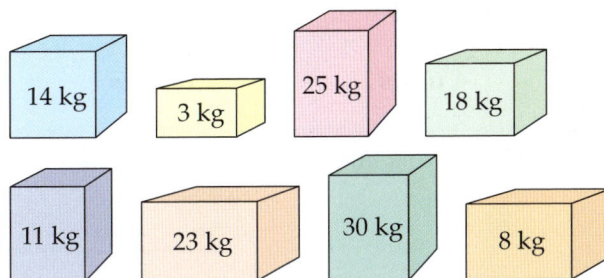

  14 kg 3 kg 25 kg 18 kg
  11 kg 23 kg 30 kg 8 kg

6 Kelly writes the heights of five students
  on cards. But then she drops the cards
  and mixes them up.

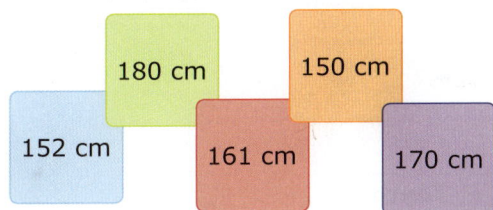

  180 cm 150 cm
  152 cm 161 cm 170 cm

  Clues: Raj is the tallest.
  Kelly is 10cm shorter than Raj.
  Nita is the shortest.
  James is taller than Ian.

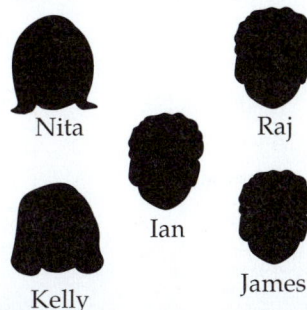

  Nita Raj Ian Kelly James

  a Use the clues to help Kelly work out each student's height.
  b Write out the name and height of each student in order,
      starting with the shortest.

MyMaths.co.uk   1217   SEARCH

7

You can zoom in on a number line.

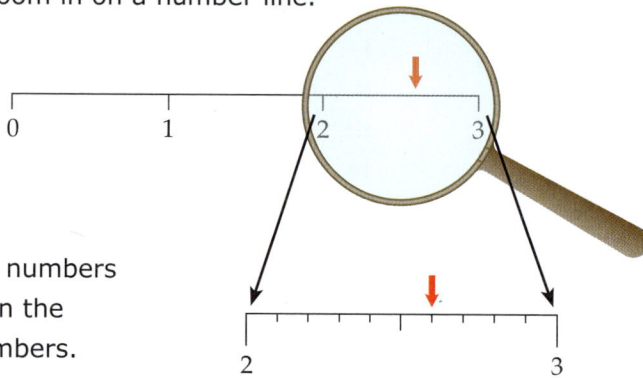

This is a decimal number. You say, "Two **point** six."

There are numbers in between the whole numbers.

Each part is one **tenth**.
The arrow is pointing at 2.6, is **2** units and **6** tenths.

p.76 > ● The **decimal point** separates the whole number part from the decimal part.

The number **4.2** can be split into

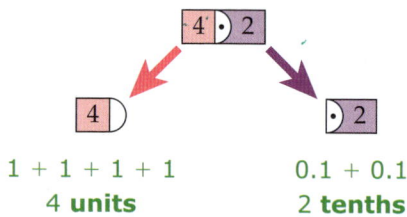

4 . 2

4

. 2

$1 + 1 + 1 + 1$
4 units

$0.1 + 0.1$
2 tenths

The dot is the decimal point.

Example

How long is this line?

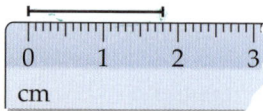

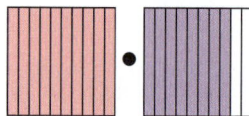

0   1   2   3
cm

1 unit + 8 tenths

The line is 1.8 cm long.

Example

What does the digit 2 stand for in each of these numbers?

a 12.1   **b** 23.5   **c** 0.2

a 2 units
b 2 tens or twenty
c 2 tenths

Tens	Units	•	Tenths
1	②	•	1
②	3	•	5
	0	•	②

If there are no units, you need to insert a 0 to hold the space.

Exercise 1c

1 What numbers do these show?

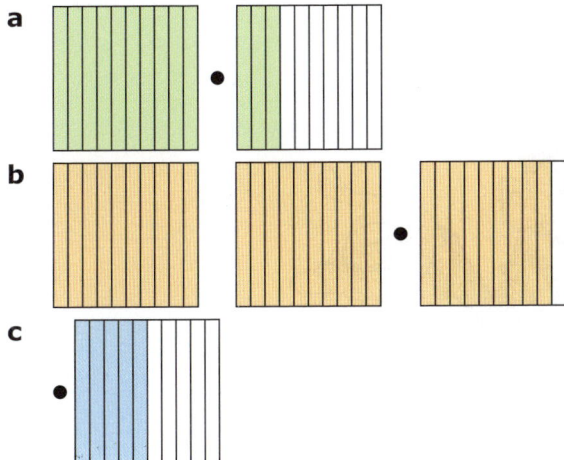

a

b

c

2 What does the red digit stand for in each number?

a 6.4   **b** 4.9   **c** 358.7   **d** 6.0

e 28.5   **f** 123.5   **g** 621.4   **h** 343.3

3 What decimal lengths are shown on this ruler?

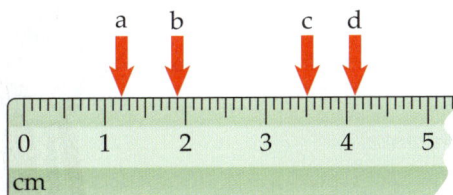

4 Use the number line to decide which is greater. Use < or > in each box.

a 2.3 ☐< 3.2   **b** 3.1 ☐ 2.9

c 5.3 ☐ 6.1   **d** 4.0 ☐ 3.8

e 3.8 ☐ 4.2   **f** 5.0 ☐ 4.9

g 3.0 ☐ 0.4   **h** 0.7 ☐ 0.9

5 Write the numbers in a copy of the grid.

a Ten point six

b Twenty-four point three

c Sixty-two point eight

d One hundred and nineteen point seven

e Six hundred and four point three

f Seven thousand and eighty five point one

Thousands 1000s	Hundreds 100s	Tens 10s	Units 1s	•	Tenths $\frac{1}{10}$s
				•	
				•	
				•	
				•	
				•	
				•	

Problem solving

6 Liam finishes his sailing course in 3.5 hours. Here are the other sailors' times:

Anna   2.3 hours

Peter   3.7 hours

Thomas   2.9 hours

Lara   2.2 hours

Put the times in order.

In what position does Liam finish?

7 An ice lolly costs £1.10.

You have 94 × 1p coins and 3 × 5p coins.

Do you have enough money to buy the ice lolly?

Did you know?

◀ Sir Ben Ainslie won his fourth sailing gold medal for the UK at the 2012 Olympic Games in London.

Gaz shares £1 equally between two charities.

£0.50 + £0.50 = £1.00

50p = £0.50

Gaz shares another £1 between 10 charities.
How much does each charity get?

p.130 >

| 0 | £0.10 | £0.20 | £0.30 | £0.40 | £0.50 | £0.60 | £0.70 | £0.80 | £0.90 | £1.00 |

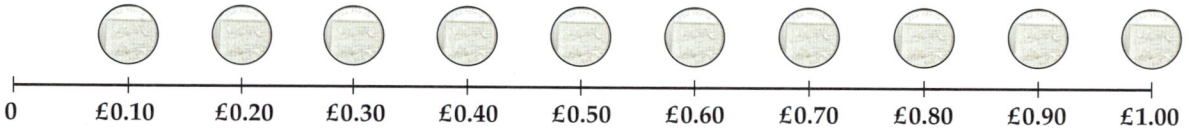

£1.00 divided by 10 is £0.10.
Each charity gets a **tenth** of the pound.

£0.10 = 10p
£0.10 is one-tenth of a pound.

⬤ You can **add** decimals, but make sure you keep the decimal
points lined up.

Example

Write each amount as a decimal number.

a

b

a   Add   0.10   10p = £0.10
              0.10
           + 0.10   Line up the decimal
           _____
            £0.30   points!

b   Add   0.50   50p = £0.50
              0.20   20p = £0.20
              0.20
           + 0.10
           _____
            £1.00   The decimals add to a whole number.

You should be able to convert between pounds and pence.

£1.50 = 150p

382p = £3.82

Exercise 1d

1 Write each of these amounts as a decimal.
  a ten pence   **b** twenty pence
  c fifty pence   **d** eighty pence

2 Write each amount as a decimal number.
  a   **b**

  c   **d**

3 What amounts are shown on this scale?

4 Use the number line on page 10 to help you add these amounts.
  a £0.10 + £0.30   **b** £0.40 + £0.50
  c £0.20 + £0.70   **d** £0.50 + £0.50
  e £0.20 + £0.80   **f** £0.40 + £0.40

5 Use these coins, to make up each amount.
How many ways can you find?
The first is done for you.
  a £0.30 → 10p + 10p + 10p OR 20p + 10p
  b £0.70   **c** £0.40
  d £0.80   **e** £0.60

Problem solving

6 Mika has £1. He buys a set of stickers for 20p, a pen for 30p and a banana for 40p. Will he have any change? How much?

7 Stuart's bus driver does not give change to customers.
  a How can Stuart make his £0.80 fare exactly with these coins?

  b Find at least one other way.

8 Floria has a bag containing 73 one pence pieces and 41 two pence pieces. She wants to change it into a smaller number of coins. What is the smallest number of coins that Floria can be given in return?

9 Spot the odd one out:
  8 pounds and fifty pence   £8.5   8 pounds and 5 pence   850p

10 What are the fewest number of coins that you need to make these amounts? The first one is done for you.
  a 46p   4 coins, 20p + 20p + 5p + 1p
  b 73p   **c** 19p   **d** 107p   **e** 36p   **f** 69p

1e Adding decimals

Where is the arrow pointing?

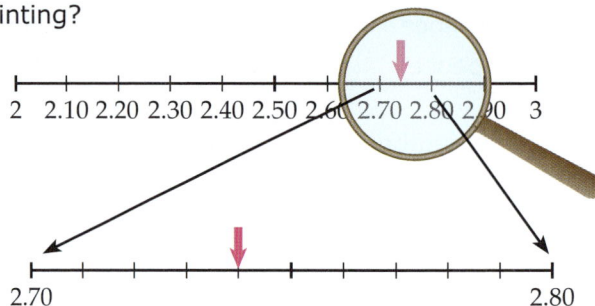

Zoom in to look at the numbers in between.

You can zoom in on decimals to get even smaller decimals!

Each part is one tenth of 10p = 1p.
The arrow is at £2.74.

1p = £0.01 = 1 **hundredth** of a pound

| 100 × 1p coins | = | 50 × 2p coins | = | 20 × 5p coins | = | 10 × 10p coins | = | £1 coin |

p.134 >

Example

Write each amount as a decimal.

a

b

a   Add   0.01   1p = £0.01
           0.01
           0.05   5p = £0.05
         + 0.05
         ─────────
          £0.12

b   Add   0.50   50p = £0.50   Line up the decimal points.
           0.50
           0.20   20p = £0.20
           0.05
         + 0.04   0.01 + 0.01 + 0.01 + 0.01
         ─────────
          £1.29   The decimals add to more than a whole.

Example

Add these decimal amounts.
a   £0.15 + £0.30 + £0.50   b   £0.55 + £0.40 + £0.32

a   0.15   b   0.55
     0.30   0.40
   + 0.50   + 0.32
   ────────   ────────
    £0.95   Nine-tenths and five-hundredths   £1.27   One whole, two tenths and seven-hundredths

Number   Whole numbers and decimals

Exercise 1e

1 Use the number line to help you add these decimals.

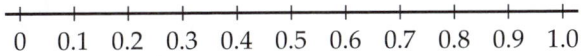

```
0   0.1  0.2  0.3  0.4  0.5  0.6  0.7  0.8  0.9  1.0
```

   a 0.1 + 0.4   **b** 0.3 + 0.5
   c 0.2 + 0.6   **d** 0.8 + 0.1
   e 0.7 + 0.3   **f** 0.9 + 0.1

2 Write each amount as a decimal.

  a
  b
  c
  d

3 Write each of these as a decimal.
  a ten pence and two pence
  b fifty pence and one penny
  c forty pence and eight pence
  d eight pence
  e three pounds and thirty pence
  f two pounds and nine pence.

4 Write each amount as a decimal number.
  a
  b
  c

5 Use the number line to help you add these decimals.

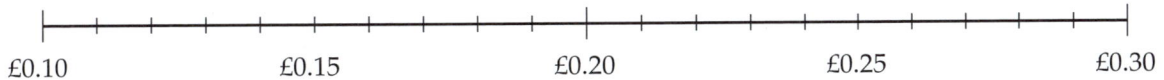

```
£0.10        £0.15        £0.20        £0.25        £0.30
```

  a £0.10 + £0.02   **b** £0.20 + £0.05   **c** £0.10 + £0.08
  d £0.15 + £0.05   **e** £0.18 + £0.02   **f** £0.22 + £0.08

> Remember to line up the decimal points.

Problem solving

6 Martin found these lost coins on the pavement.
  a Write the amount he found as a decimal.
  b Martin already had £1.91 in his pocket. How much does he have now?
  c A sandwich costs £2.10.
    How much money will Martin have left if he buys a sandwich?

7 Sangita is looking for a present for her friend. She has £10. What could she buy?

£9.50   £5.95   £2.50   £3.80

When the temperature **rises** it gets warmer.
When the temperature **falls** it gets cooler.

⬤ Numbers can go below zero.
These are **negative** numbers.

Temperature is measured in **degrees Celsius**. 'Five degrees Celsius' is 5 °C.

Example

The temperature was -6 °C. It rose 10 degrees. What is the final temperature?

Find -6 on the thermometer.
Count up 10. You get to 4.
The final temperature is 4 °C.

You can think of numbers as running left to right as well as up and down.

Example

Put these temperatures in order with coldest on the left, hottest on the right.

-1   -12   3   20   -3   12

Find the temperatures on the thermometer.
Read them in order from the bottom up.

−12   −3   −1   3   12   20

You can use a number line.

Example

The temperature was 3 °C.
An hour later it was -8 °C.
By how many degrees did the temperature fall?

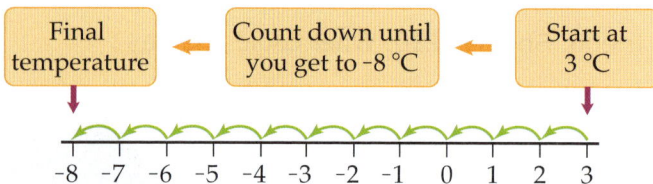

| Final temperature | ⬅ | Count down until you get to -8 °C | ⬅ | Start at 3 °C |

-8 -7 -6 -5 -4 -3 -2 -1 0 1 2 3

The temperature fell by 11 °C.

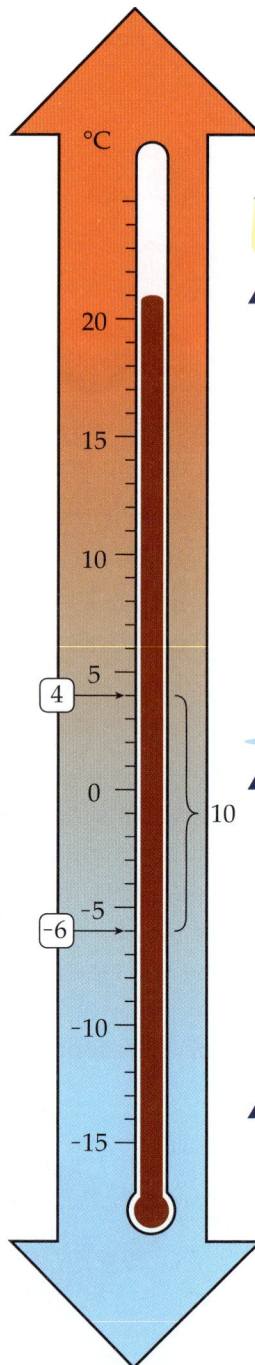

°C
20
15
10
5
4
0
-6
-5
10
-10
-15

▲ **21 °C** Your classroom should be around this temperature.

▲ Water freezes at **0 °C**.

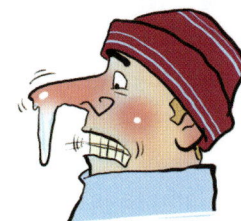

▲ **-14 °C** Very cold!

Exercise 1f

1 Write the temperatures marked on these thermometers.

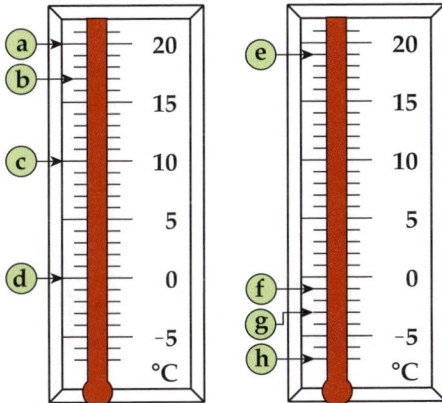

Use the number line to help you with questions **2** to **5**.

2 Find the final temperature.
  a Start at -5 °C and rise by 2 °C.
  b Start at -2 °C and fall by 5 °C.
  c Start at 8 °C and fall by 10 °C.
  d Start at -6 °C and rise by 6 °C.

3 What is the difference between these temperatures? Say whether the temperature rises or falls?
  a 4 °C to 9 °C   **b** 11 °C to 0 °C
  c 4 °C to -4 °C   **d** -5 °C to 2 °C
  e -3 °C to -8 °C   **f** 7 °C to -8 °C

4 Which is the colder temperature?
  a -4 °C or -7 °C   **b** 0 °C or -3 °C
  c -10 °C or -3 °C   **d** -7 °C or 6 °C
  e 0 °C or 4 °C   **f** -11 °C or -14 °C

5 Put these temperatures in order. Start with the coldest.
  a 3 °C, 9 °C, 0 °C
  b -2 °C, -6 °C, -5 °C
  c 4 °C, 1 °C, -6 °C
  d -5 °C, 0 °C, -8 °C
  e 6 °C, -6 °C, -10 °C
  f 0 °C, 4 °C, -7 °C
  g 5 °C, -4 °C, -6 °C

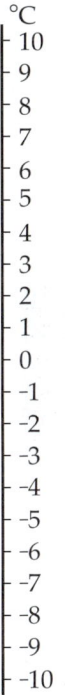

Problem solving

6 Pete wants to know what number is on the blue card. Use these clues to work it out:
  • The blue is the highest when the numbers are in order.
  • The difference between the yellow and the red is the same as the difference between the purple and the blue.

7 Match each item with its temperature.

  a mug of tea   **b** boiling kettle   **c** can of cola   **d** ice lolly   **e** you!

Did you know?

The coldest temperature ever recorded was -89.2 °C in Vostock, Antarctica.

Rounding makes numbers easier to work with.
You can round to the **nearest** 10.

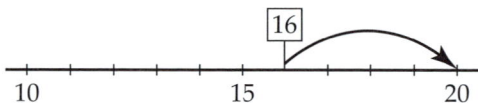

16 rounds **up**. 16 is closer to 20 than it is to 10.

> Five is actually in the middle but you round up.

Example

Round to the nearest 10.

a 25

b 184

a 30 25 rounds up

b 180 184 rounds down

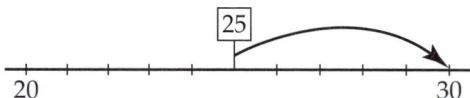

To round a number
▶ find the digit you are interested in
▶ look at the next digit to the right

Round down
0 1 2 3 4

Round up
5 6 7 8 9
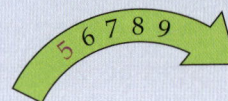

Example

Round 832

a to the nearest 100

b to the nearest 1000.

a 800 832 rounds down

b 1000 832 rounds up

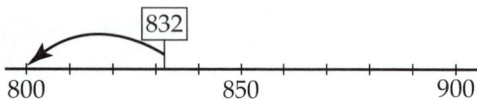

You can **estimate** first to find what the answer might be.

Example

Terrence has three jars of coffee.
The small jar weighs 150 g.
The large jar weighs 450 g.
Olivia says that she thinks the middle jar
must weigh 400 g.
Do you think she is right? Explain your answer.

> Estimating will help you to see if you have made a mistake.

The middle jar is half way in size between the small and large jars.

Estimated weight $\frac{150 + 450}{2} = \frac{600}{2} = 300\,g$

400 g is much bigger than 300 g.
Olivia is probably wrong.

Exercise 1g

1 Round the pink number to the nearest 10.

a
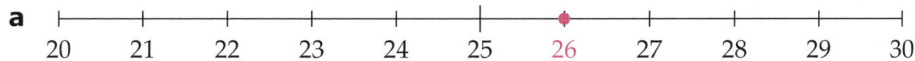

b
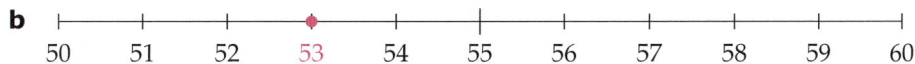

2 Round each number to the nearest 10.

a	13	**b**	27	**c**	35
d	66	**e**	51	**f**	112
g	239	**h**	215	**i**	210

4 Round each number to the nearest 1000.

a	6097	**b**	4800	**c**	3501
d	857	**e**	11263	**f**	4499
g	426	**h**	22507	**i**	6000

3 Round each number to the nearest 100.

a	231	**b**	388	**c**	810
d	555	**e**	495	**f**	786
g	123	**h**	450	**i**	1001

5 Round 12946

  a to the nearest 10

  b to the nearest 100

  c to the nearest 1000.

Problem solving

6 Chloe is 130 cm tall and Amir is 160 cm tall.

  a Give an estimate for Ben's height.

  b Give an estimate for Laura's height.

Chloe Ben Amir Laura

7 Bags of charcoal are sold in three sizes:
2 kg bags, 5 kg bags and 10 kg bags.
Give an estimate for the cost of a 5 kg bag.

8 Each person's height has been rounded to the nearest 10 cm.

Beth 170 cm   Fowsia 150 cm   Craig 140 cm   Imran 160 cm   Ian 190 cm   Karim 180 cm

The actual heights of the six people are:

144 cm	154 cm	161 cm	165 cm	184 cm	185 cm

Match each person with their actual height.

9 Sam, Oliver and Grace are playing
'Guess the number of sweets in a jar.'
Whose guess is best? Can you say why?

SAM 249   OLIVER 1023   GRACE 82

1h Order of operations

🔴 An operation (+, −, ×, ÷) tells you what to do.

$$75 + 15 - 5 = 90 - 5$$
$$= 85$$

$$8 \times 4 \times 2 = 32 \times 2$$
$$= 64$$

Mark and Sophie are calculating $6 \times 4 + 18$.

Who is right?

p.130, 132 >

p.262, 264 >

Multiply 6 by 4 and then add 18.
6 × 4 = 24
24 + 18 = 42

Add 4 to 18 first then multiply your answer by 6.
4 + 18 = 22
22 × 6 = 132

You need to use the **order of operations**.

🔴 Divide or multiply before you add or subtract.

$$6 \times 4 + 18 \qquad \text{First multiply.}$$
$$= 24 + 18 \qquad \text{Then add.}$$
$$= 42$$

So Mark is right!

Your calculator may not follow this order so be careful.

Example

Work out these calculations.

a $5 \times 9 - 22$ **b** $10 + 20 \div 5$ **c** $6 \times 4 + 18 \div 2$

a $5 \times 9 - 22 = 45 - 22$ First multiply $5 \times 9 = 45$
$\qquad\qquad\quad = 23$

b $10 + 20 \div 5 = 10 + 4$ First divide $20 \div 5 = 4$
$\qquad\qquad\quad = 14$

c $6 \times 4 + 18 \div 2 = 24 + 9$ First multiply and divide
$\qquad\qquad\qquad = 24 + 9$ $6 \times 4 = 24$ and $18 \div 2 = 9$
$\qquad\qquad\qquad = 33$ Then add.

Remember

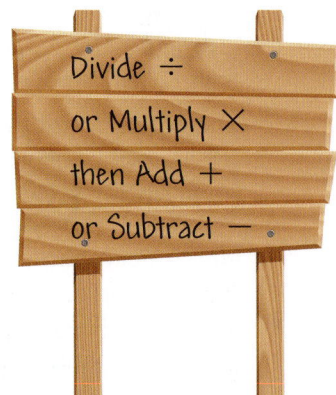

Divide ÷
or Multiply ×
then Add +
or Subtract −

Example

Insert operations to make this calculation correct:

$22 \square 5 \square 4 = 2$

$22 - 5 \times 4 = 22 - 20$ Multiply before subtracting.
$\qquad\qquad\quad = 2$

Exercise 1h

1 Work out these calculations.

   a $4 + 20 - 5$ **b** $4 \times 5 \times 2$

   c $25 - 12 - 8$ **d** $6 + 21 + 19$

   e $81 \div 9$ **f** $12 - 6 + 15$

   g $5 \times 5 \times 4$ **h** $36 \div 4 \div 3$

2 Work out these calculations.
Show your workings.

   a $4 \times 5 - 16$ **b** $12 + 32 \div 4$

   c $6 \times 9 + 4$ **d** $21 \div 7 + 18$

   e $40 \div 1 + 7$ **f** $64 + 40 \div 4$

   g $45 - 36 \div 6$ **h** $18 \div 3 + 4$

   i $100 - 9 \times 5$ **j** $12 + 32 \times 4$

   k $50 - 7 \times 7$ **l** $27 - 21 \div 3$

   m $14 \times 2 + 3$ **n** $16 \times 12 - 9$

   o $5 + 6 \times 2$ **p** $5 + 2 \times 9$

   q $15 - 3 \times 3$ **r** $25 - 18 \div 3$

   s $17 \times 3 - 12$ **t** $24 \div 8 + 4$

3 Work out these calculations with three operations.

   a $16 \times 2 + 4 \times 2$ **b** $4 \times 4 + 12 \times 2$

   c $36 \div 2 - 5 \times 2$ **d** $12 \times 5 - 2 \times 5$

   e $35 \div 7 - 45 \div 9$ **f** $30 + 4 \times 3 + 15$

   g $24 \div 3 + 4 \times 2$ **h** $15 - 2 \times 3 + 6$

   i $20 - 4 + 3 \times 2$ **j** $33 \div 3 + 3 \times 3$

   k $100 \div 5 - 16 + 4$ **l** $100 \div 10 - 1000 \div 100$

   m $40 \times 2 - 6 \times 7$ **n** $48 \div 4 - 4 \times 2$

   o $16 \div 4 \times 2 - 3$ **p** $27 \div 3 + 7 \div 7$

   q $32 \div 2 + 5 \times 4$ **r** $55 \div 5 + 22 \div 22$

   s $24 \div 3 + 2 \times 1$ **t** $70 \div 5 + 36 \div 36$

4 Work out these word calculations.
Each calculation has two operations.

   a Add 50 to 25 and then divide by 3

   b Take 5 from 21 and then divide by 4

   c Divide 60 by 5 and then add 8

   d Multiply 9 by 5 and then divide by 15

   e Divide 35 by 7 and then subtract 5

Problem solving

5 **a** Daniel has £5 and Lucy has £13. They decide to share out the money equally. How much do they each get?

   b Samira has £150 in her bank account and spends £35 on a new pair of trainers. How much money does she have left?

   c 12 friends each give £1.50 to buy ice creams. Each ice cream costs 75p. How many can they buy altogether?

£35

6 **a** Donna puts her age into code. She says, 'To find my age divide 40 by 4, then add 10 divided by 5.' How old is Donna?

   b Ayesha and Charlotte wash car windows.
This morning Ayesha earned £20.
By teatime she had doubled this amount.
Charlotte earned £15 in the morning and three times this by teatime.
How much did the two girls earn altogether?

7 Put the correct operations into each space.

   a $3 \bigcirc 5 \bigcirc 7 = 8$ **b** $3 \bigcirc 5 \bigcirc 7 = 5$

   c $3 \bigcirc 5 \bigcirc 7 = 15$ **d** $3 \bigcirc 5 \bigcirc 7 = 38$

$$\div \quad -$$
$$+ \quad \times$$

Check out

You should now be able to ...

Test it ➡

Questions

✓ Understand place value for whole numbers.	③	1
✓ Compare and order whole numbers.	③	2
✓ Use place value and decimal notation in different contexts, including money.	③	3, 4
✓ Add decimals using mental and written methods.	③	5, 6
✓ Understand and order negative numbers in the context of temperature.	③	7
✓ Round a number to the nearest 10, 100 or 1000.	④	8
✓ Use an estimate to check a result.	④	9
✓ Use the order of operations.	④	10

Language	Meaning	Example
Digit	Any of the numbers 0, 1, 2, 3, 4, 5, 6, 7, 8 or 9.	3.65 contains 3 digits
Place value	The value of a digit in a decimal number.	3.**65** contains **6** tenths
Decimal	The decimal part of a number occurs to the right of the decimal point.	3.65 has a decimal part of 0.65
Negative number	Any number less than zero.	-7 is a negative number
Round (verb)	To express a number to a given degree of accuracy.	639 is 600 rounded to the nearest 100
Estimate	An approximate answer.	149 + 302 can be estimated as 150 + 300 = 450
Operation	A rule for processing numbers.	In 6 × 4 the operation is ×

1 What is the value of the 6 in each of these numbers?

   a 4630   **b** 76

   c 82.6   **d** 967.3

2 Write these numbers in order.
Start with the smallest number.
208, 820, 88, 280, 802

3 Write each of these numbers in figures.

   a Ninety one point six

   b Four hundred and eighteen point one

   c Seventy point four

   d Eight thousand and fifty two point five

4 Place > or < into the boxes to show which number is greater.

   a 7.6 ☐ 6.7   **b** 5.5 ☐ 5.6

   c 0.9 ☐ 0.6   **d** 3.2 ☐ 8.8

5 Alice has a one pound coin. She buys an eraser for 20p and a pencil for 55p. How much change should she get?

6 Bob has a £2.40 in his pocket. He finds a 50p coin, three 10p coins and four pennies behind the sofa.

   a How much money has Bob found?

   b How much does he now have?

7 Find the final temperatures.

   a Start at -8°C and rise by 2°C

   b Start at 5°C and fall by 10°C

   c Start at -7°C and rise by 7°C

   d Start at -3°C and fall by 6°C

8 Round 4467 to

   a the nearest ten

   b the nearest hundred

   c the nearest thousand.

9 Mel is 120cm tall.
Onora is 150cm tall.

Mel   Nina   Onora   Penny

   a Give an estimate for Nina's height.

   b Give an estimate for Penny's height.

10 Work out each of these calculations.

   a $2 + 8 - 7$ **b** $3 \times 3 \times 4$

   c $28 - 16 - 5$ **d** $40 \div 5 \div 4$

   e $3 + 5 \times 6$ **f** $4 \times 6 - 16$

   g $2 \times 8 + 4 \times 5$ **h** $32 \div 4 - 2 \times 2$

What next?

Score			
	0 – 3		Your knowledge of this topic is still developing. To improve look at Formative test: 1A-1; MyMaths: 1003, 1014, 1069, 1072, 1076, 1167, 1217, 1226, 1352, 1373 and 1377
	4 – 8		You are gaining a secure knowledge of this topic. To improve look at InvisiPen: 111, 112, 113, 124 and 131
	9 – 10		You have mastered this topic. Well done, you are ready to progress!

1a

1 What does the red digit stand for in each number?

    a 42**7**   **b** 600**9**   **c** 1**5**70

    d **7**16   **e** **3**085   **f** **5**172

2 Split these numbers into 100s, 10s, and 1s. The first is done for you.

    a 224 = 100 + 100 + 10 + 10 + 1 + 1 + 1 + 1

    b 344   **c** 431   **d** 136   **e** 201

1b

3 Jamie caught five fish.

He measured the length of each fish:

21 cm   33 cm   19 cm   31 cm   27 cm

    a Write out the lengths in order, starting with the largest.

Next he weighed each fish.

190 g   181 g   238 g   310 g   218 g

    b Write out the weights in order, starting with the smallest.

1c

4 Put these decimal numbers in order, starting with the smallest.

    a 5.8, 4.9, 7.2, 6.5   **b** 8.4, 3.2, 6.9, 0.9

    c 2.4, 2.1, 2.0, 2.5   **d** 4.1, 3.9, 4.2, 3.8

5 Write each of these as decimals.

    a three-tenths   **b** seven-tenths   **c** nine-tenths

6 Use the number line to help you add these decimals.

0   0.1   0.2   0.3   0.4   0.5   0.6   0.7   0.8   0.9   1

    a 0.6 + 0.2   **b** 0.3 + 0.4   **c** 0.9 + 0.1   **d** 0.5 + 0.4

1d

7 Add these amounts.

    a £0.20 + £0.50   **b** £0.40 + £0.70

    c £0.60 + 80p   **d** £0.90 + £0.35 + 65p

    e 50p + 21p   **f** 40p + £1.20

    g £2.50 + £3.20   **h** 60p + £4.20

8 Use the number line to help you add these decimals.

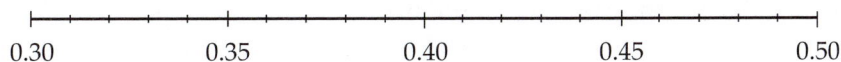

```
├──┼──┼──┼──┼──┼──┼──┼──┼──┼──┤
0.30        0.35        0.40        0.45        0.50
```

a 0.30 + 0.03   **b** 0.45 + 0.01   **c** 0.35 + 0.06   **d** 0.30 + 0.09

9 Use the number line to find each new temperature.

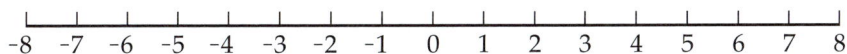

```
├──┼──┼──┼──┼──┼──┼──┼──┼──┼──┼──┼──┼──┼──┼──┼──┤
-8  -7  -6  -5  -4  -3  -2  -1  0  1  2  3  4  5  6  7  8
```

a Start at 7°C and drop by 9 degrees.
b Start at -5°C and go up by 7 degrees.
c Start at -4°C and drop by 4 degrees.
d Start at -8°C and go up by 5 degrees.
e Start at -5°C and go up by 9 degrees.

10 Complete these problems using negative numbers.

a 4 − 7 = ?   **b** 8 − 12 = ?   **c** 10 − 12 = ?   **d** 0 − 7 = ?
e -2 − 6 = ?   **f** -2 + 5 = ?   **g** -5 − 3 = ?   **h** -10 + 6 = ?
i -6 − 11 = ?   **j** -12 + 20 = ?   **k** -13 + 22 = ?   **l** -11 − 17 = ?

11 Round each number to the nearest ten.

a 54   **b** 149   **c** 65   **d** 612
e 98   **f** 185   **g** 102   **h** 3

12 Round each number to the nearest whole number.

a 4.7   **b** 8.1   **c** 5.4   **d** 11.8
e 19.5   **f** 25.4   **g** 0.7   **h** 0.4

13 Work out each calculation and say which of each group has a different answer.

a   **i** 360 ÷ 5 ÷ 3   **ii** 840 ÷ 6 ÷ 5   **iii** 200 ÷ 25 × 3
b   **i** 155 + 27 − 106   **ii** 133 − 95 + 34   **iii** 250 − 115 − 63

14 Work out each calculation and say which of each group has a different answer.

a   **i** 84 ÷ 7 + 12 × 5   **ii** 48 ÷ 3 + 8 × 7
    iii 128 ÷ 8 + 300 ÷ 5   **iv** 192 ÷ 4 + 72 ÷ 3
b   **i** 450 ÷ 6 − 13 × 3   **ii** 300 ÷ 5 − 8 × 3
    iii 360 ÷ 4 − 162 ÷ 3   **iv** 480 ÷ 8 − 84 ÷ 3

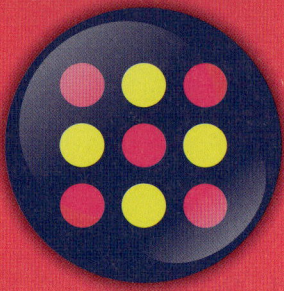

2 Measures, perimeter and area

Introduction

What is the area of the United Kingdom? It is not a very regular shape, in fact when it comes to working out its area it's quite a pointy country, yet surveyors have worked out its area as 244 820 km^2.
They do this by dividing the country into smaller regular shapes such as triangles and trapeziums and then working out the areas of each of these pieces.

What's the point?

Being able to work out the area of a country gives you an idea as to how big it is!

Objectives

By the end of this chapter, you will have learned how to …
- Measure lengths in centimetres and millimetres.
- Read and interpret scales in different contexts, including time.
- Classify 2D shapes by their properties.
- Calculate the perimeter of simple shapes.
- Calculate or estimate the area of a shape by counting squares.
- Choose and use standard metric units of measure.

Check in

1 What time is it?

a

b

c

2 Copy these headings. Put each word under the correct heading.

Length	Weight	Time

second   metre   day   gram
millimetre   year   tonne   hour
kilometre   century   week
centimetre   kilogram

Aberdeen

Bradford Leeds
 Kingston upon Hull
chester
 Sheffield

rent
Nottingham
Derby   Norwich
pton
ngham   Leicester
   Coventry

ENGLAND

Starter problem

Archaeologists have recently found what appears to be the footprint of a giant.

How tall would the giant have been?

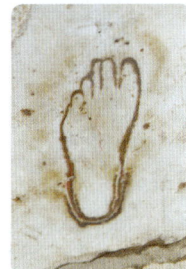

2a Measuring lines

You can use different units to measure length.

The tip of Alfie's pencil is 14 mm long.

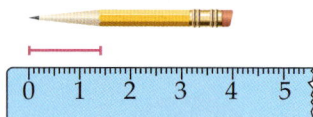

▶ Alfie is 150 cm tall.

▲ The bus is 4 m tall.
1 m is 100 cm, 4 m is 400 cm

His whole pencil is 18 cm long.
1 cm is 10 mm
18 cm is 180 mm

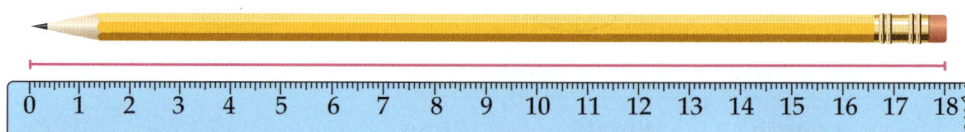

| On a ruler, each large numbered length is a **centimetre**. | Each **centimetre** has 10 smaller parts. Each smaller length is a **millimetre**. |

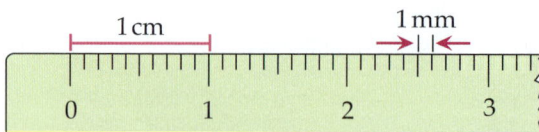

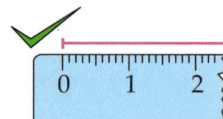

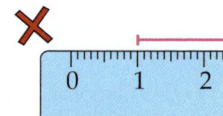

1 cm   1 mm

‹ p.8

Example

What is the length of this line?

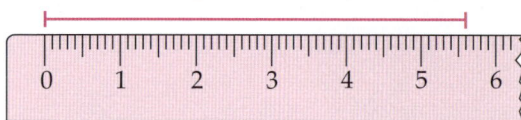

This line is 5 cm and 6 mm long.
Write this as 5.6 cm.

5.6 cm

The decimal point shows this is 5 whole cm and $\frac{6}{10}$ cm

Remember to start at 0 when you measure.

Did you know?

An average lead pencil will draw a line 48 km long, if you keep sharpening it.

Example

Write

a   50 mm in cm
b   2.2 cm in mm
c   140 cm in m
d   3.9 m in cm

a   50 mm = 5 cm
b   2.2 cm = 22 mm
c   140 cm = 1.4 m
d   3.9 m = 390 cm

Remember
1 cm = 10 mm
1 m = 100 cm

Geometry and measures Measures, perimeter and area

Exercise 2a

1 Give the length of each line. All measurements are in centimetres.

a 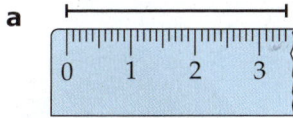 **b** 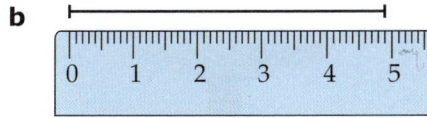 **c**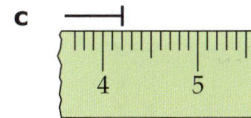

d 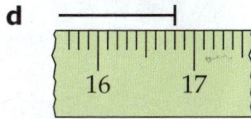 **e** 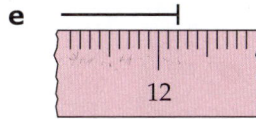 **f**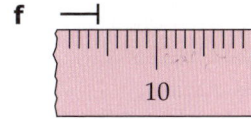

2 Use a ruler to measure each line and match it to a measurement from the box.

6.9 cm	7.5 cm
7.2 cm	6.6 cm
5.9 cm	6.3 cm

3 Draw these lines accurately.

a 3 cm   **b** 7 cm   **c** 45 mm   **d** 58 mm   **e** 11.2 cm   **f** 9.9 cm

4 Match pairs of lengths that are the same.

a 3 cm   **b** 324 cm   **c** 340 mm   **d** 32 m   **e** 3 m   **f** 32 mm

1 34 cm   **2** 30 mm   **3** 3.2 cm   **4** 300 cm   **5** 3200 cm   **6** 3.24 m

Problem solving

5 Which blue line is longer?
Check your estimate with a ruler.

6 Which unit would you use to measure ...

▲ an ice cream   ▲ your hand   ▲ a door   ▲ an ant?

MyMaths.co.uk   🔍 1146   **SEARCH**

2b Reading scales

There are many types of scales.

▲ A ruler is a scale

▲ These kitchen scales measure weight

▲ This scale measures petrol in a car

The arrow on the green scale is pointing to a number between 20 and 30.

Count on from 20. The arrow is pointing at 23.

The arrow on the blue scale is pointing to a number between 3 and 4.
Each small division is one-tenth or 0.1.

‹ p.8

The arrow is pointing at 3 whole units and 6 tenths. This is written 3.6.

Example

What reading is shown on this scale?

First, find the large numbers. ➡ Each large division = 100

Then find the value of each small division. ➡ $100 \div 10 = 10$
Each small division = 10

The arrow is pointing between 300 and 400. ➡ Count 6 small divisions.
$6 \times 10 = 60$

Count on from 300. ➡ $300 + 60 = 360$

Exercise 2b

1 Look carefully at each scale. Decide which is the best guess.

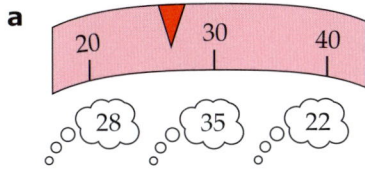

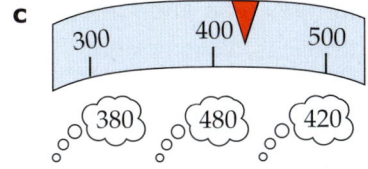

a

20　30　40

28　35　22

b

4　5

4.7　4.4　4.1

c

300　400　500

380　480　420

2 What numbers are the arrows pointing to on this decimal scale?

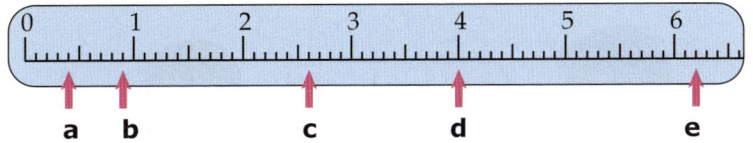

0　1　2　3　4　5　6

a　b　c　d　e

3 What does each scale show?

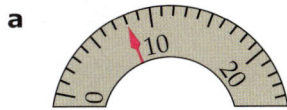

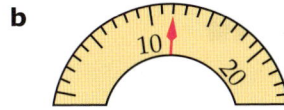

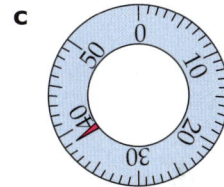

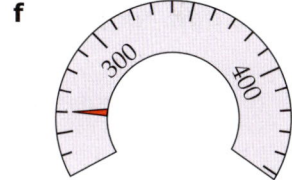

a

10　20　0

b

10　20

c

50　0　10　20　30　40

d

50　100　0　150

e

0　100　200

f

300　400

Problem solving

4 These scales have been splashed with paint.
Work out a reading or give an estimate for each one.

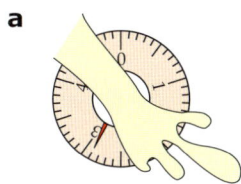

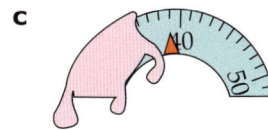

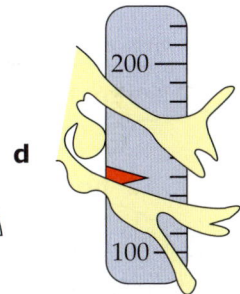

a

b

0　10　20　30

c

40　50

d

200　100

5 Petra the postal worker is weighing some parcels. Put them in order, lightest first.

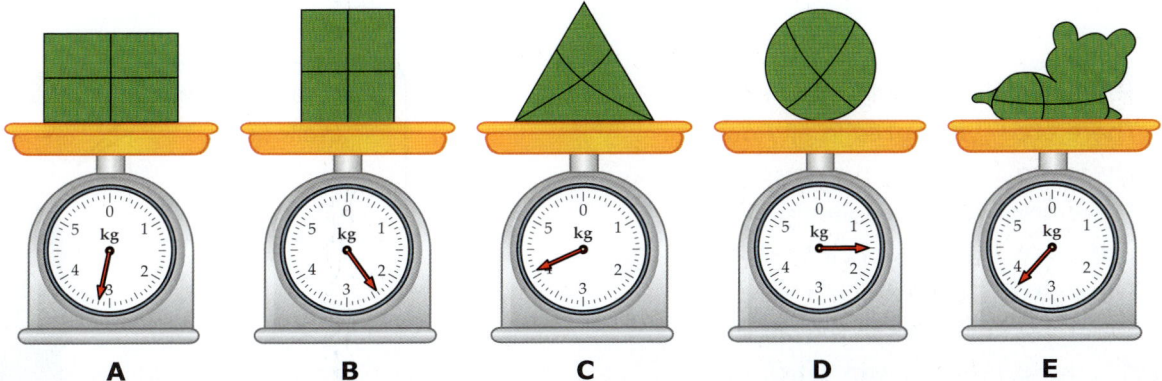

A　　B　　C　　D　　E

2c Time

Sanjeev, Mia and Lucky are working out what time it is. Who is right?

They are all right.

There are many different ways to tell the time.

No, it's 4:45 p.m.

It's a quarter to five.

No, it's 16:45.

🔴 You can use the 12-hour clock.

You use **a.m.** for times before midday.
You use **p.m.** for times after midday.

🔴 You can also use the 24-hour clock.

The hours after midday count on from 12.

▲ You do not need a.m. or p.m. for the 24-hour clock.

Example

Write this time in the 12-hour clock and the 24-hour clock.

Three thirty-four in the afternoon

12-hour

3:34 p.m.

24-hour

After midday so count on from 12

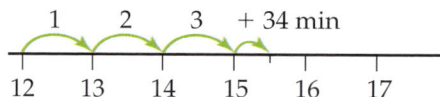

| 1 | 2 | 3 | + 34 min |
| 12 | 13 | 14 | 15 | 16 | 17 |

15:34

There are 60 **seconds** in a minute.
There are 60 **minutes** in an hour.
There are 24 **hours** in a day.
There are 7 **days** in a week.
There are 52 **weeks** in a year.
There are 12 **months** in a year.
There are 365 **days** in a year
(and 366 in a leap year).

Understanding time is really useful. You should know these quantities.

Geometry and measures Measures, perimeter and area

Exercise 2c

1 Which of these units of time would you use to measure parts **a–f**?

| seconds | minutes | hours | days | weeks | months | years |

a Tying your shoe lace   **b** You are asked how old you are

c The amount you sleep each night   **d** The length of your summer holidays

e The time it takes to run 100 metres   **f** The time it takes to boil an egg

2 Match the times.

a	b	c	d	e

a.m.	p.m.	p.m.	a.m.	p.m.

A	B	C	D	E

22:00	7:30	14:30	10:00	18:15

Problem solving

3 Here are the timings of Kim's day.

wake up	shower	breakfast	maths class

bedtime	watch tv	home	lunch

Did you know?

The Mayan civilisation in what is now Mexico used a system of two different calendars to record time.

a What is Kim doing at 7 p.m.?   **b** Does Kim have lunch at 1 a.m. or 1 p.m.?

c Where is Kim at a quarter past ten in the morning?   **d** What is Kim doing at 7.30 a.m.?

e What time does Kim go to bed?

4 Sam and Abby are taking the train to London.

a When does their train leave?

b How long is their journey?

> Cross Country Xpress
> -
> From : Newcastle   £ 72.63
> To   : London
>
> Time Depart : 09:35
> Time Arrive : 13:05

2d Shapes

Here are the most common 2D shapes.

Circle

1 curve

Square

4 sides
2 pairs of parallel sides
All sides equal

Rectangle

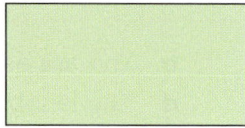

4 sides
2 pairs of parallel sides
2 pairs of equal sides

Trapezium

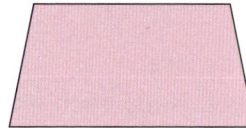

4 sides
1 pair of parallel sides

Triangle

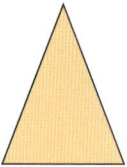

3 sides

Pentagon

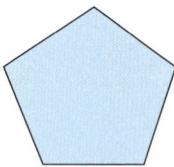

5 sides

Hexagon

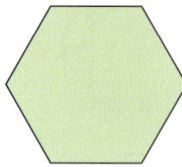

6 sides

Octagon

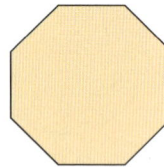

8 sides

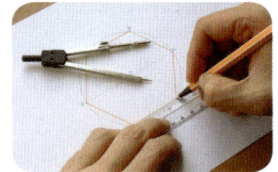

▲ Shapes you can draw on paper are called 2D. This means two-dimensional.

p.100 >

Kite

4 sides
2 pairs of equal sides

Parallelogram

4 sides
2 pairs of parallel sides
2 pairs of equal sides

Rhombus

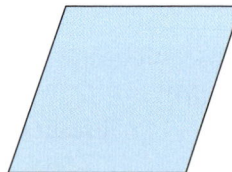

4 sides
2 pairs of parallel sides
All sides equal

Example

Use a ruler to measure the sides of each shape.
Give its name.

a
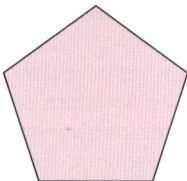

b

c

a Pentagon
Each side is 1.5 cm.

b Rectangle
The long sides are 3 cm.
The tall sides are 2 cm.

c Square
Each side is 1 cm.

▲ You can see shapes all around you, like in these tiling patterns.

Exercise 2d

1 Give the name of each shape.

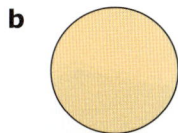

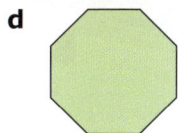

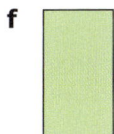

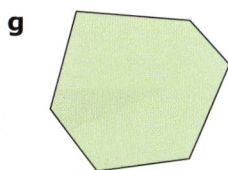

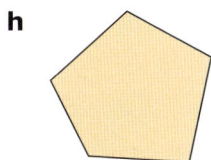

a

b

c

d

e

f

g

h

2 Measure the sides of each shape and fill in the missing information.

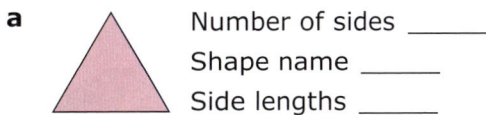

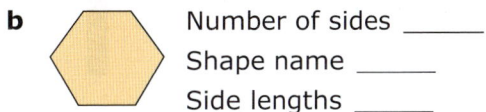

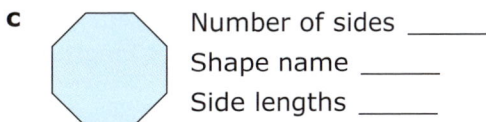

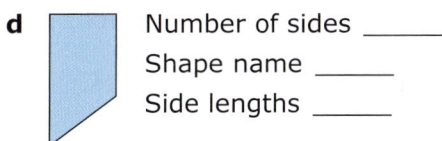

a Number of sides _____
Shape name _____
Side lengths _____

b Number of sides _____
Shape name _____
Side lengths _____

c Number of sides _____
Shape name _____
Side lengths _____

d Number of sides _____
Shape name _____
Side lengths _____

Problem solving

3 What shapes can you see in this picture?
Try to describe them using their
mathematical names.

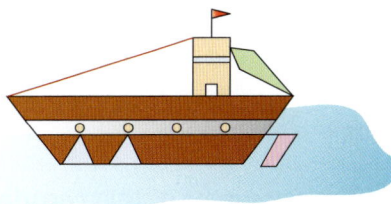

4 Here is a hexagon with its corners labelled.
Copy the shape as accurately as you can.
Draw straight lines between corners to make
  a a triangle
  b a rectangle
  c a trapezium
  d a kite
  e (harder) a rhombus

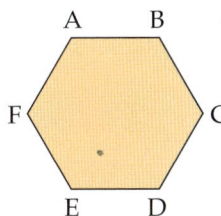

A   B
F   C
E   D

5 If you draw a shape with straight sides you can join the
middles of each side to form a new shape.
Starting with a square the new shape is also a square.
What shapes do you get if you start with a
  a rectangle   **b** trapezium   **c** kite
  d parallelogram   **e** rhombus

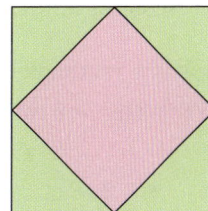

2e Perimeter

Rita is painting a white line around the edge of this table-tennis table.

When she is finished, the white line will go around the **perimeter** of the table.

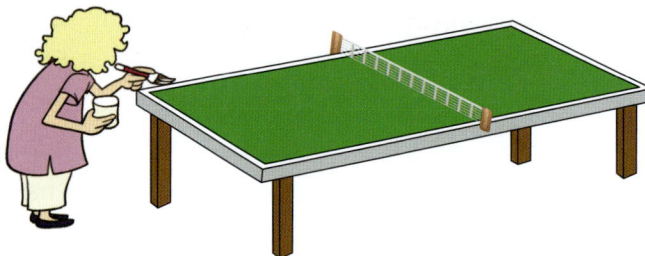

🔴 The **perimeter** is the total length around the edge of a shape.

What is the perimeter of this shape?

Add up the lengths of all three sides.

A to B = 3 cm
B to C = 4 cm
C to A = 5 cm
3 cm + 4 cm + 5 cm = 12 cm
The perimeter is 12 cm

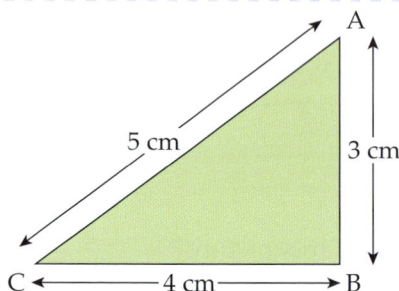

▲ The perimeter of the football pitch at Old Trafford is 350 m.

Find the perimeter of this regular pentagon.

The shape has five sides.
Each side is the same length.
Perimeter = 5 × 2 cm
         = 10 cm

⟵2 cm⟶

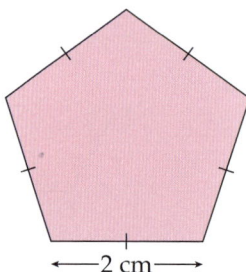

A regular shape has all sides and angles the same length.

Find the missing length of this shape.

The shape is a rectangle.
    Perimeter = 8 cm + 8 cm + ? + ?
            = 24 cm
    24 − 8 − 8 = 8
        8 ÷ 2 = 4
The missing length is 4 cm.

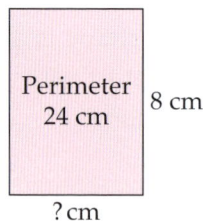

Perimeter 24 cm   8 cm

? cm

Exercise 2e

Don't use a ruler for the exercises on this page.

1 What is the perimeter of each shape?
   Give your answers in centimetres (cm).

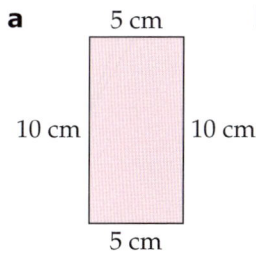

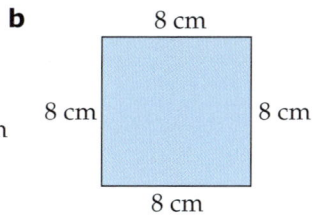

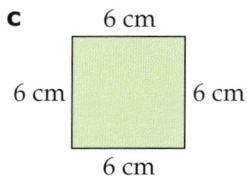

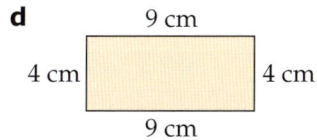

a
5 cm
10 cm   10 cm
5 cm

b
8 cm
8 cm   8 cm
8 cm

c
6 cm
6 cm   6 cm
6 cm

d
9 cm
4 cm   4 cm
9 cm

2 What is the perimeter of each regular shape?

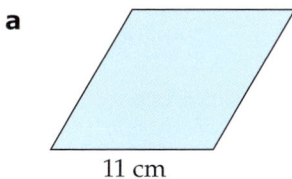

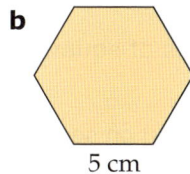

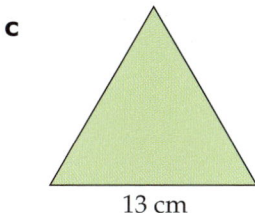

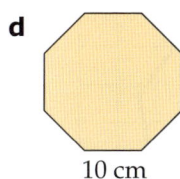

a
11 cm

b
5 cm

c
13 cm

d
10 cm

3 These shapes are **not regular**.
   Find each perimeter.

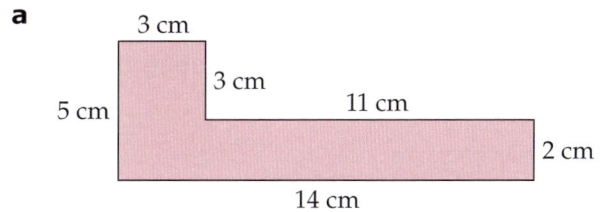

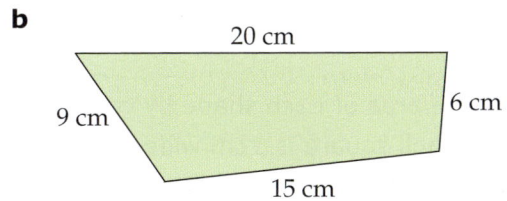

a
3 cm
3 cm
5 cm   11 cm
          2 cm
14 cm

b
20 cm
9 cm   6 cm
15 cm

4 This netball court is made of rectangles.
   Find the perimeter of
   a the full court
   b each third of the court.

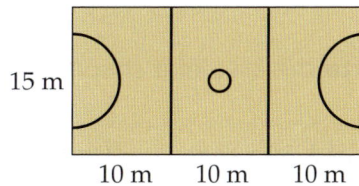

15 m
10 m   10 m   10 m

Did you know?

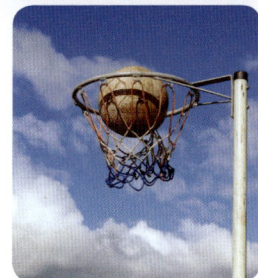

Netball developed as a women's game just after basketball was invented. In both games the courts are almost the same size and the hoops the same height off the ground.

Problem solving

5 Find the missing lengths of these shapes.

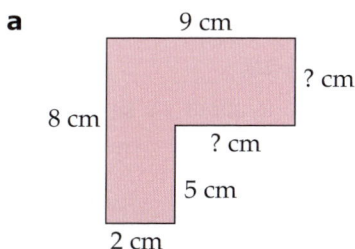

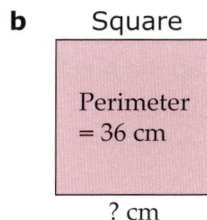

a
9 cm
? cm
8 cm
? cm
5 cm
2 cm

b Square
Perimeter = 36 cm
? cm

c What is the perimeter of the shape in part **a**?

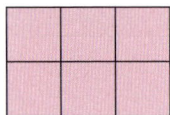

🔴 **Area** is the space inside a 2D shape.

You can find an area by counting the number of squares that fit inside a shape.

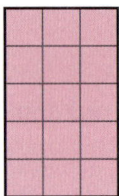

This shape is made of 6 squares.
Each square is 1 cm wide.
Its area is 6 cm².

> cm² is pronounced centimetres squared. It's a measure of area.

Example

Find the area of each shape by counting squares.
Each small square is 1 cm wide.

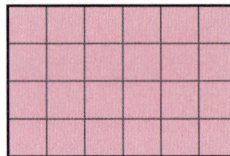

a   15 squares = 15 cm²   **b**   9 squares = 9 cm²   **c**   24 squares = 24 cm²

You can **estimate** the area of a shape if it covers parts of squares.

Example

Find the area of a 50p coin.

Draw around a 50p coin on squared paper.

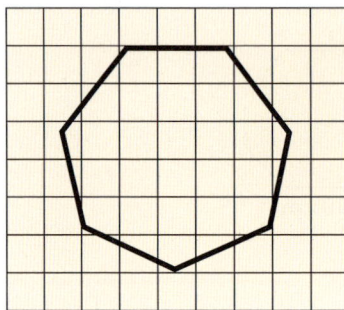

Count the whole squares.	21 squares
Count the part squares.	9 part squares → 5 whole squares
Add up the numbers of squares.	21 + 5 = 26
	The area is about 26 squares

Exercise 2f

1 Mira has a mixed bag of tiles.
   The tiles are either 1 cm squared, or they
   come in halves.
   Give the area of each shape in cm².

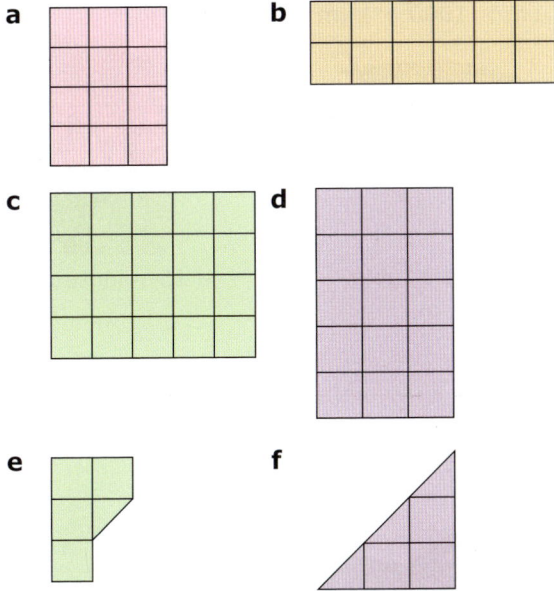

   a

   b

   c

   d

   e

   f

2 Find or estimate the area of each shape.
   Give your answer in cm².

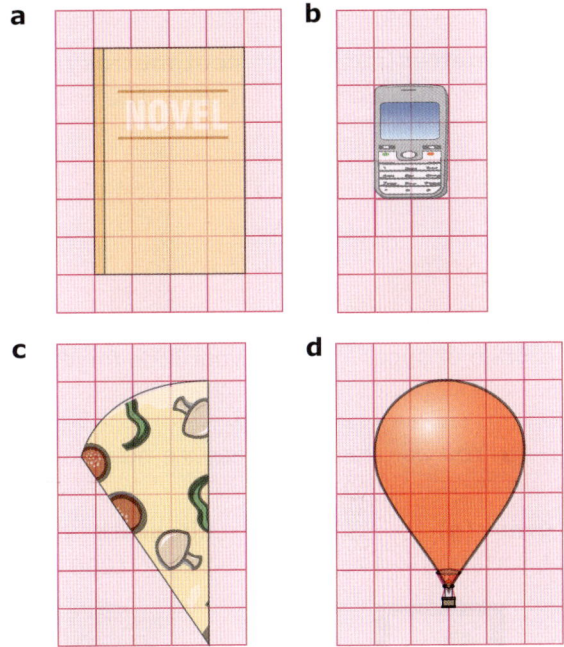

   a

   b

   c

   d

Problem solving

3 These areas have been paved with square slabs. Not all of the paving can be seen.
   Work out how many slabs are used in each area.

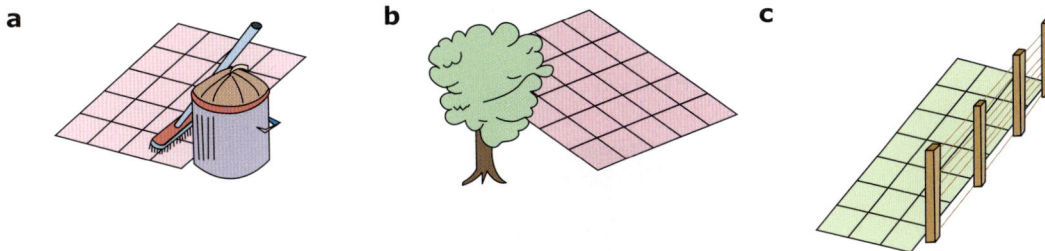

   a

   b

   c

4 Olivia, Daniel and Callum want to find the area of Olivia's hand.
   She draws around her hand on cm-squared paper.

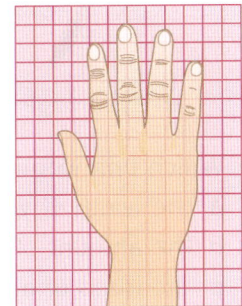

   It's 130 cm².

   It's 70 cm².

   It's 90 cm².

   Olivia   Daniel   Callum

   Who do you think is correct?
   Give reasons for your choice.

🔴 You use length to measure how long, tall or far something is.

p.260 >

millimetres (mm)
$1\,mm \times 10 = 1\,cm$

a grain of sugar

centimetres (cm)
$1\,cm \times 100 = 1\,m$

your little finger

metres (m)
$1\,m \times 1000 = 1\,km$

height of a table

kilometres (km)

a 15-minute walk

🔴 You use mass to measure how heavy something is.

gram (g)
$1\,g \times 1000 = 1\,kg$

a postage stamp

kilogram (kg)
$1\,kg \times 1000 = 1\,t$

a bag of sugar

tonne (t)

a shire horse

🔴 You use capacity to measure how much a container can hold.

millilitre (ml)
$1\,ml \times 1000 = 1$ litre

an eyedropper

litre (ℓ)

a carton of fruit juice

Example

Which unit would you use to measure
a the width of your classroom
b the amount of milk in a glass
c the mass of a loaf of bread
d the distance from Hereford to Ipswich?

a metres
b millilitres
c grams
d kilometres

Exercise 2g

1 Match each measurement with its short form.

kilogram	millimetre	gram
millilitre	metre	centimetre
litre	tonne	kilometre

ℓ	km	t	kg	cm
g	mm	ml	m	

2 Which unit would you use to measure
  a the thickness of a pencil
  b the distance from your home to school
  c the mass of a bag of grapefruit
  d the amount of fuel in a tanker
  e the size of a book
  f the mass of a ship?

3 Copy and complete each sentence by choosing the correct unit from the list in question **1**.
  a A bag of pretzels weighs 50 ___.
  b The world's tallest man was over 2.7 ___ tall.
  c A mug holds 250 ___ of tea.
  d The moon is 384 403 ___ from Earth.
  e Mount Everest is 8848 ___ high.
  f Dad filled his car with 40 ___ of petrol.
  g James weighs 62 ___.
  h The distance around my head is 56 ___.

Problem solving

4 Paul has a one-litre bottle of ginger beer.
  How many 100 ml glasses can he fill from the bottle?

5 Ribbon costs £4 per m. What is the cost of
  a 5 m   b 15 m
  c 50 cm   d 10 cm?

Ribbon
£4 per m

p.258 >

6 a Mikhaly says he is 1.46 m tall.
    What is this in mm?
  b He also says he weighs 0.05 tonnes.
    What is this in g?

7 Cheese costs £6 per kilogram.
  a How much money does
    i 100 g cost
    ii 250 g cost?
  b Molly spends £7.50 on cheese.
    How much cheese has she bought?

Did you know?

The A380-800 Air bus weighs 275 tonnes, holds 310 000 litres of fuel and has 530 km of electric cables.

8 Olive oil costs £8 per litre.
  How many litres can Rico buy for £100?

Check out

You should now be able to ...

Test it ➡

Questions

✓ Measure lengths in centimetres and millimetres.	3	1
✓ Read and interpret scales in different contexts, including time.	3	2, 3
✓ Classify 2D shapes by their properties.	3	4, 5
✓ Calculate the perimeter of simple shapes.	4	6, 7
✓ Calculate or estimate the area of a shape by counting squares.	4	8
✓ Select and use standard metric units of measure.	3	9, 10

Language   Meaning   Example

Language	Meaning	Example
Length	A measure of distance. It is often used to describe one dimension of a shape.	The length of an Olympic swimming pool is 50 m.
Mass	A measure of the amount of matter in an object. Mass is closely linked to weight.	The mass of a tennis ball is 57 g.
Capacity	A measure of the amount of space inside a container.	The capacity of a jug is 500 ml.
Perimeter	The perimeter is total length around the edge of a shape.	The perimeter of a football pitch is around 340 m.
Area	Area measures the space inside a 2D shape.	The area of a 2p coin is about 5 cm squared.

1 Use a ruler to measure each line in centimetres.

a _____

b _____

2 What does each display show?

a

b

3 Write these times in the 24-hour clock.
a half past three in the afternoon
b quarter to 7 in the morning

4 Here is a shape.
a What is this shape called?
b How many sides does it have?
c Measure the lengths of its sides.

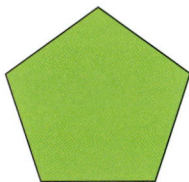

5 a What is this shape called?
b How many sides does it have?
c What are the lengths of its sides?

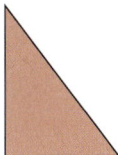

6 Find the perimeter of each shape. State the units of your answers

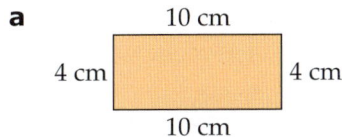

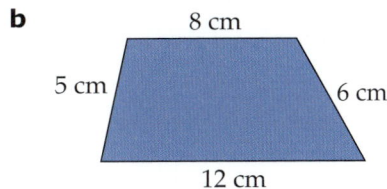

a

10 cm
4 cm   4 cm
10 cm

b

8 cm
5 cm   6 cm
12 cm

7 What is the perimeter of a regular hexagon with side length 3 cm?

8 What is the area of these rectangles?

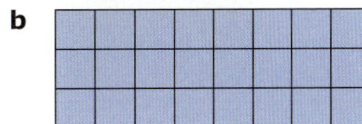

a

b

9 What unit of measurement does each of these stand for?
a mm   b kg   c ml

10 Which metric unit would you choose to measure
a the mass of a whale
b the height of a tree
c the amount of water in a raindrop
d the length of a flea?

What next?

Score			
	0 – 3		Your knowledge of this topic is still developing. To improve look at Formative test: 1A-2; MyMaths: 1084, 1101, 1104, 1105, 1110, 1124, 1146, 1229, 1232, 1234 and 1390
	4 – 8		You are gaining a secure knowledge of this topic. To improve look at InvisiPen: 311, 312, 313, 331 and 332
	9 – 10		You have mastered this topic. Well done, you are ready to progress!

MyMaths.co.uk

2 MyPractice

1 Draw a line of each length.
Write the measurement beside each line that you draw.

   a 10 cm   **b** 9 cm   **c** 13 cm

   d 10.5 cm   **e** 11.4 cm   **f** 8.2 cm

2 Measure the length of each line.

   a _____

   b _____

   c _____

   d _____

   e _____

   f _____

3 What numbers are the arrows pointing to on each scale?

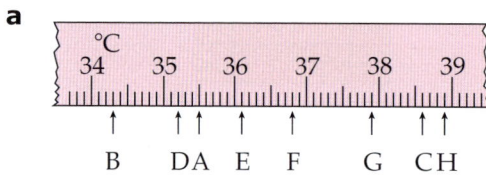

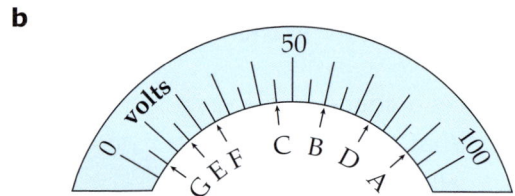

   a   **b**

4 Write these times as 24-hour clock times.

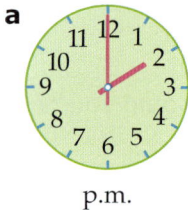

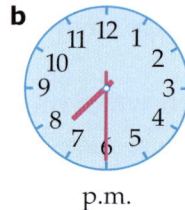

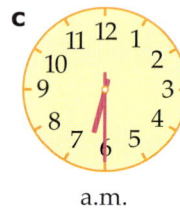

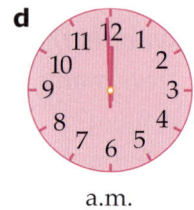

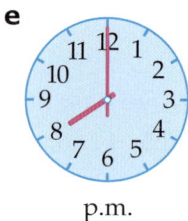

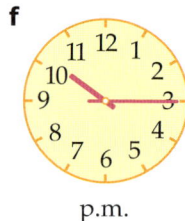

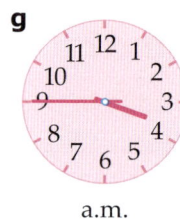

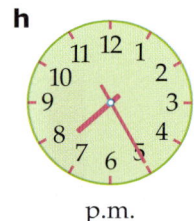

   a p.m.   **b** p.m.   **c** a.m.   **d** a.m.

   e p.m.   **f** p.m.   **g** a.m.   **h** p.m.

5 List the shapes you can see in this picture.

6 Find the perimeter of each shape.

a

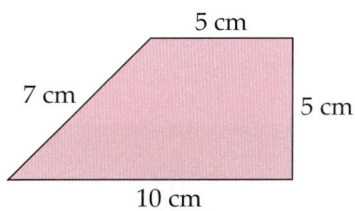

5 cm

7 cm

5 cm

10 cm

b

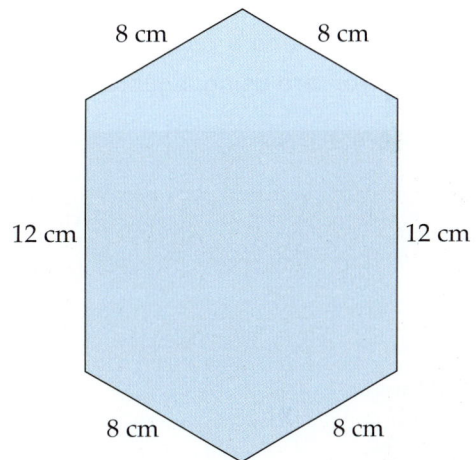

8 cm   8 cm

12 cm   12 cm

8 cm   8 cm

c

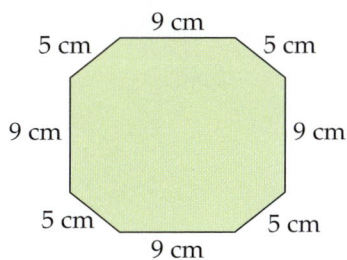

9 cm

5 cm   5 cm

9 cm   9 cm

5 cm   5 cm

9 cm

7 Find the area of each rectangle by counting squares.

a

6 cm

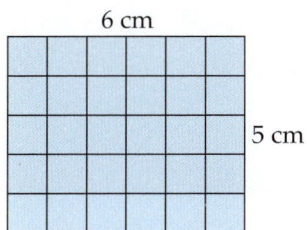

5 cm

b

2 cm

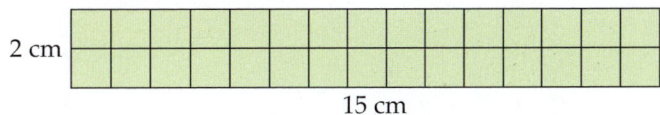

15 cm

8 **a** Sarah has 2 kg of fruit salad. How many 200 g portions can she serve?
   b Farmer Jones has 4000 kg of seeds. How many tonnes of seeds does he have?

MyMaths**.co.uk**

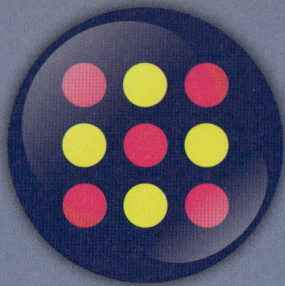

3 Expressions and formulae

Introduction

You use algebra most days without thinking about it. When you are changing your holiday money from pounds into euros, calculating the cost of using a mobile phone or converting a recipe from ounces to grams, you are using algebraic formulae.

What's the point?

A formula gives you a quick and easy way to work out unknown amounts – just by applying a simple rule.

Objectives

By the end of this chapter, you will have learned how to …

- Use letters to represent unknown numbers.
- Simplify algebraic expressions by collecting like terms.
- Substitute whole numbers into expressions and formulae.
- Derive a simple formula.

Check in

1   Lynda, John and Pat each have 20 marbles. Write the number of marbles that each of them now has if
   a   Lynda gives away 3 marbles.
   b   John buys 4 more marbles.
   c   Pat shares her marbles between 5 friends.

2   Work out the value of each of these symbols.
   a $6 + ♥ = 8$ **b** $? + 3 = 10$ **c** $10 - ☺ = 5$ **d** $3 × ✳ = 12$
   e $♣ × 2 = 6$ **f** $15 - ⊗ = 9$ **g** $♦ ÷ 2 = 4$ **h** $4 ÷ ▲ = 4$

3   Three brothers each have a bag of sweets. Their mother gives each brother 4 more sweets. Write a sum to work out the number of sweets each brother has now.

11 sweets	6 sweets	x sweets
Michael	Billy	Kevin

Starter problem

Think of a number between 1 and 10.

Double it.

Add 4.

Halve your answer.

Take away the number you first thought of.

Investigate your answer by trying different starting numbers.

Joel has a bag of marbles.

He does not know how many marbles are in the bag.

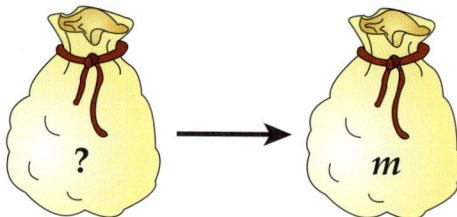

He uses the letter m to represent the number of marbles.

Joel gives away six of his marbles.

> I had **m** marbles. I gave six marbles away so now I have **m – 6** marbles.

Jenny had n marbles.
She wins 10 more marbles in a game.

> I now have **n + 10** marbles.

Peta had d marbles.
She divides them into two groups and gives one group away.

> Now I have **d ÷ 2** marbles.

> I have **k × 2** marbles.

Michael had k marbles.
He doubles this amount in a game.

James had **t** sweets.
He eats 10 of the sweets.
How many sweets has he now?

SWEETS

James has $t - 10$ sweets.

Exercise 3a

1 There are lots of marbles in this bag.
   If Joel adds five more, how many will there be?
   You can use the letter *m* for the number of marbles.

You don't have to use *m* for **m**arbles, you can use any letter!

2 There are *s* fish in a lagoon.
   If 20 fish are caught by a fisherman,
   how many fish will be left in the lagoon?

3 Jeff has *m* pounds in his wallet.
   He gives away half of his money to a charity.
   How much money has Jeff now?

4 Each girl has *n* counters.
   a If Dinesh adds 12 more, how many does she have?
   b If Alice grabs 19 more counters, how many does she have?
   c If Nicky trebles her number of counters, how many would she have then?
   d If Tina divides her counters into six equal groups, how many counters would be in each group?

5 There are *j* biscuits in this packet.
   There are some more on the plate.
   How many biscuits are there altogether?

6 There are *g* trees in a forest.
   a If 100 trees are cut down for Christmas, how many trees are left?
   b How many trees will there be in five forests?

Problem solving

7 In her maths exam, Tracy answered **P** questions.
   She got 25 of the questions right.
   How many questions did Tracy get wrong?

8 Jeso and Kat do a sponsored swim for charity.
   Jeso raises *P* pounds and Kat raises twice as much as Jeso.
   How much did they both raise in total?

Did you know?

8 million real christmas trees are sold in the UK every year.

Sam uses m to represent the number of strawberries in his box.

Take away four strawberries

$m - 4$

$m - 4$

Add five strawberries

$m + 5$

$m + 5$

Double the strawberries

m m

$2 \times m = 2m$

I don't actually know how many strawberries are in this box!

m

You can write $2 \times m$ as $2m$

p.194 > Jo also has a box of strawberries.

The box has n strawberries in it.

n

Sam and Jo add their strawberries together.

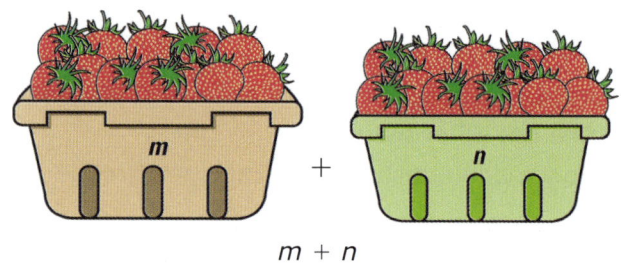

m $+$ n

$m + n$

They have $m + n$ strawberries altogether.

Exercise 3b

1 There are m strawberries in a box.
How many strawberries will there be in total if you

Start each question with m strawberries.

   a add 1   b add 3   c take away 6
   d take away 12   e add 50   f halve them
   g multiply by 3 h add p strawberries   i take away s strawberries?

2 In each question there are x cakes to start with.

   a Susan takes six of the cakes. How many are left?
   b Nick bakes 20 more cakes and adds them to the rest. How many are there now?
   c Nina works very hard and makes three times the first number of cakes. How many cakes has she made?
   d If you add Nina's cakes to Nick's cakes, how many will there be altogether?

3 This piece of string is 30 m long.

   a If Sarah cuts off p m from one end, what length is left?
   b If she cuts another p m, how much is left?

4 a There are b soldiers in a row.
      How many soldiers will there be in 12 rows?

   b If each row gets three more soldiers, what is the new number of soldiers in each row?

5 a Jack picks x kg of apples. Derek picks y kg.
      How much do they pick altogether?

   b 10 kg of the apples are bruised and get thrown away. How many kg of apples are left?

Problem solving

6 Tom has a box of biscuits with b biscuits inside.
Sara has five more biscuits on a plate.

   a How many biscuits are there in total?
   b If there are 20 biscuits altogether, how many are in the box?

7 Each box holds 12 tea cups. Each crate holds y saucers. What should the value of y be so that each tea cup has a saucer?

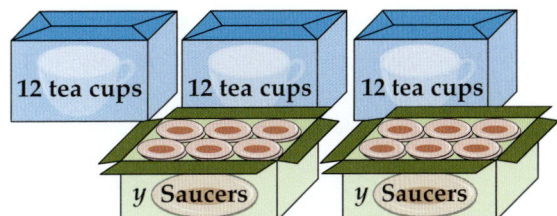

12 tea cups   12 tea cups   12 tea cups
y Saucers y Saucers

MyMaths.co.uk

3c Adding with symbols

If things are similar, they are **like**.

These are both cows.

5 cows + 6 cows = 11 cows

If things are different, they are **unlike**.

The cow and farmer are different.

4 farmers + 3 cows = 4 farmers + 3 cows

🔴 You can combine **like symbols** by adding.

Remember, you write
$5x$ for $5 \times x$.

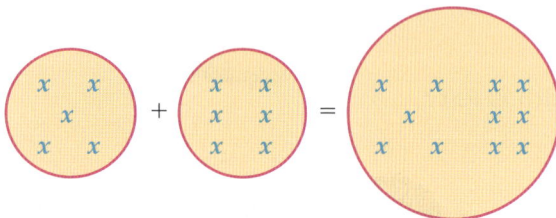

$$x\ x \quad x \quad x\ x \qquad + \qquad x\ x \quad x\ x \quad x\ x \qquad = \qquad x\ x\ x\ x \quad x \quad x\ x \quad x\ x\ x\ x$$

$$5x \quad + \quad 6x \quad = \quad 11x$$

These xs are all alike, so you can combine them.

🔴 You cannot combine **unlike symbols** by adding.

$$x\ x\ x\ x \quad + \quad y\ y\ y \quad = \quad x\ x\ x\ x \quad + \quad y\ y\ y$$

$$4x \quad + \quad 3y \quad = \quad 4x \quad + \quad 3y$$

This is a mix of xs and ys so you can't combine them.

Example

Can you combine these? Do it if you can.

a $5x + 7x$ **b** $15y + 4h$

- - - - - - - - - - - - - - - -

a ✓ Can combine
$5x + 7x = 12x$

b ✗ Cannot combine
$15y + 4h$

$5x + 7x$ is an
expression.
So is $15y + 4h$.

Example

Write these expressions as simply as you can.

a $3x + 2x + m$ **b** $8y + 3 + 2y$

- - - - - - - - - - - - - - - -

a $3x + 2x + m = 5x + m$ **b** $8y + 3 + 2y = 10y + 3$

Don't combine letters and numbers!

Algebra Expressions and formulae

Exercise 3c

1 Add these numbers together in your head as fast as you can.

a $3 + 1 + 4$ b $2 + 6 + 3$
c $4 + 5 + 6$ d $12 + 10 + 9$
e $15 + 3 + 20$ f $22 + 1 + 7$
g $19 + 12 + 1$ h $2 + 6 + 22$
i $29 + 3 + 15$ j $19 + 19 + 19$

2 Add together the symbols in each ring.

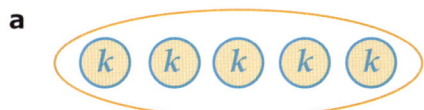

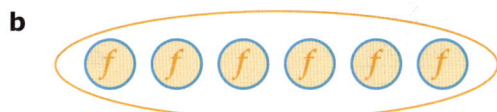

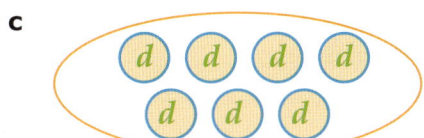

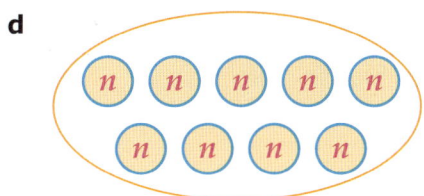

a

b

c

d

3 Write the weight on each scale as simply as you can.

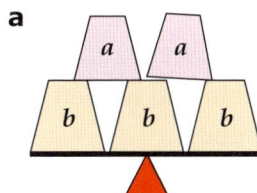

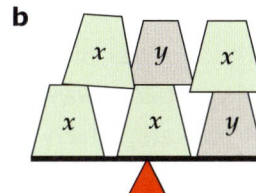

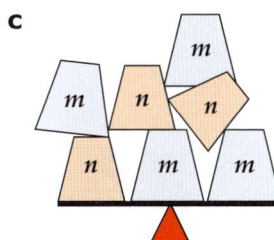

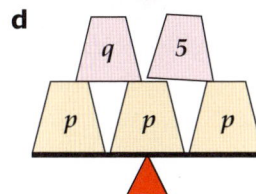

a   b

c   d

4 Simplify each of these expressions.

a $2m + 5m$ b $50f + 25f$
c $22d + 12d$ d $10k + 5k$
e $14y + 7y$ f $20z + 4z$
g $14g + 4g + 2g$ h $4q + 4q + 2q$
i $6y + 3y + 30y$ j $27w + 5w + 2w$
k $14b + 6b + 2b$ l $45j + 15j + 5j$

5 Say if these expressions have like or unlike symbols. Simplify them if you can.

a $4m + 5m$ b $3s + p$
c $x + y$ d $x + 2x$
e $2s + 3s$ f $2p + 2r$

Problem solving

6 Write the perimeter of each shape as simply as you can.

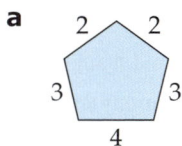

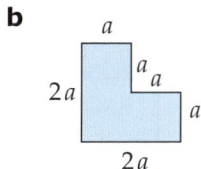

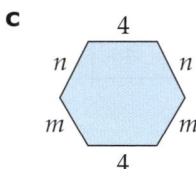

a   b   c

7 Which two shapes have the same perimeter?

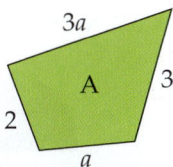

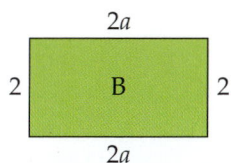

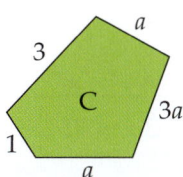

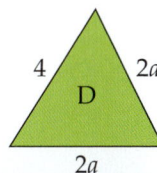

3d Simplifying expressions

These packets of seeds are all the same.
Each contains x seeds.

The number of seeds in 6 packets is $6x$.
If you take away 2 packets you are left with
4 packets, which is $4x$ seeds.

Know the language!
x is a **symbol**.
$6x$ is a **term**.
$6x - 2x$ is an **expression**.

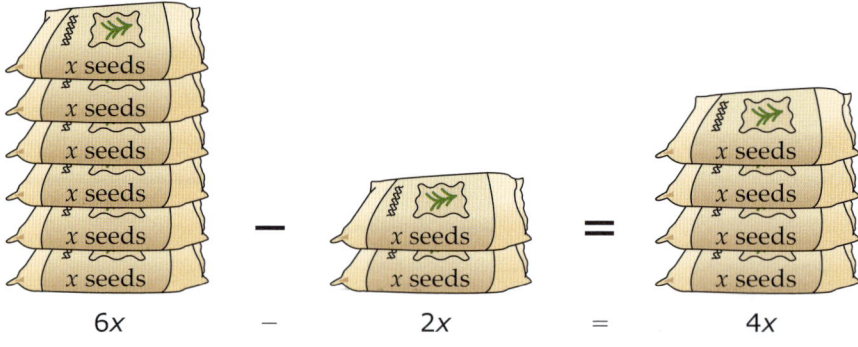

$6x$ $-$ $2x$ $=$ $4x$

💿 You can combine **like symbols** by subtracting.

Example

Simplify these expressions by combining terms.
a $5b - 2b$ **b** $10a - 6a$ **c** $3e + 6e - 5e$

a $5b - 2b = 3b$ **b** $10a - 6a = 4a$ **c** $3e + 6e - 5e = 9e - 5e$
$= 4e$

💿 You **simplify** expressions by adding and subtracting **like terms**.

You can also deal with larger expressions.

Split them into like terms. $4a + 2a + 5b - 3a + 2b$

$4a + 2a - 3a$ $5b + 2b$

Simplify.

$= 6a - 3a$ $= 7b$
$= 3a$

Make sure to include
any subtraction signs
when gathering like
symbols together.

Combine. $3a + 7b$

Algebra   Expressions and formulae

Exercise 3d

1 Work out these calculations in your head as fast as you can.

a $12 - 3 + 2$ b $32 - 3 + 15$

c $26 + 6 - 3$ d $47 - 39 + 9$

e $63 + 12 - 23$ f $100 - 93 + 13$

2 Write the symbols in each ring as simply as you can.

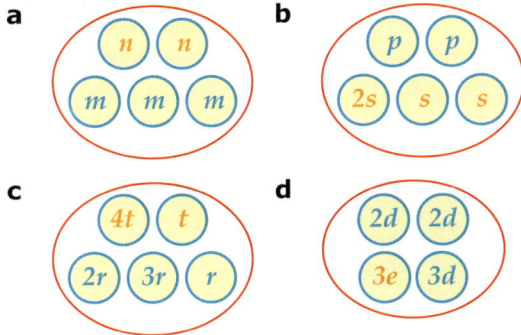

a

b

c

d

3 Simplify these expressions by subtracting like terms.

a $7t - 4t$ b $15g - 10g$

c $12h - 7h$ d $16x - 7x$

e $21p - 8p$ f $13q - 4q$

g $15m - 2m - 4m$ h $19b - 12b - 2b$

i $21c - 7c + 9c$ j $18x - 5x - 12x$

k $14y - 3y - 7y$ l $30u - 17u + 6u$

4 For each of these expressions

i Gather like terms together into boxes.

ii Simplify each box.

iii Add it all together.

a
$$16a - 4a + 7b + 4b - 3a$$

$16a\ .\ .\ .\ .$ $7b\ .\ .\ .\ .$

$=$

b
$$20x + 12y + 8x - 9y + 9y - 11x$$

$20x\ .\ .\ .\ .$ $12y\ .\ .\ .\ .$

$=$

c
$$8f - 6h - 2h + 7f + 15h - 3h$$

$8f\ .\ .\ .\ .$ $-6h\ .\ .\ .\ .$

$=$

5 Simplify these expressions.

a $2x + 4x + 3p$

b $15t + 5t + 6k$

c $22c + 4c + 2h$

d $40g + 20g + 3d + 10d$

e $5y + 2y + 4t + 2t$

f $8z + 12z + 20y + 4y$

Problem solving

6 Each step of these pyramids is made by adding the expressions in the two blocks below it.

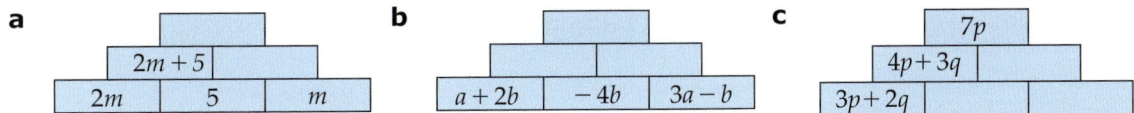

a

	$2m + 5$		
$2m$		5	m

b

$a + 2b$	$-4b$	$3a - b$

c

		$7p$
	$4p + 3q$	
$3p + 2q$		

Copy and complete the pyramids.

When you change one player for another in a football game, you use a **substitute**.

● When you swap a symbol for a number you are **substituting**.

Biscuits are sold in packets.

One gold packet holds *n* biscuits.

One green packet holds *m* biscuits.

Tonya opens each packet and counts the biscuits.

One gold packet holds 12 biscuits:

$n = 12$

One green packet holds 20 biscuits:

$m = 20$

The number of biscuits in two gold packets = $2 \times n$

$= 2 \times 12$

$= 24$ biscuits

The number of biscuits in one green and one gold packet = $n + m$

$= 12 + 20$

$= 32$ biscuits

● To substitute you replace a symbol with a number.

Example

In each expression, substitute $h = 9$ and work out the answer.

a $h + 6$ **b** $3h$

a $h + 6 = 9 + 6$
$= 15$

b $3 \times h = 3 \times 9$
$= 27$

3*h* means $3 \times h$

Exercise 3e

1 One green packet holds *m* biscuits, *m* = 20

One gold packet holds *n* biscuits, *n* = 12

How many biscuits are in

a two green packets

b two gold and one green packet

c three gold packets plus five extra biscuits

d *n* packets + 1

e *n* packets − 2

f *m* + *n* packets + 5?

2 The number of chocolates in each box is *h*.

a How many chocolates are shown in each picture?

i  **ii**

2 **iii**  **iv**

v

b If *h* is 30, how many chocolates are in each picture?

3 Work out these expressions when *n* = 10.

a $n + 5$ **b** $n + 16$

c $n - 3$ **d** $n - 10$

e $2 \times n$ **f** $5 \times n$

g $n \div 2$ **h** $n \times n$

4 If *f* = 6, work out these expressions.

a $8f$ **b** $f + 5$

c $5f$ **d** $f + f$

e $f \times f$ **f** $9f$

g $f \div 2$ **h** $f \div 6$

5 If *m* = 8 and *n* = 6, work out these expressions.

a $m + n$ **b** $m - n$ **c** $n - m$

d $2m + n$ **e** $m + 2n$ **f** $2m + 2n$

Problem solving

6 There are *k* biscuits in the green packet and *j* biscuits in the red packet.

a How many biscuits would you have if you bought one green packet and one red packet?

b If *k* = 20 and *j* = 15, how many biscuits are there in one green and one red packet?

c You need 60 biscuits. How many of each packet of biscuits would you buy?

Ellie works in a café.

She puts two teabags in every pot of tea.

She creates a **formula** to tell her how many teabags she needs in a day.

number of pots of tea × 2 teabags = number of teabags needed

A formula is a rule to help you work things out.

If Ellie makes 5 pots, she puts 5 in her formula:

5 pots of tea × 2 teabags = number of teabags needed

5 × 2 = 10 teabags needed

She can write her formula in a shorter way.

pots of tea × 2 teabags = teabags needed

p × 2 = t

She can write $p \times 2 = t$ or $2p = t$.

Example

Ellie uses 3 eggs per fry-up breakfast.

a Use words to write a formula for how many eggs she uses in a day.

b 5 people order fry-ups.
How many eggs does she use?

c Use symbols to write her formula in a shorter way.

a number of fry-up orders × 3 eggs each = total number of eggs

b The formula gives

5 orders × 3 eggs each = total number of eggs

5 × 3 = 15

She uses 15 eggs in total.

c number of fry-up orders × 3 eggs each = total number of eggs

f × 3 = e

$3f = e$

Exercise 3f

1 Ellie uses 3 tomato slices for each sandwich.

Write a number in the box to create a formula for how many tomato slices she uses each day.

number of sandwiches × ☐ = number of tomato slices

Can you write this in a shorter way?

2 Use your formula from question **1** to calculate the number of tomato slices that Ellie will need for each order.

a 4 sandwiches **b** 3 sandwiches
c 7 sandwiches **d** 9 sandwiches
e 10 sandwiches **f** 15 sandwiches

3 Ellie washes up 2 plates for every customer.

Problem solving

6 Use your formula from question **1**.
Ellie has orders for 18 sandwiches.
She has 53 tomato slices left in the fridge.
a Will she have enough tomato slices?
b Find the difference between how many slices she needs and how many are in the fridge.

3 **a** Create a formula in words to show how many plates she washes up each day. Write it in a shorter way using symbols.

b Use your formula to find how many plates she washes up if there are

i 3 customers **ii** 4 customers
iii 8 customers **iv** 10 customers
v 7 customers **vi** 9 customers
vii 20 customers **viii** 13 customers.

4 Ellie also washes up 1 cup per customer. Write a new formula to show how many plates and cups she now washes up in total. Write it in a shorter way.

5 In question **4**, you wrote a formula for Ellie's washing up if she washes 2 plates and 1 cup per customer.
Use your formula to find how many items she washes up if there are

a 3 customers **b** 4 customers
c 12 customers **d** 14 customers
e 25 customers **f** 30 customers
g 50 customers **h** 0 customers.

Did you know?

People in the UK drink 165 million cups of tea a day altogether. Laid end to end, this many cups would stretch out over 123000 miles, or roughly halfway around the middle of the earth!

3 MySummary

Check out
You should now be able to ...

Test it ➡

Questions

✓	Use letters to represent unknown numbers.	5	1 – 4
✓	Simplify algebraic expressions by collecting like terms.	5	5, 6
✓	Substitute whole numbers into expressions and formulae.	5	7, 8
✓	Derive a simple formula.	4	9, 10

Language	Meaning	Example
Symbol	A letter that is used to represent a number.	In $2a + 3b$ a and b are symbols
Expression	A collection of numbers and symbols linked by operations.	$2a + 3b$ and $13q - 4q$ are expressions
Term	A group of symbols in an expression that are separated by plus or minus signs.	In $2a + 3b$ the terms are $2a$ and $3b$
Substitute	Replace a symbol with a numerical value.	In $n + 16$ If $n = 10$, $n + 16 = 26$
Formula	A statement that links quantities.	number of sandwiches $\times 2 =$ number of slices of bread

1   There are n biscuits on a plate. Two biscuits are eaten, how many are left?

2   Grace has $£m$. Tim has twice as much money as Grace. Write an expression for the amount of money Tim has.

3   There are 15 sweets in a packet, how many sweets are there in
    a   8 packets
    b p packets
    c q packets plus r loose sweets?

4   A swimming pool is 25 m long. Bethany is swimming the length of the pool. How much further has she got left to swim after swimming d metres?

5   Simplify these expressions.
    a $a + a$
    b $2b + 5b$
    c $14c + 5c + c$

6   Simplify these expressions.
    a $5f - 3f$
    b $24g - 8g$
    c $18h - 6h - 7h$
    d $10i + 3i - 8i$

7   If $t = 5$, work out these calculations.
    a $t + 4$ b $t - 3$
    c $3 \times t$ d $t \times t$

8   If $v = 12$ and $w = 4$ work out these calculations.
    a $v \div 2$ b $v + w$
    c $w \times v$ d $w \div v$
    e $v - w$ f $w - v$

9   Two spoons are required for every person at a dinner.
    a   Copy and complete the formula

    > number of spoons
    > $= ... \times$ number of people

    b   Write your formula in a shorter way, use s for the number of spoons and p for the number of people
    c   Use your formula to calculate the number of spoons required for 12 people.

10 The length of a rectangle is 2 cm more than its width.
    a   Write a formula for the length of rectangle. Use W for the width and L for the length in cm.
    b   Use your formula to find the length of the rectangle if its width is 7 cm.

What next?

Score			
	0 – 3		Your knowledge of this topic is still developing. To improve look at Formative test: 1A-3; MyMaths: 1158, 1179 and 1187
	4 – 8		You are gaining a secure knowledge of this topic. To improve look at InvisiPen: 211, 212, 251 and 254
	9 – 10		You have mastered this topic. Well done, you are ready to progress!

3a

1 In a match box there are 50 matches.

How many matches are there in

a 2 boxes   b 3 boxes   c y boxes?

2 A bottle contains 100 tablets. How many tablets are there in

a 3 bottles   b 4 bottles   c t bottles

3b

3 Liam has m sweets.

a He gives y sweets to Sharon. How many does Liam have now?

b Then Ben gives Liam 10 sweets. How many does Liam have now?

4 Rebekah is cooking breakfast for herself, her parents and two brothers.

a She has bought q sausages, r eggs and s rashers of bacon. If everyone has one sausage, two eggs and three rashers of bacon, how many of each will she have left over?

b There were z slices of bread in the loaf and the loaf was finished after breakfast. Rebekah and her brothers each had two slices and Rebekah's parents each had one slice. What was z?

3c

5 Simplify each of these expressions.

a $2a + a$ b $5b + 2b$ c $13c + 11c$

d $10d + 6d$ e $9e + 2e + e$ f $8f + 4f + 2f$

g $4g + 4g + 4g$ h $12h + 10h + 7h$ i $19i + 6i + 5i$

6 Say if these expressions have like or unlike symbols. Simplify them if you can.

a $3p + 4q$ b $9m + 2m$ c $x + 4$

d $3y + 6 + y$ e $10 + t + 1$ f $4a + 4b$

7 Collect like terms in each of these expressions.

   a $3u + 7v + 5u$ **b** $6x + 4y + x$

   c $3p + 7q + 2p + 5q$ **d** $3a + 5b + 2a + 4b$

   e $2a + 3b + 3a + 4b + 4a$ **f** $12m + 6n + 7m + n + 3m$

   g $9x + 3y + 7x + 2y + 5x + y$

8 Collect like terms in each of these expressions.

   a $7x + 9y - 5x$ **b** $8u + 6v - 3u$

   c $2d + 7e + 3d - 4e$ **d** $5q + 9r + 2q - r$

   e $9p + 7q - 4p - 3q$ **f** $12m + 10n - 7m - 3n$

   g $20c + 11d - 8c - 7d$ **h** $8p + 6q - 3p - 2q + 4p$

9 Find the value of each expression if

   ★ = 4,   ☺ = 3,   □ = 2

   a ★ + □   **b** ★ − ☺   **c** ☺ − □

   d ★ + ☺ − □   **e** 2 × ★   **f** 2 × □

   g 4 × ☺   **h** 4 × □   **i** 6 × ☺

   j 10 × ☺

10 If $v = 4$ and $w = 6$, work out these expressions.

   a $v + w$ **b** $2v + 3$ **c** $w - v$

   d $2w - 2v$ **e** $3v - w$ **f** $2w - 3v$

11 A gate is made from five pieces of wood, all the same length.

   a Write a formula connecting the number of pieces of wood required, w, with the number of gates made, g.

   b Find the number of pieces of wood needed to make

   i 4 gates   **ii** 8 gates   **iii** 15 gates   **iv** 20 gates.

12 The distance around your neck (n) is about seven times the distance around your thumb (t).

   a Use the formula $n = 7t$ to estimate the neck measurements of people with these thumb measures.

   i 5 cm   **ii** 8 cm   **iii** 10 cm

   b Carmen has a neck measurement of 35 cm. Estimate the distance around her thumb.

A dairy farm is a business. The farmer sells the cows' milk to make a profit, so they must be well looked after.

Task 1
Put the cows in order by weight, lightest first.

Perfect for drinking

1st Class Butter

The best cheese

HOLSTEIN
Weight: 650 kg
Food: 24 kg per day
Number on farm: 25

JERSEY
Weight: 450 kg
Food: 18 kg per day
Number on farm: 10

BROWN SWISS
Weight: 585 kg
Food: 23 kg per day
Number on farm: 15

Task 2
How many cows are there in total in the herd?

Task 4
How much does the food cost per day
a in summer
b in winter?

Task 3
How much does the herd eat per day?

*** FARM FOOD *
Grass ... Free (April-Sept only)
Silage ... £10 per 100 kg

PLEASE RETAIN RECEIPT
THANK YOU.

MILK MART DAIRY
FRESH!
from farm to store

We pay

Holstein	Jersey	Brown Swiss
18 p	22 p	20 p

per litre

ONE COW:

GIVES ➤

NUMBER IN HERD ➤

HERD GIVES ➤

HOLSTEIN

20 LITRES

LITRES

JERSEY

10 LITRES

LITRES

BROWN SWISS

16 LITRES

LITRES

Task 5

If the farmer sells all the milk, does he make a profit each day?

Profit = Sales - Cost

63

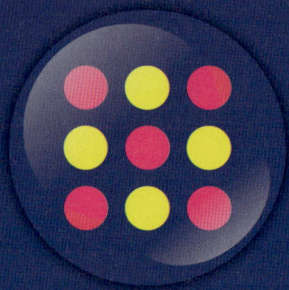

4 Fractions, decimals and percentages

Introduction

The very first fractions can be traced back to the Egyptians. They wrote all their fractions as unit fractions such as $\frac{1}{3}$ or $\frac{1}{5}$ and they didn't allow fractions such as $\frac{3}{4}$. Various other civilisations invented their own systems for fractions but it was not until the 17th century in Europe that fractions existed as we know them today.

What's the point?

A world without fractions would find it difficult to describe parts of whole numbers, or to share out quantities.

Objectives

By the end of this chapter, you will have learned how to …

- Use fractions to describe parts of a whole, including improper fractions.
- Identify equivalent fractions.
- Find fractions of a quantity.
- Calculate simple percentages, including problems involving money.
- Express a proportion as a fraction, a decimal or a percentage.

Check in

1 What fraction of these beads is pink?

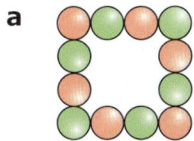

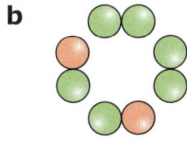

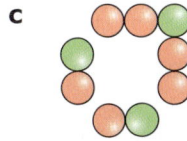

a

b

c

Starter problem

Draw a rectangle 3 cm by 4 cm.

Colour in $\frac{1}{2}$, $\frac{1}{4}$, $\frac{1}{6}$ and $\frac{1}{12}$ of the shape.

The whole rectangle should be shaded.

Draw some different sized rectangles.

Investigate which ones can be divided into unit fractions.

4a Writing fractions

● A **fraction** is a part of a whole.

Fold a piece of paper in half... ... and in half again.

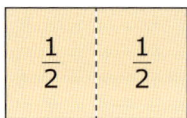

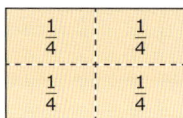

| $\frac{1}{2}$ | $\frac{1}{2}$ |

→

| $\frac{1}{4}$ | $\frac{1}{4}$ |
| $\frac{1}{4}$ | $\frac{1}{4}$ |

2 equal parts   4 equal parts

Each part is a half   Each part is a quarter

● The **numerator** shows how many parts of the whole you are working with.

➡ $\dfrac{1}{4}$ ⬅

● The **denominator** shows how many equal parts the whole has been divided into.

Example

What fraction is shaded?

There are **six** equal parts.
One part is shaded.
The shaded fraction is $\frac{1}{6}$ (one-sixth).

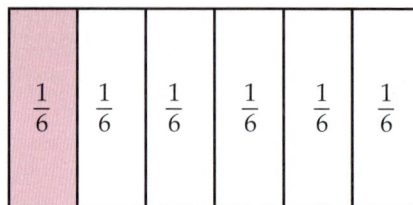

| $\frac{1}{6}$ | $\frac{1}{6}$ | $\frac{1}{6}$ | $\frac{1}{6}$ | $\frac{1}{6}$ | $\frac{1}{6}$ |

You can use fractions to describe situations in real life.

Example

a What fraction of this pizza has mushrooms?
b What fraction of this pizza has no mushrooms?

a There are eight parts.
   Five parts out of eight have mushrooms.
   $\frac{5}{8}$ (five-eighths) of the pizza has mushrooms.
b Three parts out of eight have no mushrooms.
   $\frac{3}{8}$ (three-eighths) of the pizza has no mushrooms.

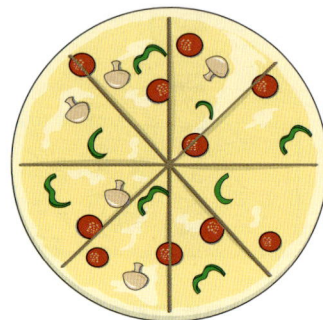

Number Fractions, decimals and percentages

Exercise 4a

1 What fraction is shaded?

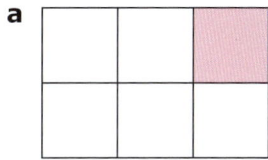

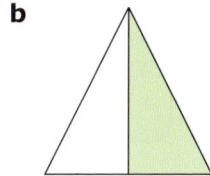

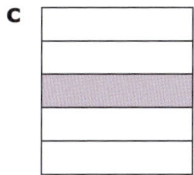

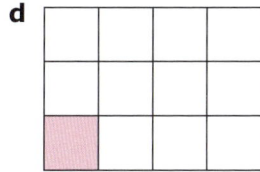

a

b

c

d

4 Match each shaded shape with its fraction.

$\frac{1}{4}$ $\frac{2}{3}$ $\frac{3}{4}$ $\frac{1}{5}$ $\frac{1}{8}$

$\frac{1}{10}$ $\frac{3}{5}$ $\frac{4}{7}$ $\frac{1}{6}$ $\frac{3}{8}$

a

b

c

d

e

f

g

h

i

j

2 Nisha baked a cake. She cuts it into eight equal pieces. She eats some of the cake.

   a What fraction has she eaten?

   b What fraction of the cake is left?

3 What fraction of each shape is shaded? What fraction is unshaded?

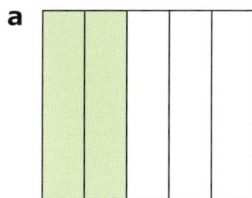

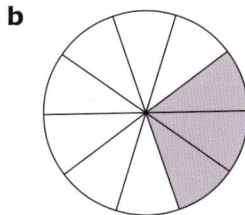

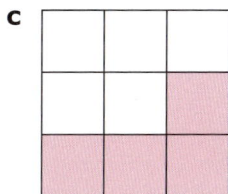

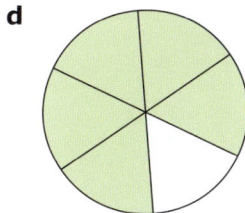

a

b

c

d

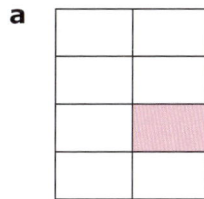

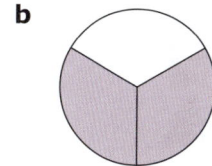

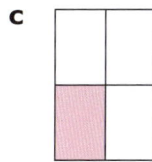

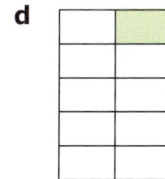

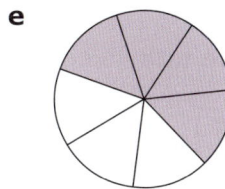

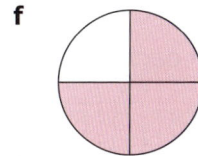

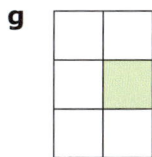

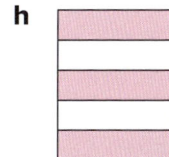

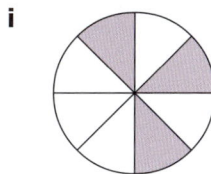

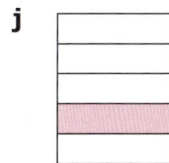

Problem solving

5 Lydia cuts up a pizza into four pieces. Is what Lydia says correct?

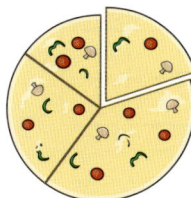

My piece is a quarter.

Lydia and Lewis are sharing a pizza.

Can I have half your pizza?

Yes, take two quarters.

Lewis knows that $\frac{2}{4} = \frac{1}{2}$.

⬤ Fractions which are worth the same but have different denominators are **equivalent**.

$\frac{2}{4}$ is equivalent to $\frac{1}{2}$.

Example

Match each shaded shape with its equivalent fraction.

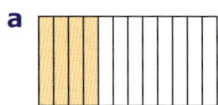

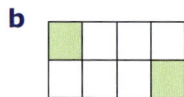

a

b

c

$\frac{1}{2}$ $\frac{1}{3}$ $\frac{1}{4}$

a $\frac{4}{12} = \frac{1}{3}$

b $\frac{2}{8} = \frac{1}{4}$

c $\frac{4}{8} = \frac{1}{2}$

⬤ You can multiply or divide the **numerator** and the **denominator** by the same number to make equivalent fractions.

$\div 3$

$\frac{3}{9} = \frac{1}{3}$

$\div 3$

$\times 2$

$\frac{1}{5} = \frac{2}{10}$

$\times 2$

Example

Which shape has $\frac{1}{4}$ shaded?

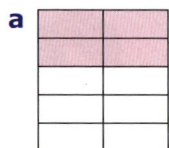

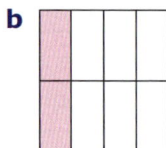

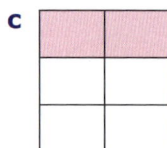

a

b

c

Shape **b** shows $\frac{1}{4}$ shaded.

$\div 2$

$\frac{2}{8} = \frac{1}{4}$

$\div 2$

Exercise 4b

1 What fraction is shaded?

Match it to an equivalent fraction: $\frac{1}{2}$, $\frac{1}{3}$, $\frac{1}{4}$.

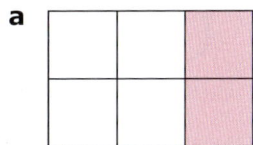

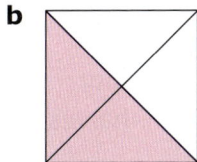

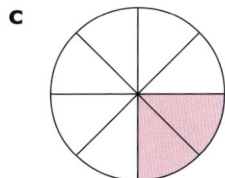

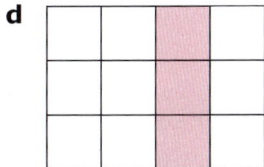

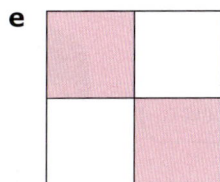

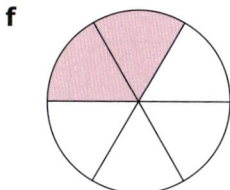

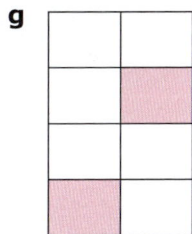

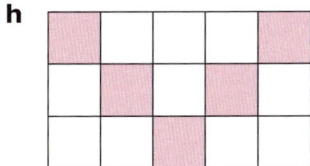

a

b

c

d

e

f

g

h

2 c

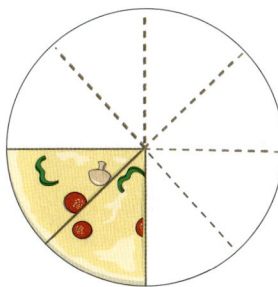

3 Find these equivalent fractions by multiplying or dividing.

a $\frac{2}{6} = \frac{1}{\square}$

b $\frac{2}{4} = \frac{\square}{2}$

c $\frac{1}{\square} = \frac{3}{6}$

d $\frac{1}{3} = \frac{3}{\square}$

e $\frac{4}{12} = \frac{1}{\square}$

f $\frac{10}{20} = \frac{\square}{2}$

2 Write two different equivalent fractions for each situation.

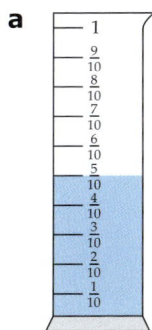

a

b

Did you know?

At least $\frac{7}{10}$ of the human body is water.

Problem solving

4 Karen bakes a cherry pie and an apple pie of equal sizes. She cuts the cherry pie into 7 equal pieces and the apple pie into 5 equal pieces.

If she eats $\frac{3}{7}$ of the cherry pie and $\frac{2}{5}$ of the apple pie, which pie do you think has the most left over? Sketch the pies to help you.

4c Improper fractions

Isla bakes two pies.
She cuts each pie in half.

$=$ $= \dfrac{4}{2}$ ← four
← halves

$\dfrac{4}{2}$ is also called a 'top heavy' fraction.

$\dfrac{4}{2}$ is an **improper fraction**.

> ⬤ The **numerator** of an improper fraction is always greater than its **denominator**. An improper fraction is always greater than 1.

Isla bakes another pie and cuts all three pies into quarters.
She eats one slice.

There are 11 quarters left over.

There are 2 and $\dfrac{3}{4}$ left over.

They are both correct.

$\dfrac{11}{4} = 2\dfrac{3}{4}$

> ⬤ A **mixed number** contains a whole number and a fraction.

$2\dfrac{3}{4}$ is a mixed number.

Example

Change the improper fraction $\dfrac{7}{3}$ into a mixed number.

$\dfrac{7}{3}$ makes 2 whole pies with $\dfrac{1}{3}$ left over.

$\dfrac{7}{3} = 2\dfrac{1}{3}$ $7 \div 3 = 2 \text{ r } 1$

Example

Change the mixed number $4\dfrac{1}{3}$ into an improper fraction.

$4\dfrac{1}{3}$ means 4 wholes with $\dfrac{1}{3}$ left over.

4 wholes are $4 \times 3 = 12$ thirds.

One third left over so $12 + 1 = 13$ thirds or $\dfrac{13}{3}$.

$4\dfrac{1}{3} = \dfrac{13}{3}$

Number   Fractions, decimals and percentages

Exercise 4c

1 Mei Ling has three bars of chocolate.
Each bar has four pieces.
She eats five pieces.
How much does she have left?
Write it as an improper fraction and a mixed number.

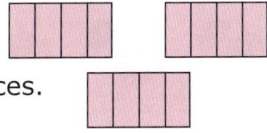

2 Write each amount as an improper fraction.

a $= \dfrac{\square}{3}$

b $= \dfrac{\square}{4}$

c $= \dfrac{\square}{\square}$

d $= \dfrac{\square}{\square}$

3 Write each amount as a mixed number.

a $= 3\dfrac{\square}{\square}$

b $= \square\dfrac{\square}{\square}$

3 c $= \square\dfrac{\square}{\square}$

d $= \square\dfrac{\square}{\square}$

4 Write each amount as
a an improper fraction
b a mixed number.

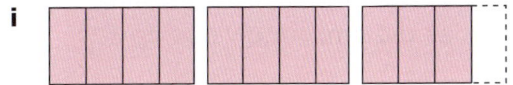

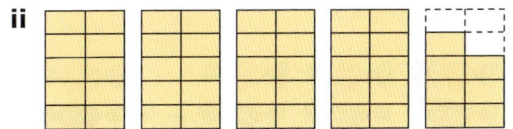

i

ii

5 Change these improper fractions to mixed numbers.

a $\dfrac{5}{2}$ **b** $\dfrac{10}{3}$ **c** $\dfrac{9}{2}$

d $\dfrac{9}{4}$ **e** $\dfrac{13}{5}$ **f** $\dfrac{11}{4}$

g $\dfrac{14}{5}$ **h** $\dfrac{19}{3}$ **i** $\dfrac{16}{7}$

6 Change these mixed numbers to improper fractions

a $1\dfrac{1}{2}$ **b** $1\dfrac{1}{4}$ **c** $2\dfrac{1}{2}$

d $2\dfrac{2}{3}$ **e** $3\dfrac{4}{5}$ **f** $3\dfrac{3}{7}$

g $2\dfrac{5}{6}$ **h** $3\dfrac{1}{9}$ **i** $4\dfrac{3}{8}$

Problem solving

7 a Isla bakes some chocolate sponge cakes. She cuts each cake into five equal pieces. She has 25 pieces when she has finished. How many cakes does Isla bake?

b If Isla's friends eat 7 pieces, how many cakes are remaining? Express your answer as a mixed number.

MyMaths.co.uk   1019   SEARCH

Ranjit has 6 apples.

She puts them into 3 equal groups of 2 apples.
She eats 2 apples.
$\frac{1}{3}$ of 6 is 2.

⬤ $\frac{1}{3}$ of an amount is the same as the amount divided by 3.

$\frac{1}{3}$ of 9 sweets

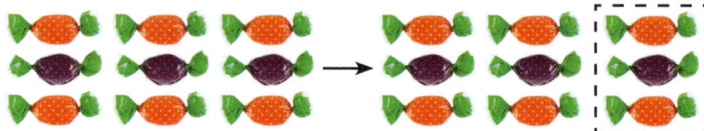

9 sweets $9 \div 3 = 3$

⬤ To find a fraction of an amount, divide the amount by the **denominator**.

$$\frac{1}{5} \text{ of } 25 = \frac{25}{5} = 25 \div 5 = 5$$

Example

Find $\frac{1}{3}$ of

a 9 kg

9 kg

b 21 stamps

c 12 cm

a $\frac{1}{3}$ of 9 = 9 ÷ 3 = 3 kg

9 can be divided into 3 equal groups of 3

b $\frac{1}{3}$ of 21 = 21 ÷ 7 = 7 stamps

21 can be divided into 7 equal groups of 3

c $\frac{1}{3}$ of 12 = 12 ÷ 3 = 4 cm

12 can be divided into 4 equal groups of 3

Exercise 4d

1 Copy and complete these divisions.

a $8 \div 2 = \square$ **b** $9 \div 3 = \square$

c $10 \div 5 = \square$ **d** $12 \div 4 = \square$

e $15 \div 3 = \square$ **f** $18 \div 6 = \square$

2 Copy and complete these statements.

a To find $\frac{1}{5}$ of an amount, divide by _____.

b To find $\frac{1}{10}$ of an amount, divide by _____.

c To find $\frac{1}{2}$ of an amount, divide by _____.

d To find $\frac{1}{8}$ of an amount, divide by _____.

3 Scruff has 10 dog biscuits.
He eats $\frac{1}{5}$ of them.
How many is this?

4 Here are some groups of sweets.

a Find $\frac{1}{3}$

b Find $\frac{1}{4}$

4 **c** Find $\frac{1}{5}$

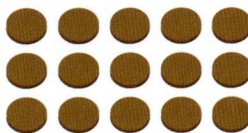

d Find $\frac{1}{2}$

e Find $\frac{1}{3}$

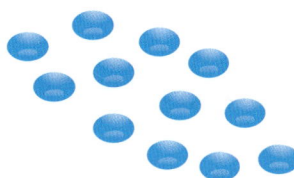

f Find $\frac{1}{4}$

Problem solving

5 Tracey is selling lemonade at the school fete.

a One jug of lemonade fills eight glasses.
What fraction of the lemonade in the jug does each glass hold?

b Tracey sells 64 glasses of lemonade. How many
full jugs will she have made?

6 Harry has a new job as a cake tester.
Each time he 'tests' a cake he has to
eat a slice that is $\frac{1}{5}$ of a cake.
At the end of the day Harry
has tested 40 cakes.
How many whole cakes has he eaten?

● Some fractions have 1 as a **numerator**.

$$\frac{1}{3}, \frac{1}{6}, \frac{1}{10}$$

The picture shows $\frac{1}{4}$ of 12 eggs.

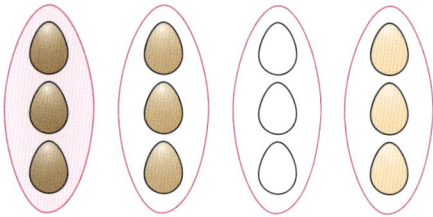

12 in 4 equal groups is

$12 \div 4 = \frac{12}{4} = 3$

$\frac{1}{4}$ of 12 is 3.

▲ Chickens can lay up to 800 eggs in their lifetime.

● Other fractions have a numerator greater than 1.

$$\frac{2}{3}, \frac{5}{6}, \frac{7}{10}$$

The picture shows $\frac{3}{4}$ of 12 eggs.

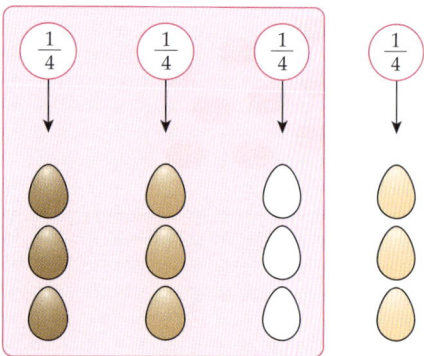

$\frac{1}{4}$ of 12 eggs $= 12 \div 4$

$= 3$ eggs

So $\frac{3}{4}$ will be 3×3

$= 9$ eggs.

$\frac{3}{4}$ is less than 1, so the answer will be less than 12

Example

What is $\frac{2}{3}$ of 15 eggs?

First find $\frac{1}{3}$ of 15

$15 \div 3 = 5$ $\frac{1}{3}$ of 15 eggs = 5 eggs

$\frac{2}{3}$ of 15 = 2 × $\frac{1}{3}$ of 15

    = 2 × 5

    = 10 eggs

Exercise 4e

1 Match the cards that have the same value.

$\frac{1}{3}$ of 9	6
5	9
$\frac{1}{3}$ of 27	4
10	$\frac{1}{4}$ of 16
3	$\frac{1}{5}$ of 40
8	7
$\frac{1}{4}$ of 24	$\frac{1}{5}$ of 25
$\frac{1}{4}$ of 28	$\frac{1}{3}$ of 30

2 Twenty people get onto a bus.

a $\frac{1}{4}$ of them support City. How many is this?

b $\frac{1}{5}$ of them support Rovers. How many is this?

c How many of the people support neither City nor Rovers?

3 Here is a collection of buttons.

a Find $\frac{2}{3}$ of this group.

b Find $\frac{3}{4}$ of this group.

4 Carla has saved £20. She decides to spend $\frac{2}{5}$ of it.
How much does Carla spend?

Problem solving

5 There are 21 people in this group.
$\frac{2}{7}$ of this group voted 'Yes'.
$\frac{2}{3}$ of this group voted 'No'.
How many did not vote?

6 Work out the legs of the spider diagram. Then choose a number to put in the centre and draw your own!

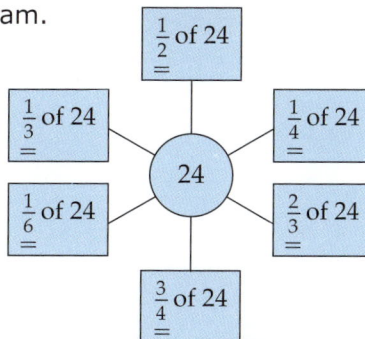

$\frac{1}{2}$ of 24 =
$\frac{1}{3}$ of 24 =
$\frac{1}{4}$ of 24 =
$\frac{1}{6}$ of 24 =
$\frac{2}{3}$ of 24 =
$\frac{3}{4}$ of 24 =
24

Did you know?

$\frac{4}{10}$ of girls born in 2013 have a good chance of living to 100!

A **percentage** is a **fraction** with denominator 100.

'Percent' means 'out of a hundred'. 100% is all of it!

10% means $\frac{10}{100} = \frac{1}{10}$. To find 10% divide by 10.

You can divide 20 marbles into 4 equal sections.

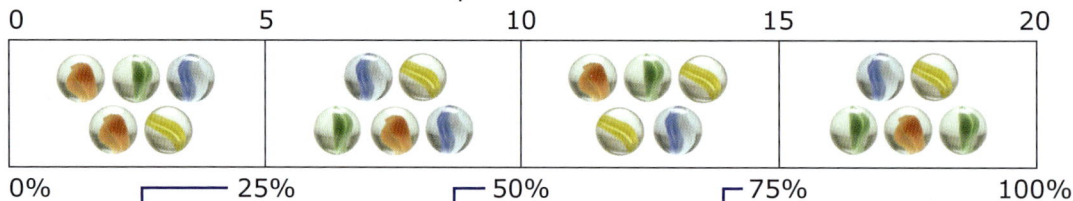

| 0 | 5 | 10 | 15 | 20 |

| 0% | 25% | 50% | 75% | 100% |

25% is half of 50%.
25% of 20 = 5

50% is half.
50% of 20 = 10

75% is 3 lots of 25%.
75% of 20 = 3 × 5 = 15

50% is **equivalent** to $\frac{1}{2}$.

To find 25%, you can just divide by 4.

You can also divide 20 marbles into 10 equal sections.

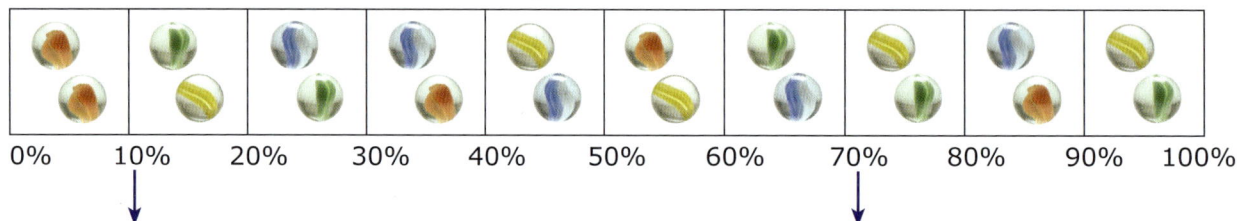

| 0% | 10% | 20% | 30% | 40% | 50% | 60% | 70% | 80% | 90% | 100% |

10% of 20 marbles = 2 marbles
$\frac{1}{10}$ of 20 marbles = 2 marbles

70% of 20 marbles = 14 marbles
$\frac{7}{10}$ of 20 marbles = 14 marbles

10% is equivalent to $\frac{1}{10}$.

Example

Find 50% of
a 100 litres   **b** 60 kg   **c** 24 students

50% is the same as $\frac{1}{2}$.

a $\frac{1}{2}$ of 100 litres
  = 100 ÷ 2
  = 50 litres

b $\frac{1}{2}$ of 60 kg
  = 60 ÷ 2
  = 30 kg

c $\frac{1}{2}$ of 24 students
  = 24 ÷ 2
  = 12 students

Exercise 4f

1 Ravi surveyed his classmates and found that

  a 40% of students in the class are boys.
      What percentage are girls?

  b 35% of students come to school by car.
      What percentage do not use cars?

> Remember, 100% is all of it!

2 What percentage of each rod is painted red, and what percentage is blue?

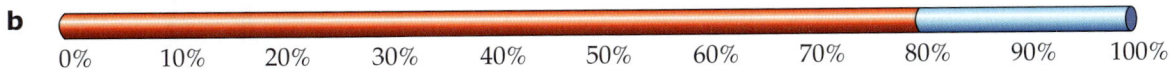

  a

| 0% | 10% | 20% | 30% | 40% | 50% | 60% | 70% | 80% | 90% | 100% |

  b

| 0% | 10% | 20% | 30% | 40% | 50% | 60% | 70% | 80% | 90% | 100% |

3 Thirty marbles are divided equally onto a ten-section strip.

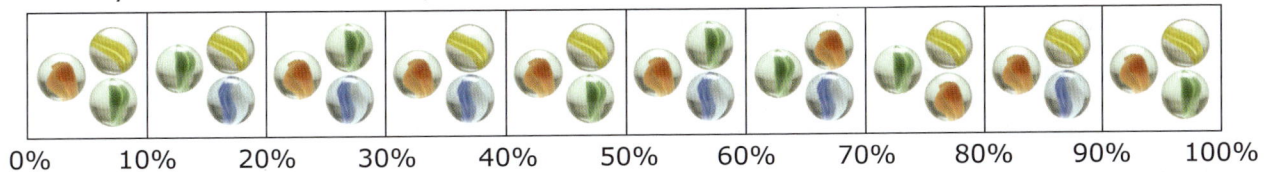

| 0% | 10% | 20% | 30% | 40% | 50% | 60% | 70% | 80% | 90% | 100% |

  Work out these percentage calculations.

  a 10% of 30   **b** 30% of 30   **c** 50% of 30

  d 80% of 30   **e** 60% of 30   **f** 100% of 30

> Use the percent strip to help you.

4 Find 10% of each of these weights.

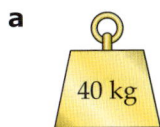

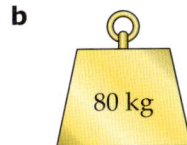

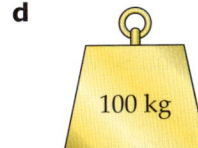

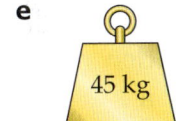

  a 40 kg   **b** 80 kg   **c** 20 kg   **d** 100 kg   **e** 45 kg

5 Find 50% of these amounts.

  a £12   **b** 30 kg   **c** 90 days

  d 50p   **e** 22 minutes   **f** 120 litres

Problem solving

6 These students are 10% of the school basketball club.

  a How many students are there in the whole basketball club?

  b Only 20% of the students turned up for training.
      How many students turned up?

7 The small print on the carton says
that 13% of the drink is juice.
What percentage is not juice?

4g Finding percentages

A **percentage** is a **fraction** with denominator 100.

$$30\% = \frac{30}{100} = \frac{3}{10}$$

Chloe sees a dress in a sale.
It is normally £20, but today
there is a 50% off sale!

50% of £20 = $\frac{1}{2}$ of £20 = £10

Chloe knows that 50%
is the same as $\frac{1}{2}$.

p.264 >

To find a percentage of an amount, you first find the
equivalent fraction with denominator 100.

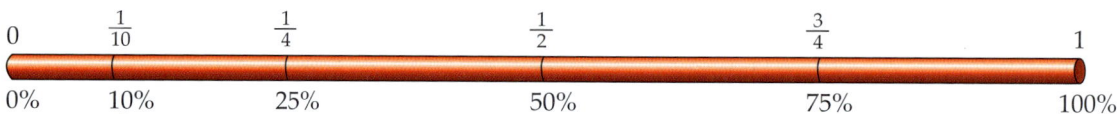

0	$\frac{1}{10}$	$\frac{1}{4}$	$\frac{1}{2}$	$\frac{3}{4}$	1
0%	10%	25%	50%	75%	100%

10% is the same as $\frac{1}{10}$.
So divide by 10.

75% is the same as $\frac{3}{4}$.
So divide by 4, then multiply by 3.

How can
you use this
information to
find 20% of
something?

Example

How much would you save in these sales?

a £80 — 10% off!

b £120 — 25% off!

a $10\% = \frac{1}{10}$

$\frac{1}{10}$ of £80 = 80 ÷ 10

80 ÷ 10 = 8

Save £8!

b $25\% = \frac{1}{4}$

$\frac{1}{4}$ of £120 = 120 ÷ 4

120 ÷ 4 = 30

Save £30!

Example

Find the missing number.

SALE
Price was £ 10
Now 50% off
Price is now £__

50% is $\frac{1}{2}$

$\frac{1}{2}$ of £10 = 10 ÷ 2 = 5

The old price − the amount off = the new price
£10   −   £5   =   £5

Exercise 4g

1 Find 10% of

   a 50m   **b** 30 starfish

   c 90kg   **d** £150

   e 250 votes   **f** 110 litres

2 Find

   a 20% of 40   **b** 60% of 80

   c 30% of 60   **d** 40% of 70

   e 70% of 30   **f** 20% of 25

3 How much would you save in these sales?

   a
> Price was £20
> Now 50% off!!

   b
> Take 10% off
> **£70!**

   c
> **SALE!!**
> 20% off £60

   d
> 30% off
> **£150!**

4 What is the new price of each item?

> Use old price − amount off = new price

a

£60
Take 10% off!!

b

£120
Take 20% off!!

c

£40
Take 25% off!!

d

£22
Take 50% off!!

e

£30
Take 60% off!!

> 60% is 6 × 10%

Problem solving

5 Three of the four percentages in each grid give the same amount.
Work out each answer and write the odd one out.

   a

25% of 40	10% of 100
50% of 20	75% of 12

   b

10% of 200	75% of 16
25% of 48	50% of 24

   c

75% of 28	25% of 84
10% of 120	50% of 42

   d

10% of 90	25% of 32
50% of 18	75% of 12

6 Take 70% of 150, and then take 20% of this amount.
Now take 20% of 150 then calculate 70% of that amount.
What do you notice?

> Try this with a number other than 150. Can you explain the results?

4h Fractions, decimals and percentages

⬤ Fractions, decimals and percentages all show parts of a whole amount.

You can divide a whole 1 into ten equal sections ...

< p.10

0%	10%	20%	30%	40%	50%	60%	70%	80%	90%	100%

| 0 | 0.1 | 0.2 | 0.3 | 0.4 | 0.5 | 0.6 | 0.7 | 0.8 | 0.9 | 1.0 |

| 0 | $\frac{1}{10}$ | $\frac{2}{10}$ | $\frac{3}{10}$ | $\frac{4}{10}$ | $\frac{5}{10}$ | $\frac{6}{10}$ | $\frac{7}{10}$ | $\frac{8}{10}$ | $\frac{9}{10}$ | $\frac{10}{10}$ |

$$=\frac{1}{5} \qquad =\frac{2}{5} \qquad =\frac{3}{5} \qquad =\frac{4}{5} \qquad \frac{5}{5}=1$$

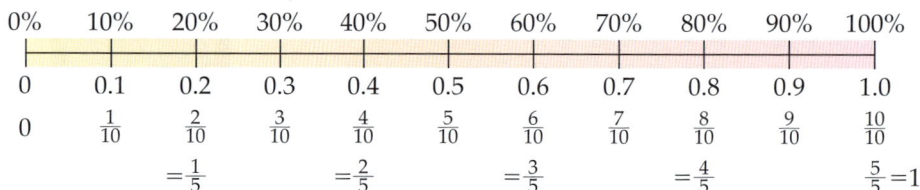

... or you can divide a whole 1 into four equal sections.

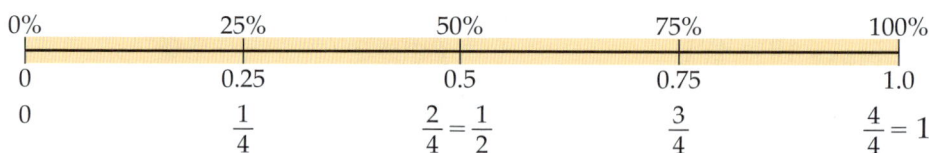

0%	25%	50%	75%	100%

| 0 | 0.25 | 0.5 | 0.75 | 1.0 |

| 0 | $\frac{1}{4}$ | $\frac{2}{4}=\frac{1}{2}$ | $\frac{3}{4}$ | $\frac{4}{4}=1$ |

What does your calculator display when you enter 3 divided by 4?

⬤ You can describe a part of an amount using fractions, decimals or percentages.

Example

For each shape, write the shaded part

i as a fraction   **ii** as a decimal   **iii** as a percentage.

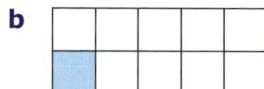

a   **b**   **c**

a **i** $\frac{6}{10}$ or $\frac{3}{5}$ **ii** 0.6   **iii** 60%

b **i** $\frac{1}{10}$ **ii** 0.1   **iii** 10%

c **i** $\frac{1}{4}$ **ii** 0.25   **iii** 25%

This hundred square is **divided** into 100 **equal** parts.

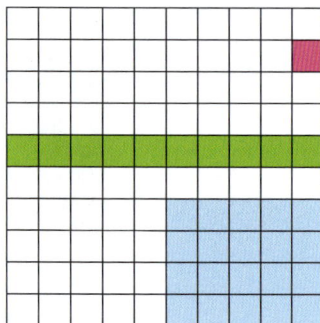

This red square is $\frac{1}{100}$ or 0.01 or 1% of the whole.

This green row of 10 squares is $\frac{1}{10}$ or 0.1 or 10%.

$\frac{20}{100}$ of the squares are shaded blue.
This is 0.20 or 20%.

Exercise 4h

1 These cakes are divided into ten equal slices.
   What **percentage** of each cake is red?

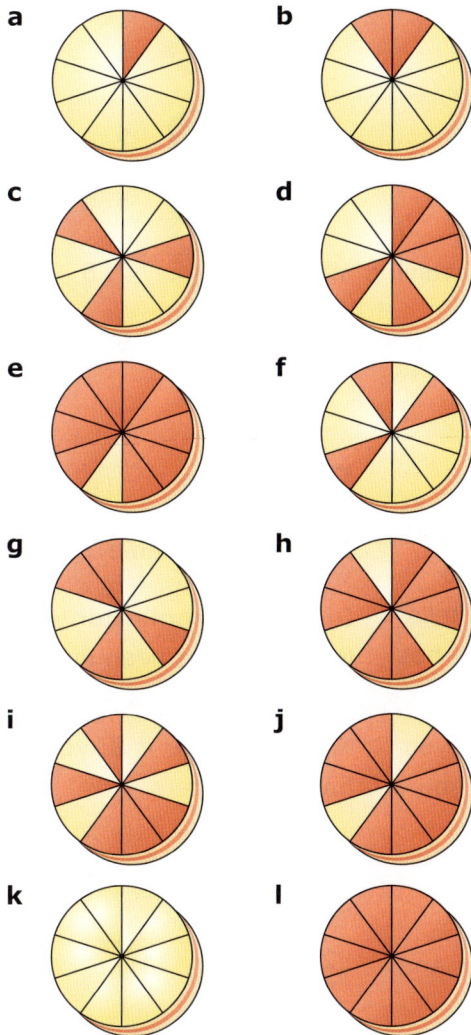

a b

c d

e f

g h

i j

k l

2 Use **fractions** to say how much of each cake in question **1** is yellow.

3 Use **decimals** to say how much of each cake in question **1** is yellow.

4 This hundred square is divided into 100 equal parts.

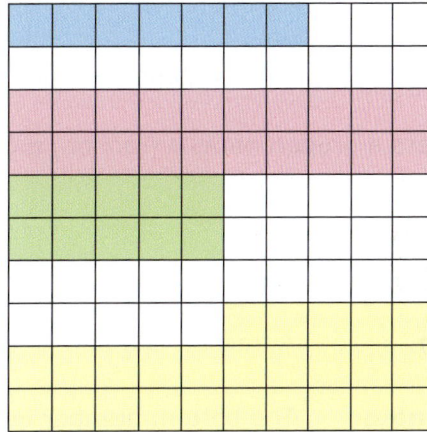

Describe the shaded areas as
i   a fraction   ii   a decimal
iii a percentage.
a blue area
b red area
c green area
d yellow area
e red and green area
f blue and yellow area
g What percentage is left unshaded?

Problem solving

5 Four cakes have been cut into different-sized pieces.
   a Which piece is the largest?
   b Match the pieces to make the four cakes.

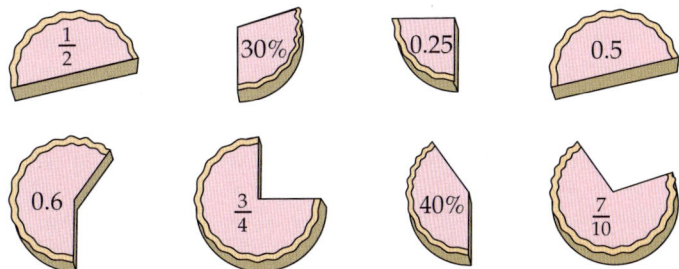

$\frac{1}{2}$ 30%   0.25   0.5

0.6 $\frac{3}{4}$ 40% $\frac{7}{10}$

Check out

You should now be able to ...

Test it ➡
Questions

✓ Use fractions to describe parts of a whole, including improper fractions.	④	1 – 3
✓ Identify equivalent fractions.	③	4
✓ Find fractions of a quantity.	⑤	5, 6
✓ Calculate simple percentages, including problems involving money.	④	7, 8
✓ Express a proportion as a fraction, a decimal or a percentage.	⑤	9

Language	Meaning	Example
Fraction	A fraction is a part of a whole.	$\frac{1}{2}$ is half of a whole
Denominator	The bottom number in a fraction. It tells you how many equal parts the whole has been divided into.	In $\frac{3}{4}$, the denominator is 4: the whole has been divided into 4 equal parts – quarters.
Numerator	The top number in a fraction. It tells you how many equal parts of the whole you have.	The numerator is 3: you have 3 quarters.
Equivalent fractions	Fractions with the same value.	$\frac{1}{2} = \frac{2}{4} = \frac{3}{6}$
Mixed number	A fraction with a whole number part and a fraction part.	$1\frac{2}{3}$
Improper fraction	A fraction with a numerator larger than the denominator.	$\frac{5}{3}$
Percentage	A fraction out of 100.	$20\% = \frac{20}{100}$

1 Write the fraction of the shape which is shaded.

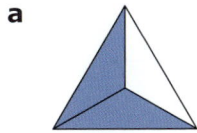

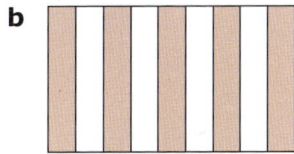

a

b

2 Convert these improper fractions to mixed numbers.

a $\frac{3}{2}$ b $\frac{7}{3}$ c $\frac{15}{4}$

3 Convert these mixed numbers to improper fractions.

a $2\frac{2}{3}$ b $1\frac{1}{4}$ c $7\frac{1}{2}$

4 Copy and complete these pairs of equivalent fractions.

a $\frac{3}{9} = \frac{\square}{3}$ b $\frac{1}{4} = \frac{\square}{20}$

c $\frac{1}{\square} = \frac{10}{20}$ d $\frac{6}{24} = \frac{1}{\square}$

5 Find

a $\frac{1}{2}$ of 10 b $\frac{1}{3}$ of 12

c $\frac{1}{4}$ of 40 d $\frac{1}{5}$ of 30

6 Find

a $\frac{2}{3}$ of 24 b $\frac{3}{4}$ of 16 c $\frac{3}{5}$ of 10

7 Find

a 10% of 40 b 20% of 40
c 30% of 40 d 50% of 40
e 60% of 40 f 25% of 40

8 Find

a 10% of 60 b 30% of 60
c 40% of 60 d 50% of 60
e 70% of 60 f 100% of 60

9 This hundred square is divided into 100 equal parts

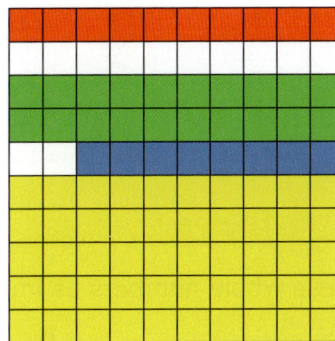

Describe the shaded areas as a

i fraction ii decimal.
  a red b green
  c blue d yellow

What next?

Score			
	0 – 3		Your knowledge of this topic is still developing. To improve look at Formative test: 1A-4; MyMaths: 1018, 1019, 1029, 1030, 1220, 1370 and 1371
	4 – 7		You are gaining a secure knowledge of this topic. To improve look at InvisiPen: 141, 142, 151 and 162
	8 – 9		You have mastered this topic. Well done, you are ready to progress!

4a

1 What fraction of each shape is shaded?

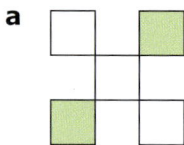

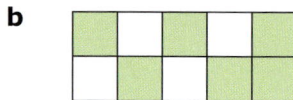

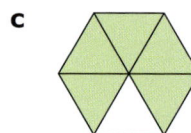

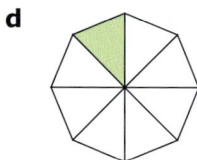

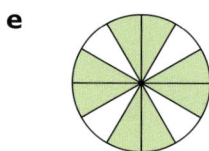

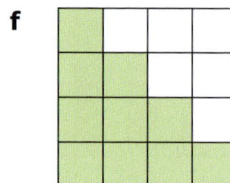

a

b

c

d

e

f

4b

2 Put these equivalent fractions into pairs as shown in the example.

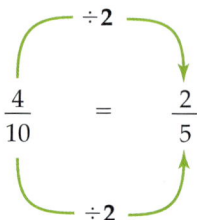

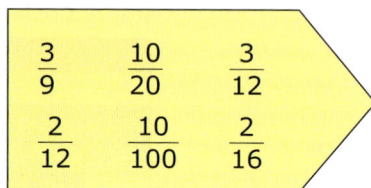

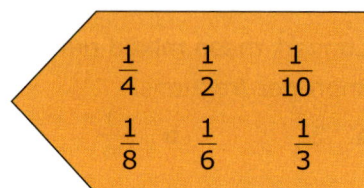

$$\frac{4}{10} = \frac{2}{5}$$

÷2 ... ÷2

$$\frac{3}{9} \quad \frac{10}{20} \quad \frac{3}{12}$$

$$\frac{2}{12} \quad \frac{10}{100} \quad \frac{2}{16}$$

$$\frac{1}{4} \quad \frac{1}{2} \quad \frac{1}{10}$$

$$\frac{1}{8} \quad \frac{1}{6} \quad \frac{1}{3}$$

4c

3 Write these whole numbers as improper fractions.

a $4 = \frac{\square}{2}$

b $3 = \frac{\square}{3}$

c $6 = \frac{\square}{2}$

d $2 = \frac{8}{\square}$

e $5 = \frac{15}{\square}$

f $5 = \frac{20}{\square}$

4 Write these improper fractions as whole numbers.

a $\frac{6}{2}$

b $\frac{8}{4}$

c $\frac{10}{2}$

d $\frac{15}{3}$

e $\frac{12}{3}$

f $\frac{28}{7}$

5 Write these improper fractions as mixed numbers.

a $\frac{7}{2}$

b $\frac{8}{3}$

c $\frac{9}{2}$

d $\frac{9}{4}$

e $\frac{11}{3}$

f $\frac{17}{5}$

6 Convert these mixed numbers into improper fractions.

a $2\frac{1}{2} = \frac{\square}{\square}$

b $3\frac{1}{2} = \frac{\square}{\square}$

c $2\frac{1}{4} = \frac{\square}{\square}$

d $3\frac{1}{3} = \frac{\square}{\square}$

e $2\frac{2}{5} = \frac{\square}{\square}$

f $3\frac{2}{7} = \frac{\square}{\square}$

7 Divide these counters into 2 equal groups.
  a There are ____ counters in each group.
  b What fraction is each group of the total?

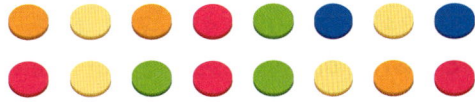

8 What is
  a $\frac{1}{10}$ of 30   **b** $\frac{1}{2}$ of 24   **c** $\frac{1}{5}$ of 30   **d** $\frac{1}{4}$ of 24   **e** $\frac{1}{8}$ of 24

9 Divide these counters into 4 equal groups.
  a There are ____ counters in each group.
  b What fraction is each group of the total?

10 A bag of 25 counters is divided into 5 groups.
  a How many counters are there in $\frac{1}{5}$ of the bag?
  b How many counters are there in $\frac{3}{5}$ of the bag?

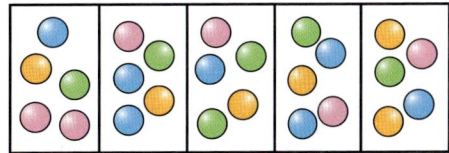

11 Find
  a $\frac{2}{5}$ of 10   **b** $\frac{2}{3}$ of 15   **c** $\frac{2}{3}$ of 12   **d** $\frac{3}{10}$ of 20   **e** $\frac{3}{5}$ of 20

12 40 teachers are surveyed about the time that school starts each morning.
   Use the percent strip below to help you.

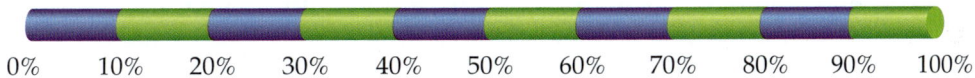

| 0% | 10% | 20% | 30% | 40% | 50% | 60% | 70% | 80% | 90% | 100% |

  a 40% vote for an earlier start. How many vote for this?
  b 30% vote to keep the same start time. How many vote for this?
  c 20% vote for a later start. How many vote for this?
  d 10% vote 'Don't Know'. How many vote for this?

13 These items are 10% off in a sale. Find their sale price.
  a Skirt costing £40   **b** Blouse costing £30   **c** Trousers costing £35

14 Copy and complete this equivalence table.

Fraction	Decimal	Percentage
$\frac{1}{10}$		
	0.2	
		60%

MyMaths.co.uk

These questions will test you on your knowledge of the topics in chapters 1 to 4.
They give you practice in the types of questions that you may see in your GCSE exams.
There are 70 marks in total.

1 a Write down the value of the 4 in words in each of these numbers.

    i 24   **ii** 476   **iii** 984   **iv** 341   (4 marks)

b Write these numbers in order from smallest to largest.

    347, 162, 971, 437, 734, 612, 791   (1 mark)

c Write down these decimal money amounts from smallest to largest.

    £4.32, £3.42, £4.23, £2.43, £2.34, £3.24   (1 mark)

2 Find the total of each of these. Do not use a calculator.

    a £0.60 + £0.27   **b** £3.27 + £9.30 + £7.41   (2 marks)

3 The recorded temperatures during seven consecutive days in a UK city were
1°C, -3°C, -2°C, 2°C, -4°C, -1°C, 3°C

    a Write these in order from coldest to warmest.   (2 marks)

    b What was the difference in temperature between the coldest and
warmest days?   (1 mark)

4 Round these numbers to

    a the nearest 10   **i** 12   **ii** 44   **iii** 63   (3 marks)

    b the nearest 100   **i** 235   **ii** 626   **iii** 967   (3 marks)

    c the nearest whole number.   **i** 3.88   **ii** 9.65   **iii** 23.54   (3 marks)

5 What are the readings given on these scales?

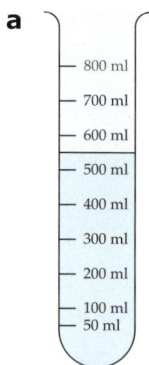

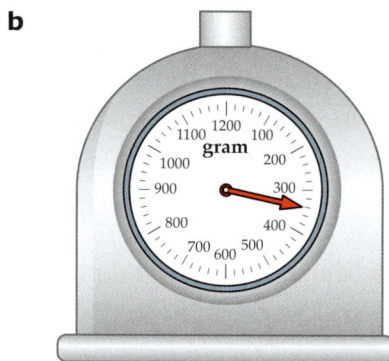

    a   **b**

    (2 marks)

6 The times shown are taken from different clocks.
Give the equivalent time in the clock given in brackets.

    a 9.30 pm (24-hour clock)   **b** 3.30 am (24-hour clock)

    c 13.45 (am/pm clock)   **d** 18:15 (am/pm clock)   (4 marks)

7 A tennis court is 78 feet long by 36 feet wide.

    a What is the perimeter of a tennis court?   (1 mark)

    b What is the name of the shape of a tennis court?   (1 mark)

8 For the irregular pentagon shown find
  a the perimeter (1 mark)
  b the area. (2 marks)

9 Express each metric quantity in terms of the new metric unit given in brackets.
  a 3.7 m (cm)
  b 195 g (kg)
  c 500 ml (litres)
  d 3.4 litres (cl) (4 marks)

10 I have picked 2 boxes of strawberries at a fruit farm.
  Each box contains x strawberries.
  a How many strawberries in total do I have?
     Write your answer in terms of x. (1 mark)
  b On the way home I eat 5 strawberries.
     How many strawberries do I now have? (1 mark)
  c If each box initially contains 42 strawberries, how many remain
     when I reach home? (2 marks)

11 Simplify these expressions by adding or subtracting like terms.
  a $4p + p$ **b** $5w + 12w - 1$
  c $6x + 4y - 3x$ **d** $9t - 2s + 6t - s$ (4 marks)

12 If $a = 3$, $b = 4$ and $c = 2$ work out the value of these expressions.
  a $3b$ (1 mark)   **b** $2c + a$ (2 marks)
  c $ac - b$ (2 marks)   **d** abc (2 marks)

13 There are 14 animals waiting to be seen by a vet. Seven are cats, four are dogs,
  two are rabbits and one is a hamster.
  a What fraction of the animals are
     i dogs   **ii** cats   **iii** rabbits   **iv** hamsters? (4 marks)
  b Write each fractions as another equivalent fraction. (4 marks)

14 Convert these fractions to either mixed numbers or improper fractions.
  a $\dfrac{8}{3}$ **b** $2\dfrac{2}{3}$ **c** $\dfrac{15}{2}$ **d** $4\dfrac{1}{4}$ (4 marks)

15 Find
  a $\dfrac{2}{5}$ of £25   **b** 50% of £30   **c** $\dfrac{1}{4}$ of 1200 g   **d** 30% of 240 litres (4 marks)

16 a Change these fractions to decimals   **i** $\dfrac{4}{5}$ **ii** $\dfrac{7}{10}$ (2 marks)
   b Change these decimals to percentages   **i** 0.6   **ii** 0.75 (2 marks)

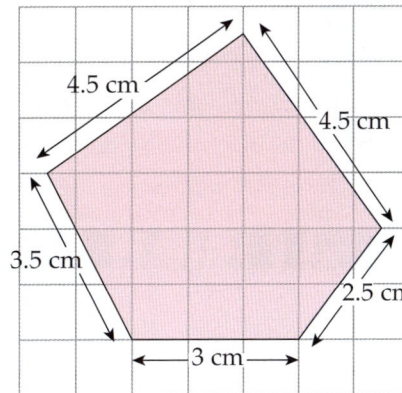

● **MyMaths**.co.uk

5 Angles and 2D shapes

Introduction

The Leaning Tower of Pisa is a very famous building in Italy. It was built in three stages over a timescale of 300 years. As it was being built it began to tilt and later the engineers tried to compensate by building rooms with one side bigger than the other. Modern restoration work has taken nearly 40 years to stabilise the tower and it now stands safely at an angle of about 4° from the vertical.

What's the point?

Accurate measurement of angles allows surveyors and engineers to construct buildings which are vertical and therefore stable – otherwise they would fall down!

Objectives

By the end of this chapter, you will have learned how to …

- Estimate angles and use a protractor to measure them.
- Distinguish between acute, obtuse and reflex angles.
- Use the sum of angles at a point, on a straight line and in a triangle.
- Classify triangles by their properties.
- Find missing angles in a triangle.
- Understand and use the points of a compass.

Check in

1 Work out these subtractions without using a calculator.

a 180 − 60 = ☐   **b** 180 − 150 = ☐   **c** 180 − 35 = ☐   **d** 180 − 90 = ☐

e 360 − 200 = ☐   **f** 360 − 130 = ☐   **g** 360 − 185 = ☐   **h** 360 − 180 = ☐

2 Write down the number that each arrow is pointing at.

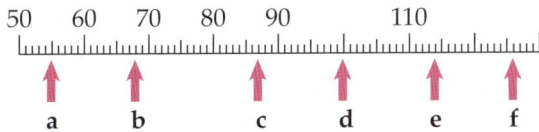

```
50   60   70   80   90        110
|littlitlittlitlittlitlittlitlittlitlittlitlittlit|
   ↑      ↑        ↑      ↑      ↑      ↑
   a      b        c      d      e      f
```

Starter problem

You will need a protractor, a plank of wood and some objects.

Place an object on the plank of wood and gradually lift up one side of the plank so the object is tilted.

Measure the angle at which the object topples over.

Repeat for different objects.

Write down what you have found out about the shapes of objects and when they topple over.

5a Angles

Rory is turning around.
He turns around to face the opposite direction.
This is a **half turn**.
He turns all the way around.
This is a **full turn**.

⬤ An **angle** is a measure of turn.

⬤ You measure angles in **degrees**, written ° for short.

There are 360° in
a full turn.

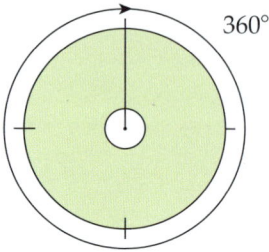

There are 180° in
a half turn.

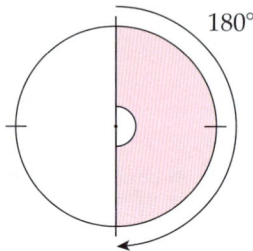

There are 90° in
a quarter turn.

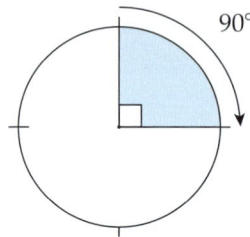

▲ You can see right
angles on many
buildings in cities.

This is a right angle.

p.178 >

An **acute** angle is smaller than 90°.	A **right angle** is exactly 90°.	An **obtuse** angle is between 90° and 180°.	The angle on a straight line is exactly 180°.

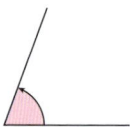

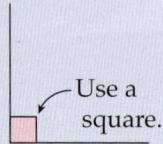

Use a square.

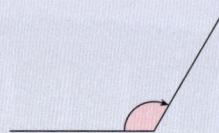

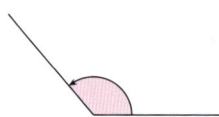

Example

Which one of these angles is 130°?

a

b

130° is between 90° and 180°
It is an obtuse angle.

a This angle is less than 90°.
   It is acute.

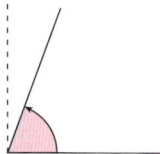

b This angle is between
   90° and 180°.
   It is obtuse so
   it must be 130°.

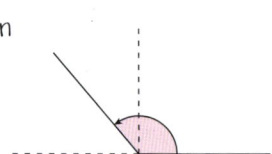

Exercise 5a

1 Name each of these angles. Choose your answers from this list.

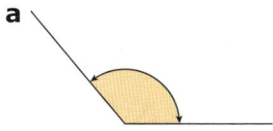 acute    obtuse   right   straight line

a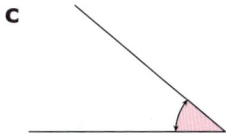

b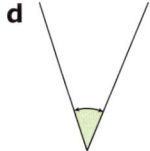

c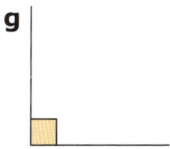

d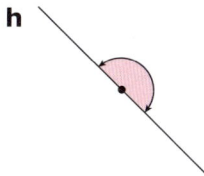

e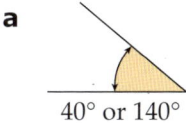

f

g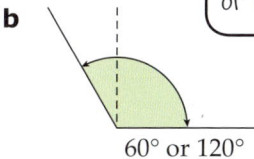

h

2 Which measurement is likely to be correct for each angle?

a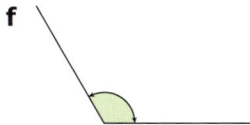
40° or 140°

Think! Is it more or less than 90°?

b
60° or 120°

2

c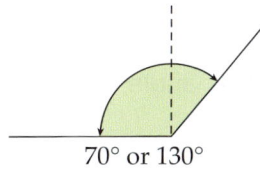
70° or 130°

d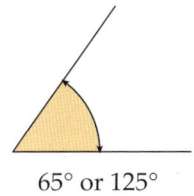
65° or 125°

e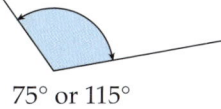
75° or 115°

f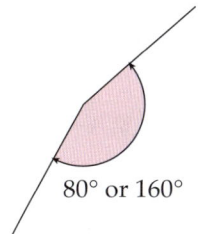
80° or 160°

3 Match each angle with a measurement from this list.

180°   30°   90°

155°   75°   120°

a

b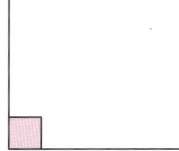

c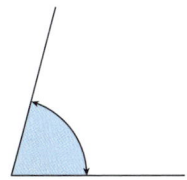

d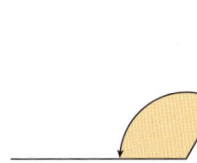

e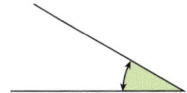

f

Problem solving

4 How many angles can you see on this bridge? What sort are they?

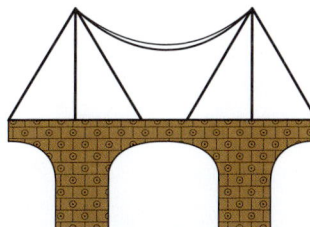

Rory is on a swing.

As he swings higher, the angle of turn gets greater.

  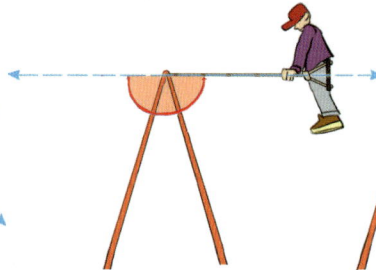 

An **acute** angle.
Less than 90°.

An **obtuse** angle.
Greater than 90°,
but less than 180°.

A **straight** line.
Exactly 180°,
or **half** a turn.

. . . oops!

Angles that add up to 180° make a straight line.

You can add any angles together.

Example

Add these angles. What is each new angle called?

a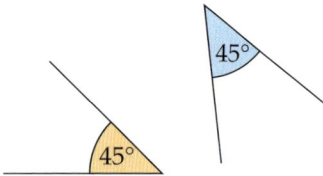

b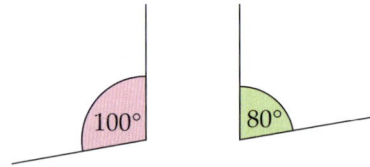

a 45° + 45° = 90°

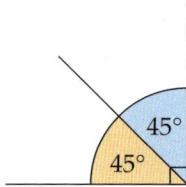

A 90° angle is a right angle.

b 100° + 80° + 180°

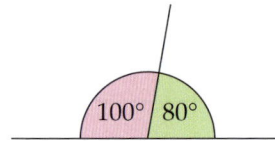

A 180° angle is a straight line.

Example

Find the missing angles in these diagrams.

a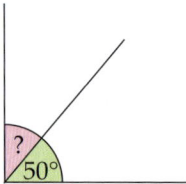

b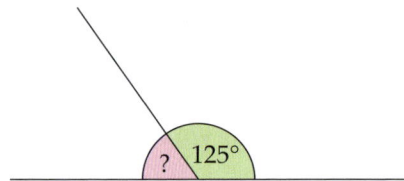

a 50° + ? = 90°
 ? = 90° − 50°
  = 40°

b 125° + ? = 180°
 ? = 180° − 125°
  = 55°

Exercise 5b

1 What do you need to add to each number to make 90?

    a 40   **b** 30   **c** 75

    d 15   **e** 45   **f** 5

2 What do you need to add to each number to make 180?

    a 120   **b** 30   **c** 90

    d 105   **e** 45   **f** 15

3 Write if each angle is acute or obtuse.

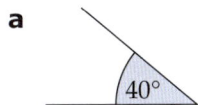

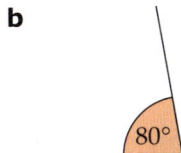

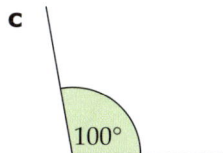

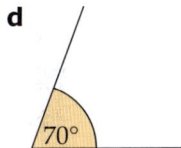

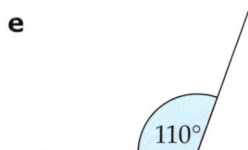

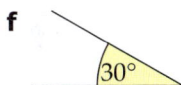

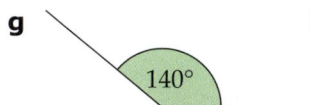

a

b

$40°$

$80°$

c

d

$100°$

$70°$

e

f

$110°$

$30°$

g

h

$140°$

$150°$

4 Find the four pairs of angles from question **3** that fit together to make a straight line.

5 How many more degrees does the pink line have to turn through to reach 90°?

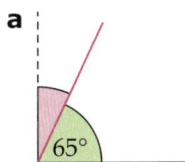

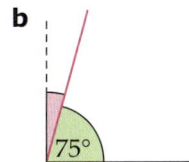

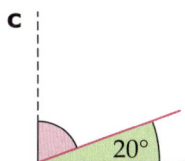

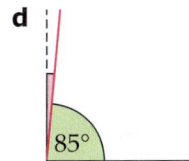

a

b

$65°$

$75°$

c

d

$20°$

$85°$

6 How many more degrees does the pink line have to turn through to reach 180°?

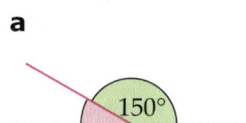

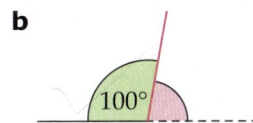

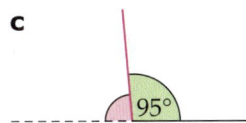

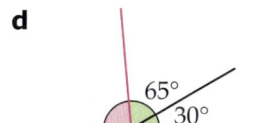

a

b

$150°$

$100°$

c

d

$95°$

$65°$

$30°$

Problem solving

7 Ryan is designing a stone arch.
Find the missing angle in Ryan's diagram.

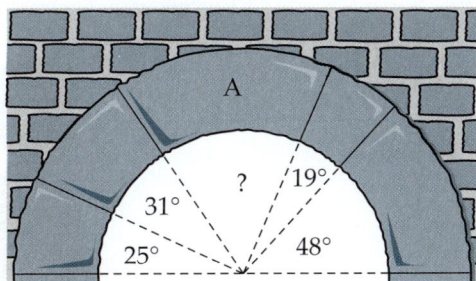

A

? $19°$

$31°$

$25°$ $48°$

8 Who has the bigger scoring angle, Alba or Marie? By how much?

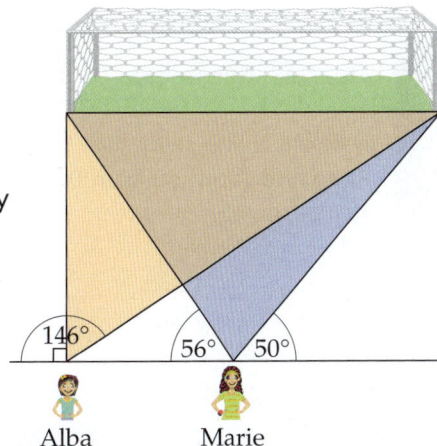

$146°$ $56°$ $50°$

Alba   Marie

You use a **protractor** to measure **angles**.

The scale is numbered in 10s and each small division is 1 **degree**.

You read one scale **anticlockwise** and the other scale **clockwise**.

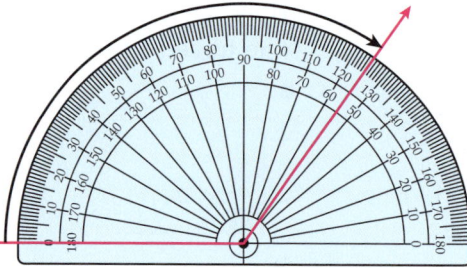

> You use the scale that starts at 0.

This angle is 125°.

It helps to **estimate** the size of the angle first.

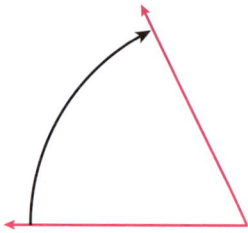

> Estimating means making your best guess.

p.228 >

This is less than 90°.
It is about 60°.

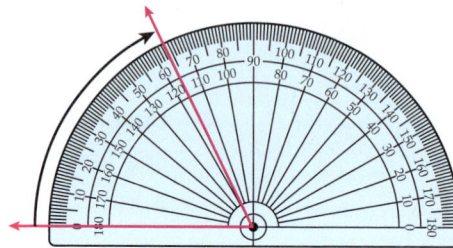

Read clockwise from zero.
The angle is 64°.

Example

What angle is shown here?

Estimate: about 60°.
Read anticlockwise from 0.
The angle is between 50° and 60°.
Count on from 50° to 55°.
The angle is 55°.

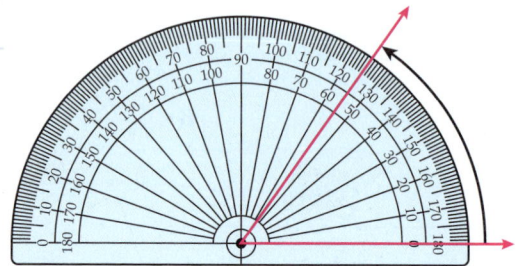

Example

Measure this angle.

Estimate: a little more than 90°.
Read anticlockwise from 0.
The angle is 100°.

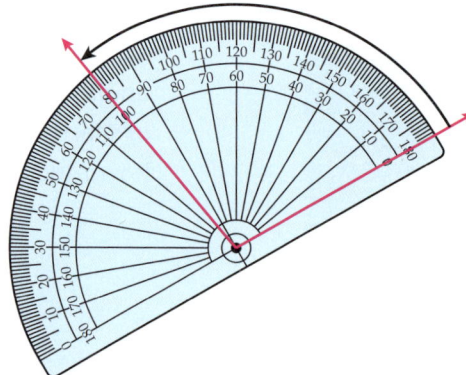

> You may need to rotate your protractor.

Exercise 5c

1 What is the size of each angle?
Say if they are acute or obtuse.
Give your answer in degrees (°).

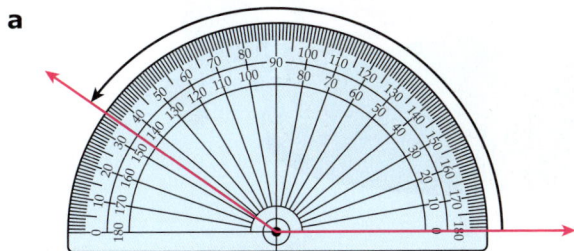

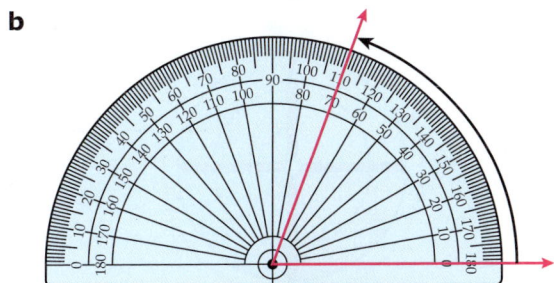

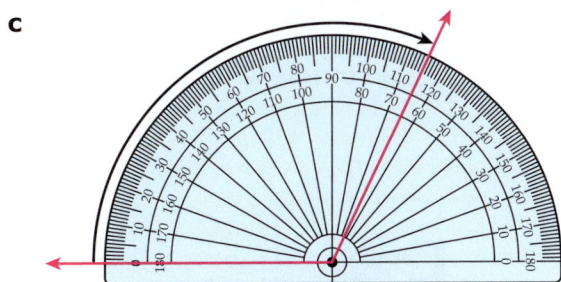

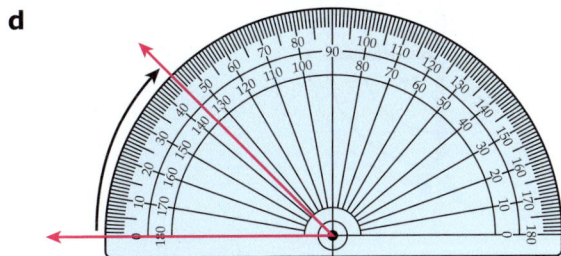

a

b

c

d

2 Measure these angles with a protractor.
Write an estimate first.
Give your answer in degrees (°).

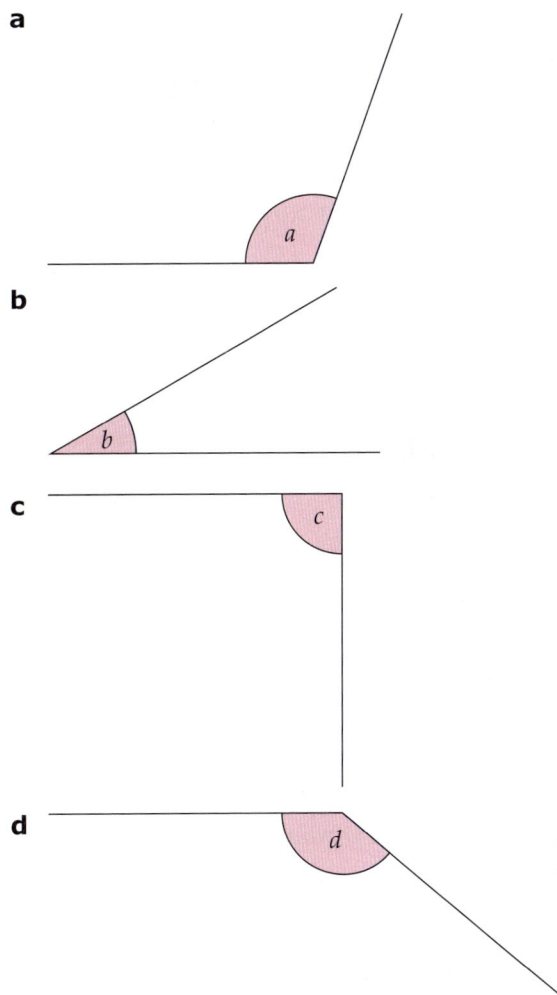

a

a

b

b

c

c

d

d

Problem solving

3 Measure the angles in this triangle.

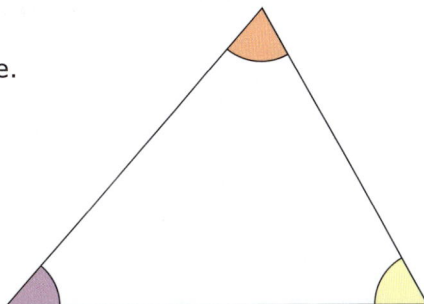

Rory is on a roundabout.
Each time the roundabout goes one full turn,
Rory turns through an angle of 360°.

As the roundabout turns the angle increases.

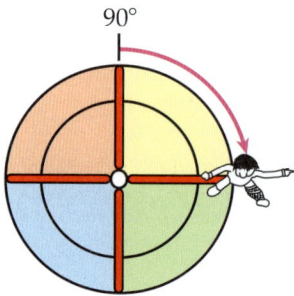

90°   180°   360°

a **quarter** turn   a **half** turn   a **complete** turn

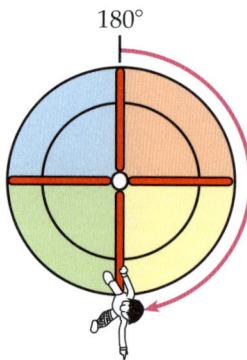

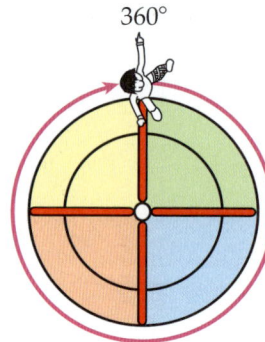

⬤ One complete turn is 360°.

Example

How many more degrees does Rory
need to turn through to reach 360°?

360° – 180° = 180°
Rory must turn 180° more to reach 360°.
Two half turns make one complete turn

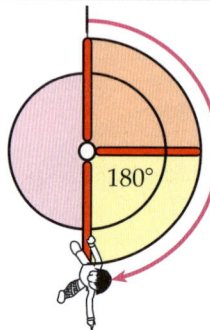

180°

⬤ An angle that is more than 180° but less that 360° is a **reflex** angle.

Example

Calculate the missing
angle.

This is a reflex angle.
360° – 110° = 250°

110° ?

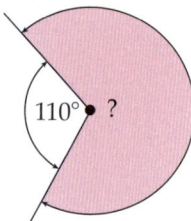

Calculate the angle! Don't
measure it with a protractor.

Exercise 5d

1 Find the missing numbers.

a 360 − 200 = ☐   b 360 − 120 = ☐
c 360 − 230 = ☐   d 360 − 250 = ☐
e 100 + ☐ = 360   f 260 + ☐ = 360
g ☐ + 60 = 360   h ☐ + 245 = 360
i 180 + ☐ = 360   j 360 − 90 = ☐
k 360 − ☐ = 210   l 130 + ☐ = 360

2 How many more degrees must Rory turn through each time to finish a complete turn?

a 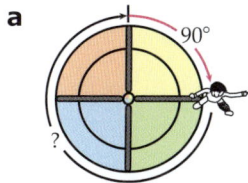   b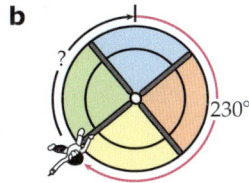

c 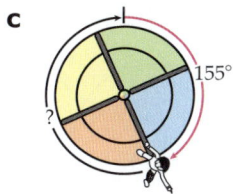   d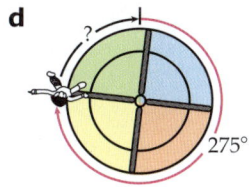

3 Find the missing angles.

a 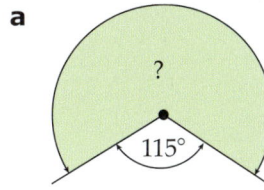   b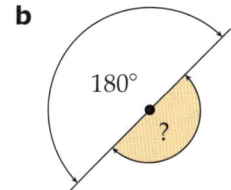

c 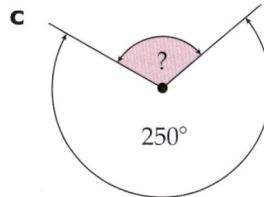   d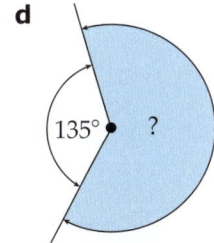

Did you know?

A traditional carousel has wooden horses rotating in a circle. The oldest was made over 200 years ago.

Problem solving

4 Choose three slices of cake that go together to make one whole cake.

 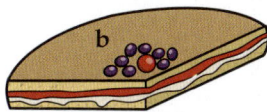 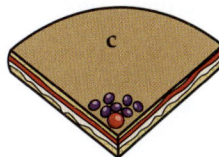 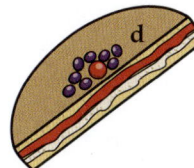 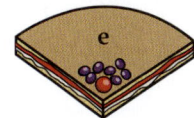

60°   150°   100°   180°   110°

5 How would you measure this angle using a protractor?

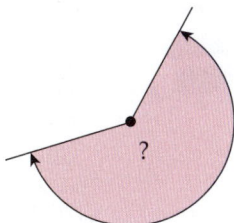

6 What is the smallest reflex angle you can make when adding three of these angles together?

35°   110°   165°
15°   75°   60°

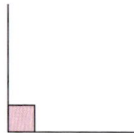

Angle facts

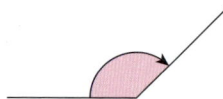
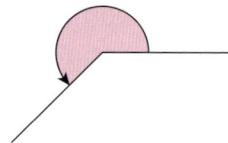

Acute angle
Less than 90°

Right angle
Exactly 90°
A quarter turn

Obtuse angle
More than 90°
less than 180°

Reflex angle
More than 180°
less than 360°

Angles on a straight line

Angles at a point

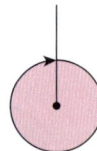

180° on a straight line, or half a turn

360° in one full turn

Example

Find the missing angles.

a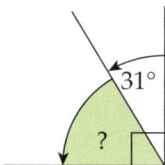

b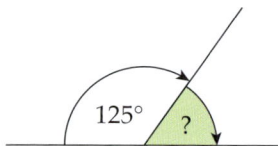

c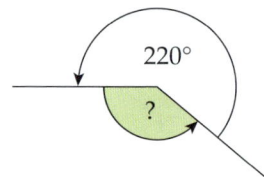

a   90° is a right angle.
The known angle is 31°.
? + 31° = 90°
? = 90° – 31°
   = 59°

b   180° is a straight line.
The known angle is 125°.
? + 125° = 180°
? = 180° – 125°
   = 55°

c   360° is a complete turn.
The known angle is 220°.
?° + 220° = 360°
? = 360° – 220°
   = 140°

Example

Priti's friends have eaten
240° of her cake.
What angle does the remaining
piece of cake make?

360° is a full turn.
360° – 240° = 120°
There are 120° left.

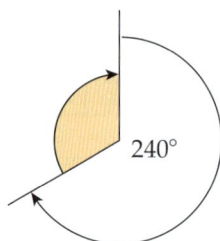

Exercise 5e

1 Choose the best **estimate** for each angle.

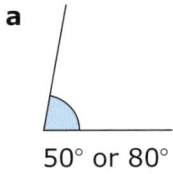

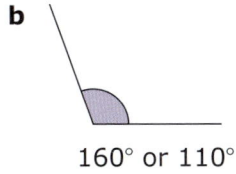

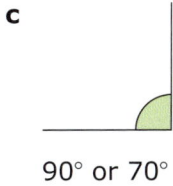

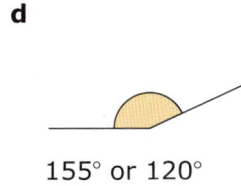

a

50° or 80°

b

160° or 110°

c

90° or 70°

d

155° or 120°

2 Are these acute angles, right angles or obtuse angles?

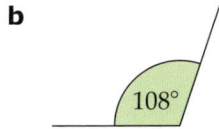

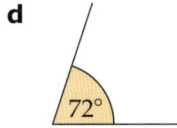

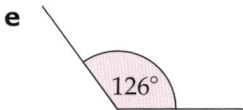

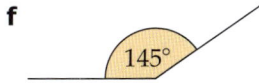

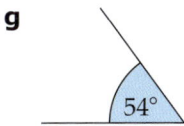

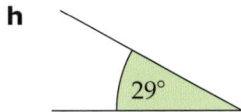

a
35°

b
108°

c
151°

d
72°

e
126°

f
145°

g
54°

h
29°

3 Which pairs of angles in question **2** fit together to make a straight line?

4 Work out the missing angle in each diagram.

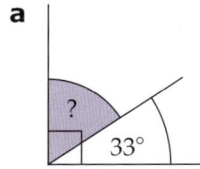

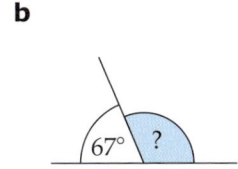

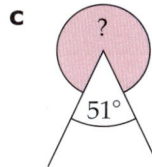

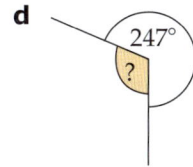

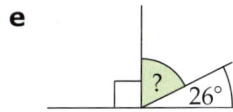

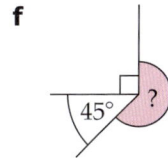

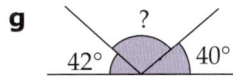

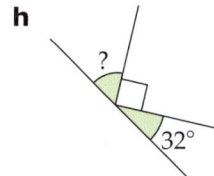

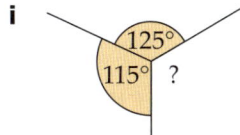

a
? 33°

b
67° ?

c
? 51°

d
247° ?

e
? 26°

f
45° ?

g
42° ? 40°

h
? 32°

i
125° 115° ?

Problem solving

5 Here are some wedges of cheese. Each wedge is cut at a different angle.
The wedges can join together to make different angles.
Which two wedges are used to make each of the angles A to G? The first one is done for you.

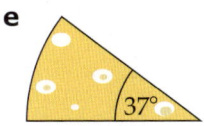

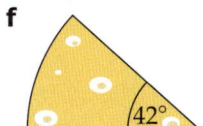

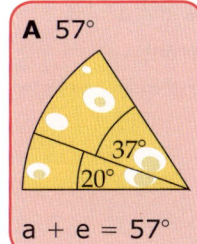

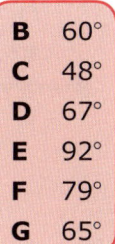

a 20°   **b** 23°   **c** 28°   **d** 30°

e 37°   **f** 42°   **g** 50°

A 57°	**B** 60°
	C 48°
37°	**D** 67°
20°	**E** 92°
a + e = 57°	**F** 79°
	G 65°

‹p.32

A **triangle** has three sides and three **angles**.

There are different kinds of triangles.

Isosceles	**Right-angled**	**Equilateral**	**Scalene**
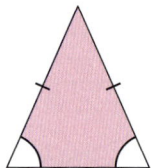	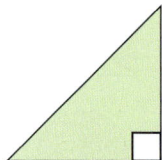	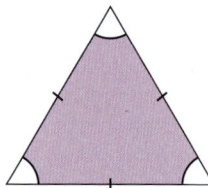	
Two sides equal. Two angles equal.	One angle 90°.	All sides equal. All angles equal.	All sides different. All angles different.

You need to know what these symbols mean.

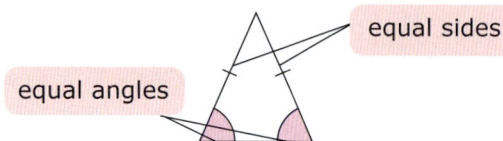

equal sides

equal angles

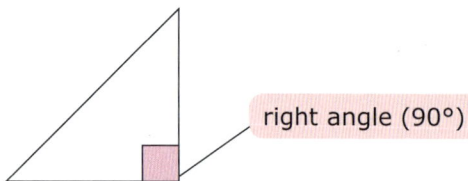

right angle (90°)

Draw two straight lines from a point. Can you position a mirror so as to create an isosceles triangle?

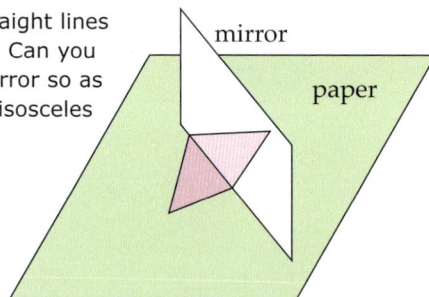

mirror

paper

Example

What kind of triangle is each of these, and why?

a
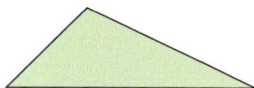

b
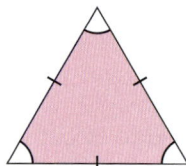

c
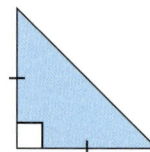

a Scalene.
All sides and angles are different.

b Equilateral.
All sides and angles are equal.

c Right-angled, isosceles triangle.
One angle is 90° and two sides are equal.

Exercise 5f

1 Name each triangle. Use the words:
isosceles, right-angled, equilateral or
scalene.

a
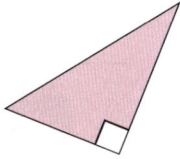

b
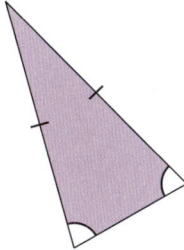

c
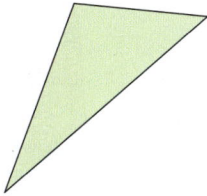

d
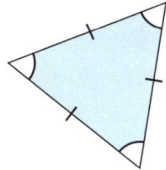

2 Paige, Janice and Alec are each thinking
of a different shape. Draw and name each
shape.

a

It has three
equal sides.

b

It has one right angle
and three sides.

2 **c**

It has three sides. No sides
are the same length.

3 For each of these triangles
  i   use a ruler to measure each side
  ii use a protractor to measure each angle
  iii name the type of triangle.

a
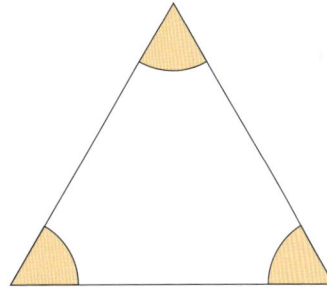

b
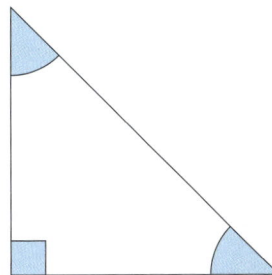

Problem solving

4 How many triangles can you see in this shape? What sort are they?

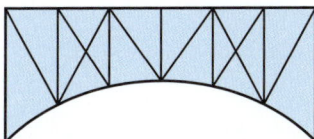

MyMaths.co.uk   🔍 1130   **SEARCH**

● The three angles in a triangle always add up to 180°.

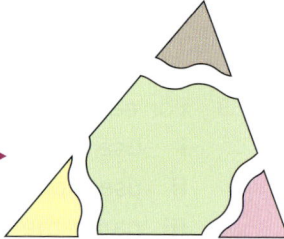

a + b + c = 180°

Why don't you measure the angles in a triangle yourself to check it!

You can use letters to stand for unknown angles.

Check it for yourself!

180°

Cut a triangle from card and colour in the three angles.

Cut the three angles from the triangle.

Put the three angles together. The angles make a straight line, adding up to 180°.

Example

Find the missing angles.

a

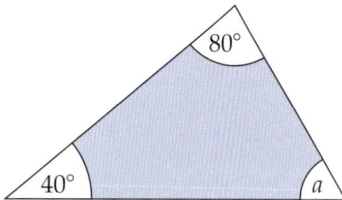

b

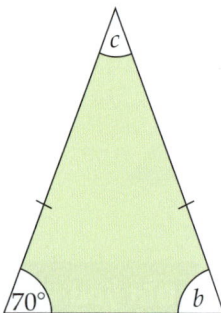

c

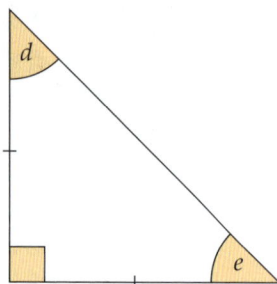

a $40° + 80° + a = 180°$
$120° + a = 180°$
$a = 180° - 120°$
$a = 60°$

b The triangle is isosceles.
$b = 70°$
$70° + 70° + c = 180°$
$140° + c = 180°$
$c = 180° - 140°$
$= 40°$

c The triangle is right angled and isosceles.
$d = e$
$90° + 2d = 180°$
$2d = 180° - 90°$
$= 90°$
$d = 90° ÷ 2$
$= 45°$

Exercise 5g

1 Find the missing angle in each of these triangles.

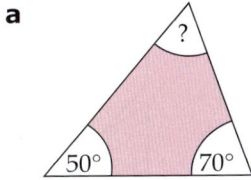

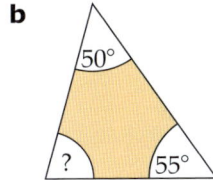

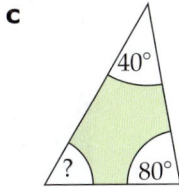

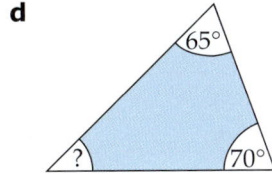

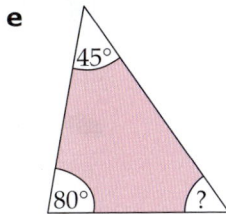

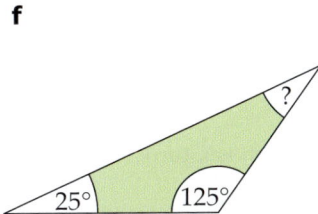

a, b, c, d, e, f

2 Find the missing angles in these triangles.

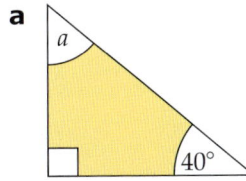

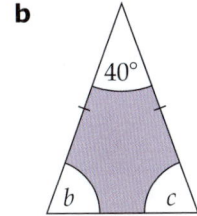

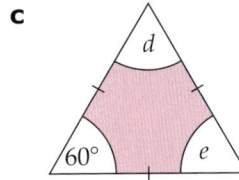

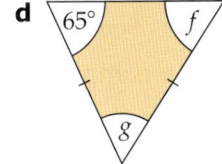

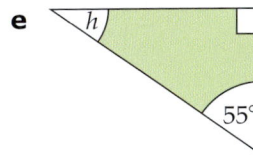

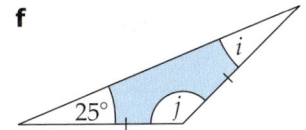

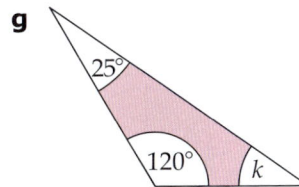

a, b, c, d, e, f, g

Problem solving

3 Megan's dog has ripped the corner off her triangle. What angle was it?

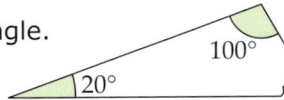

100° 20°

4 Use angle facts to find the missing angles.

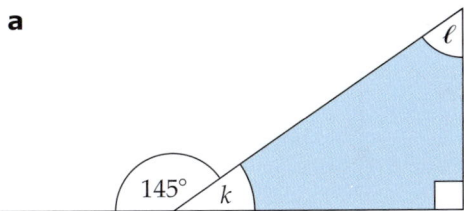

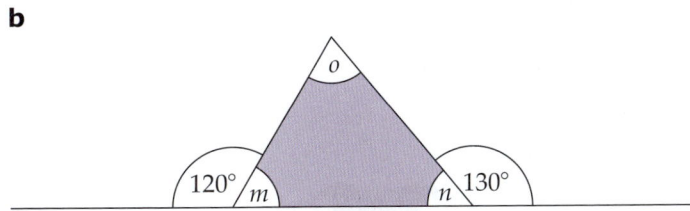

a 145° k ℓ

b 120° m o n 130°

5 Here is an equilateral triangle. What size is each angle? Are the angles always this value? How could you check?

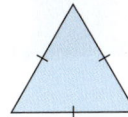

6 Which missing angle, a, b, or c, is the smallest angle?

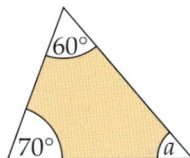

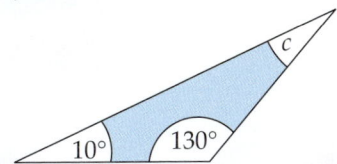

60° 70° a

b b

c 10° 130°

There are four main directions on a compass.

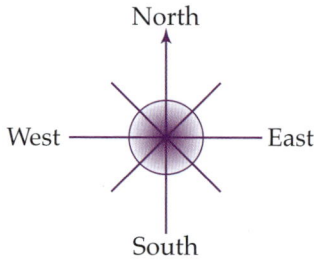

North
West ——— East
South

These directions can be split up into north-west, south-east and so on.

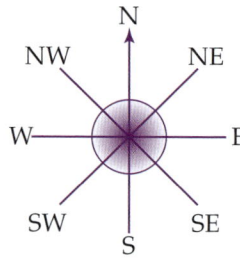

N
NW   NE
W ——— E
SW   SE
S

You could try remembering

Naughty
Elephants
Splash
Water

To use a compass, you need to remember

1 Clockwise

N
E

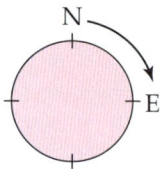

Anticlockwise

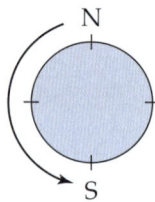

N
S

Look at an analog clock and notice how the hands move.

From North to East is $\frac{1}{4}$ turn.

From North to South is $\frac{1}{2}$ turn.

2 360° in a full turn.

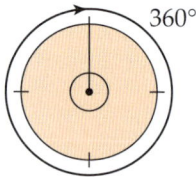

360°

180° in a half turn.

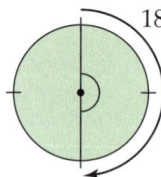

180°

90° in a quarter turn.

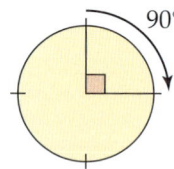

90°

Example

Zaira is standing at the school. Which direction should she go in to get to

a the shops   **b** her house?

Zaira's house

N

School

Shops

NW   N
Zaira's house   NE
W ——— School — E
SW   SE
Shops
S

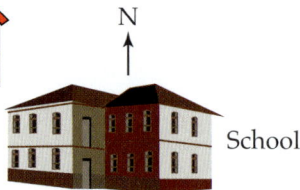

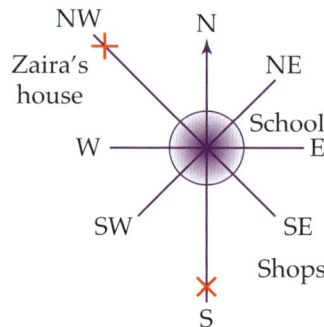

a The shops are south of the school.
b Her house is north-west of the school.

Exercise 5h

1 Amy is standing in the town square.

   a Amy looks north.
      Which road does she see?

   b She looks south.
      Which building does she see?

   c She looks south-west.
      What does she see?

   d Amy looks at Gate Street.
      In which direction is she facing?

   e Amy looks at the shopping centre.
      In which direction is she facing?

2 Charlie is facing east.

   a He turns 90° clockwise.
      In which direction is he now facing?

   b He then turns through 180°.
      In which direction is he now facing?

2 Charlie is now facing south-west.

   c He turns 180°. In which direction
      is he now facing?

   d From there he turns 90° anticlockwise.
      In which direction is he now facing?

3 Jo stands at the school.
   Which direction is the

   a bus station   **b** shops

   c farm   **d** church?

4 Lily stands in the town square from
   question **1**, facing west.

   a After how many clockwise turns of 45°
      will she be facing the station?

   b Starting with facing west again, after
      how many anticlockwise turns of 30°
      will Lily be facing High Road?

Problem solving

5 Ray and Liz each go
on a journey.
Follow the directions
to find where they
are going.

5 MySummary

Check out

You should now be able to ...

Test it ➡

		Questions
✓ Estimate angles and use a protractor to measure them.	5	1
✓ Distinguish between acute, obtuse and reflex angles.	5	2
✓ Use the sum of angles at a point, on a straight line and in a triangle.	5	3–6
✓ Classify triangles by their properties.	4	7
✓ Find missing angles in a triangle.	5	7
✓ Understand and use the points of a compass.	4	8

Language	Meaning	Example
Angle	An angle is formed when two straight lines cross or meet each other at a point.	Four angles are created
Acute angle	An angle that is less than 90°.	45° is an acute angle
Obtuse angle	An angle that is between 90° and 180°.	140° is an obtuse angle
Right angle	An angle that is exactly 90°.	90° is a right angle
Reflex angle	An angle that is greater than 180° but less than 360°.	270° is a reflex angle
Equilateral triangle	A triangle with all sides equal and all angles equal.	See page 100 for an illustration
Isosceles triangle	A triangle with two sides equal and two angles equal.	See page 100 for an illustration
Scalene triangle	A triangle with no sides equal and no angles equal.	See page 100 for an illustration

1 Measure angles *a* and *b*.

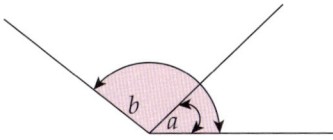

2 Describe each angle – choose from the words: *acute, obtuse, right, reflex*

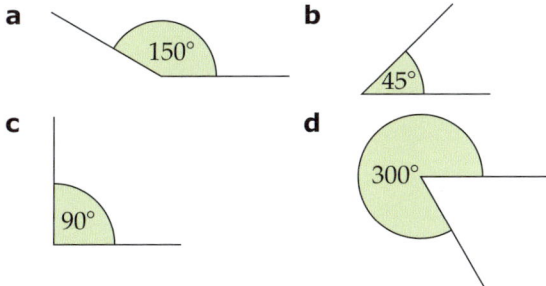

a 150°

b 45°

c 90°

d 300°

3 How many more degrees does the red line have to turn through to reach 90°?

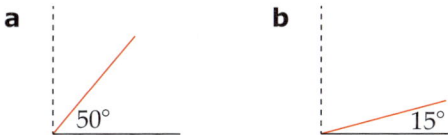

a 50°

b 15°

4 How many more degrees does the red line have to turn through to reach 180°?

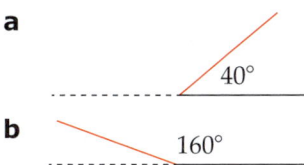

a 40°

b 160°

5 Find the missing angle for each of these

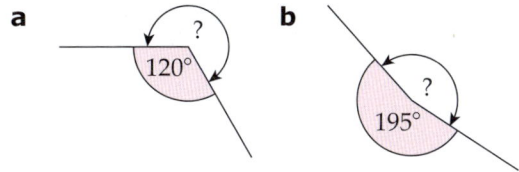

a ? 120°

b ? 195°

6 Word out the missing angle in each diagram

a ? 37°

b 112° ?

7 Calculate the value of the letters and state what type of triangles they are.

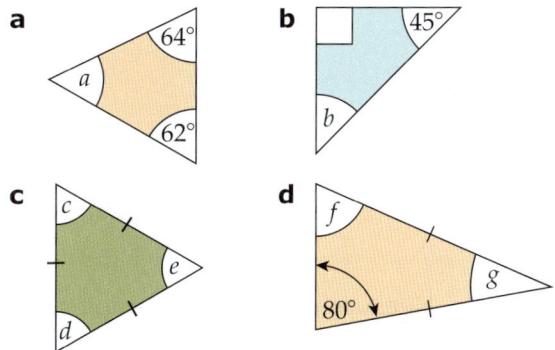

a 64° *a* 62°

b 45° *b*

c *c* *e* *d*

d *f* 80° *g*

8 Aaron is facing west, then he turns 90° clockwise. In which direction is he facing now?

What next?

Score	0 – 3		Your knowledge of this topic is still developing. To improve look at Formative test: 1A-5; MyMaths: 1081, 1082, 1130 and 1231
	4 – 7		You are gaining a secure knowledge of this topic. To improve look at InvisiPen: 341, 342 and 343
	8		You have mastered this topic. Well done, you are ready to progress!

5a

1 What kind of angle is each of these?

a

b

c

d

5b

2 Find the other angle on the straight line in each diagram.

a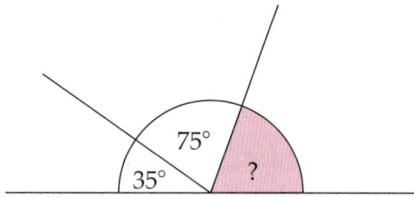

b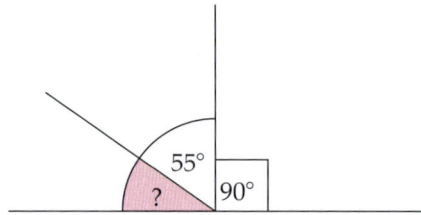

c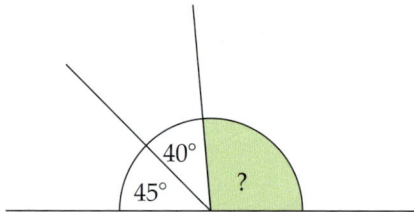

d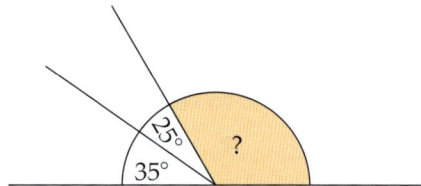

5c

3 Measure each of these angles.

a

b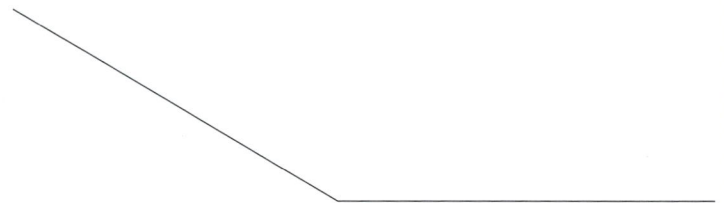

5d

4 Find the missing angle in each diagram.

a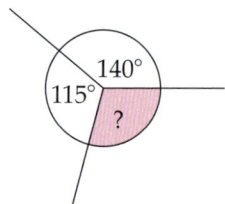

b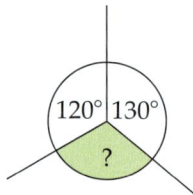

c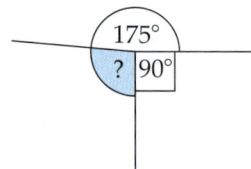

d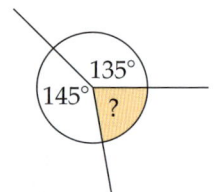

5 Find the missing angles.

a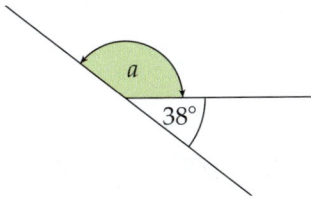

b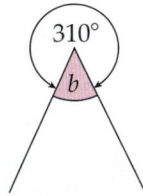

c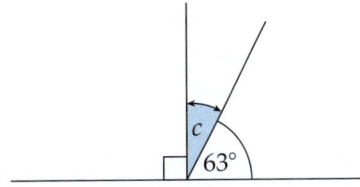

6 Match the triangle to its name and description.

a Right-angled

b Equilateral

c Isosceles

d Scalene

A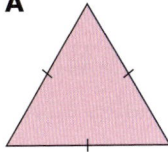

B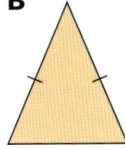

C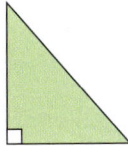

D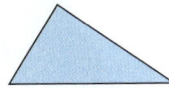

1 All sides different
All angles different

2 One angle 90°

3 Two sides equal
Two angles equal

4 All sides equal
All angles equal

7 Find the missing angles in these triangles.

a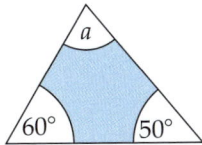

b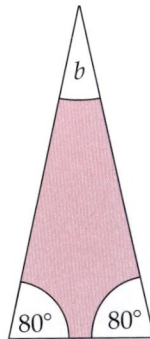

c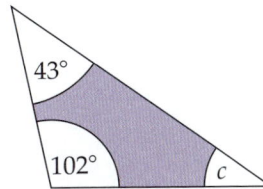

d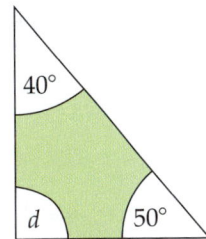

8 Vicky is facing North. She turns 135° clockwise, then 180° anticlockwise, then 90° clockwise, then 225° anticlockwise. Which direction is Vicky facing now?

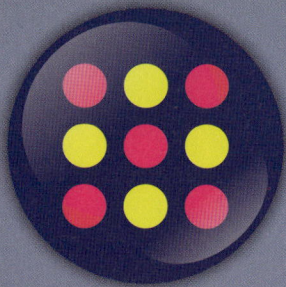

6 Graphs

Introduction

When you use the satellite navigation system in a car or search on your phone for the nearest branch of a shop, your electronic devices are using GPS coordinates. The GPS system uses coordinates which are expressed in terms of latitude and longitude, and are fixed by determining the exact distance from a number of satellites in orbit above the Earth.

What's the point?

Coordinates allow you to specify the exact position of any point on the Earth using just a pair of numbers.

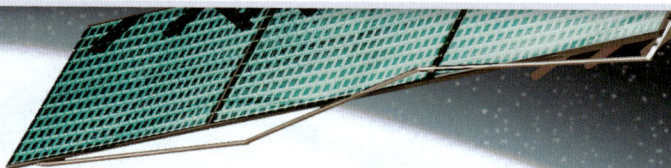

Objectives

By the end of this chapter, you will have learned how to …

- Identify and plot coordinates in all four quadrants.
- Construct and interpret line graphs in context.

Check in

1 a Draw a number line from -10 to 10.

  b Use arrows to mark these points.

   i 2   **ii** 7   **iii** -4   **iv** -9   **v** 0

2 Write down the heights of the lines labelled **a**, **b**, **c**, and **d**.

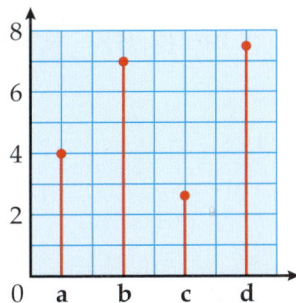

Starter problem

Martha is about to draw a right-angled triangle. She marks two points on a coordinate grid, but then her lesson ends.

Investigate where she could draw the third point to make a right angled triangle.

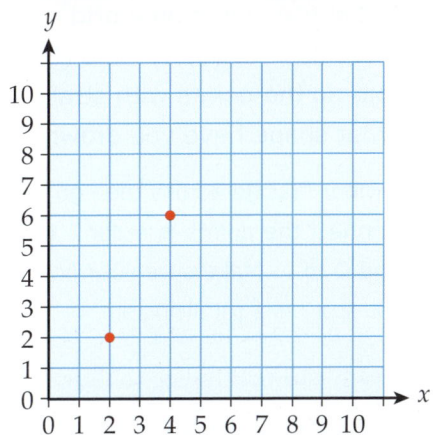

How could you describe where the bee is?

Start at the bottom left corner.

Go across first ...

... then up.

The bee is at 2 across and 4 up.

The **coordinates** of this point are (2, 4).

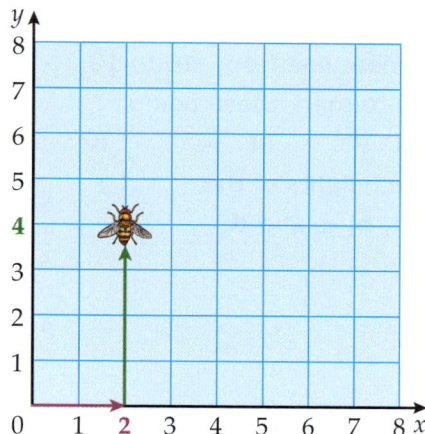

You always write coordinates in brackets, with a comma.

⬤ **Coordinates** give the position of a **point** on the grid.

Example

a   Give the coordinates for **A**, **B** and **C**.
b   Point **D** is at (1, 5). Plot point **D**.

a   A (2, 1)   2 across, 1 up
    B (5, 4)   5 across, 4 up
    C (3, 7)   3 across, 7 up
b   Plot point **D** by going 1 across and 5 up.

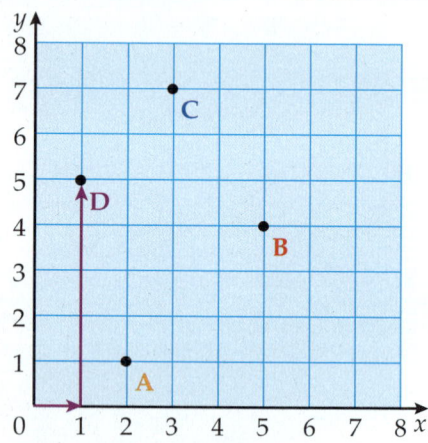

Example

a   Plot these points on a grid.
    A (2, 2)   **B** (5, 4)   **C** (5, 7)   **D** (2, 5)
b   Join up the points with straight lines.
c   What shape have you drawn?

Remember first go across then go up.
b   Connect the points in order A to B, B to C, C to D
    and D to A. Make sure your lines are straight!
c   The shape is a parallelogram.

‹ p.32

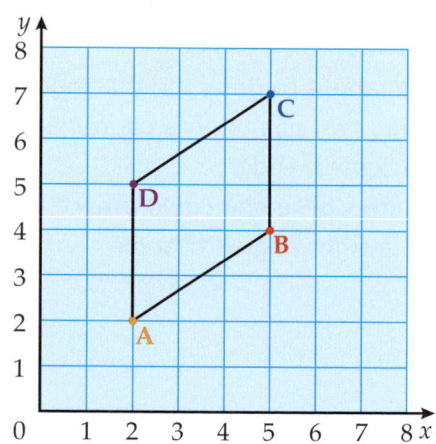

Exercise 6a

1 What are the coordinates for the objects in this garden?

    a rake   **b** flower   **c** spade

    d tree   **e** chair   **f** rock

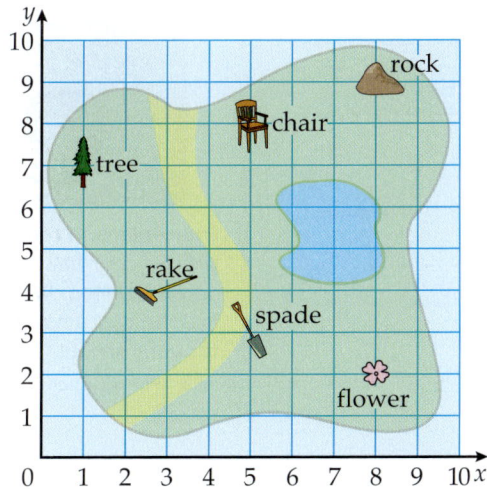

2 Write the coordinates of each point.

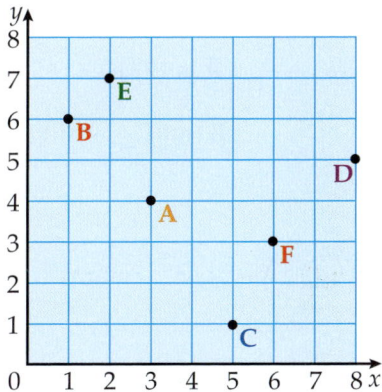

3 Plot and label each of these points on a copy of the grid in question **2**.

    A (2, 3)   **B** (1, 1)

    C (1, 6)   **D** (3, 6)

    E (7, 8)   **F** (4, 1)

    G (4, 4)   **H** (2, 8)

4 a Draw a grid from 0 to 10 in each direction. Plot and label each point.

    A (1, 1)   **B** (1, 7)   **C** (5, 7)

    D (9, 4)   **E** (5, 1)

  b Join the points to make a shape.

  c What is the name of the shape?

5 Write coordinates for each place on this map.

    a Edinburgh   **b** Glasgow

    c Uig   **d** Elgin

    e Dundee

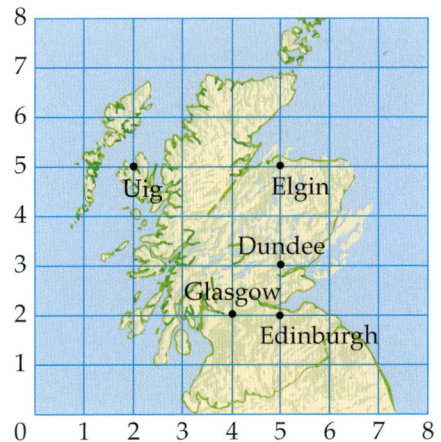

Problem solving

6 Here is a square. The coordinates of three corners are given, but there are no gridlines. What are the coordinates of the fourth corner?

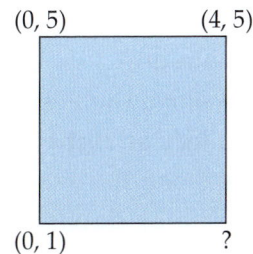

7 Another square has corners at (2, 3) (7, 3) and (7, 8). What are the coordinates of the fourth corner?

- A grid has two axes
  - ▶ a horizontal *x*-axis
  - ▶ and a vertical *y*-axis.

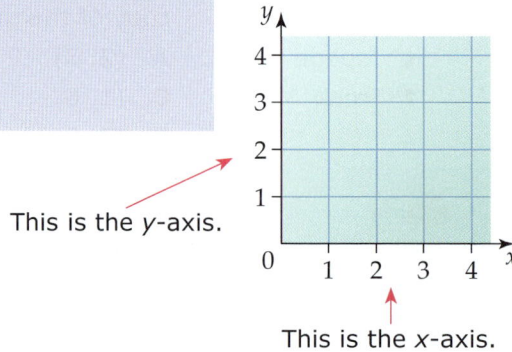

This is the *y*-axis.

This is the *x*-axis.

On a number line

- Negative numbers are to the left of 0.
- Positive numbers are to the right of 0.

⟨ p.14

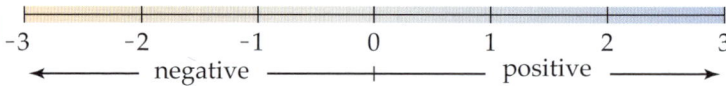

negative ⟶|⟶ positive

You can make a grid bigger by using negative axes.

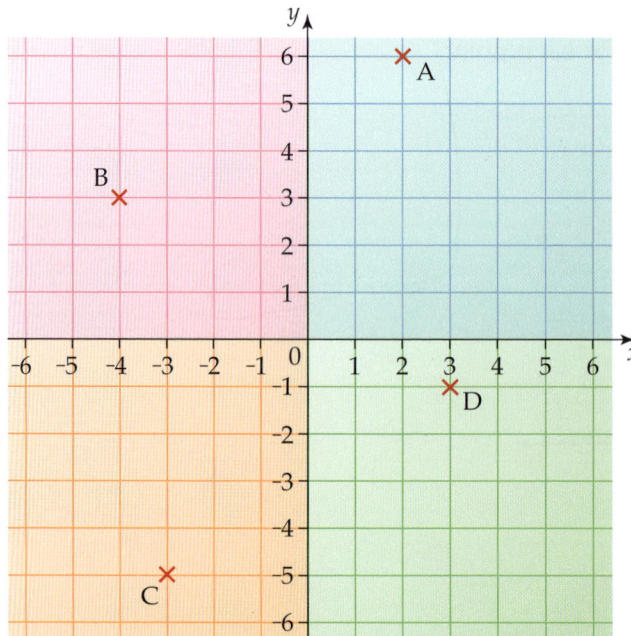

B is (-4, 3)

4 left   3 up

A is (2, 6)

2 right   6 up

C is (-3, -5)

3 left   5 down

D is (3, -1)

3 right   1 down

- On a coordinate grid
  - ▶ You move along the *x*-axis first.
    You move **left or right** (horizontally).
  - ▶ You move along the *y*-axis second.
    You move **up or down** (vertically).

Right and up are positive.
Left and down are negative.

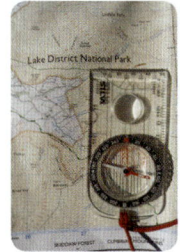

Exercise 6b

1 What are the coordinates of these places?

    a hill   **b** cave

    c village   **d** treasure

    e castle   **f** lighthouse

    g tower   **h** wreck

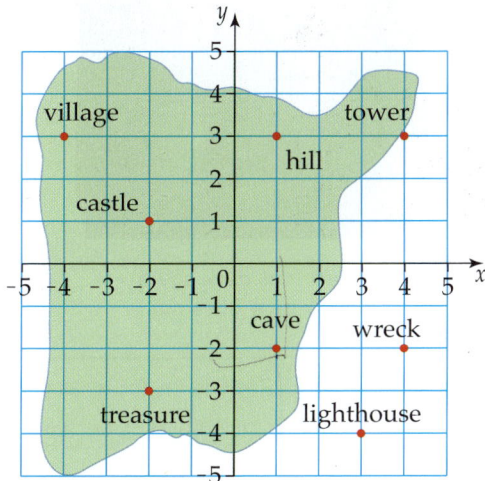

2 a Draw three grids like this one.

    b Plot one set of points on each grid.

    c Join up each set of points with straight lines.

    d Write the name of each shape.

      i (5, 3) (-5, 1) (2, -4) (5, 3)

      ii (3, 2) (2, 3) (-4, -2) (-3, -3) (3, 2)

      iii (-2, 5) (-5, 3) (-2, -4) (1, 3) (-2, 5)

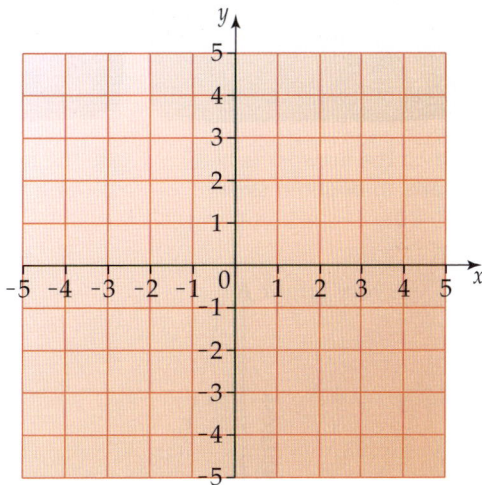

Problem solving

3 Work out this coordinate code to make a tongue-twister.

> The first word is THE.
>
> (1, 4)   (-1, 1)   (-2, 3)
>   T   H   E

(1, 4) (-1, 1) (-2, 3)

(4, 1) (2, -3) (-5, -4)

(-3, -2) (2, 3) (4, -1) (-4, 4)

(-3, -2) (4, 4) (4, -4) (-4, 2) (-2, 3) (1, -1)

(4, 1) (-5, -1) (5, -3) (-4, 2)

(4, 1) (-5, 5) (2, 3) (-4, 2) (-2, 3)

(-3, -2) (4, -1) (4, -4) (1, 2) (-2, -4)

(-2, 5) (1, -3) (4, -4) (-4, 2) (-2, 3)

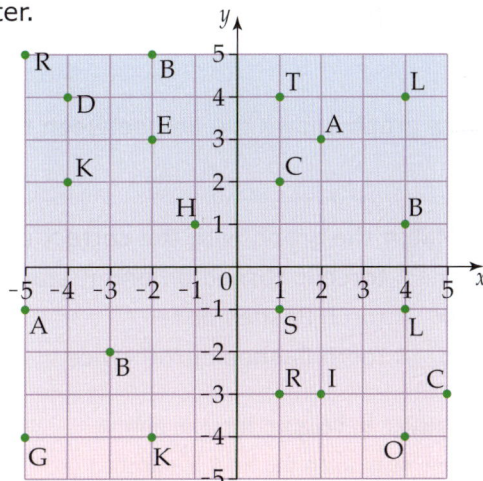

4 Here are two points, A and B. The point M is halfway between A and B. Find the coordinates of M.

         A   M   B

         x   ?   x

     (1, 5)   (1, 9)

🔴 You can often see a link between two things by looking at a **graph**.

Riley's dad is lighting a firework.

▲ When the firework is lit it starts to brighten slowly.

▲ The firework is very bright for a short time.

▲ It becomes dark again quickly as it goes out.

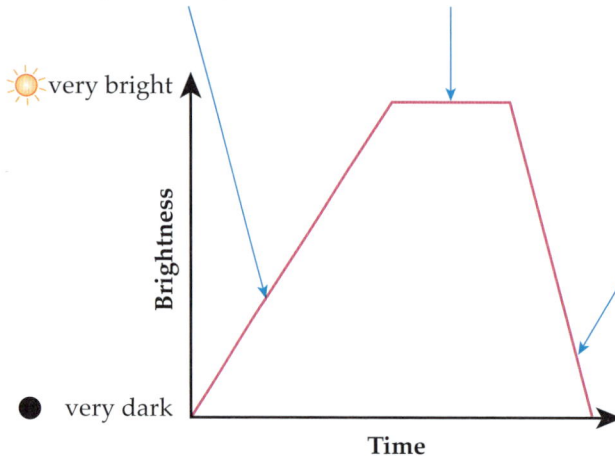

very bright

Brightness

very dark

Time

Time is on the x-axis. Brightness is on the y-axis.

This graph shows the link between time and the brightness of the firework.

Example

Match the graph with the correct description.

a   A torch is turned on and it stays on.

b   A torch flashes once.

c   A torch flashes on/off twice.

Answer **b**, because there is only one peak when the light is switched on.

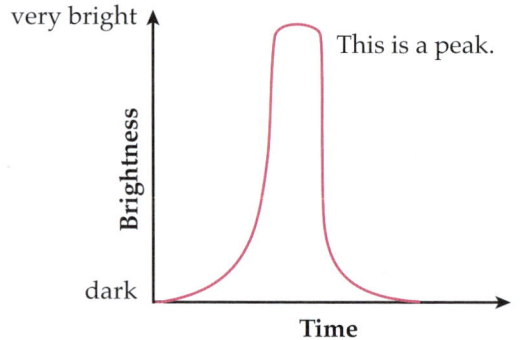

very bright

This is a peak.

Brightness

dark

Time

Exercise 6c

1 Match each description with its correct graph.

  a A car's indicator keeps flashing on and off.

  b Cinema lights are dimmed quickly.

  c Cinema lights are dimmed slowly.

  d A light is turned on in a room.

A

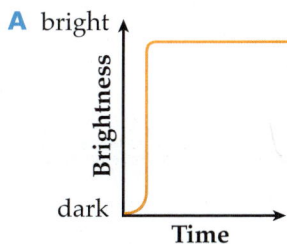

B

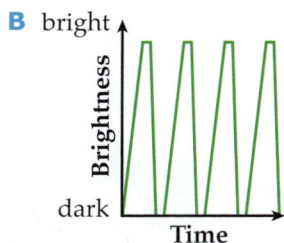

C

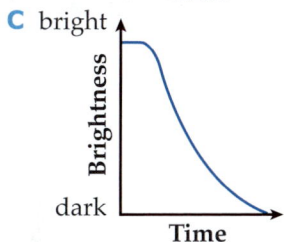

D

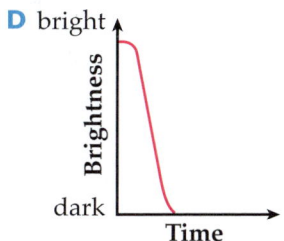

2 Match each description with a possible graph.

  a The temperature slowly climbs from 0 °C.

  b The temperature rises and falls quickly.

  c The temperature starts high and falls very quickly.

  d The temperature climbs, stays the same for a while and climbs again.

  e The temperature starts above 0° and rises slowly.

  f The temperature rises quickly, stays the same for a while and then falls.

A

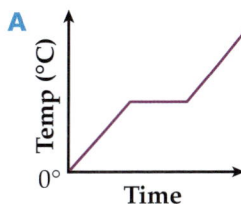

B

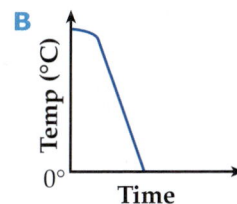

C

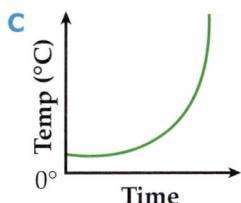

D

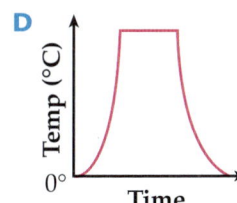

E

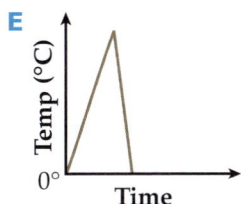

F

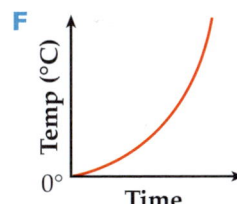

Problem solving

3 The graph shows a cyclist's journey to the park.

Write a short description of this journey.

Use words like

- getting faster
- slowing down
- cycling steadily.

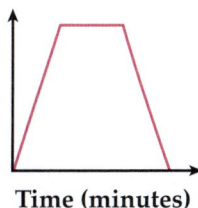

Did you know?

The temperature in the UK can sometimes change by 20 °C over one day in some places.

MyMaths.co.uk

A **line graph** shows how things change over time.

> When you read a line graph
> ▶ **Time** goes along the horizontal axis.
> ▶ The vertical axis shows what you are measuring.
> ▶ The points show the information that you are given.
> ▶ The points are joined with a line.

This line graph tells you how many people were on the Number 17 bus each day during one week.

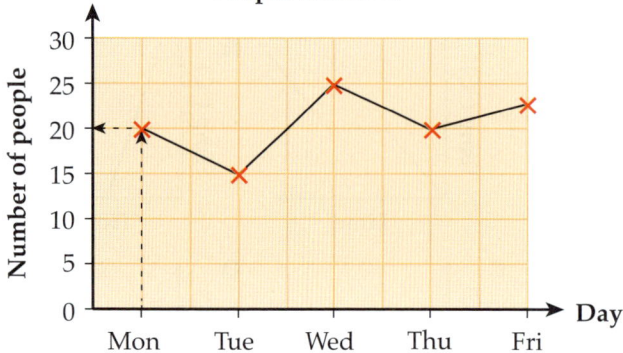

To find the number of people on the bus on Monday
- Read up from Monday to the graph.
- Read across from that point to the vertical axis.

20 people were on the bus on Monday.

Example

James drew a line graph to show the temperature of his oven.

a What time was the oven turned on?

b What was the highest temperature in the oven?

c What time was the oven turned off?

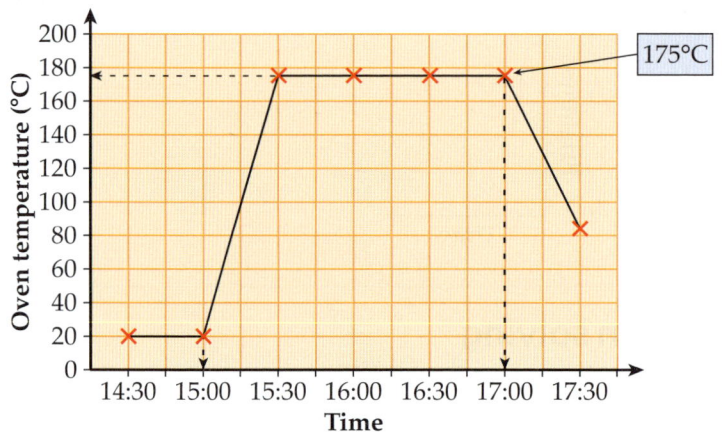

a The oven was turned on at 15:00 (3 p.m.).   The graph starts to rise at 15:00.

b The highest temperature was 175°C.   Look at the highest points on the graph.

c The oven was turned off at 17:00 (5 p.m.).   The graph begins to fall at 17:00.

p.156 ›

Exercise 6d

1 This line graph shows the height of a hot air balloon in metres (m).
 a What time did the balloon take off?
 b What was the greatest height of the balloon?
 c How long did the whole flight last?

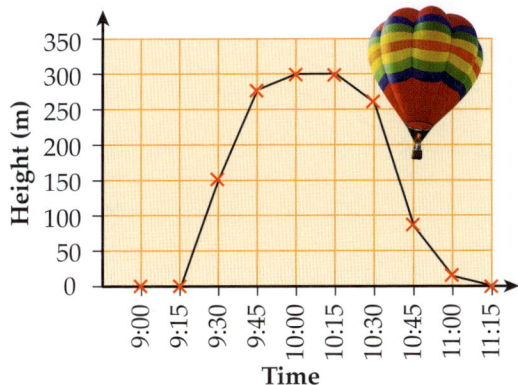

2 This line graph shows how the outside temperature changed one summer day.
 a What was the temperature at 10 a.m.?
 b What was the highest temperature recorded?
 c When was the temperature 15 °C?

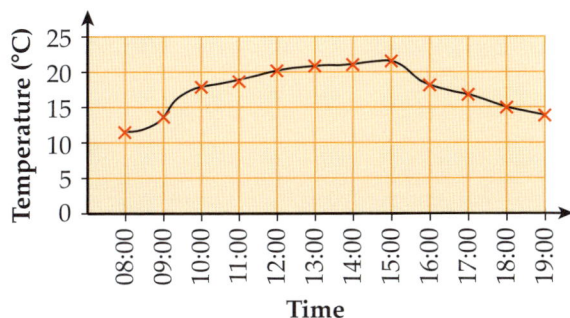

3 Grandad planted a tree when he was young and measured it every 10 years.
 a How tall was the tree in 1970?
 b Use the graph to find when the tree was exactly 10 m tall.
 c What was the height of the tree in 1995?

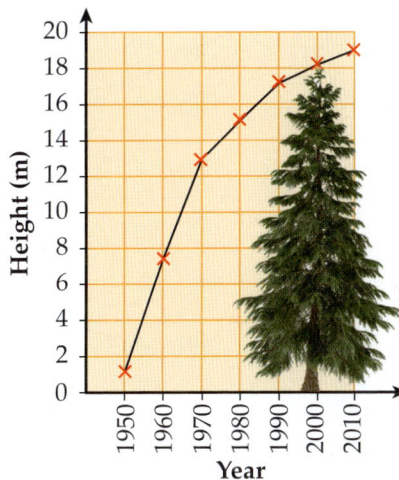

4 Draw a line graph to show how the height of a sunflower changed over a 30-day period. Use the data provided in the table.

Day	0	5	10	15	20	25	30
Height (cm)	0	1	2	6	14	26	33

Problem solving

5 The graph shows the story of Ruby's bath. It plots the depth of the water in cm over time. Write the story of her bath, including when she got in and out. Include as much detail as you can.

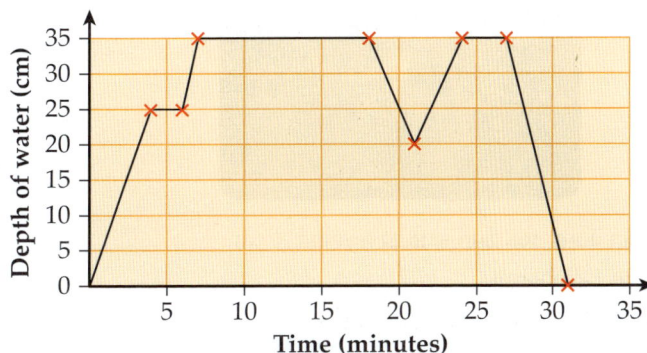

6e Line graphs 2

You can draw two sets of data on a graph to compare them.

p.156 >

Example

This graph shows the water level in Grey's Reservoir over two years.
Describe the main features of the graph.

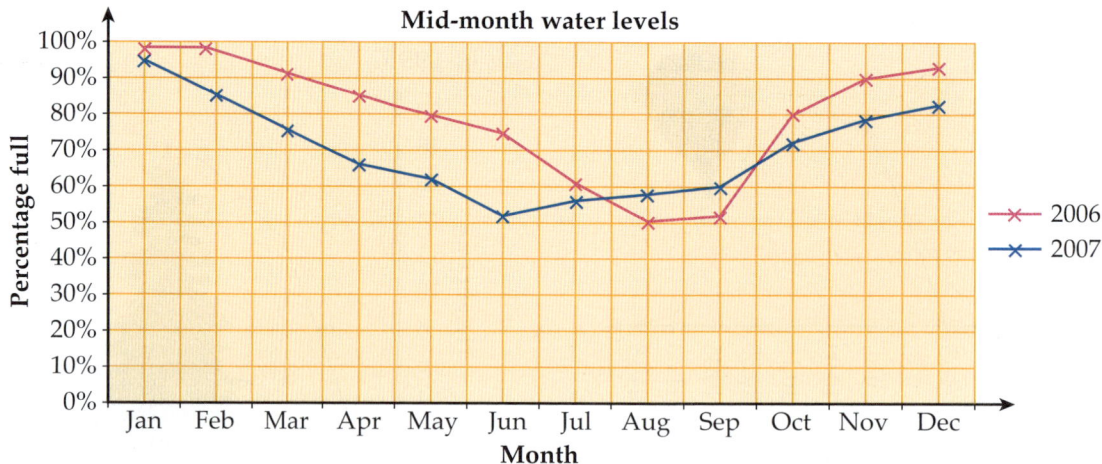

Mid-month water levels

Possible things you could write include

*   In both years, the reservoir is highest during the winter months
    and lowest during the summer months.
*   The water levels were generally higher in 2006 than in 2007.
*   The lowest level was just over 50% in both years.
*   This level was in June for 2007, and in August for 2006.

You do not always join the dots on a line graph.
To show a trend you can use a curve.

Example

The sun sets in the UK at a different time every day.
What time does it set in Edinburgh in June?

Edinburgh Sunset times

In June, the Sun sets at around 10 p.m.
in Edinburgh.

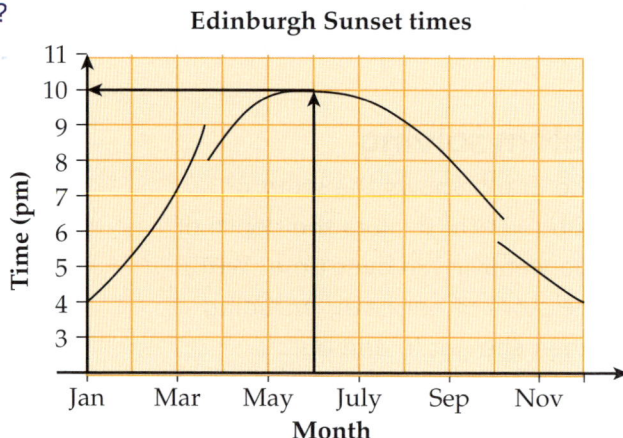

Exercise 6e

1 This line graph shows the height of grass on a lawn.

   a What was the grass height on day 1?

   b What was the greatest height of grass?

   c On which day was the grass cut?

   d What height might the grass be on day 15?

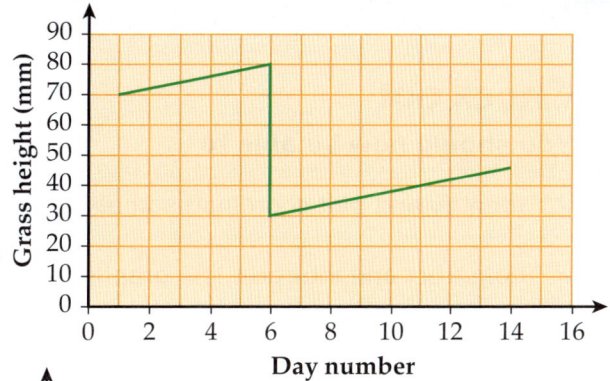

2 This line graph shows how the tide level at Dewey Harbour changed during one day.

   a There were two low tides. When did these happen?

   b What were the times of the two high tides?

   c What was the height of the tide at 10 a.m.?

   d Captain Jack needs the height of the tide to be at least 8 m, so that he can sail his ship into the harbour. Between which times can he enter the harbour?

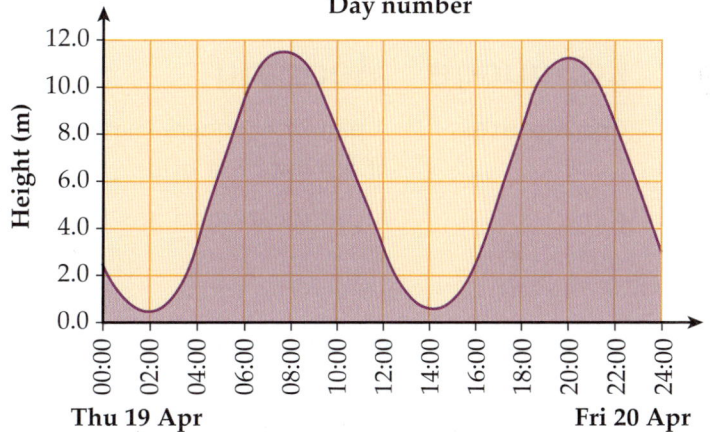

3 This line graph shows the monthly temperatures in two cities.

   a What might the temperature be in each city in January?

   b During which months would you expect the temperature in Moscow to be higher than it is in Sydney?

   c For how many months of the year would you expect the temperature in Moscow to be below freezing?

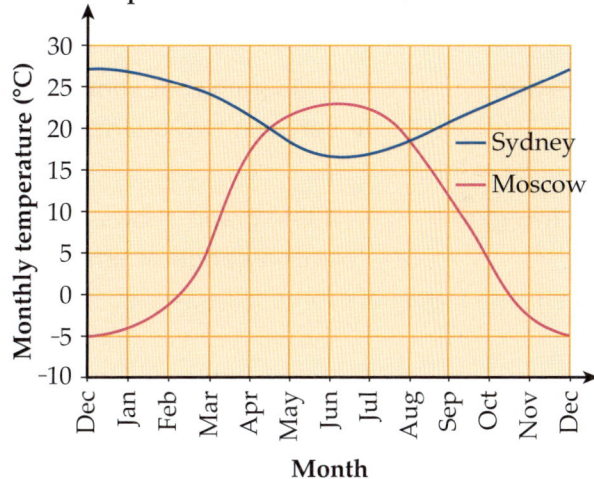

Problem solving

4 This line graph shows the average daily maximum temperature for a part of Libya. The highest temperature ever recorded was in Al' Aziziyah, Libya in July at 57.7 °C.

   Where would that temperature be on this graph? What would that do to the line?

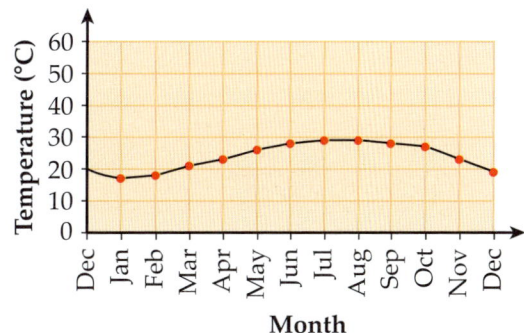

6 MySummary

Check out
You should now be able to ...

Test it ➡
Questions

✓	Identify and plot coordinates in all four quadrants.	5	1 – 3
✓	Construct and interpret line graphs in context.	4	4 – 5

Language	Meaning	Example
Coordinates	A pair of numbers that give the position of a point on a grid.	(4, 3) means 4 along and 3 up starting from the origin
Axis	A coordinate grid has two axes.	The horizontal axis is called the x-axis. The vertical axis is called the y-axis.
Quadrant	One of four quarters on a coordinate grid separated by the x- and y-axes.	The first quadrant is in the top right corner. Both the x and y coordinates of points in this quadrant are positive.
Graph	A diagram that shows a relationship between two quantities.	A graph could show the link between number of ice creams sold and temperature
Line graph	A line graph shows how quantities change over a period of time.	A line graph could show the height of a tree over a number of years

6 MyReview

1 Give the coordinates of points A, B, C and D.

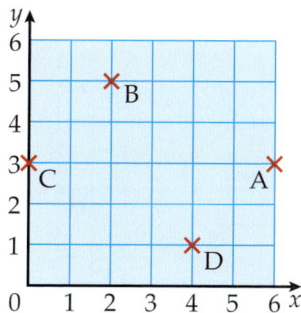

2 Give the coordinates of points E, F, G and H.

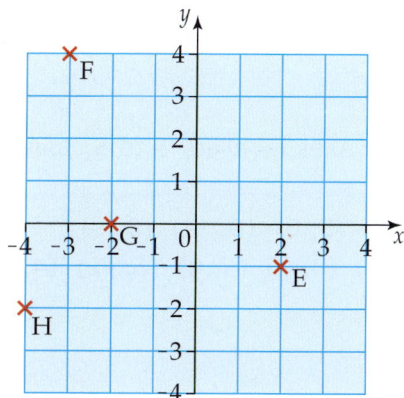

3 Copy the axes and mark on the points.

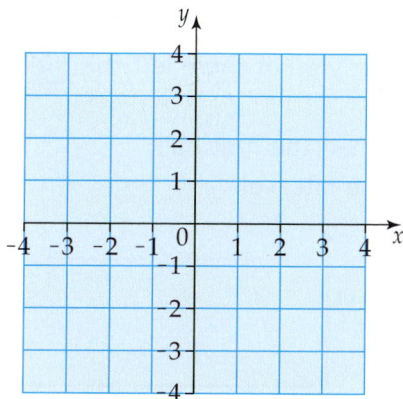

3
  a (-2, 3), label it A.
  b (-1, -2), label it B.
  c (-4, 2), label it C.
  d (2, 0), label it D.

4 Which of the graphs fits this description?
The noise level rises slowly then falls quickly.

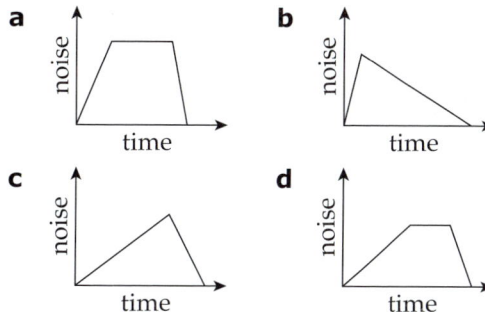

5 The line graph shows the height of a seedling in the days after it was planted.

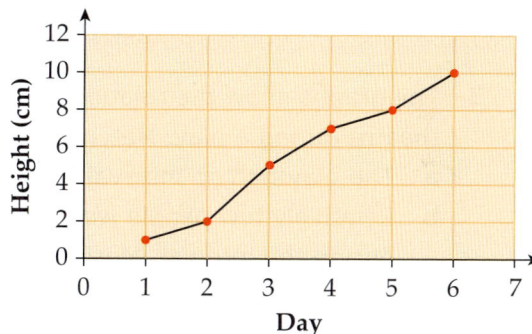

  a How tall was the seedling at the end of day 4?
  b When was the seedling exactly 5 cm tall?

What next?

6a

1 Write the coordinates of each point.

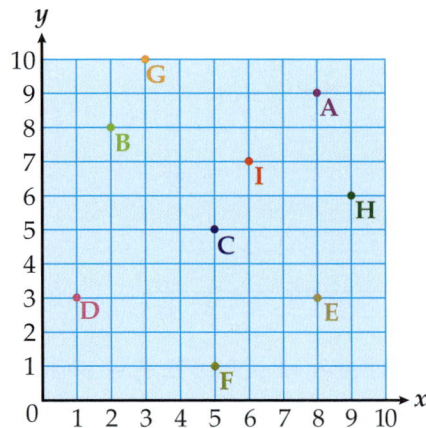

6b

2 For each part, plot the points given on a grid with axes labelled -5 to 5. Join each point to the next with a straight line.

   a (0, -4) (0, -2) (-5, 0) (-5, 1) (0, -1) (0, 0) (5, 0) (5, -4) (0, -4)

   b (-4, -3) (-4, -1) (-5, -1) (-5, 0) (2, 0) (3, 2) (4, 2) (5, 0) (5, -1) (4, -3)
      (3, -3) (2, -1) (-2, -1) (-2, -3) (-4, -3)

6c

3 The graphs show the relationship between time and the number of people in a theatre during a play. Match each of the descriptions with a possible graph.

   a The play had no interval.

   b Relatively few people went to the play and nearly all of them left the theatre during the interval. Most didn't come back.

   c The second half of the play was much longer than the first half.

   d Relatively few people left the theatre during the interval.

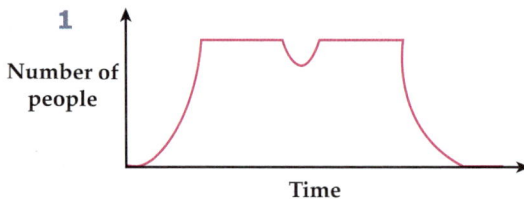

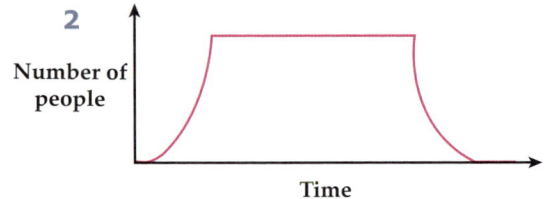

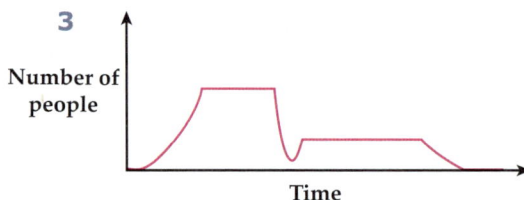

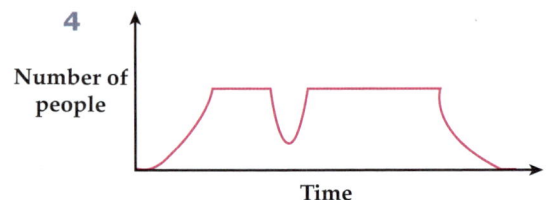

4 This line graph shows how the temperature in a room changed.

   a At what time was the temperature 18°C?

   b What was the temperature at 10:00?

   c How many hours did it take for the temperature to drop from 21°C to 15°C?

   d At what time was the temperature the same as it was at 10:00?

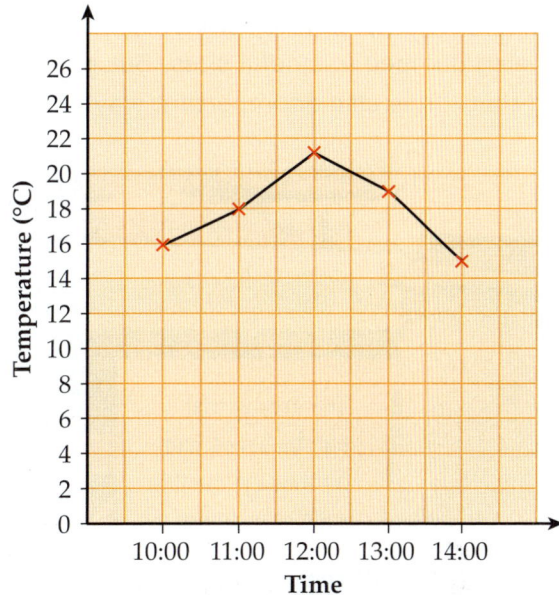

5 A group of hikers walked 20 km between 10 a.m. and 2:30 p.m. The line graph shows details of their progress.

   a What distance had they walked by
      i   10:45 a.m.
      ii 11:15 a.m.
      iii 12:15 p.m.

   b How far did they walk during the first half hour?

   c During which half hour interval did they walk the furthest? How far was this?

   d Between which times did they stop for lunch?

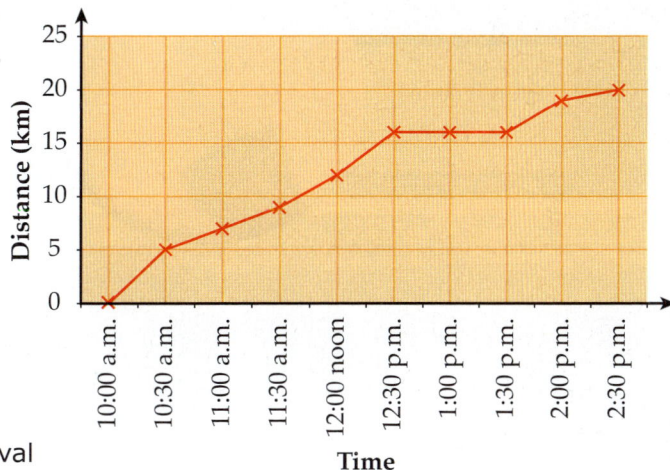

MyMaths.co.uk

Case study 2: Recycling and energy

Recycling waste products means that not all of our rubbish ends up being dumped in landfill sites. But recycling does much more than that – it is also an important way of saving energy.

The energy that can be saved from an average dustbin each year could:

power a television for 5 000 hours

light a bulb for 10 000 hours

Task 1

a How many days is 5 000 hours, to the nearest day?

b Will the energy saved from a dustbin each year be enough to power your telly for a year?

c Will it be enough to power your bedroom light bulb for a year?

Task 2

a How many hours of television could you power by recycling 20 cans?

b How many hours of television could the average person power per year by recycling aluminium cans?

Aluminium drink cans

> 20 aluminium drink cans can be recycled for the same amount of energy that it takes to make just 1 new can.

> Each aluminium can that is recycled saves enough energy to run a television set for three hours.

> The average person uses around 80 aluminium cans per year.

Steel cans

< Recycling one steel can saves enough energy to power an energy-saving 18 watt light bulb for about 12 hours.

< The average household uses 50 steel cans per month.

Task 3

a How many hours of an 18 watt bulb could the average household power per month by recycling steel cans?

b What about per year?

Glass

< One recycled glass bottle saves enough energy to power a computer for about 30 minutes.

< Recycling glass uses 50% of the energy needed to make new glass.

Task 4

a How many hours could 10 recycled glass bottles power a computer for?

b How many recycled bottles can be made for the same energy as 1 new bottle?

Task 5

a How many plastic bottles need to be recycled to save enough energy to run the fridge for a day?

b Challenge Look up what 1 tonne means. How many two litre drinks bottles would you get from 1 kilogram of plastic?

Plastic

> One recycled plastic bottle would save enough energy to run a fridge for 4 hours.

> One tonne of plastic is equivalent to 20 000 two litre drinks bottles.

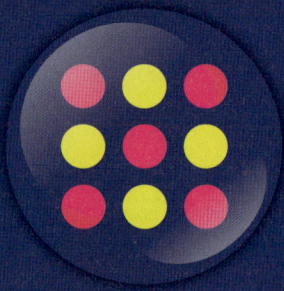

7 Adding and subtracting

Introduction

Whether you are checking your change in a shop, or working out the cost of downloading five items, calculation skills are an important part of your life. These same skills are equally important for adults in all walks of life.

What's the point?

A good grasp of arithmetic is a vital skill for everyday life. People with poor calculation skills often struggle to succeed with money.

Objectives

By the end of this chapter, you will have learned how to ...

- Strengthen and extend mental methods of addition and subtraction.
- Use efficient written methods to add and subtract whole numbers.

Check in

1. What number should you add to these numbers to make 10?

   a 7   **b** 2   **c** 5   **d** 1   **e** 3

2. What is the result of adding these numbers?

   a 4 + 7   **b** 20 + 70   **c** 13 + 11   **d** 120 + 140

3. What is the result of subtracting these numbers?

   a 9 − 4   **b** 80 − 60   **c** 27 − 15   **d** 89 − 54

Starter problem

Here is a game for 2 players. You will need a dice.
The first player rolls the dice and writes the number
in one of the boxes of their own additions or one of
their opponent's.
The second player rolls the dice and does likewise.
After all the boxes have been filled the players work
out each of their additions mentally, and check their opponent's.
The winner is the player who has made the highest total.

Kia is practising her **mental addition**.

She would like to work out problems quickly when ...

Add 150 g of plain flour to 75 g of ...

... she is busy with her hands

I got 25 downloads for 75 p each. How much is that?

... she is on the move

£1.35 and £2.00 That's £5.35

Hang on!

... she is shopping.

‹ p.2 Adding in 10s

31 + 40

↓

10 + 10 + 10 + 10

= 71

Adding in 10s and units

34 + 23

↓

10 + 10 + 1 + 1 + 1

= 57

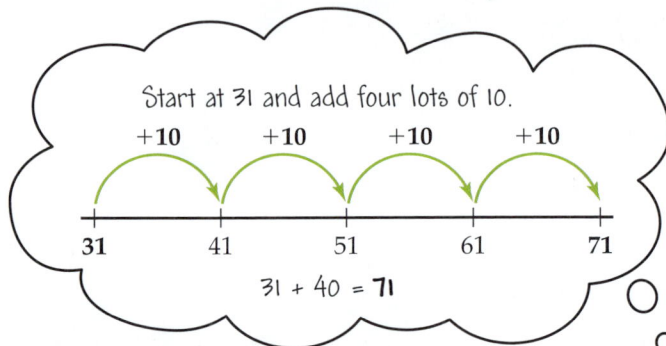

Start at 31 and add four lots of 10.

+10   +10   +10   +10

31   41   51   61   71

31 + 40 = 71

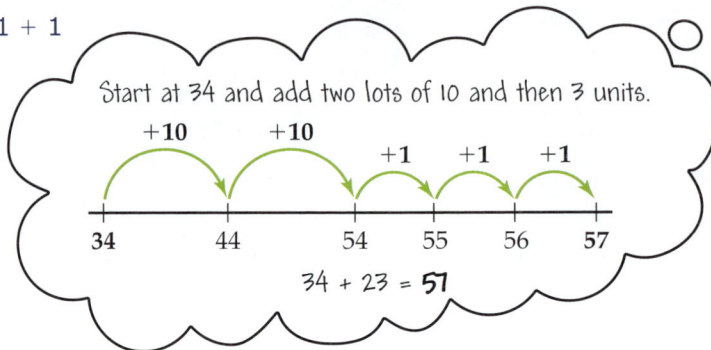

Start at 34 and add two lots of 10 and then 3 units.

+10   +10   +1   +1   +1

34   44   54   55   56   57

34 + 23 = 57

Example

Add 36 and 142.

Count on from the larger number.

+10   +10   +10   +5   +1

142   152   162   172   177   178

142 + 36 = 178

You could also draw your number line like this.

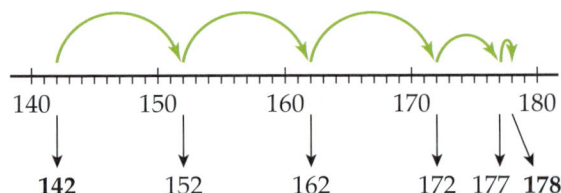

140   150   160   170   180

142   152   162   172 177 178

Exercise 7a

1 Write out all the number pairs that add up to 20 using these cards.

You will end up with six pairs of numbers.

| 1 | 12 | 19 | 9 | 17 | 10 |

| 15 | 3 | 5 | 10 | 8 | 11 |

2 Work out these problems in your head.

  a 10 + 6   **b** 5 + 13
  c 0 + 12   **d** 8 + 9
  e 16 + 3   **f** 7 + 13
  g 3 + 2 + 5   **h** 10 + 6 + 8
  i 12 + 5 + 7   **j** 31 + 9 + 3

3 Add 20 to each number. Do the working out in your head.

  a 9   **b** 17   **c** 20   **d** 45
  e 53   **f** 74   **g** 90   **h** 114

4 By counting on in jumps of 100, complete these number patterns.

  a 110, 210, ☐, ☐, ☐, 610
  b 243, ☐, ☐, ☐, 643, ☐
  c 76, ☐, ☐, ☐, 476, ☐

5 What sum is shown in these mental calculations?

  a
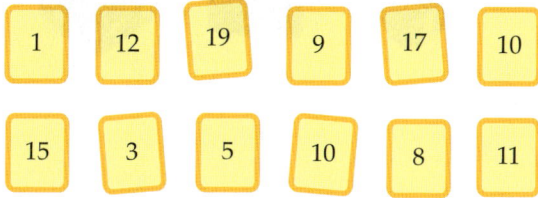

  b
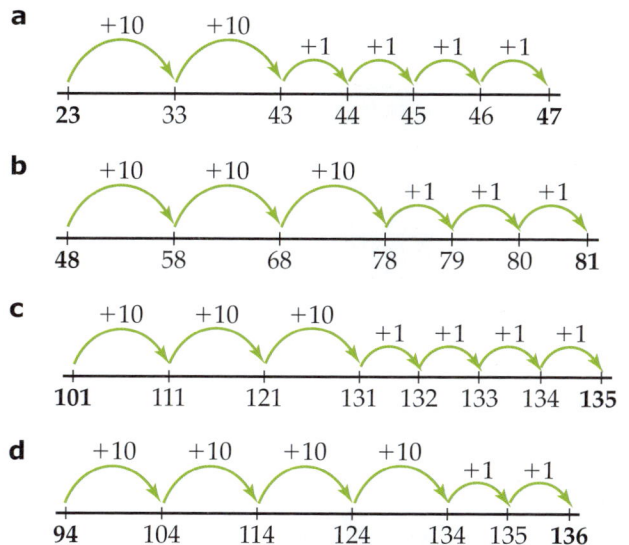

  c

  d

6 Calculate these sums.

You can use a number line to help you.

  a 25 + 20   **b** 33 + 40
  c 17 + 30   **d** 39 + 50
  e 25 + 21   **f** 34 + 41
  g 27 + 32   **h** 56 + 33
  i 44 + 32   **j** 28 + 24
  k 94 + 13   **l** 144 + 23
  m 262 + 115   **n** 25 + 188

Problem solving

7 Work out these addition problems in your head.

  a 20p + 35p   **b** 20p + 45p   **c** 120p + 30p

8 Members of the Angling Club went fishing and caught fish of these weights (in kg).

2, 1, 4, 3, 2, 5, 3, 4, 3, 5

Work out the **total** weight of the fish in your head.

7b Mental methods of subtraction

Ben is practising his mental subtraction.
He plays a game by rolling three dice.
He adds to find the total then subtracts from 20.

$4 + 5 + 3 = 12$
Then, $20 - 12 = 8$

‹ p. 14

Subtracting in 10s

$51 - 30$
$\downarrow$
$-10 - 10 - 10$
$= 21$

Start at 51 and **take away** three lots of 10.

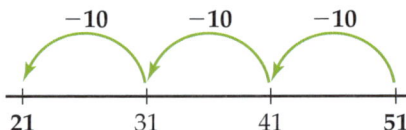

$-10 \qquad -10 \qquad -10$

21   31   41   51

$51 - 30 = \mathbf{21}$

Subtracting in 10s and units

$45 - 23$
$\downarrow$
$-10 - 10 - 1 - 1 - 1$
$= 22$

Start at 45 and take away two lots of 10 and then 3 units.

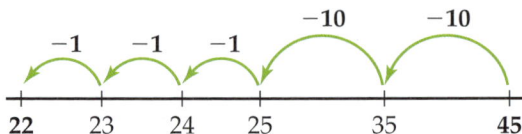

$-10 \qquad -10$
$-1 \quad -1 \quad -1$

22   23   24   25   35   45

$45 - 23 = \mathbf{22}$

Example

What is $57 - 25$?

Start at 57. Make two jumps of -10.   OR   Find the **difference** between 57 and 25 by
This takes you to 37.   counting on.
Then one jump of -5 brings you to 32.

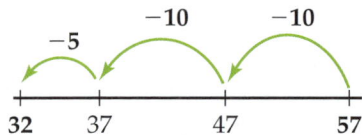

$-10 \qquad -10$
-5

32   37   47   57

$57 - 25 = 32$

$+10 \qquad +10 \qquad +10$
$\qquad\qquad\qquad\qquad +1 \quad +1$

25   35   45   55   56   57

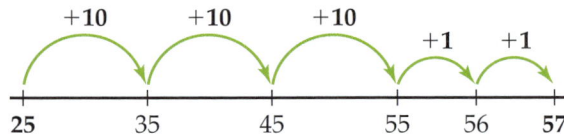

three 10s   and   two 1s $= 32$

Number Adding and subtracting

Exercise 7b

1 Work out these subtraction problems.

a 20 − 7 **b** 20 − 12
c 20 − 5 **d** 20 − 11
e 20 − 9 **f** 20 − 17

2 Add the scores from the three dice.
Subtract the total from 20 in your head.

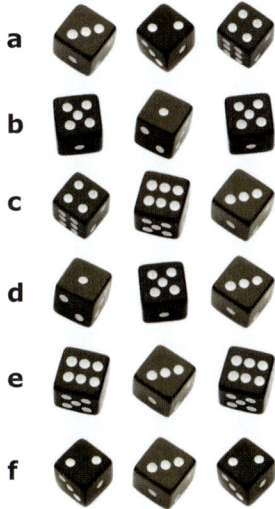

a
b
c
d
e
f

3 Work out these problems in your head.

a 10 − 7 **b** 12 − 9
c 15 − 4 **d** 11 − 0
e 19 − 15 **f** 18 − 18
g 92 − 3 − 4 **h** 103 − 2 − 2
i 75 − 9 − 3 **j** 35 − 4 − 7

4 Subtract 30 from each number.
Do the working out in your head.

a 39 **b** 51
c 60 **d** 88
e 95 **f** 100
g 120 **h** 127

5 Work out these subtraction problems in
your head. Choose your own method.

a 28 − 18 **b** 45 − 11
c 29 − 17 **d** 78 − 23
e 70 − 33 **f** 40 − 18
g 81 − 28 **h** 90 − 55

Problem solving

6 Members of the Athletics Club decide that
they will get fit. They start training.
After 12 weeks they are weighed.
Here are four results.
Work out each member's weight loss in
your head. Give your answers in kilograms.

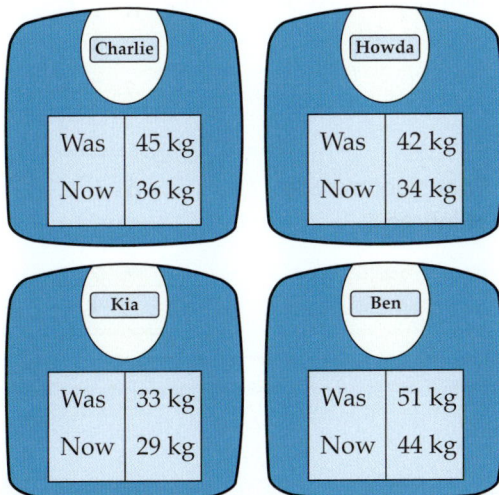

Did you know?

Alexander Aitken 1895–1967
was famous for being able to
do very complex calculations
in his head.
For example, he could
multiply two 8-figure numbers
mentally.

There are lots of ways to add and subtract.

1 Use a number line.

$41 - 24 = ?$

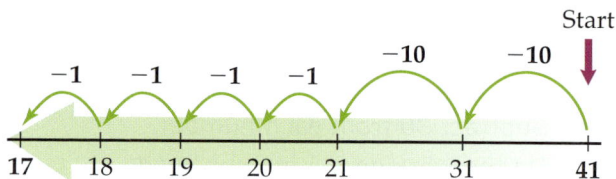

Four jumps of −1
subtracts 4

Two jumps of −10
subtracts 20

$41 - 24 = 17$

2 Split into tens and units.

$48 + 23 = ?$

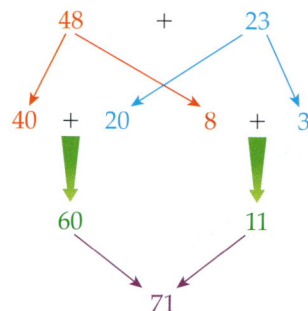

$48 + 23 = 71$

3 Set out your working in columns.

Example

Use columns to work out:

a $324 + 145$ **b** $548 - 235$

a Set out the numbers
in columns.

```
H T U
3 2 4
+1 4 5
```

Add the **U**nits.
4 add 5 = 9

```
H T U
3 2 4
+1 4 5
      9
```

Add the **T**ens column.

```
H T U
3 2 4
+1 4 5
   6 9
```

Then add the
Hundreds.

$324 + 145 = 469$

```
H T U
3 2 4
+1 4 5
4 6 9
```

b Set out the numbers
in columns.

```
H T U
5 4 8
-2 3 5
```

Subtract the **U**nits.
take 5 from 8 = 3

```
H T U
5 4 8
-2 3 5
      3
```

Subtract the **T**ens column.

```
H T U
5 4 8
-2 3 5
   1 3
```

Then subtract the
Hundreds.

$548 - 235 = 313$

```
H T U
5 4 8
-2 3 5
3 1 3
```

Exercise 7c

1 Use a number line to complete this addition grid.
The first is done for you.

34 + 23 =

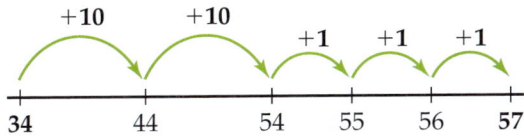

+	34	43	14
23	57		
63			
52			
17			

2 Use a number line to solve these subtraction problems.
The first is done for you.

a 43 − 22 =

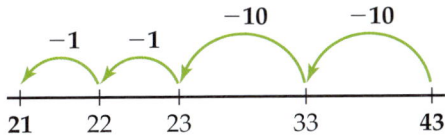

b 48 − 17   **c** 60 − 24
d 43 − 27   **e** 34 − 19

3 Copy and complete these work cards.

Addition

a
```
  2 5
+ 1 4
─────
```

b
```
  3 1
+ 2 7
─────
```

c
```
  1 6
+ 5 3
─────
```

d
```
  2 4 2
+ 1 3 2
───────
```

e
```
  3 3 5
+ 2 0 4
───────
```

f
```
  5 8 1
+ 3 1 6
───────
```

Subtraction

a
```
  5 5
− 2 4
─────
```

b
```
  6 7
− 2 3
─────
```

c
```
  8 6
− 5 0
─────
```

d
```
  4 6 4
− 1 5 3
───────
```

e
```
  8 5 3
− 5 0 3
───────
```

f
```
  4 6 6
− 4 0 6
───────
```

Problem solving

4 In these triangles you add the numbers in the circles to find the numbers in the rectangles.
Copy and complete them.

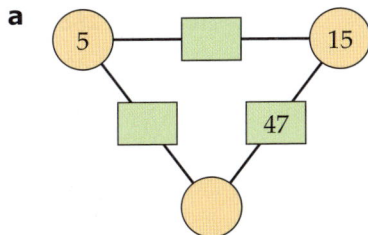

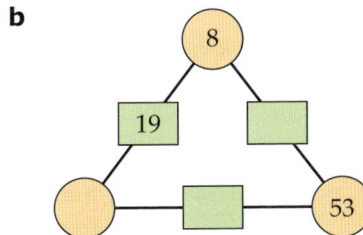

a

b

Did you know?

You can use an **abacus** to add, subtract, multiply and divide quickly.

5 Which is greater?
     a 24 + 13 or 88 − 14   **b** 101 + 77 or 49 + 120   **c** 98 − 53 or 23 + 16
     d 87 − 26 or 198 − 158   **e** 214 + 23 or 108 + 144   **f** 88 + 120 or 463 − 261

Luja is doing some arithmetic.
She wants to work out 58 + 25

and 161 − 25.

Add the units 8 + 5.
I've got more than 10.
What do I do?

I can't take 5 from 1.
What do I do?

```
    5  8
+   2  5
_____
```

8 + 5 = 13
Break the 13 into tens and units.
13 = 10 + 3

```
    5  8
+   2  5
_____
       3
_____
    1
```

Move the 1 below
the line to remind
you to add it on.

Add the tens column.

```
    5  8
+   2  5
_____
    8  3
_____
    1
```

```
    1  6  1
−      2  5
_____
```

Take a ten from the tens column and put it
into the units column.
161 = 150 + 11

```
    1  ⁵6̸ ¹1
−      2  5
_____
          6
```

Remember to write
how many tens
you have left in the
tens column.

Subtract the tens column.

```
    1  ⁵6̸ ¹1
−      2  5
_____
       3  6
```

Subtract the hundreds column.

```
    1  ⁵6̸ ¹1
−      2  5
_____
    1  3  6
```

You can check your
answer by doing the
arithmetic in reverse.
For example, in part **b**,
check that 282 + 345
= 627 by adding.

Example

a Work out
437 + 181

b Work out
627 − 282

```
    4  3  7
+   1  8  1
_____
    6  1  8
_____
    1
```

437 + 181 = 618

```
   ⁵6̸ ¹2  7
−  2  8  2
_____
   3  4  5
```

Take 100 from the
hundreds column
to put it into the
tens column.

627 − 282 = 345

Exercise 7d

1 Match the boxes that have the same value.

93 − 17	91
49 + 39	88
302	152 − 61
76	235 + 67

2 Use columns to work out these additions.
  a 251 + 427   **b** 106 + 371
  c 544 + 352   **d** 262 + 533

3 Use columns to work out these subtractions.
  a 357 − 143   **b** 584 − 252
  c 298 − 160   **d** 871 − 551

4 Without actually doing the calculations, how can you tell that each of these answers is incorrect?
  a 279 − 144 = 133
  b 422 − 166 = 588
  c 728 − 699 = 129

5 Work out these additions and subtractions.

Workcard 1
Addition

a
```
  417
+ 255
------
```
b
```
  309
+ 263
------
```
c
```
  291
+ 340
------
```
d
```
  365
+ 164
------
```
e
```
  120
+ 585
------
```
f
```
  759
+ 168
------
```

Workcard 2
Subtraction

a
```
  580
− 155
------
```
b
```
  762
− 435
------
```
c
```
  918
− 452
------
```
d
```
  707
− 237
------
```
e
```
  419
− 290
------
```
f
```
  635
− 365
------
```

Problem solving

‹ p. 38

6 a A bag of flour weighs 1 kg.
    250 g of flour is removed from the bag.
    How many grams are left?
  b Jack has three containers of juice.
    Each container holds 750 ml.
    How much juice does he have altogether?

7 Here is some major arithmetic!
  a
```
  1234567890123456789 0
+ 9876543210987654321 0
---------------------
```
  b
```
  8640864086408640
− 1234123412341234
----------------
```

7 MySummary

Check out

You should now be able to ...

Test it ➡

Questions

✓ Strengthen and extend mental methods of addition and subtraction.	3	1, 2
✓ Use efficient written methods to add and subtract whole numbers.	4	3 – 6

Language	Meaning	Example
Addition	The act of summing two numbers.	12 + 7 is an addition of 12 and 7
Sum	The result of an addition.	19 is the sum
Subtraction	The act of taking away one number from another.	12 − 7 = 5 is the subtraction of 7 from 12
Column arithmetic	An efficient method of adding or subtracting two numbers.	$$\begin{array}{r} 4\,3 \\ +\,6\,9 \\ \hline 1\,1\,2 \end{array} \qquad \begin{array}{r} {}^{6}\!\!\not{7}\,{}^{1}1 \\ -\,2\,3 \\ \hline 4\,8 \end{array}$$

1 Work out these additions in your head.

a	50 + 30	**b**	75 + 20
c	15 + 35	**d**	40 + 38
e	7 + 0	**f**	23 + 7
g	14 + 21	**h**	18 + 51
i	47 + 35	**j**	97 + 23
k	235 + 144	**l**	99 + 99

2 Work out these subtractions in your head.

a	50 − 9	**b**	67 − 20
c	41 − 21	**d**	65 − 30
e	87 − 32	**f**	73 − 38
g	56 − 18	**h**	177 − 116
i	257 − 129	**j**	408 − 212

3 Copy and complete these calculations.

a
```
   5 7
 + 2 1
 ─────
```

b
```
   8 1 6
 + 1 7 1
 ───────
```

c
```
   6 5
 − 2 4
 ─────
```

d
```
   5 7 4
 − 1 6 3
 ───────
```

4 Copy and complete these calculations.

a
```
   6 3
 + 2 9
 ─────
```

b
```
   3 3 5
 + 7 1 8
 ───────
```

c
```
   8 3
 − 6 5
 ─────
```

d
```
   3 0 4
 − 1 8 5
 ───────
```

5 Work out these calculations using a written method.

a	46 + 123	**b**	316 − 202
c	478 + 767	**d**	553 − 47

6 You buy a chocolate bar for 84p and a magazine for £2.50

a How much money have you spent?

b If you pay with a £5 note how much change should you get?

What next?

Score			
	0 – 2		Your knowledge of this topic is still developing. To improve look at Formative test: 1A-7; MyMaths: 1020, 1028 and 1345
	3 – 5		You are gaining a secure knowledge of this topic. To improve look at InvisiPen: 121 and 125
	6		You have mastered this topic. Well done, you are ready to progress!

7a

1 Calculate these additions.

    a 54 + 16   **b** 48 + 22

    c 53 + 17   **d** 51 + 19

    e 65 + 39   **f** 79 + 13

2 A lorry of length 25 m is towing a trailer of length 15 m. What is the total length?

3 Use the method of 'adding tens and then units' to find each answer.

    a 54 + 31   **b** 70 + 14   **c** 62 + 22   **d** 79 + 12

4 Use a number line to find the answer if you need to.

    a 77 + 35   **b** 88 + 26   **c** 60 + 54   **d** 83 + 28

5 In these pyramids, each number is found by adding the two numbers below it. Copy the pyramids and fill in the missing numbers.

a

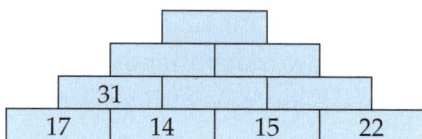

b

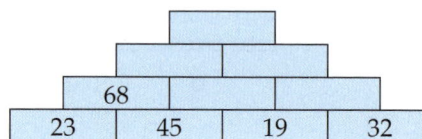

7b

6 Calculate these.

    a 74 − 31   **b** 47 − 32   **c** 54 − 12

    d 64 − 19   **e** 62 − 48   **f** 84 − 8

7 At Manor Lane School there are 89 students in year 7. There are 41 boys. How many girls are there?

8 Use the method of 'subtracting tens and then units' to find each answer.

    a 89 − 43   **b** 68 − 22   **c** 96 − 51   **d** 81 − 39

9 Find the answers. Use a number line if you need to.

    a 102 − 57   **b** 110 − 65   **c** 91 − 48   **d** 102 − 43

10 In these pyramids, each number is found by subtracting the two numbers below it. Copy the pyramids and fill in the missing numbers.

a

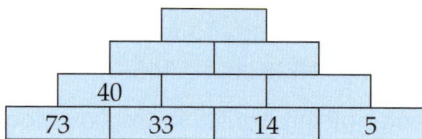

b

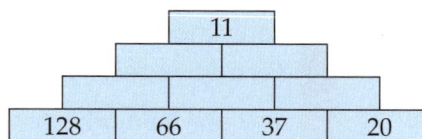

11 Complete these column additions and subtractions.

a 4 3
  + 2 5
  ──────
  ══════

b 7 2
  + 2 6
  ──────
  ══════

c 6 6
  − 3 2
  ──────
  ══════

d 9 5
  − 7 3
  ──────
  ══════

12 Work out these using column arithmetic.

a 245 + 352
b 628 + 371
c 307 + 651
d 273 + 516
e 356 − 134
f 728 − 617
g 856 − 35
h 764 − 560

13 Complete these column additions and subtractions.

a 4 6 4
  + 3 1 8
  ──────
  ══════

b 2 1 8
  + 3 0 2
  ──────
  ══════

c 5 8 4
  − 3 8 0
  ──────
  ══════

d 6 7 0
  − 2 3 5
  ──────
  ══════

14 Add or subtract using columns.

a 5 9 6
  + 3 2 7
  ──────
  ══════

b 6 4 1
  + 2 3 9
  ──────
  ══════

c 4 5 2
  − 1 0 6
  ──────
  ══════

d 8 1 7
  − 2 8 0
  ──────
  ══════

15 Write these problems in columns and then add or subtract.

a 539 + 254
b 107 + 448
c 472 − 209
d 703 − 362

16 The passenger numbers for a train service are:
Monday 562, Tuesday 703, Wednesday 481
  a Find the total number of passengers for the three days.
  b Find the difference between the number of passengers on Tuesday and the number of passengers on Wednesday.

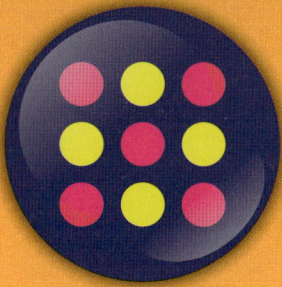

8 Statistics

Introduction

Designer clothes are big business. Shops have to decide how many items to stock in each size - too few and the customers complain, too many and they have lots of unsold items on the shelves!

Clothes shops conduct surveys to find out the 'distribution' of sizes of their customers so they can work out the correct number of items to stock in each size.

What's the point?

Market research allows businesses to find out information about their customers' needs. If they do not have this awareness, they will most likely go out of business.

Objectives

By the end of this chapter, you will have learned how to …

- Plan how to collect and organise small sets of data from surveys and experiments.
- Solve problems by interpreting data in lists and tables.
- Construct and interpret statistical diagrams, including pictograms, bar charts, pie charts and line graphs.
- Calculate statistics for small sets of data, including the mode, median and range.

Check in

1   In a pictogram the symbol represents 10 cars.

   a   Which of these represents 20 cars?

   i   ii

   iii

   b   Which of these represents 5 cars?

   i   ii

   iii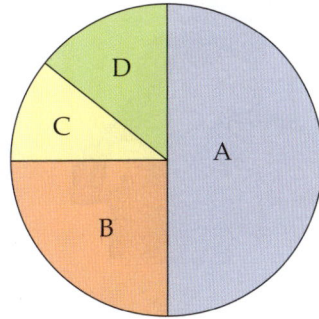

2   Write down the fraction of the whole circle
    represented by each of the letters A, B, C and D.

Starter problem

What is the difference between the 'average' boy and the 'average' girl?
You will need to work out some averages and gather some information from the rest of
your class.

Tracy wants to find out how students get to school.

She **collects** data by **surveying** students.

She writes a **questionnaire** for each student to fill in.

What if lots of students travel to school by train?

1) How old are you?

_____

2) How do you get to school each day?

Car   Bus   Walk   Cycle   Other

☐   ☐   ☐   ☐   ☐

3) When do you get to school?

Before 8:00 am   8:00 to 8:30 am   After 8:30 am

☐   ☐   ☐

What if it varies depending on the day?

She has to ask the right questions to make sure she collects useful data.

Tracy also wants to find out about their favourite subject.
She is not sure which of these questions is the best one to ask.

a) Do you like Maths?

b) Which subject is your favourite?

English Maths PE Geography French Other

☐   ☐   ☐   ☐   ☐   ☐

c) What is your favourite subject? _____

Her friends have some comments on the questions.

In **a**, what about the other subjects?

The best question is **b**. It gives a choice of subjects. It includes 'Other' in case a student's favourite subject isn't listed.

In **c** there could be any answer! It would be hard to keep track of all the answers but at least it could be a good reflection.

Exercise 8a

1 Anna wants to know students' favourite kind of music. Which question would be best to ask? Suggest how it could be improved.

a) Do you like rap music? Yes/No

b) What is your favourite kind of music? _____

c) Which kind of music is your favourite?
Indie Hip-hop Pop
☐ ☐ ☐
Dance Other
☐ ☐

2 Anna now wants to know **how** students listen to music. Write a question for her questionnaire.

Did you know?

Every 10 years the government gives every household in the UK a questionnaire called a census.

3 Anna wants to know which DJs students prefer. She wrote these questions. How could she make each question better?

a Do you like DJ Backbeat?

b Which DJ is your favourite?
DJ Fraction ☐
Grooverider ☐
Elektra ☐

c Do you want to be a DJ when you grow up?

Problem solving

4 Journalists need to ask the right questions to get correct data.
What questions do you think the journalist asked to get these responses?

a I like the holidays!

b Springtime is best.

c Pizza!

d I live for football season!

e Summer is wonderful!

f France.

Example

You can organise data in a **frequency table**.

Sammi wants to find out the most popular mobile phone colour.
She records the colours of 12 of her friends' phones.

Red   Black   Black   Brown   Black   White
Pink   Black   Black   Silver   Red   Silver

Organise this set of data into a table.

> Frequency means "how many"

The table shows the **frequency** for each colour.

Colour	Red	Black	Brown	White	Silver	Pink
Frequency	2	⑤	1	1	2	1

The table shows clearly that black is the most popular colour.

If you have a large set of data, it is easier to make a frequency table using a **tally chart**.

Example

Ben did a survey to find the most popular vegetable.
Draw a tally and frequency table for this set of data.

To make a tally chart, go through the data crossing off each item and putting a tally mark in the correct row.

Favourite vegetable	Tally	Frequency
Carrot	ЖII I	6
Beetroot	ЖII	5
Tomato	II	2
Sweetcorn	III	3
Peas	ЖII III	8

> Add the tallies to find the frequency.

> Every five tallies makes a five-bar gate. This makes it easier to count up.

Exercise 8b

1 The children in class 7F ate these fruits one lunchtime.
Draw a frequency table for this set of data.

2 The tally chart shows the numbers of people at three school clubs one evening.
Draw a frequency table for this set of data.

Club	Tally
Art Club	JHT JHT JHT I
Netball Club	JHT JHT JHT JHT II
Computer Club	JHT JHT III

3 Heather took part in a bird-watching project.
The diagram shows all the birds that she saw in one hour.

a Make a tally chart for this set of data.

b Use your tally chart to produce a frequency table.

Key: = Sparrow   = Robin   = Magple   = Pigeon

Problem solving

4 Ronnie and Johnny recorded their dart scores differently. Who won?

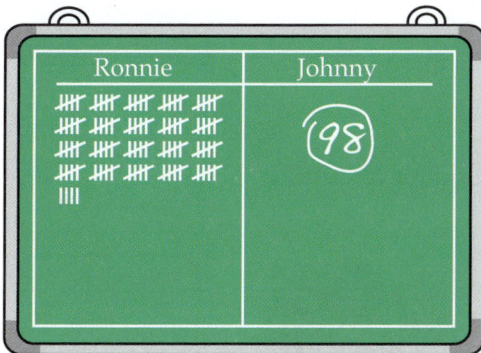

5 Find three things wrong with this tally chart.

Language	Tally	Frequency
Cebuano	III	3
Guaymi	JHT II	6
Berber	JHT III	8
Bemba	JHT JHT I	11
Gurma	II	2
Farsi	JHT	5
Bengali	JHT I	6
Guaymi	IIII	4
		Total = 47

MyMaths.co.uk

Q 1235 SEARCH

8c Reading lists and tables

🔵 A list shows data in a clear way so that it is easier to understand.

Lists also make it easy to add up things, like amounts of money.

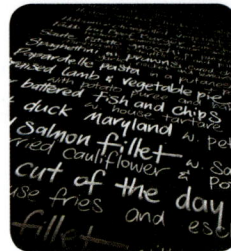

▲ The menu at a café is a kind of list.

p. 266 >

Example

At the end of a meal in a restaurant four friends looked at the bill.

a How many drinks did they have?

b If the four friends share the bill equally, how much should each person pay?

---

a They had four drinks altogether.

Just count the number of drinks shown on the bill.

b 64 ÷ 2 = 32
32 ÷ 2 = 16
Each person pays £16.

To divide by four you can halve the total and then halve again.

CARLA'S RESTAURANT	
YOUR RECEIPT	
STARTER	3.75
STARTER	3.75
MAIN COURSE	8.90
MAIN COURSE	7.95
MAIN COURSE	8.20
MAIN COURSE	8.75
DESSERT	4.20
DESSERT	4.20
DESSERT	4.75
DRINK	2.60
DRINK	2.60
DRINK	2.60
DRINK	1.75
*****************	******
TOTAL	64.00
*****************	******
THANK YOU - CALL AGAIN SOON	

🔵 Frequency tables make it easier to show larger amounts of data.

Example

The manager at Carla's Restaurant keeps a record of the main courses sold one lunchtime.

a What was the most popular dish?

b How many main courses were sold altogether?

Look at the totals in the table. There were more chef's salads sold than any other dish.

a The chef's salad was the most popular dish.

b Add together the totals for each dish.
7 + 4 + 8 + 2 + 4 = 25
There were 25 main courses sold.

Dish	Frequency
Dover Sole	7
Lasagne	4
Chef's Salad	⑧
Stuffed Courgette	2
Crab Cakes	4

Exercise 8c

1 Here is the four friends' restaurant bill again.

  a How many starters did they have?

  b How much did the most expensive dessert cost?

  c How can you tell that the four friends all had different main courses?

  d The friends paid £70 for the meal, including a tip. How much was the tip?

CARLA'S RESTAURANT ****YOUR RECEIPT****	
STARTER	
STARTER	3.75
MAIN COURSE	3.75
MAIN COURSE	8.90
MAIN COURSE	7.95
MAIN COURSE	8.20
DESSERT	8.75
DESSERT	4.20
DESSERT	4.20
DRINK	4.75
DRINK	2.60
DRINK	2.60
DRINK	2.60
*******************	1.75
TOTAL	*****
********************	64.00
	*****
THANK YOU - CALL AGAIN SOON	

2 Look at the table in the second example.

  a How many people ordered lasagne?

  b What was the least popular dish?

  c What was the second most popular dish?

3 This list shows the prices for a range of furniture. How much has each person spent?

  a Hari buys a 2-seater settee and a reclining armchair.

  b Antonio buys a 3-seater settee, a corner unit and a 2-seater settee.

  c Jane buys two armchairs and a 3-seater settee.

New!! Furniture range

Corner unit	£45
Armchair	£50
Reclining armchair	£85
2-seater settee	£95
3-seater settee	£125

4 The table shows the number of minutes Jenna spent doing her homework one week.

Sunday	Monday	Tuesday	Wednesday	Thursday	Friday	Saturday
75	30	45	25	60	0	0

  a On which day did she do the most homework?

  b On which days did she do no homework?

  c How long did Jenna spend doing homework that week?

Problem solving

5 Sam noted the time he spent doing homework. He spent 30 minutes doing homework on Monday and the same on Tuesday. He did one hour of homework on Wednesday, and 75 minutes on Thursday. On Friday he spent just 15 minutes on homework, but on Saturday he did 90 minutes. He did no homework on Sunday.

  a Make a table to show how long Sam spent on his homework each day.

  b Find the total time Sam spent on his homework.

  c What fraction of the days did he do no homework?

❮p. 66

A **pictogram** shows data as a series of pictures.

Example

Mr Brown records the number of computers in three classrooms.
What is the total number of computers?

Room 17	🖥 🖥 🖥 🖥 🖥
Room 18	🖥 🖥 🖥
Room 19	🖥 🖥 🖥 🖥

Key: 🖥 = 1 computer

There are 5 computers in Room 17, 3 in Room 18 and 4 in Room 19.

The total number of computers is 5 + 3 + 4 = 12 computers.

With larger numbers, one symbol can stand for a **group** of things.

Choose something easy to draw!

Example

Andy's teacher asks him to record the number of books in each classroom.
Use Andy's data to create a pictogram.

ROOM 17	30
ROOM 18	40
ROOM 19	15

First, choose a **symbol**.

Then choose a **key**.
Next, work out how many symbols you need for each room.
Finally, draw your pictogram.
Don't forget to give a key.

Key: 📖 = 10 books
$30 \div 10 = 3$ symbols
$40 \div 10 = 4$ symbols
$15 \div 10 = 1.5$ symbols

If he used one 📖 per book there would be a lot of drawing to do!

Room 17	📖 📖 📖
Room 18	📖 📖 📖 📖
Room 19	📖 📖

Key: 📖 = 10 books

The 📖 symbol stands for 5 books.

Exercise 8d

1 This pictogram shows the number of people living in three houses in a street.

House number	Number of people
1	👤👤👤👤👤👤
2	👤👤👤👤
3	👤👤👤

Key: 👤 = 1 person

a Make a table to show the number of people living in each house.

b How many people live in the three houses?

2 Celine bought some food for her cat. She bought 2 cans of beef flavour, 2 cans of tuna flavour and 5 cans of chicken flavour.
Draw a pictogram to show this information.

3 The pictogram shows the number of houses in three villages.

Village	Number of houses
Apton	🏠🏠
Bapton	🏠🏠🏠🏠🏠🏠
Capton	🏠🏠🏠

Key: 🏠 = 10 houses

3 a How many houses are there in each village?

b Find the total number of houses in the three villages.

4 The pictogram shows the number of meals served in Max's restaurant.

Day	Number of meals
Monday	◯ ◯ ◗
Tuesday	◯ ◯ ◯
Wednesday	◯ ◗
Thursday	◯ ◖
Friday	◯ ◯ ◯
Saturday	◯ ◯ ◯
Sunday	◯ ◯ ◯

Key: ◯ = 20 meals

a How many meals were served on Tuesday?

b How many meals were served on Thursday?

c What was the least busy day?

d How many meals were served over the whole week?

5 Erica surveyed the birds in her garden. She counted 4 chaffinches, 6 pigeons, 12 starlings and 18 sparrows.
Draw a pictogram to show her results.

Problem solving

6 Moira did a survey on what pets people preferred but her cat walked all over it! Help her complete her table and pictogram. How many people did she ask?

Type of pet	Cat	Dog	Fish	Other
No. of people	6	🐾	4	🐾

Cat	🐾🐾🐾🐾🐾
Dog	🐾😊😊😊😊
Fish	🐾🐾🐾🐾🐾🐾
Other	😊😊🐾🐾

Key: 😊 = 2 people

You can use data from a pictogram or frequency table to draw a **bar chart**.

Title

Frequency

Labels

⟨ p.118

> When you draw a bar chart
> ▶ Leave gaps between the bars.
> ▶ Make sure all the bars are the same width.
> ▶ Write a label on each **axis**.
> ▶ Make sure that the vertical axis has a clear scale.

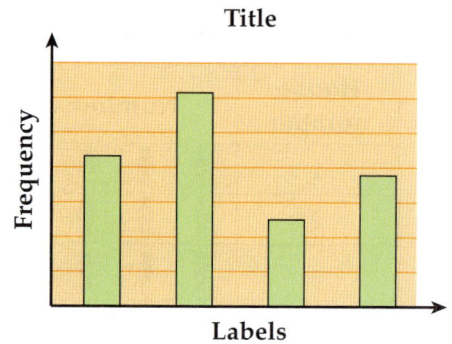

Sarah is investigating class 7A's favourite drinks.
She turns her pictogram into a bar chart.

7A's favourite drinks

Favourite drink	Number of students
Cola	🥛 🥛 🥛 🥛
Squash	🥛 🥛 🥛 🥛
Orange juice	🥛 🥛 🥛 🥛 🥛
Water	🥛

Key: 🥛 means 2 students

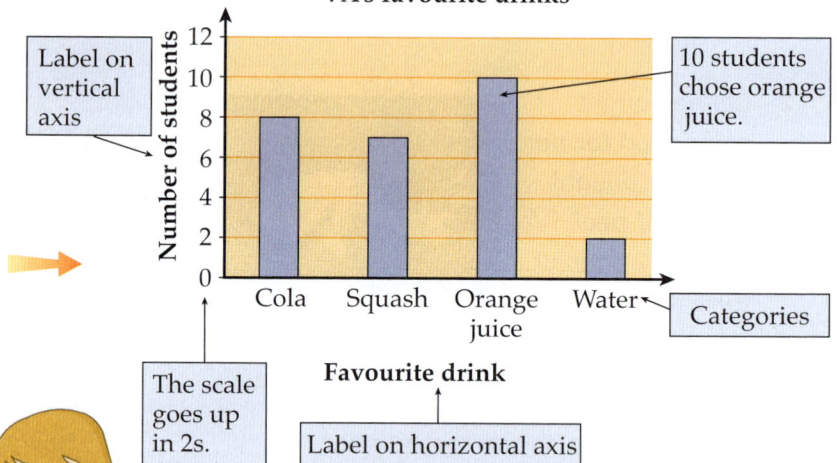

Label on vertical axis

The scale goes up in 2s.

7A's favourite drinks

Number of students

Cola   Squash   Orange juice   Water

Favourite drink

Label on horizontal axis

10 students chose orange juice.

Categories

If you turn my pictogram on its side it looks a bit like my bar chart!

Example

The bar chart shows the number of computers in four classrooms.

a Which room has the most computers?
b How many computers are there altogether?

a Room 24 has the most computers (7).
b The total number of computers is
5 + 4 + 5 + 7 = 21

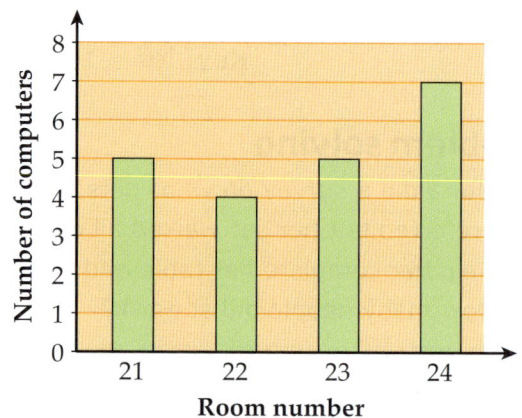

Number of computers

21   22   23   24

Room number

Exercise 8e

1 This bar chart shows the number of students in each class who play rugby.

- **a** How many students in class 7A play rugby?
- **b** Which class has the most rugby players?
- **c** Which class has the fewest rugby players?
- **d** How many students play rugby in total?

Students who play rugby

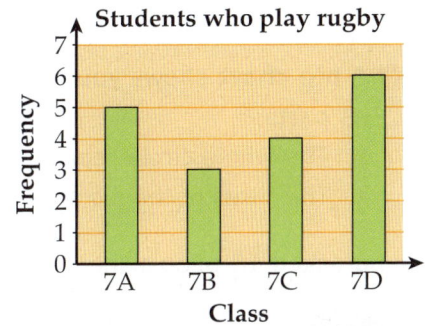

2 This table shows the number of students who were absent from class 7C at Clearview High School. Copy and complete the bar chart for this set of data.

Day	Mon	Tue	Wed	Thu	Fri
Absences	3	2	0	1	2

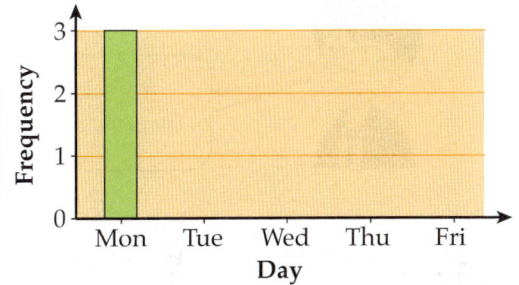

3 Draw a bar chart for the data in this pictogram.

Number of books read during Year 7 Reading Challenge

Key: = 10 books

4 Draw a bar chart for the data in this frequency table.

Packs of cat food eaten by Cheryl's cat in one week

Flavour	Lamb	Tuna	Cod	Beef
Frequency	4	1	5	2

Problem solving

5 Here are the sports options chosen during Year 7 Activity Week at Speedwell Middle School.

For this set of data
- **a** draw a tally chart and frequency table
- **b** draw a bar chart.

Key: = Hockey = Football = Netball

6 a Draw a bar chart for the data in this Frequency table.
- **b** Look back at question **4**. How are the two graphs the same and how do they differ?

Packs of cat food eaten by Cheryl's cat in one month

Flavour	Lamb	Tuna	Cod	Beef
Frequency	12	4	8	16

MyMaths.co.uk 1193, 1205 SEARCH

153

A **pie chart** shows you how a total is divided up into its parts.

▶ The whole circle represents the total.

▶ The slices of the pie show you how big the parts are.

Favourite dessert

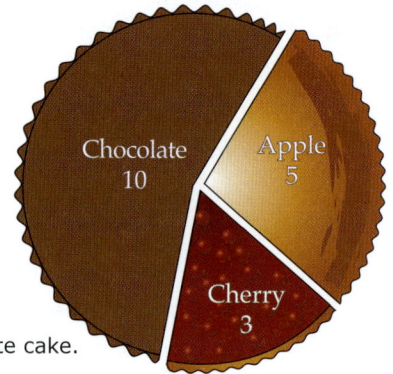

Liang asked 18 people this question.

What's your favourite dessert?

10 people chose chocolate cake.

5 people chose apple crumble.

3 people chose cherry flan.

Example

This pie chart shows the types of films that a cinema showed one month.

a How many types of film were there?

b Which type of film was shown the most?

Types of film

a 4 types of film

There are 4 pie slices.

b Action films were shown most.

Action has the biggest pie slice.

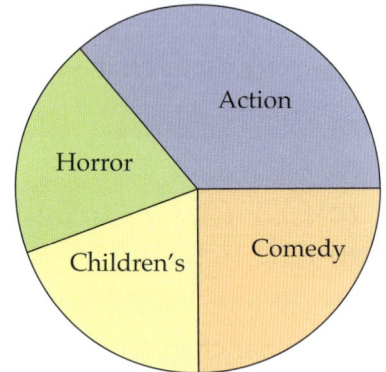

Pie charts allow you to describe fractions of an amount.

Example

This pie chart shows the flavours of ice cream served one day in a shop. What fraction of the total is each flavour?

Chocolate $\frac{1}{2}$,

Vanilla $\frac{1}{4}$,

Strawberry $\frac{1}{4}$

Ice cream flavours

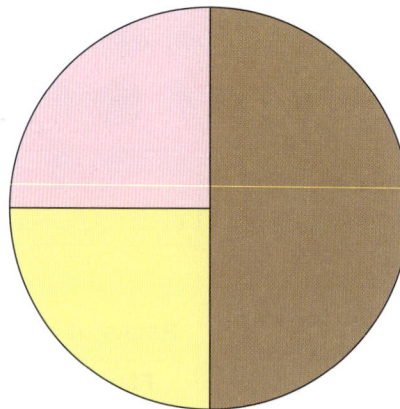

Key:

Strawberry

Chocolate

Vanilla

p.66

Exercise 8f

1 This pie chart shows class 7A's eye colours.

Eye colour

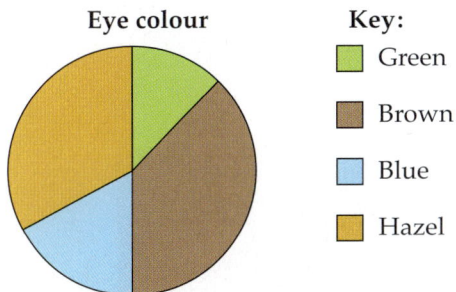

Key:
- ▢ Green
- ▢ Brown
- ▢ Blue
- ▢ Hazel

a How many eye colours are there?
b Which colour is the least common?
c Which colour is the most common?

2 Camilla carried out a survey to find out what kind of pet her classmates have. The pie chart shows her results.

Favourite pets

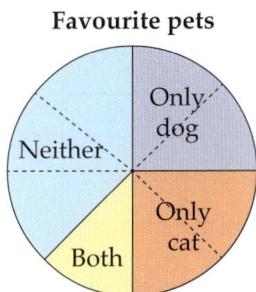

2 What fraction of the class own
a only a dog
b only a cat
c neither a dog nor a cat
d a cat *and* a dog?

3 This pie chart shows how the Barnes family spent their money in one month.

Spending

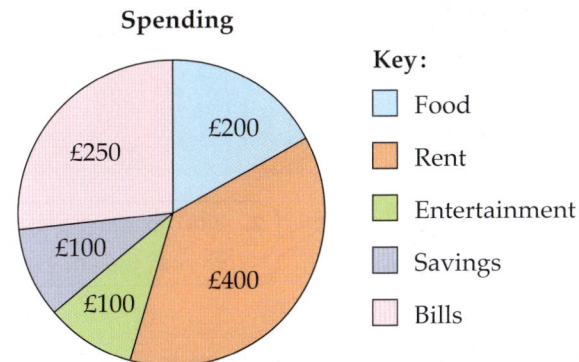

Key:
- ▢ Food
- ▢ Rent
- ▢ Entertainment
- ▢ Savings
- ▢ Bills

a How much did they spend on food?
b On which item was about $\frac{1}{4}$ of the money spent?
c On which item was the most money spent?

Problem solving

4 Algie asked his class what their favourite fruit was. He drew a pie chart of the results.
a What fraction chose **i** bananas **ii** apples?
b What fraction did not choose oranges or pears?
c Can you say how many people are in Algie' class?

5 This unlabelled pie chart shows the Barlow family's expences for a night out at the cinema. They spent money on tickets, popcorn, parking and baby-sitting. Which slice do you think could represent each of the four costs?

Spending

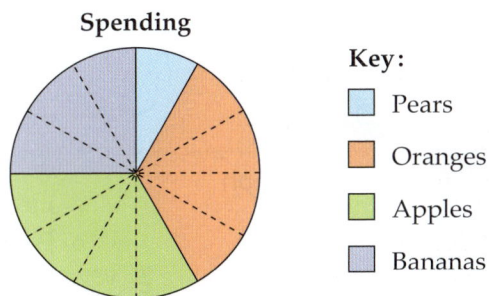

Key:
- ▢ Pears
- ▢ Oranges
- ▢ Apples
- ▢ Bananas

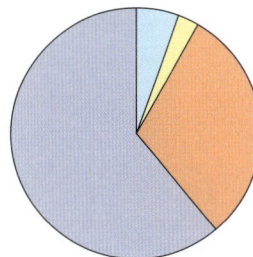

8g Reading diagrams

Sarah's top tips to reading diagrams.

1. Different types of diagram show different things.

Bar charts and pictograms compare totals.

Line graphs show how things change over time.

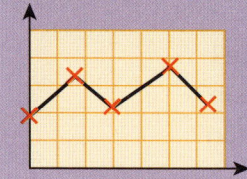

Pie charts show how big the parts of a total are.

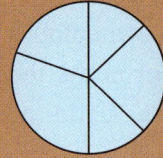

2. When reading a diagram with a **key**, you need to read the key carefully.

Pie charts and pictograms use keys.

Example

Andrew said, 'This diagram is wrong. You can't have half a student!' Is Andrew correct?

Andrew hasn't read the key correctly. The half symbol represents 1 student.

Football	🎾 🎾 🎾 🎾
Rugby	🎾 🎾 🎾 🎾 🌙
Tennis	🎾 🎾 🌙
Netball	🎾 🎾

Key: 🎾 = 2 students

3. When reading a **diagram** with a **scale**, you need to
   – look at the correct axis
   – and read the scale carefully.

Bar charts and line graphs use scales.

< p.118

Example

This line graph shows the attendance at Meadway School. Which week had the lowest attendance?

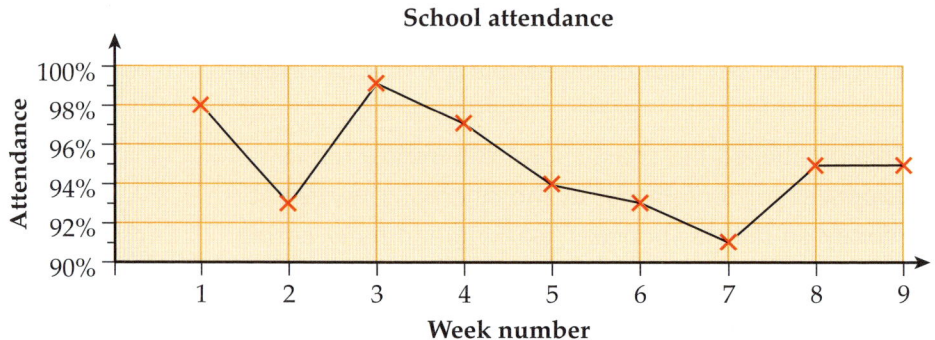

School attendance

The lowest attendance was in week 7.

The question asks *when*, **not** *what*, the lowest attendance was.

Exercise 8g

1 This bar chart shows the number of boys and girls in four classes.
The blue bars represent boys. The green bars represent girls.

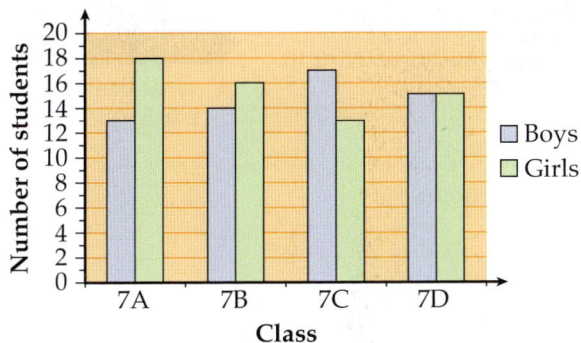

a How many boys are there in class 7B?
b Which class has equal numbers of boys and girls?
c Which class has more boys than girls?
d Which class has more students than the others?

2 Steve drew this line graph to show the number of songs he downloaded each month.

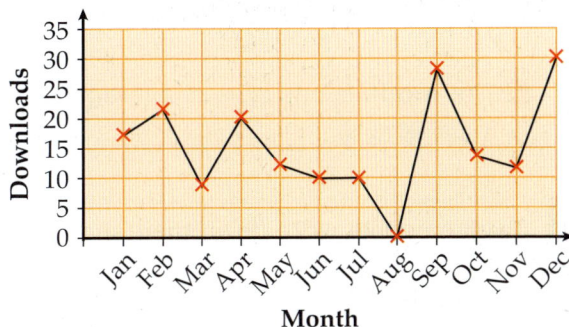

a How many songs did Steve download in April?
b In which month did Steve download no songs?
c What was the greatest number of songs he downloaded in a month? When did this happen?

Problem solving

3 The pie charts show the types of tree in two woods. In each wood 500 trees were looked at to see what type they were.

a What was the most common type of tree in each wood?
b Richard says, 'The charts show that there are more oak trees in Cantor Wood than there are in West Wood'. Explain why Richard is wrong.
c George says, 'The charts show that Cantor Wood has more oak trees than birch trees'. Explain why George is right.

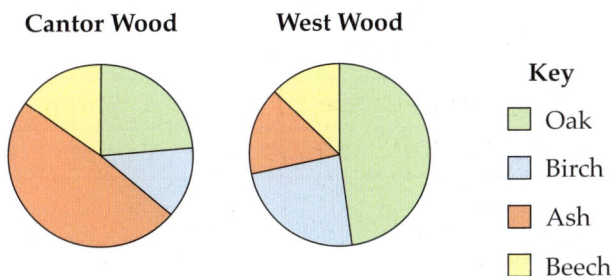

Cantor Wood   West Wood

Key
Oak
Birch
Ash
Beech

4 The deputy head teacher at Passmore School wants to draw a diagram to show the number of absences each term.
What sort of diagram should she use?
Explain your answer.

8h Averages – the mode

The average 12-year-old girl in the UK is 1.5m tall.

⬤ An **average** is a single value that represents a whole set of values.

⬤ The **mode** is one type of average. It is the most frequent value in a set of data.

▲ What does an average person look like?

Example

Twelve people write down their shoe sizes. Find the mode.

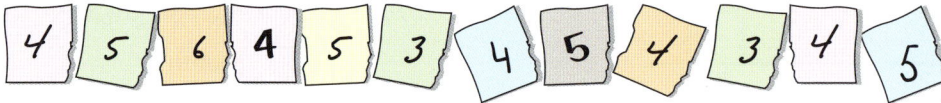
4 5 6 4 5 3 4 5 4 3 4 5

Write the data as a **frequency table**.

Shoe size	3	④	5	6
Frequency	2	⑤	4	1

The most popular shoe size is 4.

The mode of this set of data is size 4.

The mode is the size with the highest frequency.

The mode does not have to be a number.

This table shows the eye colours of 25 students.

Eye colour	Blue	Green	Brown	Hazel
Frequency	7	5	⑫	1

Brown is the **modal** colour.

⬤ A set of data may have more than one mode or it may have no mode.

Example

Find the mode of each set of data.

a 4 4 5 8 9 9 10

b 2 5 7 8 11

c 6 7 5 9 3 7 5 1 9 5

It helps to put data in order to find the mode.

a This set of data has two modes.
    The modes are 4 and 9.

b Each value occurs once.
    There is no mode.

c 1 3 5 5 5 6 7 7 9 9
    The mode is 5.

❮ p. 6

Exercise 8h

1 Find the mode of each set of numbers.

  a 3 5 5 8

  b 1 4 4 6 6 6 7 8 8 10

  c 14 17 17 19 22

  d 1 1 2 3 5 5 8

2 Find the mode of each set of numbers.

  a 5 7 8 5 8 4 6 8 3 8

  b 19 17 18 19 15 18 16 18

2 **c** 3.1 3.5 3.4 3.3 3.4 3.4

  d 1.7 2.3 0.9 1.8 1.9 2.4

3 Find the modal number of goals from this frequency table.

Goals	0	1	2	3	4
Frequency	5	3	6	2	1

< p. 8

Problem solving

4 Pat recorded the number of people travelling in each car going past a check point.

  a Make a **tally chart**.

  b Draw a frequency table.

  c Use your frequency table to find the mode of the set of data.

```
1 3 3 4 3 3 4 3 5 3
3 1 4 2 2 2 2 3 2 2
2 1 3 3 4 3 4 2 1 3
```

5 Suresh asked 50 people to keep a record of how many telephone calls they received during one week, the results are shown in this spreadsheet.

  a Make a tally chart and a frequency table for this set of data.

  b Use your frequency table to produce a **bar chart** for the data.

  c Find the mode of the number of calls received.

Phone Calls

File Edit View Insert Format Tools Data Window Help Acrobat

4	9	11	7	8
8	8	9	6	10
9	6	5	12	9
9	9	9	9	6
6	4	5	8	9
15	12	6	4	8
9	9	8	5	2
7	9	8	6	9
4	7	7	10	8
11	7	10	7	11

6 Liang recorded the time it took for him to get dressed every day. Here are his times.

10s, 10s, 40s, 41s, 43s, 47s, 52s, 53s

Is 10s a good average to represent the data?

> The mode is 10s, so that is the average time.

8i   Averages – the median

The **median** is another type of average.

❮ p. 6

🔴 To find the median, put the data in **order**, and then find the middle value.

3   3   4   ⑤   5   6   7
5 is the median.

Example

Jules asks nine people their ages.

| 12 | 34 | 56 | 21 | 13 | 9 | 4 | 17 | 34 |

Find the median age for this group of people.

Put the data in order.
Count down from each of the end numbers in pairs.

4   9   12   13   ⑰   21   34   34   56

The middle number is 17.

The median age is 17.

> You can cancel out each of the end numbers in pairs.

It is easy to find the middle number when you have an odd number of data values.

🔴 To find the median of an even number of data values
▶ add the two numbers nearest the middle
▶ divide the total by two.

Example

Find the median age of Sanjit's family.
26   81   45   53

First, put the values in order.

26   (45   53)   81

There is no 'middle number'.
45 + 53 = 98
98 ÷ 2 = 49
The median age is 49.

Add the two numbers nearest the middle.
Divide the total by 2.

Exercise 8i

1   Work out the median of each set of numbers.
   a 2   3   4   4   7
   b 4   9   12
   c 3   6   8   11   12

Remember, mark off the ends in pairs.

2   Work out the median of each set of numbers.
   a 5   7   4
   b 2   9   8   3   4
   c 1   9   6   8

3   At the London Olympics, the men's 100 m final times were

Place	1st	2nd	3rd	4th	5th	6th	7th	8th
Time (s)	9.63	9.75	9.79	9.80	9.88	9.94	9.98	11.99

Find the median finishing time for the race.

‹ p. 8

4   Arrange each set of data in order. Find the median.
   a Nine children's shoe sizes.   3, 6, 4, 6, 6, 5, 4, 7, 6
   b Ten people's ages.   21, 18, 35, 48, 16, 26, 30, 18, 14, 10
   c Lengths (in cm) of six worms.   11, 9, 12, 10, 12, 13
   d Number of people in ten families.   4, 5, 3, 2, 4, 3, 4, 3, 2, 6

5   The populations of five cities are
   Leicester   280 000
   Brighton & Hove   248 000
   Manchester   422 000
   Cardiff   305 000
   Edinburgh   449 000
   a Write this list of populations in order of size.
   b Find the median population of the five cities.

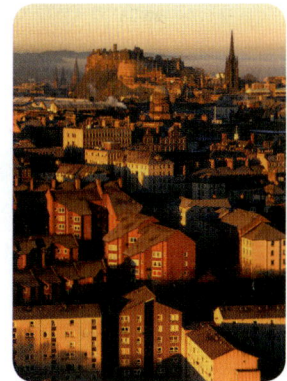

▲ Edinburgh

Problem solving

6   Find the median of each data set.
   a 4, 5, 6, 100, 100
   b 1, 3, 4, 5, 8, 9
   c 10, 11, 15, 205, 318, 906
   Is the median a good representation of the data in each case?

MyMaths.co.uk   1203   SEARCH

● The **range** is the difference between the largest value and the smallest value in a set of data.

Here is a set of shoe sizes. ③ 3 4 4 5 7 ⑨

9 − 3 = 6

The range is 6.

Debbie asks eight people how many cups of coffee they had made today.
Find the range of this set of data.

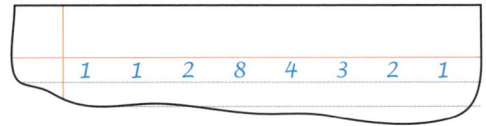

| 1 | 1 | 2 | 8 | 4 | 3 | 2 | 1 |

① 1 1 2 2 3 4 ⑧   Order the data.

Range = 8 – 1   The range = highest value − lowest value

The range is 7.

● Use an **average** to compare the **size** of values in two data sets.

● Use the **range** to compare the **spread** of values in two data sets.

Remember, the mode is the most frequent value and the median is the middle value.

Example

For a science experiment, Mandy measures leaves (in millimetres) from two different trees.

| Oak | 42 | 42 | 44 | 45 | 47 | 47 | 47 | 47 | 50 | 50 | 51 |
| **Birch** | 24 | 27 | 32 | 34 | 38 | 38 | 38 | 43 | 44 | 47 | 48 |

Compare the two sets of data.

Oak   Mode = 47 mm
        Range = 51 mm – 42 mm = 9 mm

Birch   Mode = 38 mm
        Range = 48 mm – 24 mm = 24 mm

The oak leaves are usually longer than the birch leaves.
The birch leaf lengths have more **variation** than
the oak leaf lengths. They have a greater spread of values.

Oak

Birch

Variation means differences.

Exercise 8j

1 Write each set of data in order. Then find the range.

a 4   11   6

b 3   8   6   7   9

c 5   5   1   9

d 6   12   5   8

2 Calculate the range of the heights of these skyscrapers.

Building	Height (m)
Taipei 101, Taipei, Taiwan	508
Petronas Tower 1, Kuala Lumpur, Malaysia	452
Petronas Tower 2, Kuala Lumpur, Malaysia	452
Willis Tower, Chicago	442
Jin Mao Building, Shanghai	421

3 Mrs Jones recorded the test scores for five students in Class 7A and five students in Class 7B.

7A test scores	4	8	9	9	10
7B test scores	2	3	5	10	10

a Find the modal score for each class.

b Find the range of the scores from each class.

Problem solving

5 Look again at the test scores in question **3**.

a Find the median score for each class.

b Which class did best on the test? Explain your answer.

c Is your answer for part **b** the same as you got in question **3**?
Which of your answers do you think is the best one? Explain your answer.

6 The data shows the times taken, in seconds, for 10 students to tie their shoelaces.
Two of the pieces of data are missing. 10, 7, □, 9, □, 11, 15, 12, 9, 11
The mode is 11 seconds and the range is also 11 seconds.

a Find the two missing values.

b Write a different set of 10 data values with the mode and range both as 11 seconds.
Is the median the same as in the first set?

3 **c** Which class did best on the test? Explain your answer.

d Which class had the most variation in scores? Explain your answer.

4 Class 7M recorded the number of pieces of homework they handed in last week.

Boys	8	7	7	6	8
	7	6	8	8	7
Girls	4	11	9	11	7
	9	10	11	2	5

a Calculate the mode for **i** the boys **ii** the girls.

b Which group usually hands in the most homework? Explain your answer.

c Find the range for **i** the boys **ii** the girls.

d Was the boys' or the girls' homework more varied? Explain your answer.

Did you know?

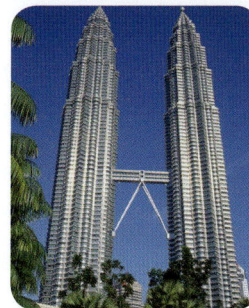

The shape of the Petronas towers is based on the Rub el Hizb symbol - two overlapping squares - with circles added at the overlap points.

Check out

You should now be able to...

		Questions
✓ Plan how to collect and organise small sets of data from surveys and experiments.	3	1, 2
✓ Solve problems by interpreting data in lists and tables.	3	3
✓ Construct and interpret statistical diagrams, including pictograms, bar charts, pie charts and line graphs.	4	4, 5
✓ Calculate statistics for small sets of data, including the mode, median and range.	5	6, 7

Language	Meaning	Example
Questionnaire	An organised list of questions, often with options for answers.	Examples of questionnaires are on page 144
Frequency table	A table that shows how often a particular item of data occurs. It often includes a tally column.	Examples of frequency tables are on page 146
Pictogram	A diagram that shows data as a series of pictures.	Examples of pictograms are on page 150
Bar chart	A diagram that uses rectangles to represent frequency.	Examples of bar charts are on page 152
Pie chart	A diagram that uses a circle to display data in proportion.	Examples of pie charts are on page 154
Average	A representative value for a set of data.	The average 12-year old girl in the UK is around 1.5 m tall
Mode	The data value that occurs most often.	2, 3, 4, 4, 5, 6, 7, 8, 9
Median	The middle value when the data are sorted into numerical order.	The mode is 4 The median is 5
Range	The difference between the highest and lowest values in a set of data.	The range is $9 - 2 = 7$

1 You have been asked to find out about the people who go to see films at a local cinema. Write two questions you could use on a questionnaire.

2 A number of different shaped counters are as shown.

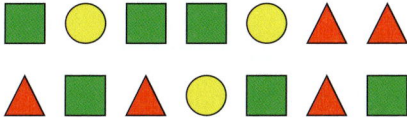

Draw a frequency table for this set of data.

3 The table shows how many hours Dave spends driving in a week.

M	T	W	Th	F	Sa	Su
2.5	1.5	2	2	3.5	5	0

a On what day does he drive most?
b How long did he drive for on Friday?

4 The pictogram shows how many books people borrowed from a library in a week.

Number of Books	People
0	🧍 🧍 🧍 🧍 🧍
1	🧍 🧍
2	🧍
3	🧍 🧍 🧍
4	🧍 🧍 🧍 🧍

key: 🧍 = 10 people

4 a How many people borrowed exactly 2 books?
b How many people borrowed no books?
c How would you represent 40 people on this pictogram?
d Draw a bar chart for the data in this pictogram.

5 Students in year 8 at a school can bring a packed lunch, go to the canteen, or go home for lunch.

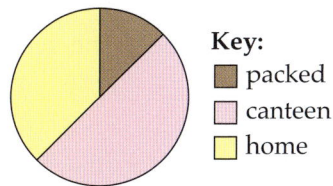

Key:
■ packed
■ canteen
■ home

a What is the least popular lunch choice?
b What fraction of the students go to the canteen for lunch?

6 Find the mode for each set of numbers, if there is one.

a 3   5   7   3
b 12   14   16   18
   14   15   16   19
c 27   29   26   28   28   27
   24   26   29   24   28
d 3   5   7   5   3   7
   5   5   7   3   7   3

7 For the data in question **6** find
a the medians   b the ranges.

What next?

Score			
	0 – 3	🟥	Your knowledge of this topic is still developing. To improve look at Formative test: 1A-8; MyMaths: 1193, 1198, 1200, 1203, 1205, 1206 and 1235
	4 – 6	🟧	You are gaining a secure knowledge of this topic. To improve look at InvisiPen: 411, 415, 411, 421, 423, 424, 441 and 445
	7	🟩	You have mastered this topic. Well done, you are ready to progress!

MyMaths.co.uk

8a

1   Eva decides to ask all of the students in her group at college how they get to college each day.

How do you travel to college each day?

Walk	Bus	Train
☐	☐	☐

Suggest any improvements that might be made to Eva's questionnaire.

8b

2   A dice is rolled 30 times. The scores are:

2 5 1 3 1 3 4 1 6 4 4 4 4 2 5
5 5 3 5 4 3 5 2 3 4 2 3 2 6 6

a   Make a tally chart for this set of data.
b   Use your tally chart to produce a frequency table.

8c

3   Ben recorded the number of times his computer crashed. It crashed three times on Monday, and twice on Tuesday. On Wednesday his computer crashed five times, but on Thursday it did not crash at all. On Friday there were four crashes.

a   Draw a table to show this information.
b   Write down the total number of crashes.

8d

4   The table shows the number of credits awarded to students in Year 7 at Hollybank High School.

Class	7W1	7W2	7W3	7W4
Credits	8	7	4	6

Draw a pictogram to show this information.
Make sure you choose a suitable symbol.

8e

5   This table shows the number of pieces of homework that Kelly was set each day.

Day	Monday	Tuesday	Wednesday	Thursday	Friday
Pieces of homework	2	3	2	4	5

Draw a bar chart to represent this set of data.

6 This pie chart shows the methods used to generate electricity in the USA.

a What method is $\frac{1}{4}$ of the total?

b What method is $\frac{1}{2}$ of the total?

c What two methods together make up $\frac{1}{4}$ of the total?

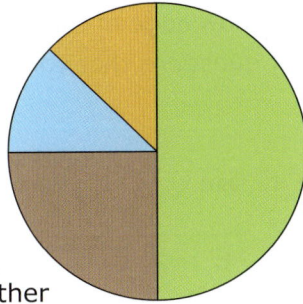

Key:
- Coal
- Nuclear
- Natural gas and oil
- Hydroelectric and others

7 The bar chart shows the number of boys and girls in five year groups.

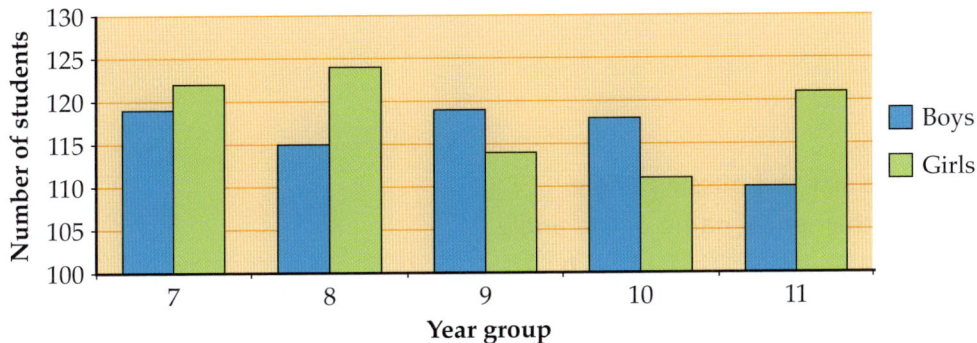

Number of students / Year group

Boys
Girls

a List the year groups that had more boys than girls.

b Estimate the total number of girls in each of the five year groups.

c Estimate the total number of students in all five year groups combined.

d Say which year group had the largest total number of students.

8 Near to where Shani works there are two cafés. She timed how long in minutes it took the waitress to bring her lunch on 10 different occasions at both cafes.

Cafe A   5, 3, 3, 6, 6, 8, 3, 5, 3, 8

Cafe B   8, 8, 6, 4, 6, 3, 8, 8, 5, 4

a For each of the two data sets find

   i   the mode

   ii the median

   iii the range.

b Describe two differences between the two cafés.

These questions will test you on your knowledge of the topics in chapters 5 to 8.
They give you practice in the types of questions that you may see in your GCSE exams.
There are 55 marks in this test.

1 For each angle
   i use a protractor to measure its size (2 marks)
   ii give its mathematical name. (2 marks)

   a   **b**

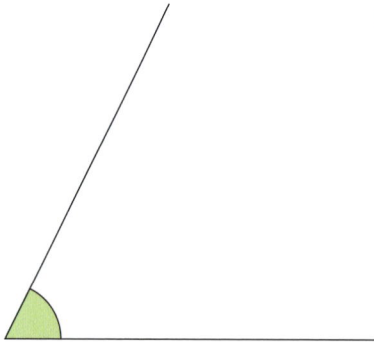
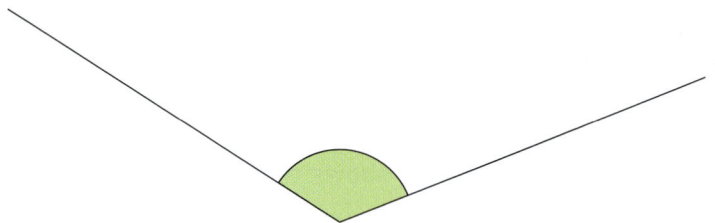

2 For each diagram
   i calculate the size the missing angle (2 marks)
   ii give the mathematical name of the angle. (2 marks)

   a   **b**

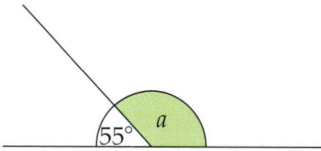
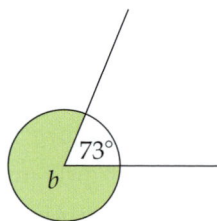

3 **a** What is the name given to a triangle that has all sides of a different length
   and all angles of a different size? (1 mark)
   b What is the name given to a triangle that has all sides of equal length? (1 mark)
   c For the triangle in part **b**, what is the common angle? (1 mark)

4 Find the missing angles in these triangles. (4 marks)

   a   **b**

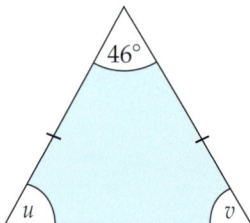
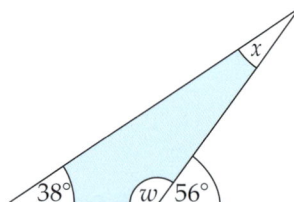

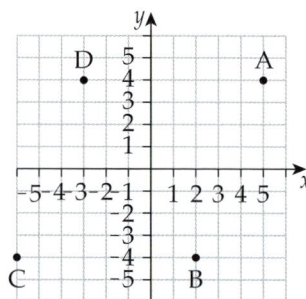

5 **a** In the diagram write down the coordinates (4 marks)
   of the points marked A, B, C and D.
   b Connect the points with straight lines.
   What is the name of the shape? (1 mark)

6 This line graph shows how the outside
temperature changed during a particular week.

   a What day was the lowest temperature recorded?   (1 mark)

   b What day(s) was the temperature 22°C?   (2 marks)

   c What was the difference in temperature
     between **i** Sunday and Thursday and
     ii Sunday and Wednesday?   (2 marks)

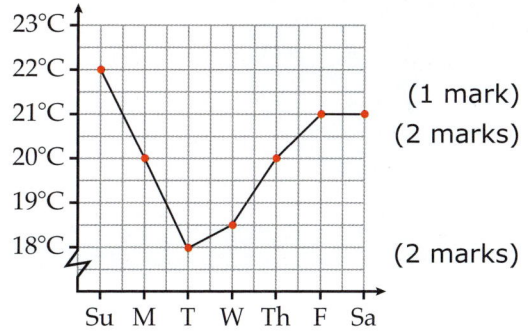

7 Work these out in your head.

a	29 − 14	(1 mark)	**b**	17 + 14	(1 mark)
c	85 − 9	(1 mark)	**d**	63 + 15	(1 mark)
e	103 − 30	(1 mark)			

8 Use a number line or columns to work out these problems.

a	38 + 62	(1 mark)	**b**	87 − 35	(1 mark)
c	197 + 28	(1 mark)	**d**	492 − 275	(1 mark)
e	852 − 394	(1 mark)	**f**	321 + 213	(1 mark)

9 Use columns to work out these problems.

a	608 + 154	(1 mark)	**b**	762 − 387	(1 mark)
c	569 − 256	(1 mark)	**d**	346 + 861	(1 mark)

10 The following table shows the sales of canned
drinks from a school canteen.
Draw a pictogram to represent these sales.
Use the symbol of a can to represent 5 drinks.

Drink	Sales
Cola	35
Diet Cola	26
Orange	11
Water	4

(4 marks)

11 The table shows the frequency of vowels in the first four lines of a well-known play.

   a Draw a bar chart for this data.   (4 marks)

Vowel	a	e	i	o	u
Frequency	9	16	11	9	5

   b What was the mode for the vowels found?   (1 mark)

12 Eleven boys and eleven girls have had their height measured to the nearest centimetre
as follows.

Boys: 126, 131, 147, 153, 154, 154, 156, 159, 160, 163, 175

Girls: 124, 129, 133, 135, 135, 142, 151, 153, 153, 164, 167

   a Find the mode and median of these heights

     i for the boys only   (2 marks)

     ii for the girls only.   (2 marks)

   b **i** What was the range for the boys data?   (1 mark)

     ii What was the range for the girls data?   (1 mark)

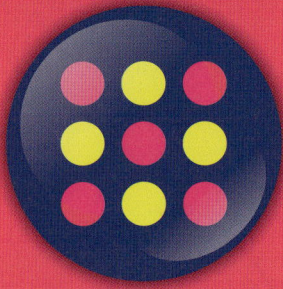

9 Transformations and symmetry

Introduction

Dance is an art form in which people move their body rhythmically to music. It features in most cultures for many different purposes. Each dance contains a series of steps which are performed in various combinations to form a routine.

What's the point?

Transformations move points and shapes from one place to another. The steps of a dance routine can be described by mathematical transformations – slides (translations), flips (reflections) and spins (rotations).

Objectives

By the end of this chapter, you will have learned how to …

- Identify lines of symmetry in a 2D shape.
- Transform a shape by reflection in a mirror line.
- Transform a shape by translation and describe a translation.
- Transform a shape by rotation about a point.
- Create tessellations using reflections, rotations and translations.

Check in

1 Jason is looking at photographs on a computer. He must click either 'rotate clockwise' or 'rotate anticlockwise'. Write the correct instruction for these photographs.

a

b

c

2 Write the coordinates for the corners of each shape.

a
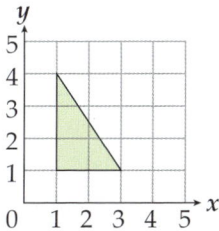

b
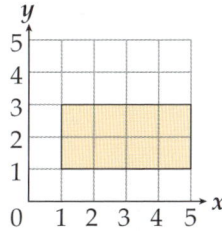

c
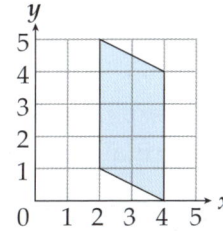

Starter problem

Design a 30 second dance routine for robots which involves the mathematical transformations of translation, rotation and reflection.

You can make a symmetric shape as follows.

1 Fold a piece of card in half.

2 Cut a shape along the folded edge.

3 Unfold your symmetric shape.

> The fold line is a **line of symmetry**.

A shape has reflective **symmetry** if it folds exactly onto itself. It is **symmetrical**.

These shapes have one line of symmetry.

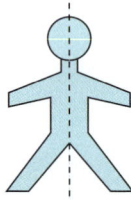 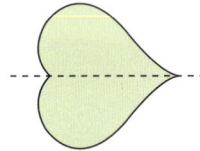

> You use a dashed line to show a line of symmetry.

These shapes have more than one line of symmetry.

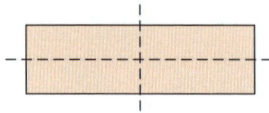 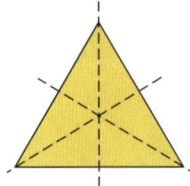

These shapes have no lines of symmetry.

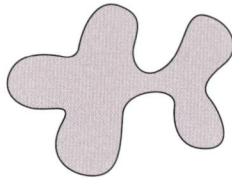 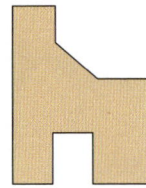

▲ Butterflies have natural symmetry.

Here are some more shapes with their lines of symmetry drawn.

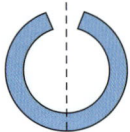  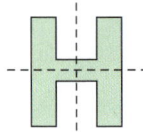

One   None   One   Two

> Hold a mirror on a line of symmetry to see the whole shape.

Exercise 9a

1 Are these shapes symmetrical?

a    **b**

c    **d**

e    **f**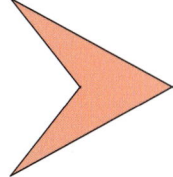

g   **h**

2 These shapes have only one line of symmetry.
Copy or trace them and draw the line of symmetry.

a   **b**

2 **c** 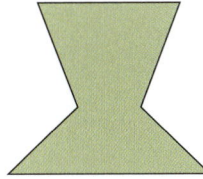   **d**

3 These shapes have more than one line of symmetry.
Copy or trace them and draw all the lines of symmetry.

a 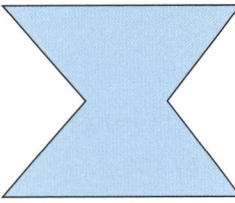   **b**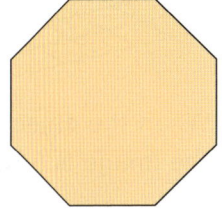

c    **d**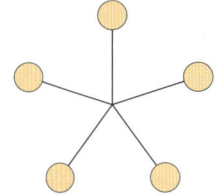

e

Problem solving

4 Kiran is looking at car logos.

a How many lines of symmetry does each logo have?

i    **ii**    **iii**    **iv**

b Draw any other symmetrical car logos that you know.

5 How many ways can you fold a rectangular piece of paper exactly in half?
What about a square piece of paper?

← 19 mm →

MyMaths.co.uk   1114   SEARCH

🔴 You can **reflect** a shape in a **mirror line**.

The **object** is in front of the mirror. You can see the **image** in the mirror.

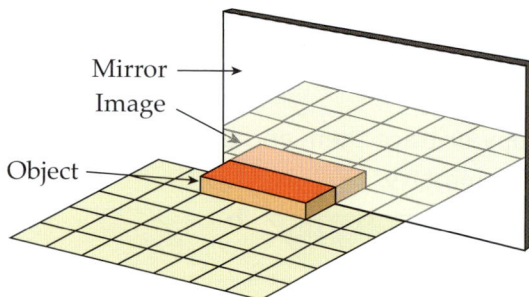

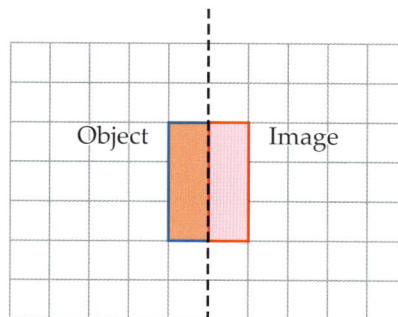

Mirror Line

When the object is moved further away the image is further away too.

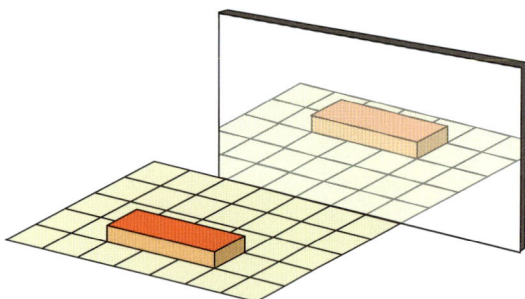

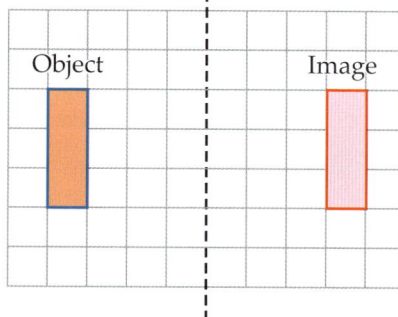

The image appears to be the same distance from the mirror as the object.

Example

Reflect shape A in the mirror line.

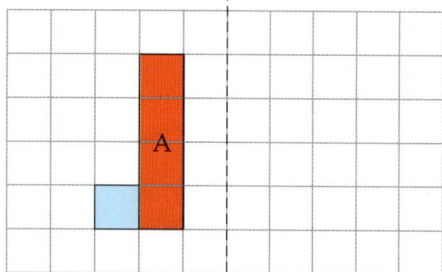

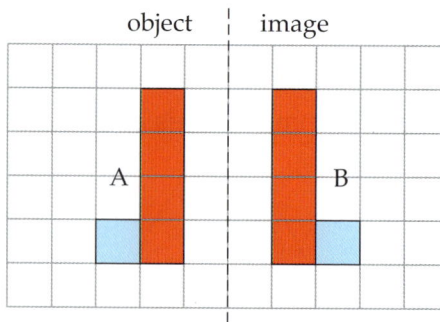

The red squares are all one square away from the mirror line.

The blue square is two squares away from the mirror line.

Exercise 9b

1 Copy these shapes onto squared paper. Complete the reflection and name the resulting shape.

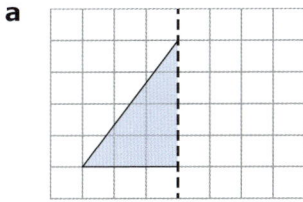

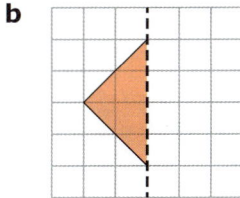

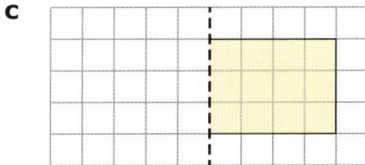

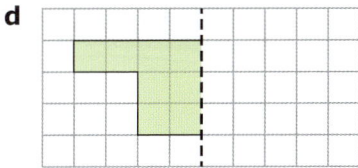

a

b

c

d

2 Copy each shape and mirror line onto squared paper.
Draw the reflection of each shape in the mirror line.

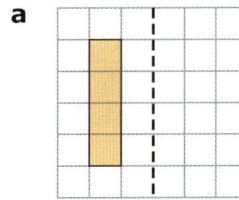

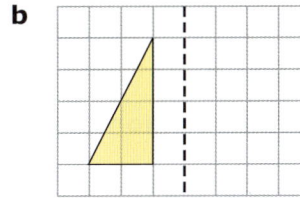

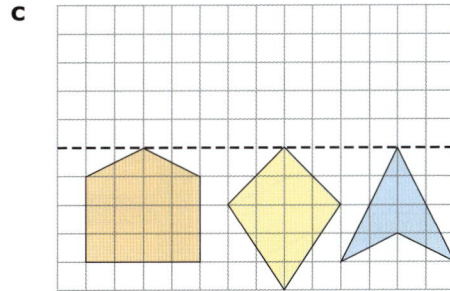

a

b

c

Problem solving

3 Kiko looks into a mirror. Which image is her true reflection?

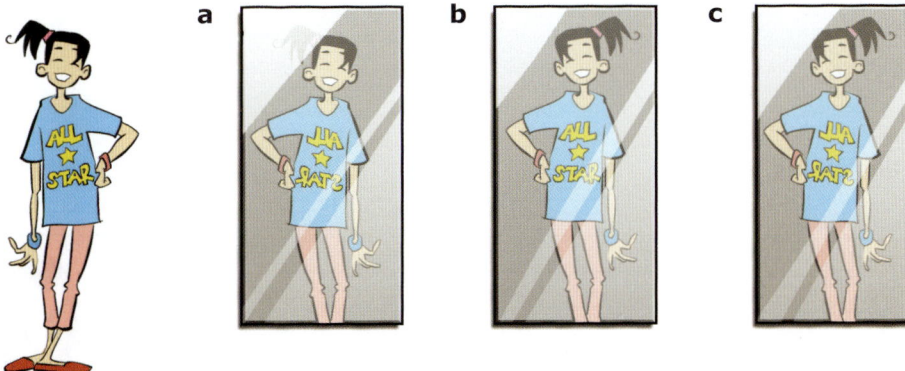

a   **b**   **c**

4 These shapes are reflected in a horizontal mirror line. Trace or copy the shapes onto squared paper. Reflect them. What words do they make?

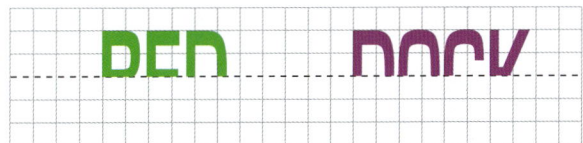

BED   DOCK

9c Translation

Members of class 7G are practising dance steps for the end of term show.
They are meant to move around the stage together ... but it's not working.

> RIGHT, RIGHT, FORWARD ...

> RIGHT, RIGHT, FORWARD ...

> BACK, TURN, SPIN, JUMP...

> RIGHT, RIGHT, FORWARD ...

Their teacher draws diagrams of the steps
so that the dancers can see the moves.

They are performing a **translation** across the stage.

⬤ A translation is a **slide**.

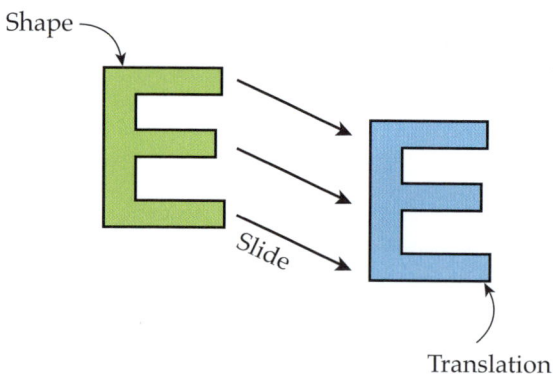

Shape

Slide

Translation

> 4 STEPS UP STAGE
> 2 STEPS RIGHT

⬤ In a translation, a shape moves
  ▶ first, right or left
  ▶ second, up or down.

Example

Describe these translations.

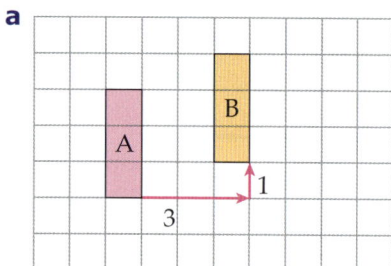

a

B

A

3

1

b

2

3

C

D

> Count across first, then up or down.

a   3 to the right, then 1 up   b   2 left, 3 down

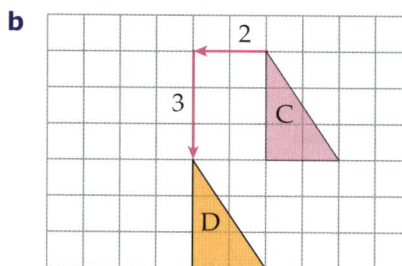

< p.112

Exercise 9c

1 Which letter will the dancer reach
if she follows each of these directions?
The first is done for you.

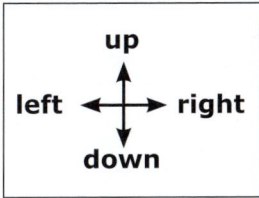

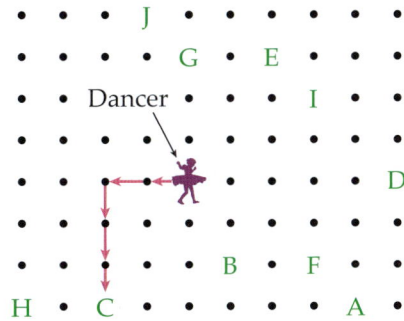

```
•   •   •   J   •   •   •   •   •   •
•   •   •   •   G   E   •   •   •   •
•   •  Dancer •   •   •   I   •   •
•   •   •   •   •   •   •   •   •   •
•   •   •   ←←← 💃  •   •   •   •   D
•   •   •   •   •   •   •   •   •   •
•   •   •   •   •   •   •   •   •   •
•   •   •   •   •   B   F   •   •
H   •   C   •   •   •   •   •   A   •
```

up
left ←→ right
down

a 2 steps left, 3 steps down = C
c 4 steps right, 3 steps down
e 4 steps left, 3 steps down
g 3 steps up
i 2 steps right, 3 steps up

b 3 steps right, 2 steps up
d 1 step left, 4 steps up
f 5 steps right
h 1 step right, 2 steps down
j 3 steps right, 2 steps down

Always start from the dancer.

2 Complete the description for each translation.

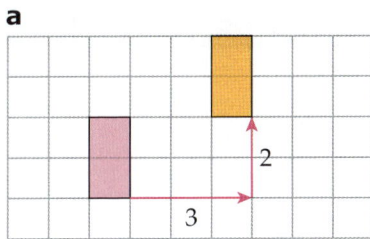

a

2
3

_____ to the right, _____ up

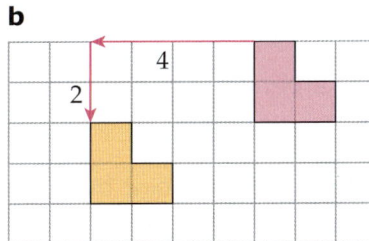

b

4
2

_____ to the left, _____ down

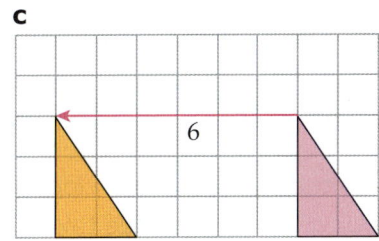

c

6

_____ to the left, _____ down

Problem solving

3 Each translation moves
triangle A to another position.
Give the number of the
position it moves to.
a 1 to the right, 4 up
b 4 to the left, 3 down
c 5 to the right, 6 down
d 5 to the left, 0 up or down

4 Describe how triangle A
translates to these positions.
a A to B
b A to C
c A to D
d A to E

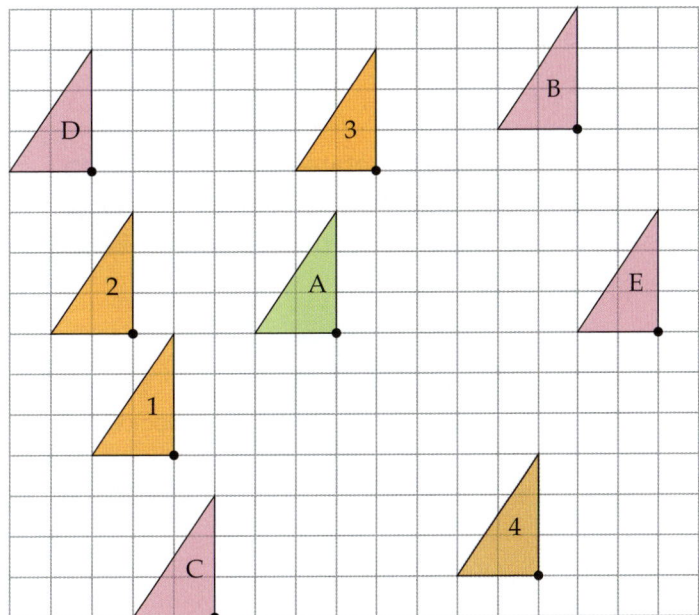

9d Rotation

The blades on a wind turbine **rotate** around the centre.

> 🔴 A **rotation** is a turn.

You need to know three things for a rotation:

1 The **direction** of turn.

Anticlockwise   Clockwise

‹ p.90 **2** The **angle** of turn.

$\frac{1}{4}$ turn $\frac{1}{2}$ turn   full turn

90°   180°   360°

3 The point that the shape rotates around.
This is the **centre of rotation**.

This triangle is rotated clockwise about the red point by 90°.
Four of these rotations take it back to where it started.

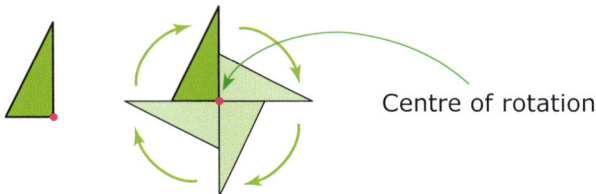

Centre of rotation

- Trace around the shape.
- Put your pencil on the dot.
- Rotate the shape $\frac{1}{4}$ turn clockwise.
- Draw around the shape again.

Example

Draw this shape after it rotates
a 90° clockwise about the red point
b 90° anticlockwise about the red point.

90° anticlockwise

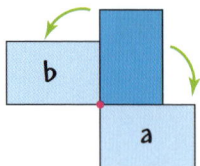

b

90° clockwise

a

'Rotate **about** a point' just means 'rotate **around** the point.'

Exercise 9d

1 Draw these shapes after they turn 90° anticlockwise about the red dot.

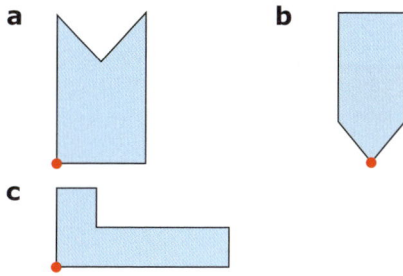

a

b

c

2 **a** Copy this shape on squared paper.

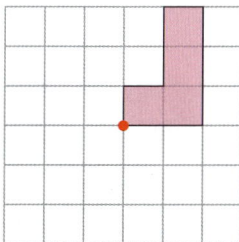

b Rotate the shape about the red dot clockwise through 90° and draw the rotated shape.

c Rotate the shape through 90° clockwise again and draw the rotated shape.

d Repeat this until the shape is back where it started.

You should have four shapes in your pattern.

3 Copy each shape onto squared paper. Follow the instructions to rotate each shape.

The centre of rotation is marked with a red dot.

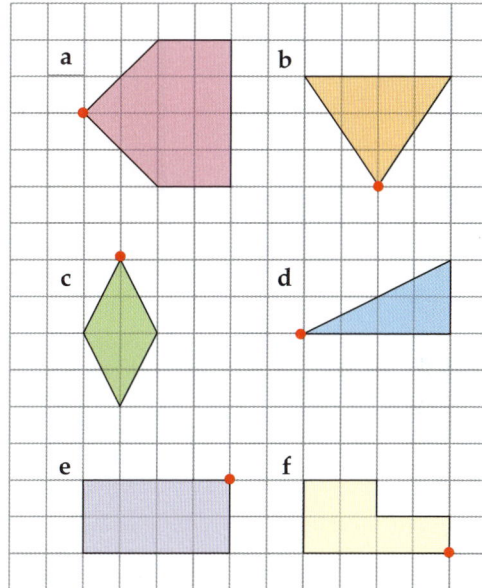

a   b   c   d   e   f

Shape **a**   Clockwise 90°

Shape **b**   Anticlockwise 180°

Shape **c**   Anticlockwise 90°

Shape **d**   Clockwise 180°

Shape **e**   Anticlockwise 270°
(270° is $\frac{3}{4}$ of a turn)

Shape **f**   Clockwise 90°.

Problem solving

4 Draw these letters after a rotation of 180° clockwise about the dot.

U S b f m

You can turn the page upside down to see a 180° turn.

Did you know?

The Isle of Man has a rotating pattern of three legs on its flag.

MyMaths.co.uk

9e Tessellations

🟤 A tessellation is a pattern made up by repeating the same shape with no gaps or overlaps.

This tile shape is repeated across the wall.

The tiles are two different colours, but they are all the same shape.

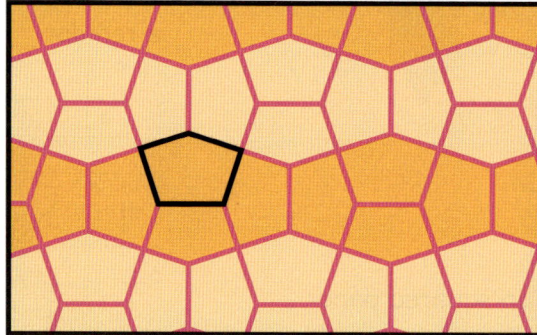

▲ The tile has been reflected and rotated.

🟤 You can **reflect, translate** or **rotate** shapes to make them tessellate.

This tessellation is made by translations.

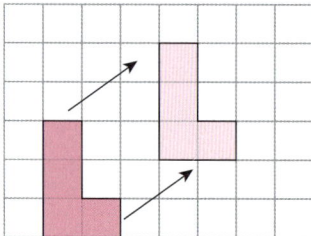

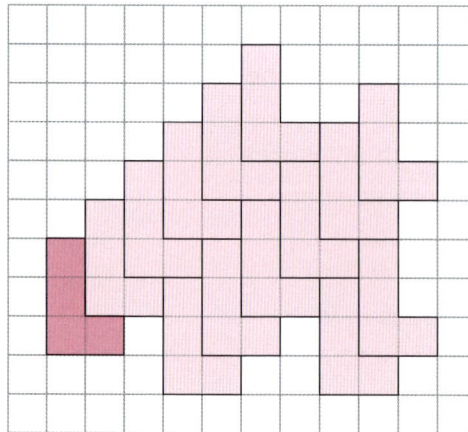

Did you know?

You can see tiling patterns on many old buildings, like this one.

Example

Use reflections and translations to complete this tessellation.

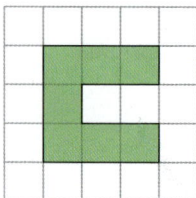

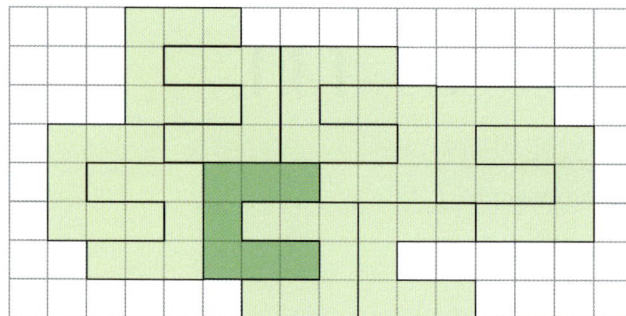

Add enough copies of the original shape to make the pattern obvious.

Geometry Transformations and symmetry

Exercise 9e

1 Draw these shapes on squared paper.
Use translations to make a tessellation.
The first has been started for you.

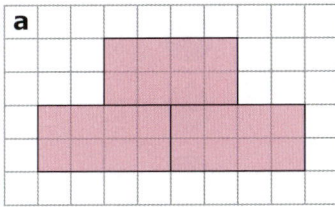

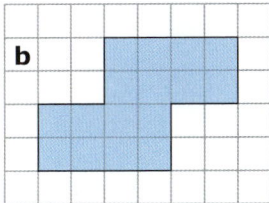

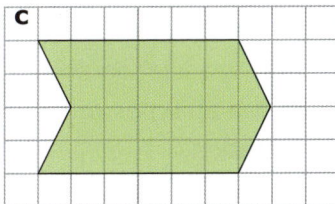

a

b

c

2 Copy each shape onto squared paper.
Repeat each shape 10 times to show how
it can tessellate.

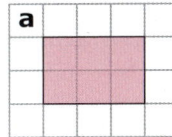

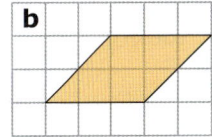

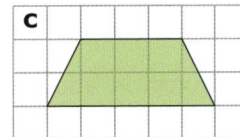

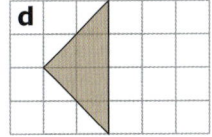

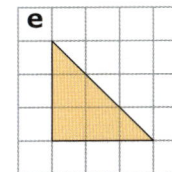

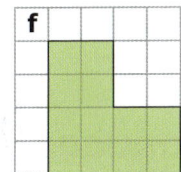

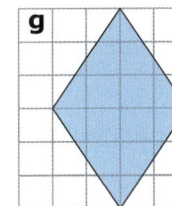

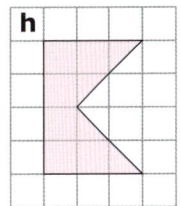

a

b

c

d

e

f

g

h

Problem solving

3 Bees make honeycombs from wax.
They build hexagonal cells where they
rear their young and store honey.
Tessellate a hexagon to make a
honeycomb pattern.

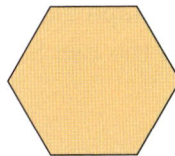

Does this shape tessellate?

4 Draw a rectangle onto
card and cut it out.

Cut out a triangle and slide it
over to make a new shape.

Make other shapes like this and see which shapes tessellate.

MyMaths.co.uk

9 MySummary

Check out

You should now be able to ...

Test it ➡

		Questions
✓ Identify lines of symmetry in a 2D shape.	3	1
✓ Transform a shape by reflection in a mirror line.	4	2
✓ Transform a shape by translation and describe a translation.	5	3
✓ Transform a shape by rotation about a point.	4	4, 5
✓ Create tessellations using reflections, rotations and translations.	4	6

Language · Meaning · Example

Language	Meaning	Example
Transformation	The act of moving a shape from one place to another.	Reflection, translation and rotation are all types of transformation
Object	The shape before a transformation.	
Image	The shape after a transformation.	object image
Line of symmetry	You can fold a shape along a line of symmetry, and the two halves will match exactly.	A square has four lines of symmetry
Reflection	A transformation in which the object flips through a mirror line.	Examples of reflections on page 174
Translation	A transformation in which the object slides.	Examples of translations on page 176
Rotation	A transformation in which the object turns about a point.	Examples of rotations on page 178
Tessellation	The same shape arranged in a tiling pattern with no gaps.	Examples of tessellations on page 180

1 Copy or trace each shape and draw all the lines of symmetry. How many lines of symmetry do these shapes have?

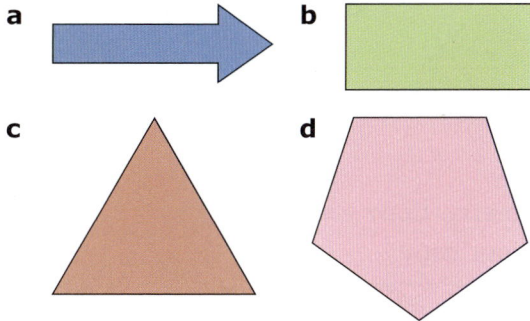

a

b

c

d

2 Copy the shapes on squared paper and reflect the shapes in the mirror lines.

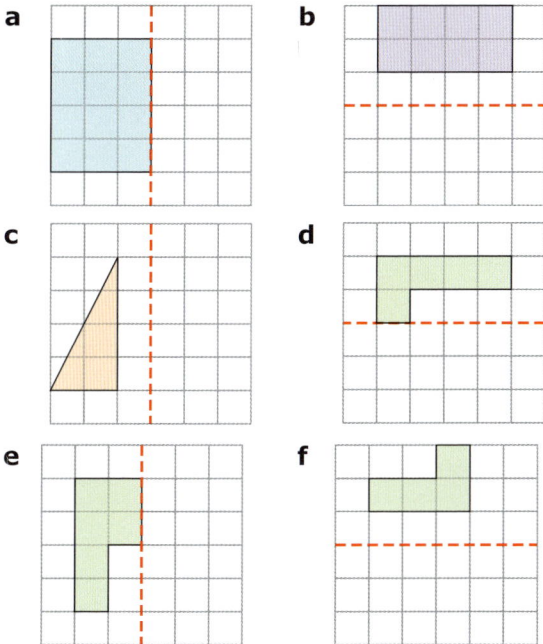

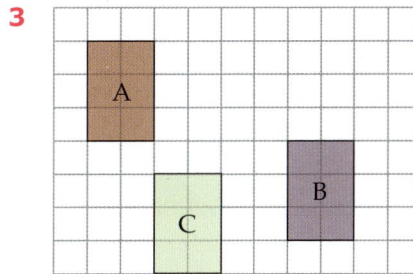

a

b

c

d

e

f

3

Describe the translations of

a   A to B
b   B to A
c   A to C
d   C to A
e   B to C
f   C to B.

4 Copy the rectangle on squared paper and rotate the rectangle 90° clockwise about the red point.

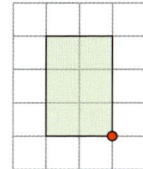

5 Copy the triangle on squared paper and rotate 180° about the red point.

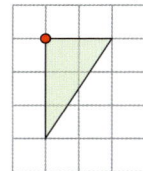

6 Copy the triangle on square grid paper and tessellate it six times.

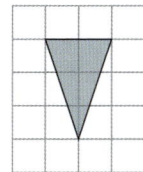

What next?

Score			
	0 – 2		Your knowledge of this topic is still developing. To improve look at Formative test: 1A-9; MyMaths: 1114
	3 – 5		You are gaining a secure knowledge of this topic. To improve look at InvisiPen: 361, 362, 363, 364 and 365
	6		You have mastered this topic. Well done, you are ready to progress!

MyMaths.co.uk

9a

1 Each shape has only one line of symmetry.
Copy each shape and draw the line of symmetry on your copy.

a 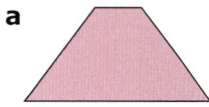 b 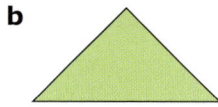 c 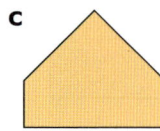 d 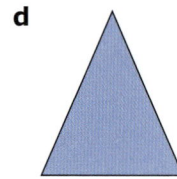 e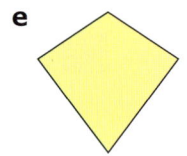

2 Each shape has more than one line of symmetry. Copy each
shape and draw the lines of symmetry on your copy.

a 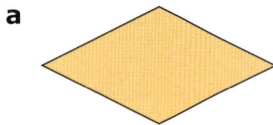 b 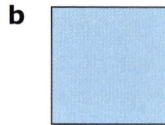 c 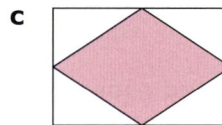 d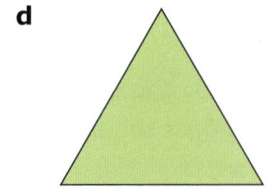

9b

3 Copy each shape onto squared paper and reflect it in the mirror lines.

a 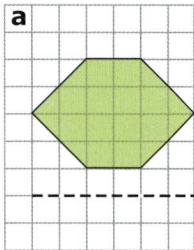 b 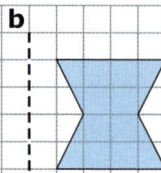 c 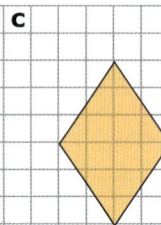 d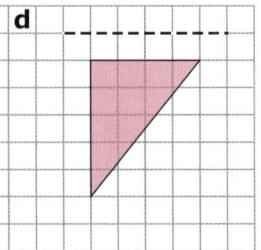

9c

‹ p.112

4 **a** Copy this shape onto squared
paper and reflect it in the mirror line.
b Give coordinates for the corners
of the image.

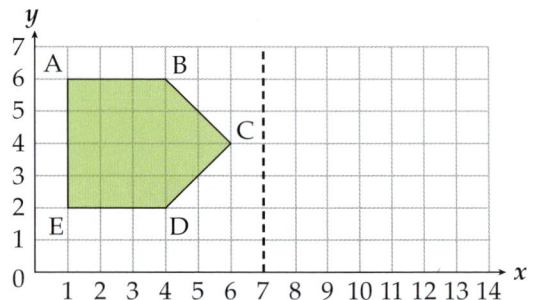

5   Copy this shape onto squared
    paper and translate it.
    a   4 left, 3 up
    b   3 right, 3 down
    c   5 left, 2 down
    d   1 right, 4 up

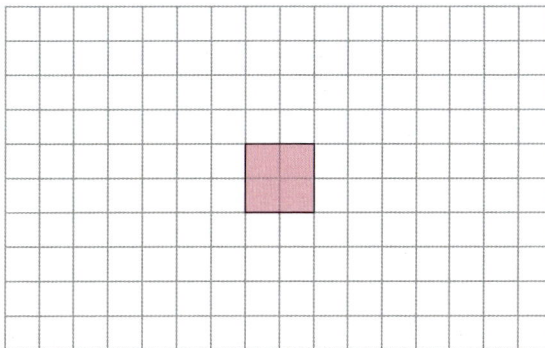

6   Copy the diagram onto squared paper.
    Draw the images of the object after following
    each of these transformations.
    a   A reflection in the mirror line.
    b   A translation by 4 to the right and 4 down.
    c   A clockwise rotation about the red dot of
       i   90 degrees
       ii   180 degrees and
       iii 270 degrees.

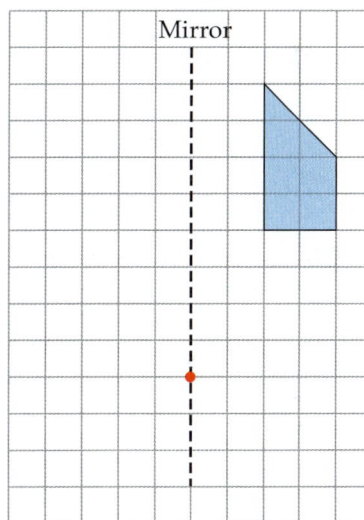

7   Test each shape to see if it will tessellate.
    (Remember there must be no gaps or overlaps.)

a
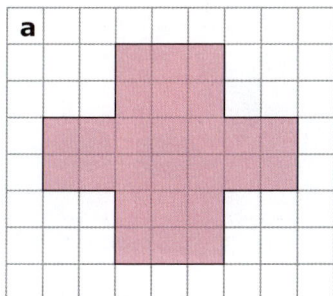

b
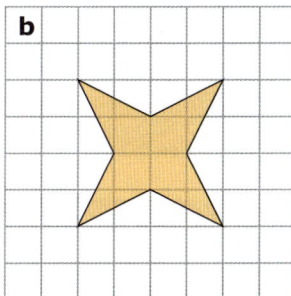

c
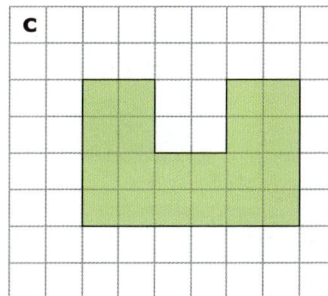

A Rangoli pattern is a Hindu design traditionally made during the Diwali festival to welcome guests. The designs can be made with rice powder, coloured chalk, beads, flowers and beans.

Task 1

Rangoli patterns are based on symmetry. Find the lines of symmetry in these Rangoli patterns.

For each pattern, state how many lines of symmetry it has. (Be careful: one of them does not have any! What kind of symmetry does this pattern possess?)

A
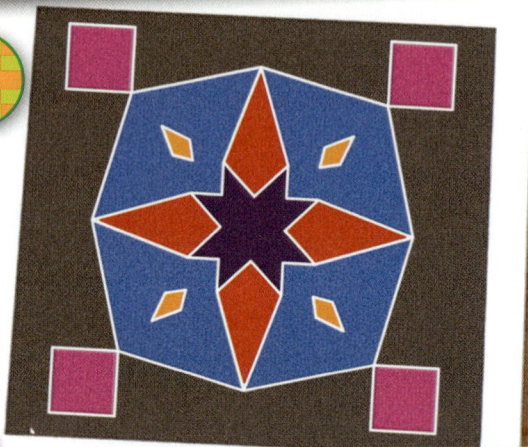

B

C

D

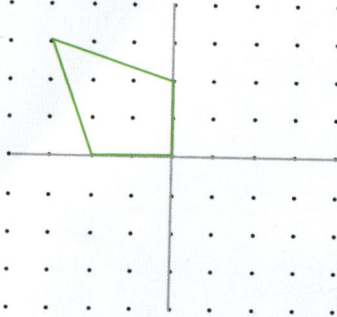

a Draw a horizontal and a vertical axis on square dotty paper. Draw a simple design in the top left-hand quadrant.

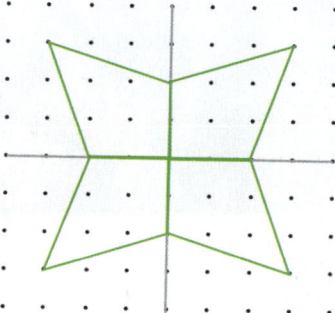

b Reflect the lines in the horizontal axis and then reflect the whole pattern in the vertical axis.

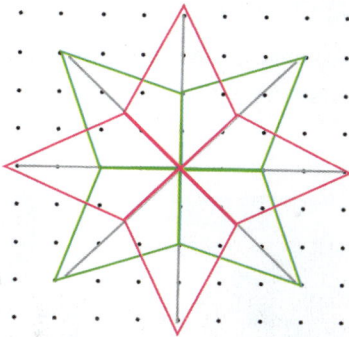

c Draw diagonal lines through the origin. Turn your paper so these lines are axes and draw your pattern in the new top left-hand quadrant.
Repeat step **b**.

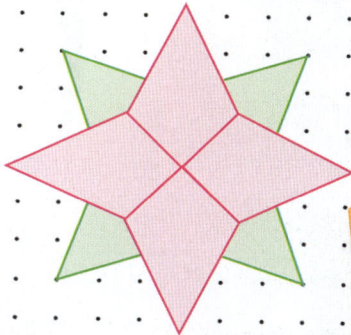

d Erase the axes and diagonal lines. Colour in the regions if you want to.

Task 3

a Draw the lines of reflection symmetry on your pattern.

b What is the order of rotation symmetry?

Task 4

Make up your own design as in step **a** of Task 2. Create a Rangoli pattern from your design.

10 Equations

Introduction

The word **algebra** comes from the title of a book 'Hidab **al-jabr** wal-muqubala' written in 825 AD by the Arab mathematician Abu Abdullah Mohammed Ibn Musa al Khawarizmi. The title of his book loosely translates as 'the science of reunion and opposition' – it describes the steps that are used to solve equations.

What's the point?

Even to this day, algebra allows lots of real life problems to be solved by using maths.

Objectives

By the end of this chapter, you will have learned how to …

- Represent functions as sequences of operations.
- Understand and use inverse operations.
- Use letters to represent unknown numbers.
- Construct and solve simple equations.

Check in

1 Calculate

    a $5 + 17$ **b** $17 - 5$ **c** $23 + 8$ **d** $23 - 8$

    e 12×3 **f** $36 \div 4$ **g** 4×6 **h** $24 \div 3$

2 Write an expression for each of these situations.

    a Adam has p downloaded songs. He buys 5 more songs.

       How many songs does Adam have now?

    b Noah has a tree that is k cm tall. He cuts 100 cm from the top of the tree.

       How tall is the tree now?

Starter problem

This grid is an empty magic square.

a	3	4
1	5	b
6	c	d

$1 \quad 3$
$2 \quad 4 \quad 8$
$6 \quad 9$
$5 \quad 7$

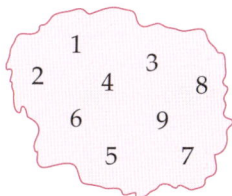

In a magic square every row, column, and diagonal adds up to 15.

Place each of the numbers from 1 to 9 into the grid to make this a magic square.

10a Operations

> A **function** uses a **rule**.

The **input** goes in... ...you apply the **rule**... ...the **output** comes out.

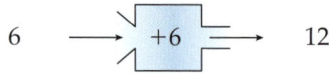

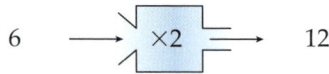

$$6 \longrightarrow \boxed{+6} \longrightarrow 12$$

$$6 \longrightarrow \boxed{\times 2} \longrightarrow 12$$

> An operation is a rule for processing numbers. The basic operations are addition, subtraction, multiplication and division.

Example

What are these functions doing?

a input output
   $3 \longrightarrow 9$

b input output
   $5 \longrightarrow 12$

c input output
   $16 \longrightarrow 4$

a $3 \boxed{+ 6} = 9$
   or
   $3 \boxed{\times 3} = 9$

b $5 \boxed{+ 7} = 12$

c $16 \boxed{- 12} = 4$
   or
   $16 \boxed{\div 4} = 4$

Each of these rules has only one **operation**.

You can use more than one operation in a function.

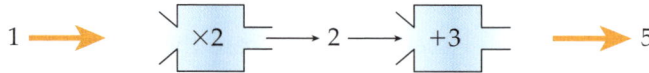

$$1 \longrightarrow \boxed{\times 2} \longrightarrow 2 \longrightarrow \boxed{+3} \longrightarrow 5$$

Example

Work out the missing operations.

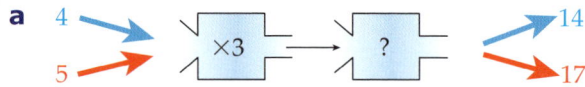

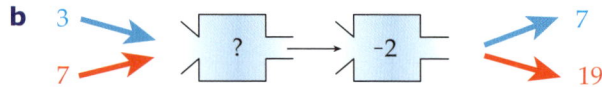

a $4 \longrightarrow \boxed{\times 3} \longrightarrow \boxed{?} \longrightarrow 14$
   $5 \longrightarrow \qquad\qquad\qquad\qquad \longrightarrow 17$

b $3 \longrightarrow \boxed{?} \longrightarrow \boxed{-2} \longrightarrow 7$
   $7 \longrightarrow \qquad\qquad\qquad\qquad \longrightarrow 19$

a $4 \times 3 = 12 \rightarrow 12 \boxed{} = 14$ $5 \times 3 = 15 \rightarrow 15 \boxed{} = 17$
   $\qquad\qquad\qquad 12 \boxed{+2} = 14$ $\qquad\qquad\qquad 15 \boxed{+2} = 17$

The second operation is +2

b $3 \boxed{} - 2 = 7$ $7 \boxed{} - 2 = 19$
   $3 \boxed{} \quad = 9$ $7 \boxed{} \quad = 21$
   $3 \boxed{\times 3} \quad = 9$ $7 \boxed{\times 3} = 21$

The first operation is ×3

Exercise 10a

1 Find the missing outputs.

a 3 → +4 → ?

b 4 → ×3 → ?

c 7 → +9 → ?

d 3 → ×10 → ?

2 Find the output when the input is 6.

a 6 → +3 → ?

b 6 → -4 → ?

c 6 → ×3 → ?

d 6 → ÷2 → ?

3 Work out the missing operations.

a 18 → ? → 20

b 2 → ? → 20

c 9 → ? → 15

3

d 18 → ? → 9

e 4 → ? → 24

f 21 → ? → 7

g 3 → ? → 36

h 24 → ? → 8

i 45 → ? → 15

In question **3** there may be more than one answer.

4 Work out the missing outputs.

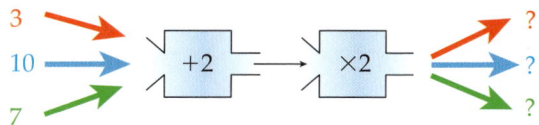

3, 10, 7 → +2 → ×2 → ?, ?, ?

5 Find the missing operations.

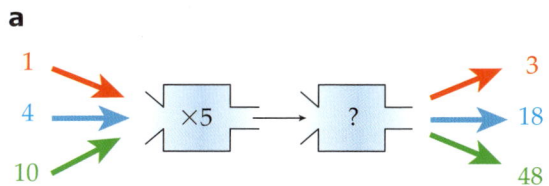

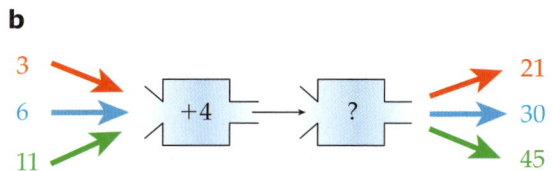

a 1, 4, 10 → ×5 → ? → 3, 18, 48

b 3, 6, 11 → +4 → ? → 21, 30, 45

Problem solving

6 A train ticket costs £30 per week. Bradley has a rail card which gives him £10 back if he buys tickets for 4 weeks. Find out how much Bradley spends over a 4-week period.

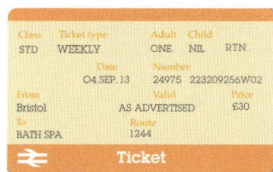

7 Find the two operations for this function.

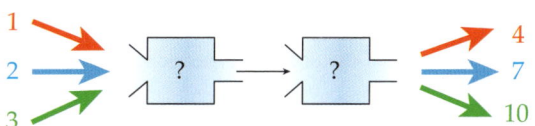

1, 2, 3 → ? → ? → 4, 7, 10

MyMaths.co.uk

Justin has 14 pencils.

He gives 3 to his friend.

What does he need to do to get back to 14 pencils?

> I need to add 3 pencils, of course!

You can undo a number operation by using the opposite or inverse operation.

> An **inverse operation** takes you back to where you started.
> ▶ The opposite of + is − ▶ The opposite of × is ÷

$$4 + 2 = 6 \longleftrightarrow 6 - 2 = 4 \qquad 3 \times 4 = 12 \longleftrightarrow 12 \div 4 = 3$$

▲ Lots of actions have opposites. The inverse of turning a light on is turning it off again.

Example

Olivia thought of a number and divided by 4. Her answer was 6. What was her number?

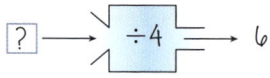

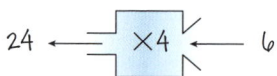

$$? \longrightarrow \boxed{\div 4} \longrightarrow 6$$

The inverse of ÷ is ×.

$$24 \longleftarrow \boxed{\times 4} \longleftarrow 6$$

The starting number was 24.

Opposites

+	→ −
−	→ +
×	→ ÷
÷	→ ×

You can use inverse operations to solve real life problems.

Example

a Over the past twenty years, the population of Swinefield has trebled in size to 1200.
How many inhabitants did Swinefield originally have?

b Over the past twenty years, the number of houses in Swinefield has increased by 200 to 310.
How many houses did Swinefield originally have?

a Original population × 3 = 1200
1200 ÷ 3 = 400
The population was originally 400.

b Original houses + 200 = 310
310 − 200 = 110
There were originally 110 houses.

Exercise 10b

1 Match each operation with its inverse.

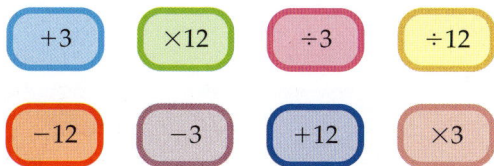

| +3 | ×12 | ÷3 | ÷12 |

| −12 | −3 | +12 | ×3 |

2 Find the inverse operations.

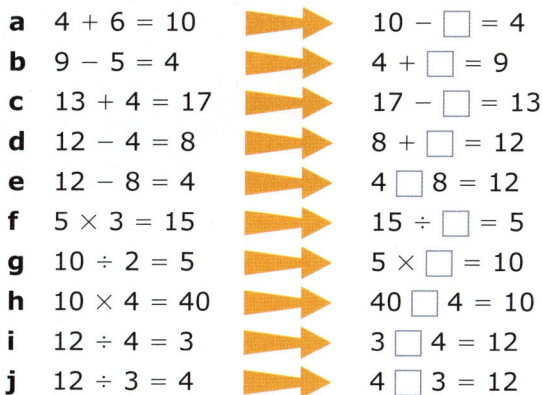

a	4 + 6 = 10	10 − ☐ = 4
b	9 − 5 = 4	4 + ☐ = 9
c	13 + 4 = 17	17 − ☐ = 13
d	12 − 4 = 8	8 + ☐ = 12
e	12 − 8 = 4	4 ☐ 8 = 12
f	5 × 3 = 15	15 ÷ ☐ = 5
g	10 ÷ 2 = 5	5 × ☐ = 10
h	10 × 4 = 40	40 ☐ 4 = 10
i	12 ÷ 4 = 3	3 ☐ 4 = 12
j	12 ÷ 3 = 4	4 ☐ 3 = 12

3 Find the missing inverse operation.

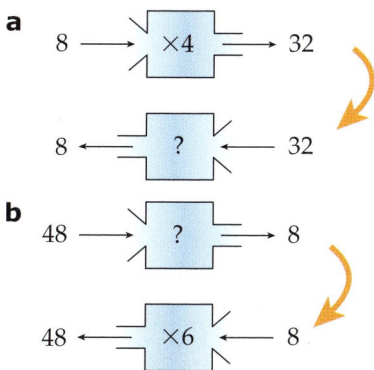

a
8 → ×4 → 32

8 ← ? ← 32

b
48 → ? → 8

48 ← ×6 ← 8

4 Find each starting number.

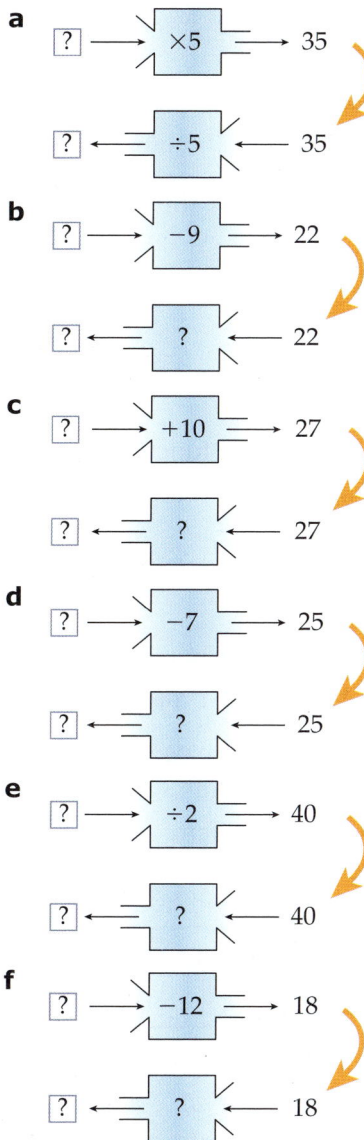

a
? → ×5 → 35

? ← ÷5 ← 35

b
? → −9 → 22

? ← ? ← 22

c
? → +10 → 27

? ← ? ← 27

d
? → −7 → 25

? ← ? ← 25

e
? → ÷2 → 40

? ← ? ← 40

f
? → −12 → 18

? ← ? ← 18

Problem solving

5 Use inverse functions to find the starting numbers.
- **a** Start with a number. Add twelve to the number. The answer is forty.
- **b** Start with a number. Multiply the number by three. The answer is twenty-seven.

6 Simon is thinking of a number. He adds 5 to it and says his answer is 25.
Harry says his number must be 5.
Why is Harry not right? What was Simon's number?

🔴 You can use a letter to stand for an unknown number.

Martino the Great has seven doves in an hat.
He takes two doves from the hat.

<p. 46

Martino uses n to stand for the number of doves left in the hat.

$n + 2 = 7$

Draw a function machine.

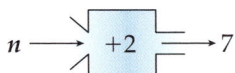

$n \longrightarrow \boxed{+2} \longrightarrow 7$

To find n draw the inverse function machine.

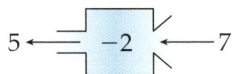

$5 \longleftarrow \boxed{-2} \longleftarrow 7$

So, $n = 5$.

Example

a Kaisa had £20 in her purse.
   She has £12 left. How much did she spend?

b Justin had some marbles.
   He played a game and lost four of them.
   He has five marbles left.
   How many did he have at the start?

---

a

I will use c to represent how much I spent.

$c + 12 = 20$
$20 - 12 = 8.$ I spent £8

$c \longrightarrow \boxed{+12} \longrightarrow 20$

$8 \longleftarrow \boxed{-12} \longleftarrow 20$

b

I will use n to stand for the number of marbles that I had.

$n - 4 = 5$
$5 + 4 = 9$
I had 9 marbles.

$n \longrightarrow \boxed{-4} \longrightarrow 5$

$9 \longleftarrow \boxed{+4} \longleftarrow 5$

Exercise 10c

1 Calculate the values of these letters.

   a $c + 4 = 7$ **b** $d + 5 = 9$

   c $t + 8 = 9$ **d** $h + 6 = 10$

   e $p + 7 = 7$ **f** $b + 4 = 8$

   g $20 + g = 30$ **h** $15 + u = 20$

   i $16 + v = 21$ **j** $16 + a = 24$

   k $17 + s = 21$ **l** $35 + y = 40$

   m $32 + f = 40$ **n** $25 + j = 50$

   o $30 + h = 45$ **p** $1 + k = 100$

> These problems are like Kaisa's.

2 Calculate the values of these letters.

   a $h - 4 = 7$ **b** $d - 2 = 9$

   c $k - 8 = 10$ **d** $c - 6 = 3$

   e $p - 7 = 0$ **f** $g - 7 = 3$

   g $t - 10 = 15$ **h** $j - 6 = 24$

   i $m - 7 = 21$ **j** $u - 10 = 10$

   k $g - 5 = 32$ **l** $f - 20 = 40$

   m $j - 6 = 9$ **n** $y - 8 = 12$

   o $a - 14 = 6$ **p** $k - 1 = 100$

> These problems are like Justin's.

Problem solving

3 You can describe situations using letters.

> Jon had 7 marbles. He found some more in his bag. Now he has 12 marbles.

Use v to stand for the number of marbles that Jon found.

Then $7 + v = 12$.

Write these situations using your own letters.

a
> Deepak has some money in his wallet. He spends £5 and he has £10 left.

b
> Katie weighed 30 kilograms. Her weight increases and now she weighs 45 kilograms.

c
> Sarah read 30 pages of her book. She reads more pages and now she has read 55 pages.

d
> Lizzie collects 30 CDs. Some of them will not work on her player. Fourteen CDs will work.

4 Calculate the value of each of your letters in question **3**.

5 Two aliens are weighing themselves on the same scales.
Alien 1 weighs 12 kg.
Together they weigh 30 kg.
How much does Alien 2 weigh?

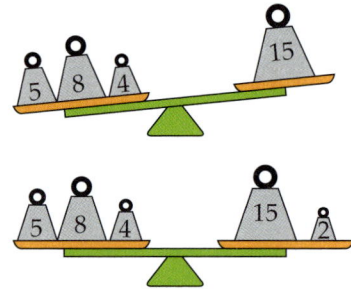

Justin is putting some weights on his scales.

His scales do not balance.

He adds an extra 2 kg to the right-hand side to balance them.

He writes this as

$5 + 8 + 4 = 15 + 2$

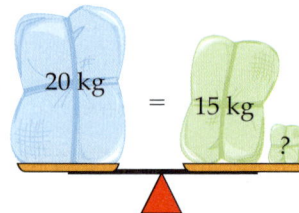

🔴 An equals sign acts like a **balance**.

Example

What is the missing weight on these scales?

Write an equation.

$20 = 15 + ?$

$? = 20 - 15$ — You could do this subtraction in

$? = 5$ — your head by counting on.

The missing weight is 5 kg

Check: $20 = 5 + 15$ ✔

🔴 An equation contains an equals sign and an unknown number.

$20 = ? + 15$ is an equation.

You can also write an equation using letters to stand for unknown numbers.

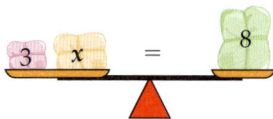

$3 + x = 8$

So, x must be 5.

Check: $3 + 5 = 8$ ✔

You could draw

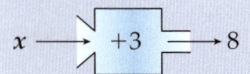

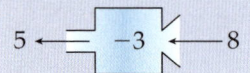

Example

Find the value that makes the equation balance.

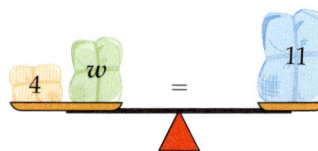

Write the equation.

$4 + w = 11$

$w = 11 - 4$

$w = 7$

Check: $4 + 7 = 11$ ✔

Exercise 10d

1 a Write an equation for each set of scales.

i

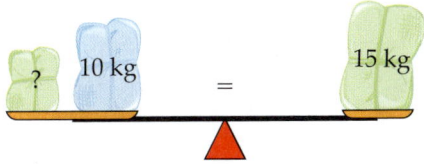

? 10 kg = 15 kg

ii

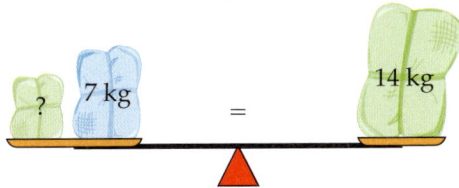

? 7 kg = 14 kg

iii

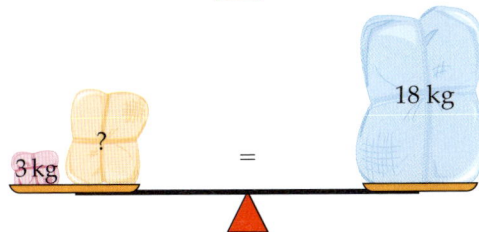

3 kg ? = 18 kg

iv

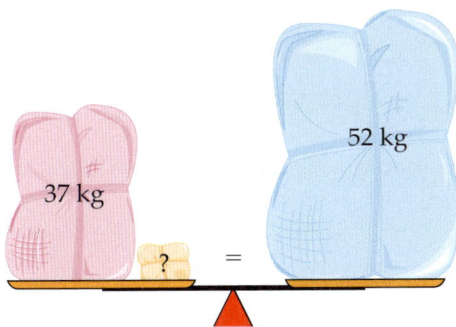

37 kg ? = 52 kg

b Find the weight that makes each equation balance.

2 Find the value that makes each equation balance.

   a $5 + x = 10$ **b** $y + 10 = 14$

   c $w + 6 = 17$ **d** $6 + m = 12$

   e $15 + z = 20$ **f** $t + 23 = 30$

3 Find the value that makes each equation balance.

   a $4 + 7 = 5 + x$ **b** $6 + 6 = 10 + y$

   c $20 + z = 34$ **d** $13 = 1 + g$

   e $6 \times 2 = 10 + b$ **f** $3 \times 6 = 12 + p$

   g $p - 10 = 10$ **h** $14 + f = 22$

   i $7 + d = 7$ **j** $q + 17 = 30$

   k $24 + b = 28$ **l** $c + 7 = 18$

Did you know?

The Ancient Egyptians used balances to weigh gold.

Problem solving

4 Theo is making 425 g of muesli.
What weight of hazelnuts should he add?

Muesli

200 g porridge oats
25 g wheat germ
___ hazelnuts
50 g almonds
50 g sultanas
25 g dried apricots

5 a In this pyramid, each brick is made by adding together the two bricks below it. Fill in the missing bricks and work out the value of n.

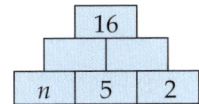

16
n 5 2

b Now try this one!

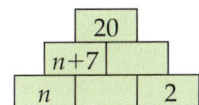

20
$n+7$
n 2

Danielle has a purse full of pound coins and a £5 note.
She knows she has £14 in total.

You can write this as an equation.
$x + 5 = 14$

Use **inverse operations** to work out how
many pound coins are in Danielle's purse.

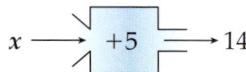

The input is x, the number of pound coins in
her purse.

Danielle has £9 in her purse.

Remember
inverses

$+ \rightarrow -$

$- \rightarrow +$

$\times \rightarrow \div$

$\div \rightarrow \times$

Example

James had £30 in his wallet.
He spent half of the money.
Find how much money James spent.

Use a letter to represent the money that James spent.

The money James spent $= x$

$2x = 30$

The value of x is 15.

So James spent £15.

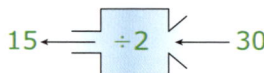

Check: £15 + £15 = £30 ✔

Example

I think of a number. I multiply the number by 4 and get 40.
What number did I start with?

Let the start number $= y$.

$4y = 40$

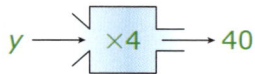

$40 \div 4 = 10$

so $y = 10$

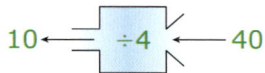

You started with 10.

Example

Solve these equations by finding the value of the letter.

a $x + 15 = 25$ **b** $y - 7 = 20$ **c** $z \times 3 = 18$

a $x + 15 = 25$
   $x = 25 - 15$
   $x = 10$

b $y - 7 = 20$
   $y = 20 + 7$
   $y = 27$

c $z \times 3 = 18$
   $z = 18 \div 3$
   $z = 6$

Exercise 10e

1 Find the starting number in each of these puzzles.
You can probably do most of them in your head.

a I think of a number and add 3.
Now I have 10.

b I think of a number and add 20.
Now I have 30.

c I think of a number and subtract 6.
Now I have 5.

d I think of a number and multiply it by 4. Now I have 8.

e I think of a number and divide it by 3.
Now I have 10.

2 Use inverses to find the value of the letter in each equation.

a $x + 17 = 25$ b $m + 20 = 45$
c $d + 23 = 47$ d $h + 15 = 15$
e $3p = 24$ f $r \div 5 = 6$
g $12m = 48$ h $y \div 3 = 9$

3 a Write this sentence as an equation.
Use x for the missing number.

'I think of a number and I add 17 to it. The answer is 42.'

b Find x.

4 Find the value of the letter in each equation.

a $w + 16 = 17$ b $t + 13 = 28$
c $b - 20 = 45$ d $f - 12 = 11$
e $2 \times t = 24$ f $5 \times j = 40$
g $e \div 3 = 10$ h $d \div 3 = 7$

Problem solving

5 Mark is going to the county fair.

a Write the total cost as an equation.
Use n for the number of rides.

b How much would it cost in total if Mark went on three rides?

County Fair
Entrance £3
Each ride £2

Did you know?

When you program a computer to solve a problem you use letters to stand for all the numbers involved.

10 MySummary

Check out
You should now be able to ...

Test it ➡
Questions

✓ Represent functions as sequences of operations.	4	1, 2
✓ Understand and use inverse operations.	5	3
✓ Use letters to represent unknown numbers.	5	4, 5
✓ Construct and solve simple equations.	5	6, 7

Language	Meaning	Example
Operation	A rule for processing numbers.	$+$, $-$, $\times$ and $\div$ are arithmetical operations
Inverse operation	An operation that reverses the effect of an original operation.	$+$ is the inverse of $-$ $\times$ is the inverse of $\div$
Equation	A statement that says that two expressions are equal. An equation always contains an equals sign. It may also contain an unknown number. We use a letter to stand for the unknown number.	$y - 12 = 3$ y is the unknown value
Solve	The act of finding the unknown value in an equation.	When you solve this equation, you find that $y = 15$

1 Find the missing outputs.

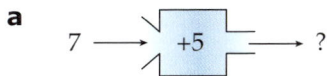

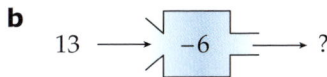

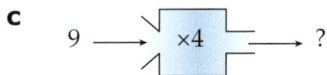

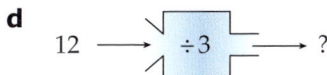

a

$7 \longrightarrow \boxed{+5} \longrightarrow ?$

b

$13 \longrightarrow \boxed{-6} \longrightarrow ?$

c

$9 \longrightarrow \boxed{\times 4} \longrightarrow ?$

d

$12 \longrightarrow \boxed{\div 3} \longrightarrow ?$

2 Find out the missing operation. There may be more than one correct answer.

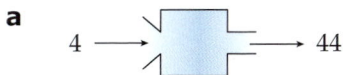

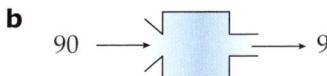

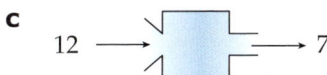

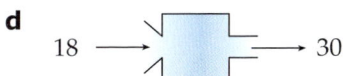

a

$4 \longrightarrow \boxed{} \longrightarrow 44$

b

$90 \longrightarrow \boxed{} \longrightarrow 9$

c

$12 \longrightarrow \boxed{} \longrightarrow 7$

d

$18 \longrightarrow \boxed{} \longrightarrow 30$

3 Complete these statements.

a The inverse of $+7$ is …

b The inverse of -9 is …

c The inverse of $\times 4$ is …

d The inverse of $\div 3$ is …

4 Calculate the values of these letters.

a $a + 9 = 15$ **b** $b + 8 = 26$

c $c - 5 = 9$ **d** $d - 4 = 8$

e $9 + e = 25$ **f** $f - 13 = 37$

5 Find the value that makes each equation balance.

a $6 \times g = 24$ **b** $10 \times h = 50$

c $15 + i = 24$ **d** $21 = j \times 3$

e $3 + k = 3$ **f** $4 \times 2 = m - 3$

6 Find the weight that makes the equation balance.

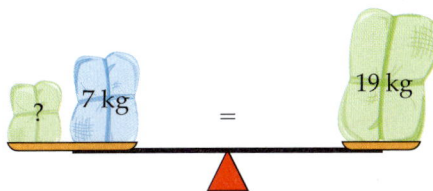

7 Find the starting number in each of these puzzles.

a *I think of a number and add 7. Now I have 13.*

b *I think of a number and subtract 10. Now I have 25.*

c *I think of a number and multiply it by 3. Now I have 33.*

d *I think of a number and divide it by 4. Now I have 8.*

What next?

Score			
	0 – 2		Your knowledge of this topic is still developing. To improve look at Formative test: 1A-10; MyMaths: 1154 and 1159
	3 – 5		You are gaining a secure knowledge of this topic. To improve look at InvisiPen: 211, 233, 234, 239 and 253
	6 – 7		You have mastered this topic. Well done, you are ready to progress!

10a

1 Calculate the input in each case.

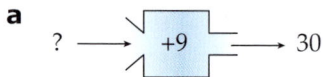

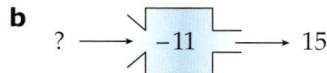

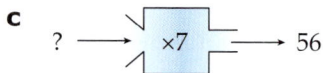

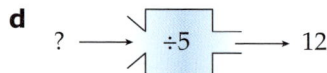

a ? → [+9] → 30

b ? → [−11] → 15

c ? → [×7] → 56

d ? → [÷5] → 12

2 Work out the missing operations. There may be more than one answer.

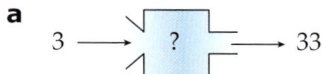

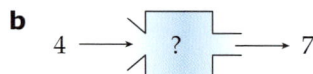

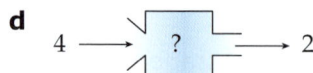

a 3 → [?] → 33

b 4 → [?] → 7

c 4 → [?] → 8

d 4 → [?] → 2

3 Find the missing operations.

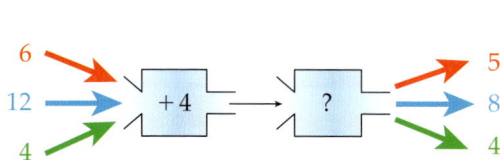

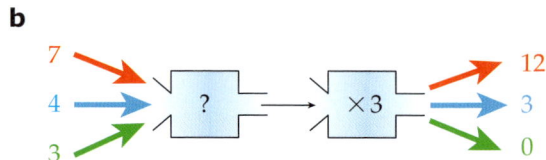

a
6, 12, 4 → [+4] → [?] → 5, 8, 4

b
7, 4, 3 → [?] → [×3] → 12, 3, 0

10b

4 Use inverse operations to find the missing inputs.

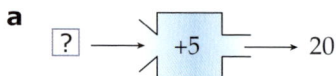

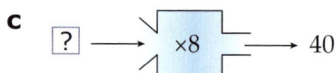

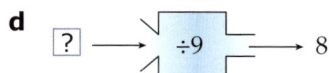

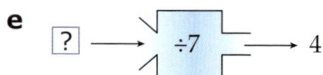

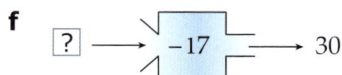

a [?] → [+5] → 20

b [?] → [−7] → 11

c [?] → [×8] → 40

d [?] → [÷9] → 8

e [?] → [÷7] → 4

f [?] → [−17] → 30

10c

5 Work out the value of these letters.

a $4 + a = 10$

b $12 = b + 10$

c $c + 6 = 15$

d $14 = 7 + d$

e $15 + e = 20$

f $f - 4 = 2$

g $g - 10 = 10$

h $20 = 16 + h$

i $9 - i = 9$

j $j - 15 = 5$

k $23 + k = 30$

l $l - 8 = 12$

6 Write equations using letters for these drawings. Do not give a value for ?.

a

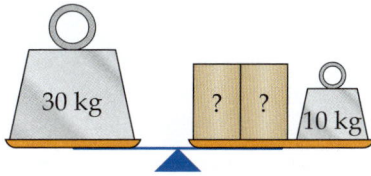

b

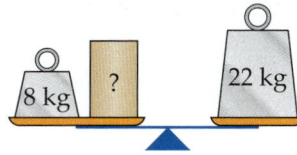

7 Find the value that makes each equation balance.

a $3 + 6 = 4 + a$ **b** $7 + 5 = b + 10$

c $18 + 2 = c + 8$ **d** $20 - 5 = 10 + d$

e $20 - 7 = 1 + e$ **f** $6 \times 2 = 9 + f$

g $15 - 6 = 5 + g$ **h** $30 - 11 = h + 2$

8 Find the value of the letter in each of these equations.

a $t + 6 = 10$ **b** $y + 8 = 12$ **c** $x + 9 = 14$

d $g + 19 = 23$ **e** $m - 4 = 7$ **f** $n - 10 = 6$

g $v + 23 = 25$ **h** $r - 4 = 16$ **i** $g + 5 = 21$

j $q - 14 = 6$ **k** $t + 16 = 20$ **l** $h - 5 = 1$

9 Find the value that makes each equation balance.

a $y - 9 = 15$ **b** $5t = 75$ **c** $60 \div v = 12$

d $n \div 6 = 3$ **e** $p + 11 = 26$ **f** $50 - r = 39$

g $m \div 4 = 12$ **h** $t + 21 = 30$ **i** $6a = 60$

10 Find the value of the letter in each equation.

a $y + 35 = 60$ **b** $t - 39 = 15$ **c** $5 \times m = 90$

d $7 \times p = 224$ **e** $r \div 12 = 8$ **f** $6a = 24$

g $9b = 63$ **h** $c \div 4 = 32$ **i** $p \div 10 = 10$

11 For each puzzle **i**   write an equation

   ii find the unknown starting number.

a   I think of a number and divide it by 6. Now I have 8.

b   I think of a number and multiply it by 6. Now I have 36.

c   I think of a number and add 19. Now I have 47.

d   I think of a number and subtract 23. Now I have 38.

e   I think of a number and multiply it by 7. Now I have 49.

f   I think of a number and add 22. Now I have 55.

g   I think of a number and subtract 15. Now I have 12.

h   I think of a number and divide it by 4. Now I have 9.

11 Factors and multiples

Introduction

If you want to listen to music and surf the internet at the same time without your computer slowing down you need plenty of RAM (Random Access Memory), which is measured in gigabytes (GB). The speeds and memories of computers are becoming so fast and so big that mathematicians have to use increasing multiples of 1000 to describe them.

1000 Megabytes = 1 Gigabyte
1000 Gigabytes = 1 Terabyte
1000 Terabytes = 1 Petabyte
1000 Petabytes = 1 Exabyte

What's the point?

Being able to appreciate very large numbers as multiples of familiar numbers allows you to understand the technical specifications of your computer.

Objectives

By the end of this chapter, you will have learned how to ...

- Recognise and list factors and multiples.
- Use simple tests of divisibility.
- Recognise the squares of numbers up to 10×10.

Check in

1   Copy and complete.

    a $\square \times 3 = 30$ **b** $10 \times 7 = \square$ **c** $\square \times 5 = 35$

    d $15 \div 3 = \square$ **e** $2 \times \square = 18$ **f** $\square \times 6 = 60$

2   Write whether each of these numbers is odd or even.

    a 12   **b** 15   **c** 100   **d** 2657   **e** 3001   **f** 22 223

Starter problem

You are going to play a game
against an imaginary computer.
Here are the rules of the game.

1   Start by taking any card.
2   The computer takes all of the cards that are factors of
    your number.
3   Now take another card that still has factors remaining.
4   The computer takes the remaining factors of your
    new card.
5   Repeat steps 3 and 4 until no cards with factors remain.
6   Your score is the total of your cards.
7   The computer's score is the total of its cards plus any remaining.

Can you beat the computer?

205

11a Factors

Alec is making rectangular patterns with eight counters.
He can make four different patterns:

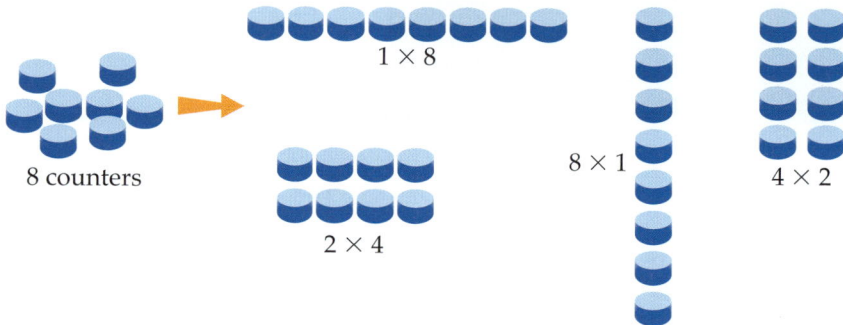

I can see what multiplies to make 8!

1×8

2×4

8×1

4×2

8 counters

He looks for the number 8 in his multiplication table.

$8 = 1 \times 8$	$8 = 8 \times 1$
$8 = 2 \times 4$	$8 = 4 \times 2$

1×8 and 2×4 are the same as 8×1 and 4×2.

×	1	2	3	4	5	6	7	8	9	10
1	1	2	3	4	5	6	7	8	9	10
2	2	4	6	8	10	12	14	16	18	20
3	3	6	9	12	15	18	21	24	27	30
4	4	8	12	16	20	24	28	32	36	40
5	5	10	15	20	25	30	35	40	45	50
6	6	12	18	24	30	36	42	48	54	60
7	7	14	21	28	35	42	49	56	63	70
8	8	16	24	32	40	48	56	64	72	80
9	9	18	27	36	45	54	63	72	81	90
10	10	20	30	40	50	60	70	80	90	100

● Numbers that **multiply** together to make a given number are called **factors**.
▶ Factors always come in factor pairs.

The factors of 8 are 1, 2, 4 and 8.
The factor pairs are 1 and 8, and 2 and 4.

You can also describe factors using division.

A number that divides a given number exactly is a factor of the given number.

$8 \div 4 = 2$ (no remainder!)
4 is a factor of 8
$8 \div 2 = 4$
and 2 is a factor of 8

Example

Find the factors of 6.

Put 6 counters into rectangular patterns.
Write the multiplication for each pattern.

6×1 1×6 2×3 3×2

The factors of 6 are: 1, 2, 3 and 6.
The factor pairs are 1 and 6, and 2 and 3.

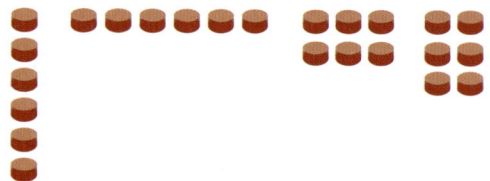

Exercise 11a

1 a Put these 12 counters into rectangular patterns.
b Write a multiplication for each pattern.
c Check your answers with the multiplication table.
d List all the factors of 12.

2 Here are 20 counters.
a Find all the different ways to put them in rectangles.
b List all the factors of 20.
c Which factors are not in the multiplication table?

3

> **Factor Facts!**
> Have you noticed that
> • 1 is a factor of every number.
> • Every number is a factor of itself.
> $20 = 20 \times 1$ $12 = 12 \times 1$ $6 = 6 \times 1$

Use these facts and the multiplication table to list the factors of

a 9 **b** 12 **c** 15
d 16 **e** 18 **f** 21
g 24 **h** 27 **i** 25

> You know that 1 is a factor. Now ask, 'Is 2 a factor?', then 3, then 4 …

Problem solving

4 Match each number in a green box with its set of factors.
Beware, there is a mystery! There is a fifth unknown number and each set of numbers contains one of its factors.
What are the extra factors and what is the unknown numbers?

13   60   30   27   ?

a 1 2 3 5 6 10 15 28 30
b 1 3 7 9 27
c 1 2 3 4 5 6 10 12 14 15 30 60
d 1 4 13

5 Look at these shapes. Which one has the greatest area? What do you notice?
a **b** **c**

6 Some numbers have only two factors: one and the number itself.
The factors of 5 are 1 and 5. The number 5 has no other factors.
Which of these numbers have only two factors?

12 9 7 14 13

Can you find a number that has just three factors?

11b Multiples

🔴 **Multiples** are made by multiplying numbers together.

$2 \times 9 = 18$ $2 \times 10 = 20$

18 and 20 are both multiples of 2.

Sophie is looking for multiples of 2.

She draws a diagram …   … and looks in a multiplication table.

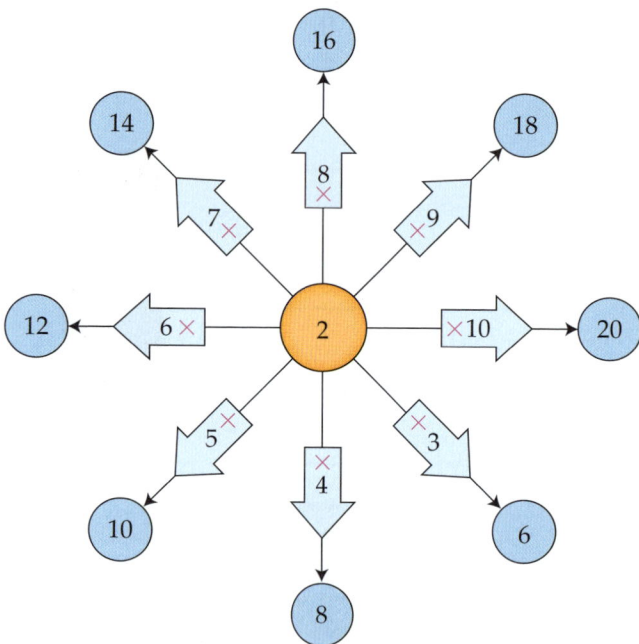

×	1	2	3	4	5	6	7	8	9	10
1	1	2	3	4	5	6	7	8	9	10
2	2	4	6	8	10	12	14	16	18	20
3	3	6	9	12	15	18	21	24	27	30
4	4	8	12	16	20	24	28	32	36	40
5	5	10	15	20	25	30	35	40	45	50
6	6	12	18	24	30	36	42	48	54	60
7	7	14	21	28	35	42	49	56	63	70
8	8	16	24	32	40	48	56	64	72	80
9	9	18	27	36	45	54	63	72	81	90
10	10	20	30	40	50	60	70	80	90	100

Example

What are the multiples of 3 up to 20?

$3 \times 1 = 3$ $3 \times 2 = 6$ $3 \times 3 = 9$

$3 \times 4 = 12$ $3 \times 5 = 15$ $3 \times 6 = 18$

3, 6, 9, 12, 15 and 18. $3 \times 7 = 21$
                            21 is a multiple of 3
                            but it is bigger than 20.

Hey! These are just numbers in the 3 times table.

Example

Find two numbers that have these multiples: 8, 12, 16, 20

Look at the factors.

$2 \times 4 = 8$ $2 \times 6 = 12$ $2 \times 8 = 16$ $2 \times 10 = 20$

                        $3 \times 4 = 12$ $4 \times 4 = 16$ $4 \times 5 = 20$

2 and 4 have 8, 12, 16 and 20 as multiples.

Exercise 11b

1 Copy the diagram to find multiples of 5.
Fill in all of the circles.

2 a Repeat Question **1** for multiples of 3 by placing
3 at the centre.
  b Then repeat for multiples of 6.

3 a Write a list of multiples of 2 up to 30.
  b Write a list of multiples of 3 up to 30.
  c What numbers up to 30 are multiples of
both 2 and 3?

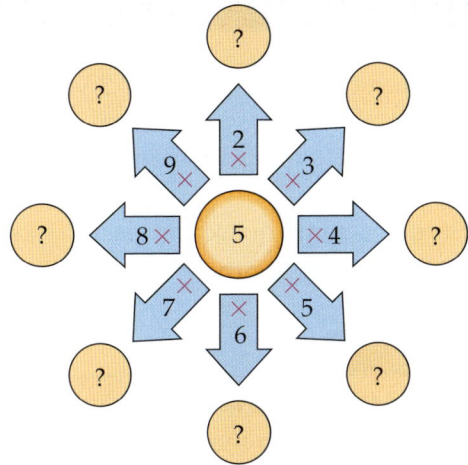

Problem solving

4 Starting with each number in the green box, follow through the maze to one of the capital
letters. You can only land on numbers that are multiples of your starting number.
Which number matches each capital letter?

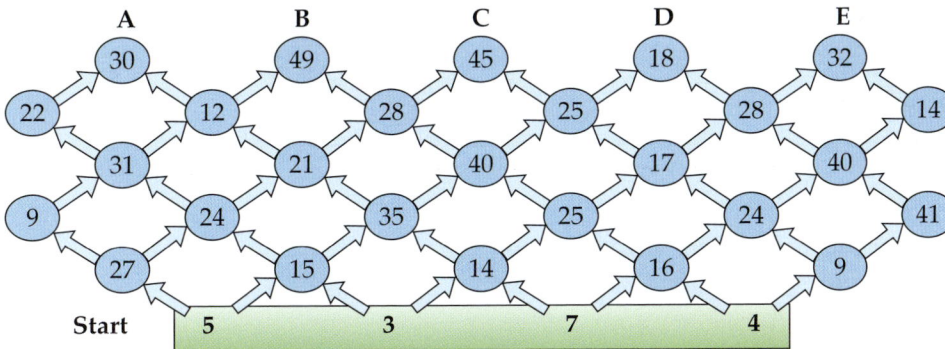

5 a Which numbers have all these multiples?
  b What would be the next number in the ring?

6, 12, 36, 18, 24

6

If a number is a multiple of 3, when you
add its digits together and the sum is also
a multiple of 3.

For example, 1 + 2 + 3 = 6 and 6 is a
multiple of 3. So, 123 is a multiple of 3.

Use Jenny's rule to check whether these numbers are multiples of 3.
a 69 **b** 175 **c** 174 **d** 711 **e** 253 **f** 2058

11c   Tests of divisibility

If a number is a multiple of 3 you can say it is **divisible** by 3.

> 🔴 Divisible means divides exactly.

Here are some quick and easy tricks to see if your number is divisible by another.

p.266 >

· 2

Is the last digit **even** (2, 4, 6, 8, 0)? Then 2 will divide into the number exactly.

28	8 even ✓	$28 \div 2 = 14$
23	3 odd ✗	$23 \div 2 = 11\frac{1}{2}$

· 10

Does it end with 0? Then 10 will divide into the number exactly.

350	✓	$350 \div 10 = 35$
238	✗	$238 \div 10 = 23\frac{4}{5}$

· 5

Does it end with 0 or 5? Then 5 will divide into the number exactly.

45	✓	$45 \div 5 = 9$
37	✗	$37 \div 5 = 7\frac{2}{5}$

Example

Which two numbers in this list are *not* **multiples** of 5?

25,   57,   60,   205,   208,   325

Multiples of 5 end in 5 or 0.

57 and 208

· 3

Do the digits add up to a multiple of 3 (3, 6, 9, 12 …)?
Then 3 will divide into the number exactly.

216	$2 + 1 + 6 = 9,$	$9 \div 3 = 3$	✓	$216 \div 3 = 72$
217	$2 + 1 + 7 = 10,$	$10 \div 3 = 3\frac{1}{3}$	✗	$217 \div 3 = 72\frac{1}{3}$

· 4

Are the last two digits **divisible** by 4? Then 4 will divide into the number exactly.

420	$20 \div 4 = 5$	✓	$420 \div 4 = 105$
326	$26 \div 4 = 6\frac{1}{2}$	✗	$326 \div 4 = 81\frac{1}{2}$

Exercise 11c

1 **a** Will 2, 5 and 10 all divide exactly into 20?

   b Will 2, 5 and 10 all divide exactly into 40?

   c Will 2, 5 and 10 all divide exactly into 35?

   d What do you notice about the numbers that 2, 5 and 10 **will** all divide into exactly?

2 Which three numbers from the list cannot be divided exactly by 2?

26	44	31	68
180	109	15	662

3 Which two numbers from the list cannot be divided exactly by 5?

30	85	55	58
125	103	160	105

4 Caroline has 94 biscuits and three sisters. She wants to share her biscuits out fairly between all four of them. Will there be any left over for the dog?

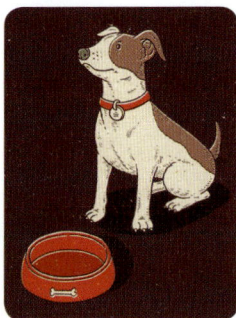

5 Here are some numbers.
28, 120, 168, 255, 300, 360
Choose a number from the list that is
   a divisible by 10   **b** a multiple of 2
   c a multiple of 4   **d** divisible by 3
   e divisible by 5   **f** a multiple of 6.

6 Answer **yes** or **no** to each question.
   a Can 5 divide into 47 860 exactly?
   b Can 2 divide into 63 657 exactly?
   c Can 4 divide into 31 724 exactly?
   d Can 3 divide into 3141 exactly?
   e Can 10 divide into 16 145 exactly?
   f Can 3 divide into 3521 exactly?
   g Can 2 divide into 84 130 exactly?
   h Can 4 divide into 53 214 exactly?
   i Can 5 divide into 15 151 exactly?
   j Can 10 divide into 45 040 exactly?

7 **a** Write down a number between 100 and 140 that is divisible by 3 and 5.
   b Write down a number between 150 and 190 that is divisible by 4 ad 5.
   c Write down a number between 400 and 500 that is divisible by 3 and 10.

Problem solving

8 Carlos has £416.
   a Can he share it exactly 3 ways?
   b Can he share it exactly 4 ways?
   c Can he share it exactly 5 ways?

9 Which number from this group **cannot** be divided exactly by at least one of: 2, 3, 4, 5 or 10?

135	340	229	312

MyMaths.co.uk   🔍 1218 **SEARCH**

Alec is using counters again. He starts with one counter, and adds one counter at a time and tries to make squares.

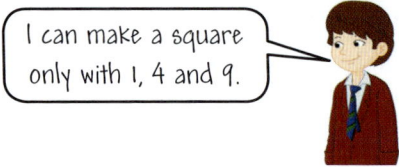

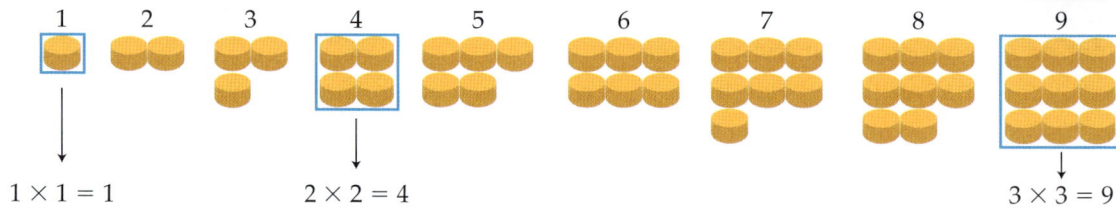

I can make a square only with 1, 4 and 9.

| 1 | 2 | 3 | 4 | 5 | 6 | 7 | 8 | 9 |

$1 \times 1 = 1$ $2 \times 2 = 4$ $3 \times 3 = 9$

⬤ A number multiplied by itself is a **square number**.

$3 \times 3 = 9$ 9 is a square number.

You say three squared.

You write it like this.

$$3^2$$

×	1	2	3	4	5	6	7	8	9	10
1	1	2	3	4	5	6	7	8	9	10
2	2	4	6	8	10	12	14	16	18	20
3	3	6	9	12	15	18	21	24	27	30
4	4	8	12	16	20	24	28	32	36	40
5	5	10	15	20	25	30	35	40	45	50
6	6	12	18	24	30	36	42	48	54	60
7	7	14	21	28	35	42	49	56	63	70
8	8	16	24	32	40	48	56	64	72	80
9	9	18	27	36	45	54	63	72	81	90
10	10	20	30	40	50	60	70	80	90	100

Can you see the pattern in this multiplication table?

$1 \times 1 = 1$
$2 \times 2 = 4$
$3 \times 3 = 9$
$4 \times 4 = 16$

9 814 072 356

▲ What's the biggest square number you can think of? This is 99 066 squared!

Example

What is missing in these calculations?

a $5 \times \square = 5^{\square} = 25$

b $6 \times 6 = \square^2 = \square$

a $5 \times 5 = 5^2 = 25$

b $6 \times 6 = 6^2 = 36$

Exercise 11d

1 Jack makes a sketch to find the first three square numbers.

Copy Jack's pattern and find the next two square numbers.

$\times$

$1 \times 1 = 1$

$\times\times$
$\times\times$

$2 \times 2 = 4$

$\times\times\times$
$\times\times\times$
$\times\times\times$

$3 \times 3 = 9$

? **?**

2 Here are the first 10 square numbers in no particular order.

Complete the list. The first two are done for you.

a $3^2 = 3 \times 3 = 9$ **b** $1^2 = 1 \times 1 = 1$
c 6^2 **d** 4^2
e 9^2 **f** 2^2
g 10^2 **h** 8^2
i 5^2 **j** 7^2

3 Find two more square numbers.

Problem solving

4 Follow only the square numbers through the maze.

As you arrive at each square number write the letter written in the box. What word have you spelt?

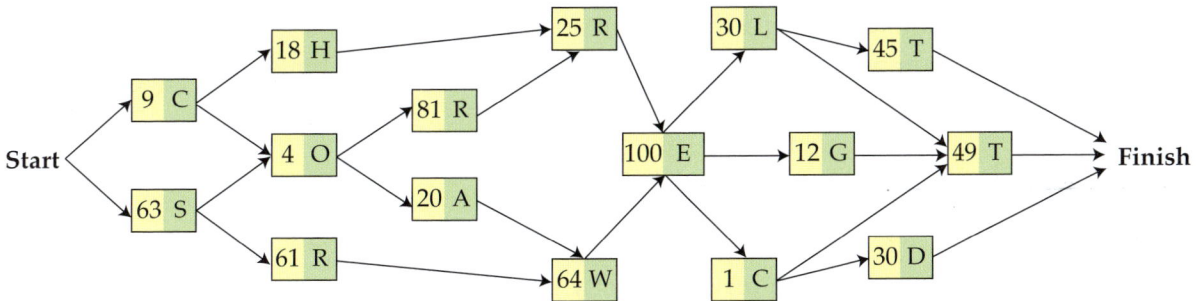

Start

9 C — 18 H — 25 R — 30 L — 45 T
63 S — 4 O — 81 R — 100 E — 12 G — 49 T — Finish
61 R — 20 A — 64 W — 1 C — 30 D

5 Kiran has a pile of 2p coins. She arranges them in squares.

p.244 ❯

The first square is worth 2p

The second square is worth 8p

The third square is worth 18p

a What would the fourth square be worth?

b What would the tenth square be worth?

c Kiran has 40p worth of 2p coins.
What is the biggest square she can make?

Did you know?

▲ A chess board is made up of $8^2 = 64$ squares.

11 MySummary

Check out

You should now be able to...

Test it ➡

Questions

✓ Recognise and list factors and multiples.	4	1 – 6
✓ Use simple tests of divisibility.	4	7 – 10
✓ Recognise the squares of numbers up to 10 × 10.	4	11

Language	Meaning	Example
Factor	A number that divides exactly into another number.	1, 2, 5 and 10 are factors of 10
Factor pair	Two factors of a number which give the number when multiplied together.	1 and 10, and 2 and 5 are the factor pairs of 10.
Multiple	A number A is a multiple of another number B if B divides into A exactly. A is a multiple of B if A appears in the times table for B.	10, 15, 20 and 25 are all multiples of 5
Square number	A whole number multiplied by itself.	$5^2 = 5 \times 5 = 25$ 25 is a square number
Divisible	If a number A divides exactly into another number B, then B is divisible by A.	3 divides exactly into 9 9 is divisible by 3

1 List all the factors of

   a 4   **b** 6

   c 20   **d** 25

   e 26   **f** 30

   g 36   **h** 44

2 a List all the factors of 12.

   b List all the factors of 15.

   c Which numbers are factors of both 12 and 15?

3 a List the first 15 multiples of 3.

   b List the first ten multiples of 5.

   c Which of these numbers are multiples of both 3 and 5?

4 Write a list of multiples of 7 up to 70.

5 Which numbers have all these as multiples?

10, 20, 30, 40, 50

6 Write down all of the multiples of 10 between

   a 101 and 137   **b** 212 and 262

   c 509 and 545   **d** 1011 and 1089

7 Which of these numbers can you divide by 2 without leaving a remainder?

   a 87 or 88   **b** 146 or 147

   c 1001 or 1002   **d** 1010 or 1011

8 Which of these numbers can you divide exactly by 4?

   a 70 or 72   **b** 238 or 240

   c 158 or 160   **d** 442 or 444

9 Which of these numbers are multiples of 3?

   a 86 or 87   **b** 363 or 364

   c 588 or 589   **d** 675 or 676

10 a Write down a number between 201 and 280 that is divisible by 3 and 10.

    b Write down a number between 401 and 450 that is divisible by 4 and 5.

    c Write down a number between 301 and 350 that is divisible by 3 and 5.

11 Calculate

   a 5^2 **b** 7^2

   c 1^2 **d** 11^2

What next?

Score		
0 – 4		Your knowledge of this topic is still developing. To improve look at Formative test: 1A-11; MyMaths: 1032. 1035, 1053 and 1218
5 – 9		You are gaining a secure knowledge of this topic. To improve look at InvisiPen: 171 and 181
10 – 11		You have mastered this topic. Well done, you are ready to progress!

11a

1 **a** Arrange 6 counters in equal rows in as many ways as you can.

b For each diagram, write down a multiplication.

c Write down all the factors of 6.

Check your answers in the multiplication table.

2 Find all the factors of the number 8. Use counters to help you.

Check yours answers in the multiplication table.

3 List as many factors as you can for these numbers:

a 8   **b** 10   **c** 20   **d** 22   **e** 28   **f** 30   **g** 36   **h** 50

11b

4 **a** The numbers that belong in the circles are multiples of 4.

Copy the diagram. Start at the top and work clockwise to fill in the circles.

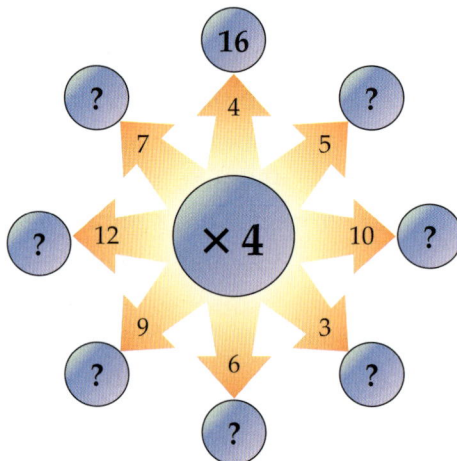

b How could you use multiples of 4 to calculate multiples of 8?

5 **a** Write a list of the multiples of 3 up to 30.

b Write a list of the multiples of 5 up to 30.

c Which of these numbers are multiples of both 3 and 5?

6 **a** Which numbers have all the numbers in the ring as multiples?

b What is the next number that would go into the ring?

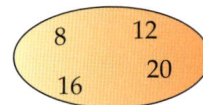

7 24 is a multiple with eight factors. Find as many of these factors as you can.

8 Which numbers are factors of all the numbers in the ring?

9 Copy and complete the table. Write *yes* or *no* in all the spaces on your copy.

Number	Divisible by 2?	Divisible by 3?	Divisible by 4?	Divisible by 5?	Divisible by 10?
154					
315					
364					
990					
1008					

10 Square numbers can be arranged into a square pattern. Which of these groups of tiles can be arranged in a square pattern? Answer **Yes** or **No**.

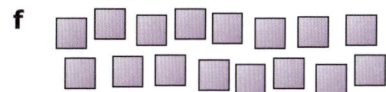

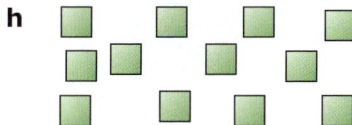

a

b

c

d

e

f

g

h

The number of tiles in a row will be the same as the number of tiles in a column.

11 Use a multiplication table to write as many square numbers as you can.

12 Which of these calculations have a square number as their answer? Answer 'Square' or 'Not square'.

a 7×7 **b** 9×8 **c** 12×12

d 6×4 **e** 20×3 **f** 3×3

g 11×10 **h** 15×10 **i** 6×6

13 Find as many factors as you can for each of these numbers. Use a multiplication table to help you.

a 2   **b** 4   **c** 10   **d** 16

e 30   **f** 24   **g** 35   **h** 40

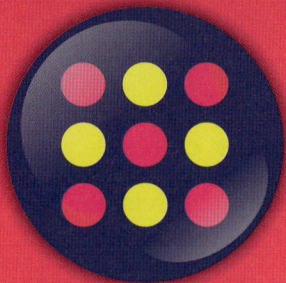

12 Constructions and 3D shapes

Introduction

How do you make a football? When you look at a football, it is made of regular mathematical shapes joined together to make a sphere.

The manufacturer first makes and cuts out a 2D plan, or net, of the material from which the football is made. The net is fastened or sewn together to make the 3D football.

What's the point?

An understanding of 2D shapes allows designers and manufacturers to combine them to make many of the 3D shapes which you see every day.

Objectives

By the end of this chapter, you will have learned how to ...

- Recognise and name common 3D shapes.
- Construct simple nets of 3D shapes.
- Use 2D representations to visualise 3D shapes.
- Use a protractor to measure and draw angles.
- Use a ruler and protractor to construct a triangle.
- Know the parts of a circle.

Check in

1 Estimate the size of these angles.

a 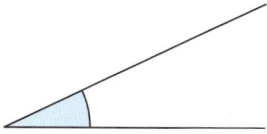   **b** 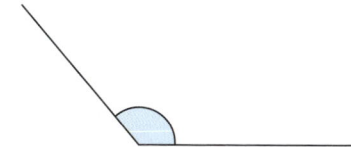   **c**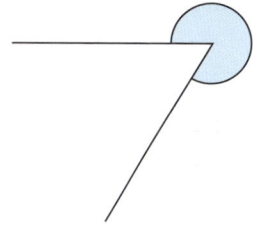

2 Using a pair of compasses, draw a circle that is exactly 10 cm across.

Starter problem

Here is a model of a house made from paper.
The model is made from different nets which are then
folded into 3D shapes. Each net makes part of the house
and the pieces are then glued together to make what you
see in the picture.

Design and build your own 3D paper house.

You see **3D** shapes everywhere.
3D stands for **three-dimensional**.

< p.32

Did you know?

The Egyptian pyramids all have square bases.

Here are some 3D shapes.

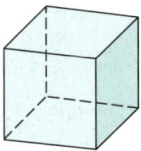

Cube

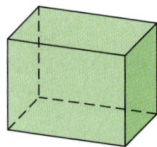

Cuboid

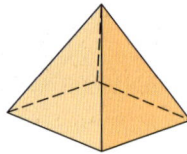

Square-based pyramid

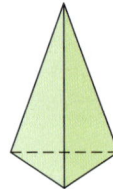

Triangular-based pyramid

Sphere

Cylinder

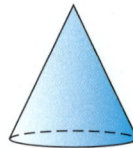

Cone

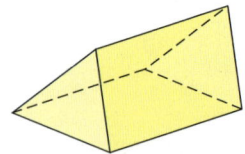

Triangular prism

● A 3D shape has **faces**, **edges** and **corners**.

This cube has
  6 faces – all squares
  12 edges – all the same length

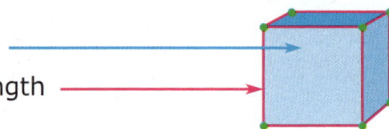

8 corners

Example

What are these 3D shapes?
a One curved face
     No edges or corners

b Six rectangular faces
     Edges not the same length

c Circular base and top
     No straight edges

a

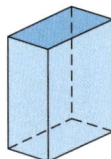

Sphere

b

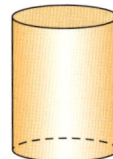

Cuboid

c

Cylinder

Exercise 12a

1 Class 7W are making 3D models of buildings near their school.
List the 3D shapes used to make each model. The first is done for you.

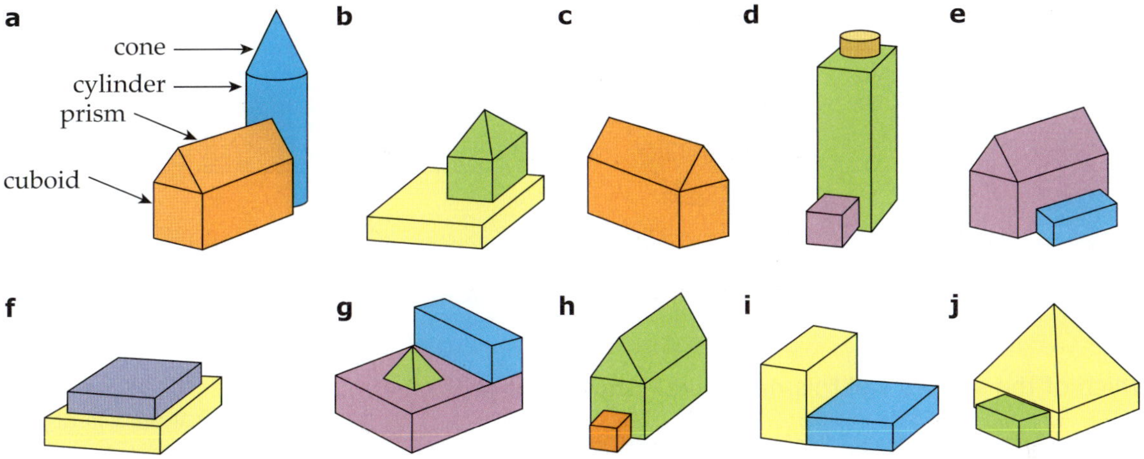

a

cone ⟶
cylinder ⟶
prism ⟶

cuboid ⟶

b   **c**   **d**   **e**

f   **g**   **h**   **i**   **j**

2 Here is an overhead view of the buildings near the school.
Match each 3D model above with the 2D view below.

Problem solving

3 Paige and Adio are describing two shapes.
What 3D shapes could they be?

a It has a square base and five faces.

b It has one flat face and one curved surface.

When a 3D shape is opened out, the flat shape it makes is called its **net**.

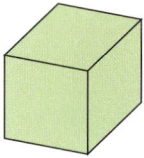

Cube

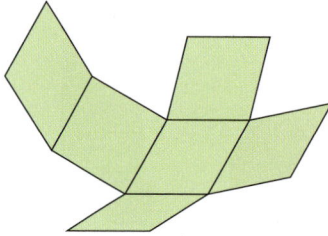

Unfold it

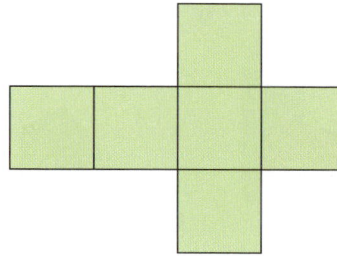

A net of the cube

Example

◄ p.32

Which of the shapes will this net make? Show your reasoning.

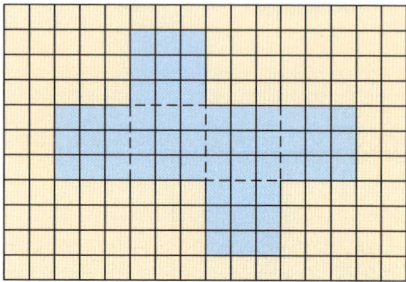

a 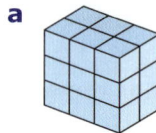   b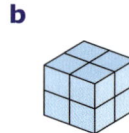

c 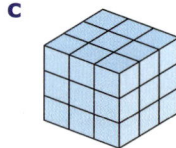   d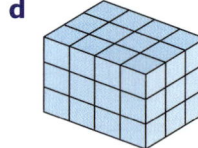

a and **d** have different-sized faces.
b has only four squares on each face.
c has nine squares on each face.
So, **c** matches the net.

> The word 'net' was first used to describe a piece of paper that could be folded to make a model of a crystal.

How to make a cube

- Draw the outline of this net on squared paper.
- Draw a dotted line where the net needs to be folded.
- Draw 'glue flaps' to stick it together.
- Cut it out carefully, fold it and glue it.
- Voilà!

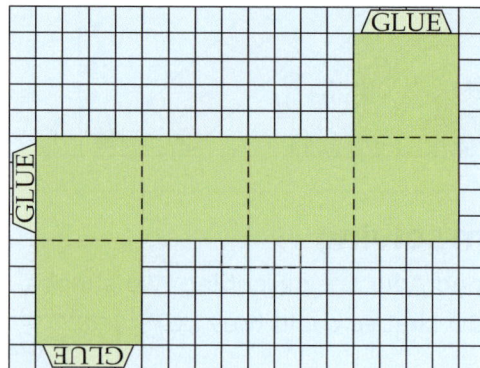

Exercise 12b

1 Two of these nets will **not** fold to make a cube. Which ones are they?

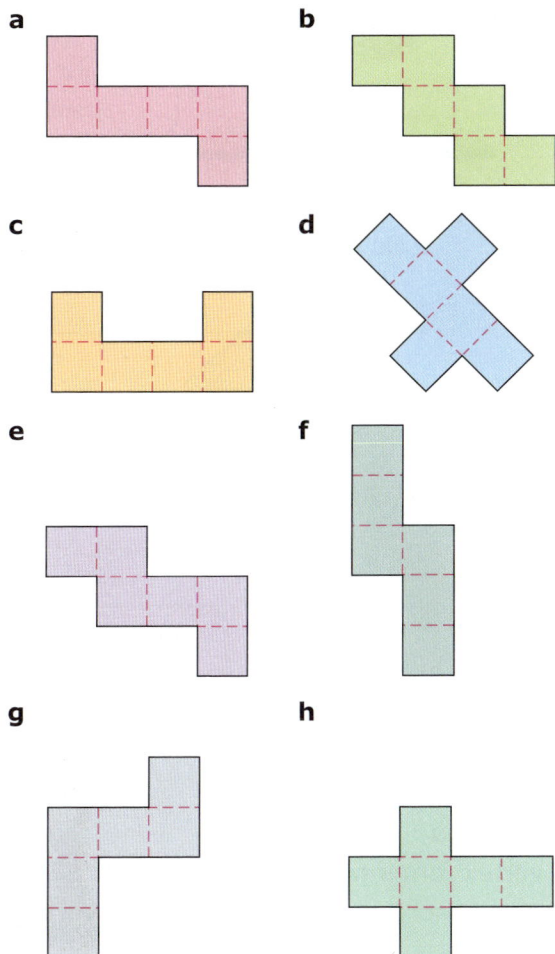

a

b

c

d

e

f

g

h

2 Copy this net of a cube onto squared paper.

Draw the 'glue flaps' and the fold-lines.

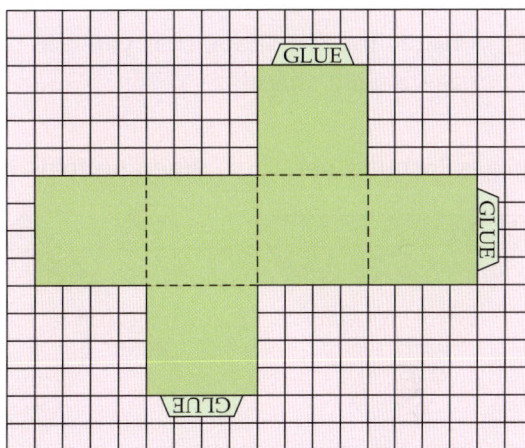

Cut out, fold and glue your cube.

It's easier to decorate your cube before you fold it.

Did you know?

Pablo Picasso and other cubist artists used shapes to depict 3D objects. What shapes can you see in this picture?

Problem solving

3 **a** Draw the net of a cube on squared paper.

A dice has six faces, marked with dots representing numbers.

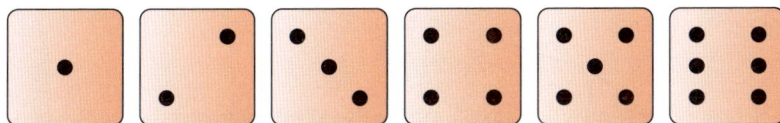

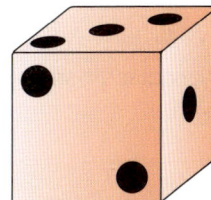

The opposite faces of a dice always add up to 7.

b Draw dots on the net of your cube, so that when folded, opposite faces always add up to 7.

Joshua is making a volcano in the shape of a triangular-based pyramid.
What shape should he draw on the cardboard?

I'm making an exploding volcano triangular-based pyramid!

⬤ A **net** is the flat shape that you fold to make a solid shape.

Here is Joshua's net.   When he folds it together ...   ... He gets a pyramid.

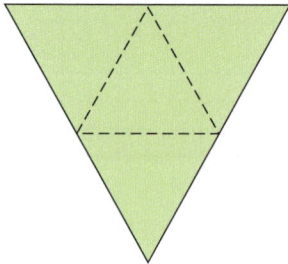   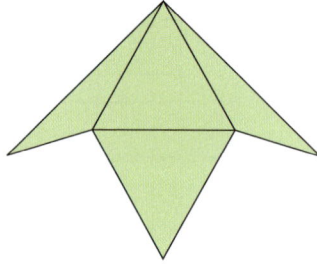   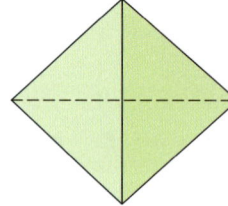

Joshua's triangular-based pyramid has

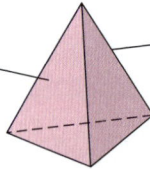

4 faces

6 edges
An edge forms when two faces meet.

4 vertices
A vertex forms when three or more edges meet.

The plural of vertex is vertices.

Example

Which solid shape will this net make when cut out and folded?
a   cuboid
b   triangular-based pyramid
c   triangular prism

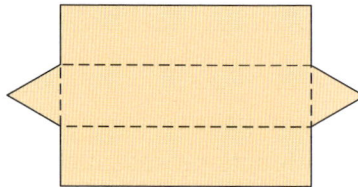

Draw the edges you can't see as broken lines.

c   A triangular prism

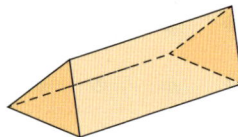

Exercise 12c

1 Match each 3D shape (**a–f**) with its net (**1–6**)

a

b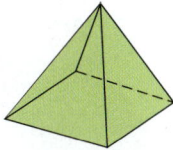

c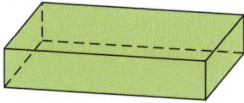

d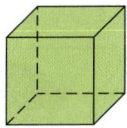

e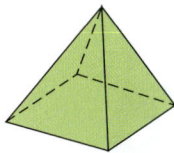

f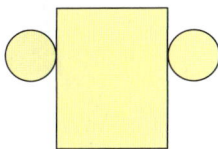

1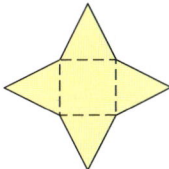

2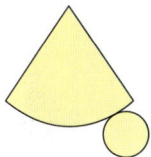

3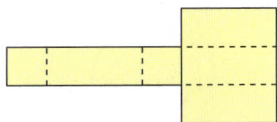

4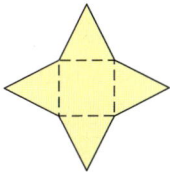

5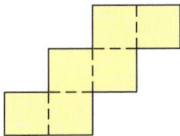

6

2 On squared paper draw the net for this cuboid.

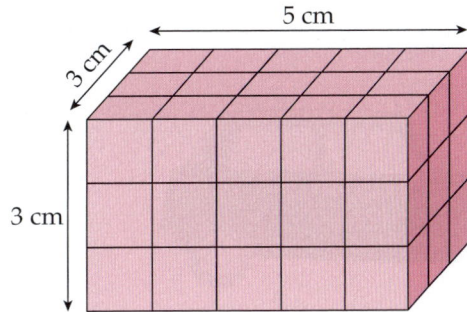

3 For each shape say how many

   i faces   **ii** edges   **iii** vertices

   it has.

a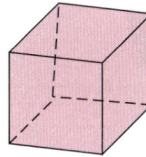

Cube

b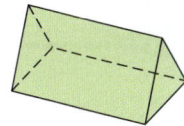

Triangular prism

c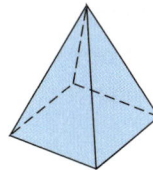

Square-based pyramid

d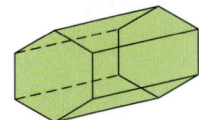

Hexagonal prism

Problem solving

4 Oliver has drawn a net for a triangular prism. Will it work?

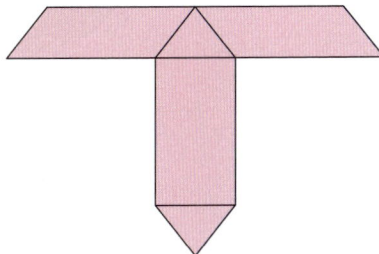

MyMaths.co.uk   1106   **SEARCH**

Keisha is putting her car for sale on the Internet.
She takes a photo ...

... from the side,

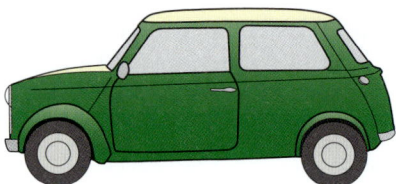

p.288 >

... from the top

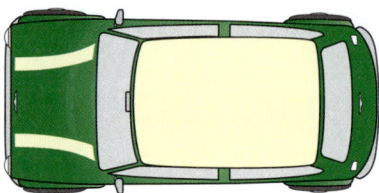

... and from the front.

MINI

Architects use these types of 2D drawings.

Example

< p. 32

Here is a can of beans.
a Describe it as a mathematical shape.
b Draw this can of beans from
  i the top   **ii** the side

Top view

Side view

a A can of beans is a cylinder.
b **i**   **ii**

The top view of the can is a circle.

The side view of the can is a rectangle.

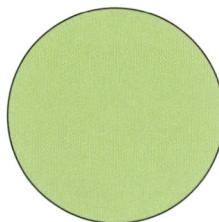

Exercise 12d

1 Draw this cube from
   a the top
   b the side.

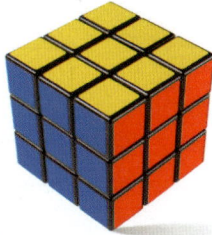

2 Draw this square-based pyramid from
   a the top   **b** the side

3 Draw this cone from
   a the top
   b the side

4 Here are the top and two side views of a solid shape.

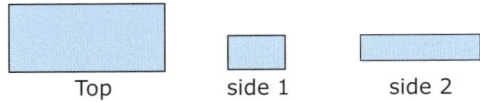

Top   side 1   side 2

Is the shape A, B or C?

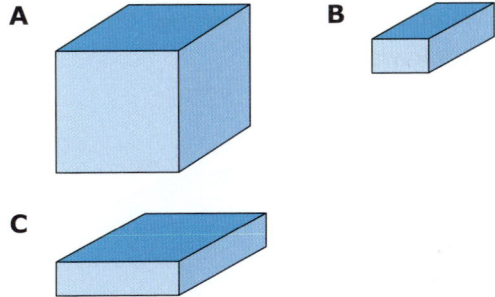

A

B

C

Did you know?

The GCHQ building in Cheltenham is called the 'Doughnut Building.' Can you see why?

Problem solving

5 Draw the view from the top and side for each of these shapes.
   a   **b**   **c**

You need a protractor, a ruler and a pencil to measure and draw angles.

‹ p. 94

And you need to be able to use them correctly!

Example

a Write the angles measured on the **clockwise** scale.

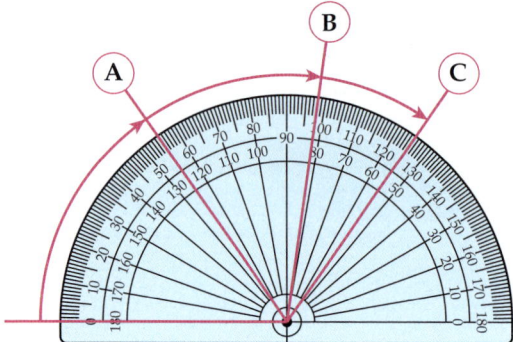

A 55°   B 98°   C 125°

b Write the angles measured on the **anticlockwise** scale.

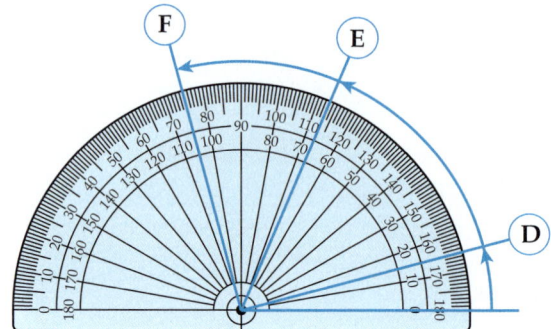

D 15°   E 67°   F 105°

Example

Draw an angle of 60°.

1 Draw a line about 7 cm long.

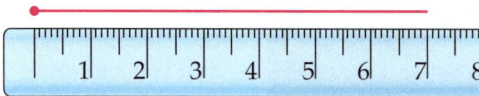

Put a dot at one end.

2 Place the protractor on the line.

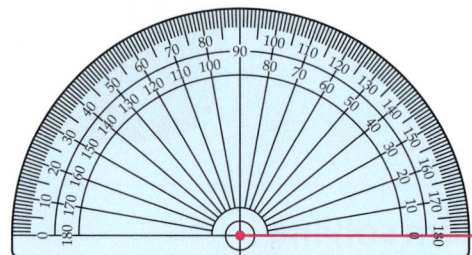

Put the cross-line on top of the dot.

3 Read round the scale from 0.

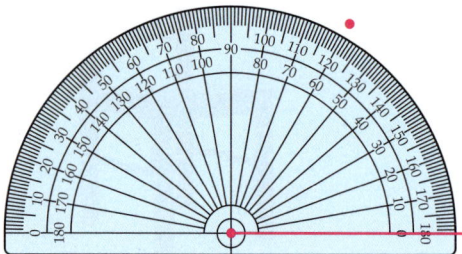

Mark 60° with a dot.

4 Join the dots to complete the angle.

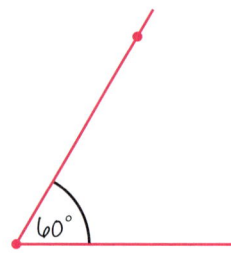

60°

This is an angle of 60°.

Exercise 12e

1 What is the size of each angle? Give your answer in degrees (°).

a

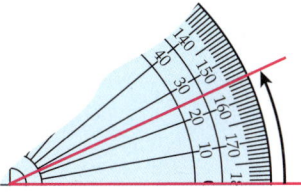

b

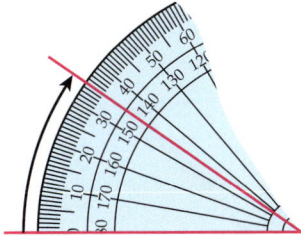

c

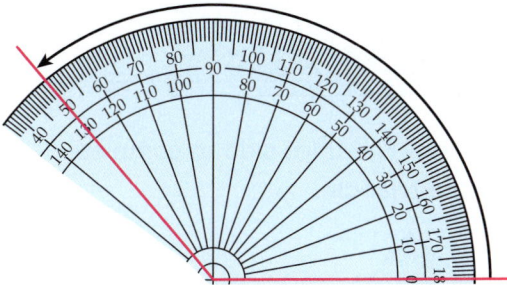

2 a Write these angles using the clockwise scale.

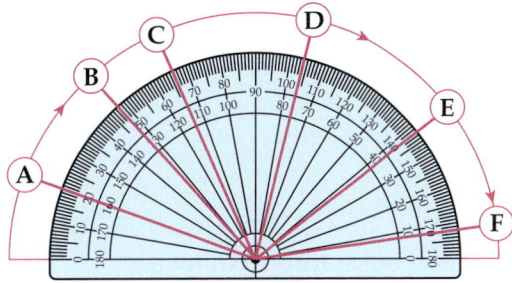

b Write these angles using the anticlockwise scale.

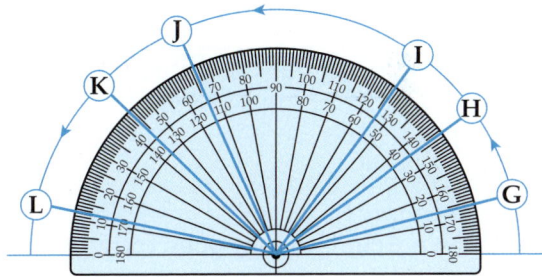

3 Draw these angles.

a 35°	**b** 60°	**c** 100°
d 135°	**e** 165°	**f** 20°
g 145°	**h** 55°	**i** 115°
j 85°	**k** 125°	**l** 75°

Problem solving

4 Michael is aiming a ball of paper at three waste paper bins.

Attempt **a**, at angle 30° missed.

Attempt **b**, at angle 60° missed.

Estimate the three angles at which he should launch the ball of paper to land in bins 1, 2 and 3.

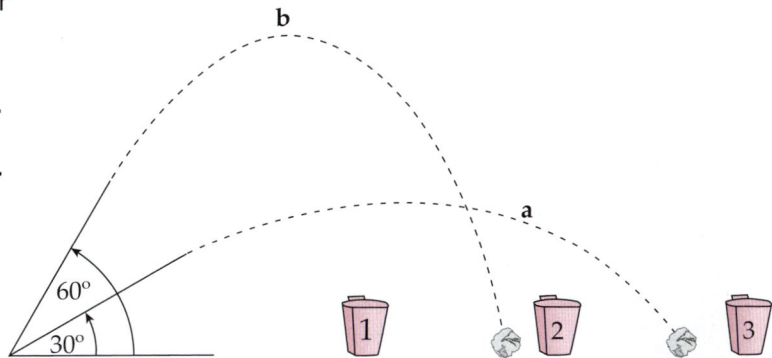

5 How would you measure an angle of 230°? How would you draw it?

230° is a **reflex** angle

MyMaths.co.uk 🔍 1081 **SEARCH**

p. 100

You can **construct** a **unique** triangle, using a **ruler** and protractor, given the right information.

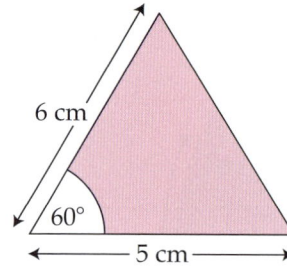

6 cm

60°

5 cm

1   Draw a **base line** 5 cm long.

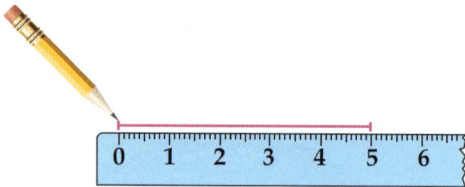

p. 94

0 1 2 3 4 5 6

2   Measure and mark an angle of 60° at one end of the line.

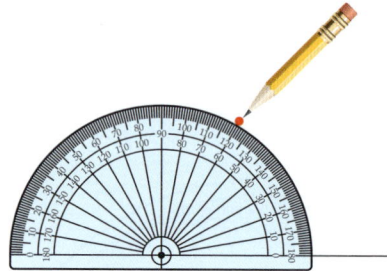

3   Draw a 6 cm line that goes through your mark.

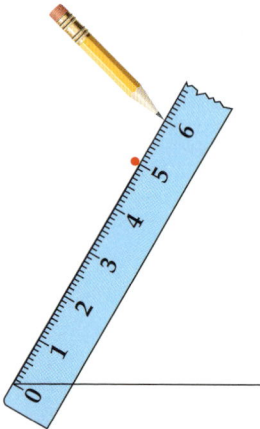

0 1 2 3 4 5 6

4   Draw the third side to complete the triangle.

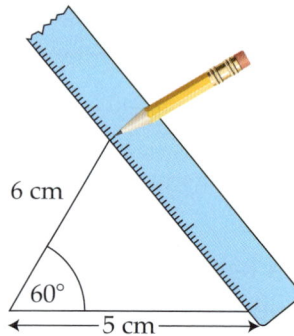

6 cm

60°

5 cm

These are often called SAS triangles because you are given two sides and the angle between them.

Did you know?

Triangulum is a constellation in the northern sky, meaning 'the triangle' in Latin. Its three brightest stars form an almost isosceles triangle.

Exercise 12f

1 Draw these angles.

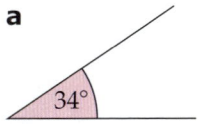

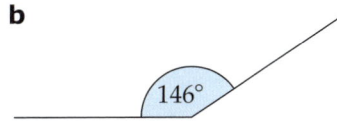

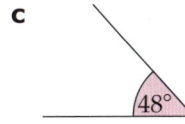

a
34°

b
146°

c
48°

2 a Draw each of these triangles accurately.

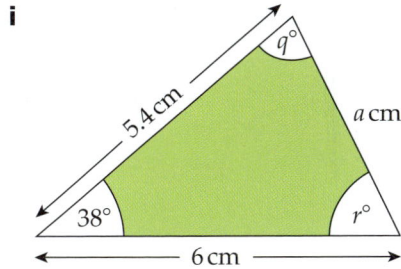

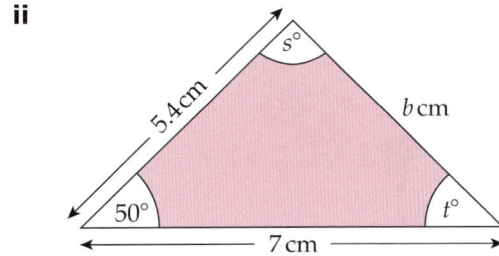

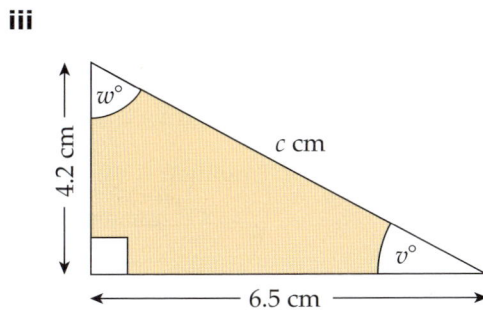

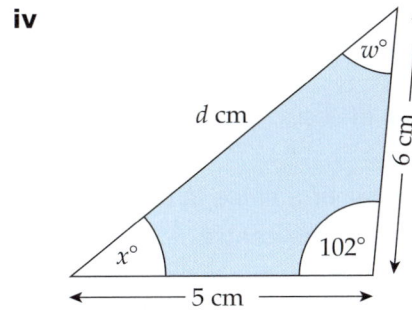

i
$q°$
5.4 cm
a cm
38°
$r°$
6 cm

ii
$s°$
5.4 cm
b cm
50°
$t°$
7 cm

iii
$w°$
4.2 cm
c cm
$v°$
6.5 cm

iv
$w°$
d cm
6 cm
$x°$
102°
5 cm

b On your drawings, measure the angles labelled q, r, ..., z.

c On your drawings measure, the sides labelled a, b, ..., f.

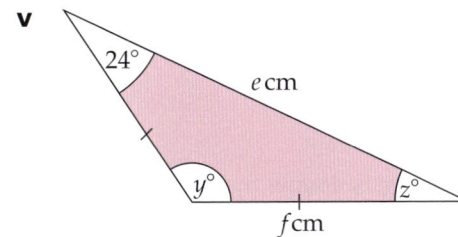

v
24°
e cm
$y°$
$z°$
f cm

‹ p.102

Problem solving

3 Del, Claire and Adam are standing in a triangle, labelled CAD, throwing a Frisbee.

Claire throws it to Adam at 60° to the line CD.

Adam throws it to Del at 60° to the line CA.

Del throws it to Claire at 60° to the line AD.

Are they standing equal distances apart?

C

A

D

12g Introducing circles

Rosie is drawing a circle to make a
Christmas tree bauble.
She uses a pair of compasses.

She sets her compasses
at a distance of 5 cm.

She keeps the point
still in the centre ...

... and spins them to
to draw a smooth circle.

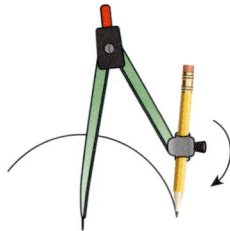

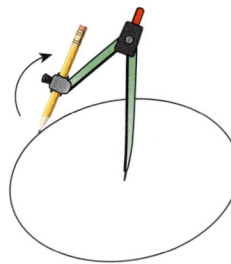

5 cm

The **radius** of the circle is 5 cm.
This is the distance you set your
compasses to draw the circle.

The **diameter** of the circle is 10 cm.

> ⬤ The **radius** of a circle is the distance from the centre to
> the edge.
> ⬤ The **diameter** of a circle is the distance all the way
> across through the centre.
> ▶ The diameter is double the length of the radius.

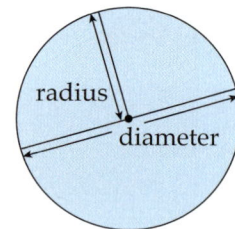

radius

diameter

Example

a   Use a ruler to measure the radius of this circle.
b   What is its diameter?

a   The radius is 1.5 cm.
b   Its diameter is double the radius.
    2 × 1.5 = 3 cm

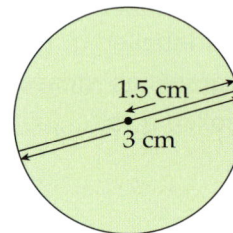

1.5 cm

3 cm

Rosie wants to put tinsel around the edge of her bauble.

> ⬤ The distance all the way around the edge
> of a circle is its **circumference**.

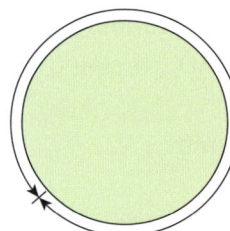

Circumference

Exercise 12g

1   Measure **i** the radius **ii** the diameter of each circle.

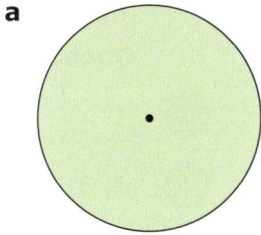

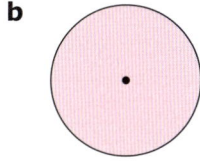

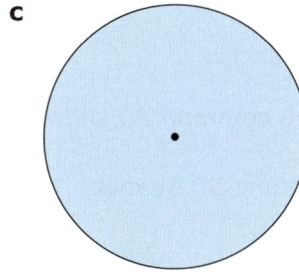

a

b

c

Did you know?

When you drop a stone into a still lake, you get circular ripples on the surface.

2   Peter has drawn three sketches of his design for a Christmas card.
Draw his designs accurately.

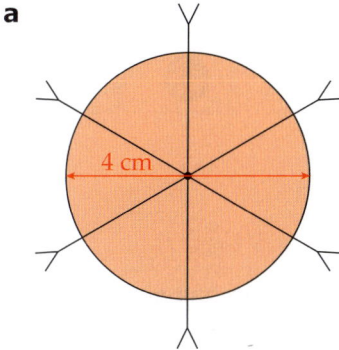

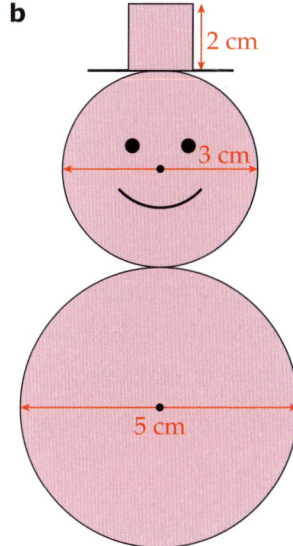

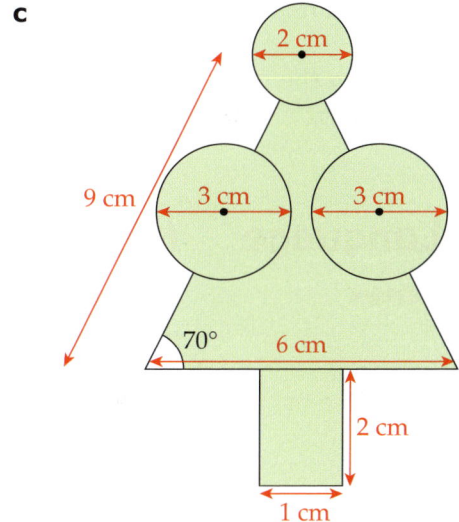

a

4 cm

b

2 cm

3 cm

5 cm

c

2 cm

9 cm

3 cm   3 cm

70°   6 cm

2 cm

1 cm

Problem solving

3   Here is a circle of diameter 5 cm.
Can you estimate the circumference using a
piece of string and a ruler?

5 cm

4   The Yin-Yang symbol is made from circles and parts of circles.
Can you draw it accurately?
Think carefully about how it is put together.

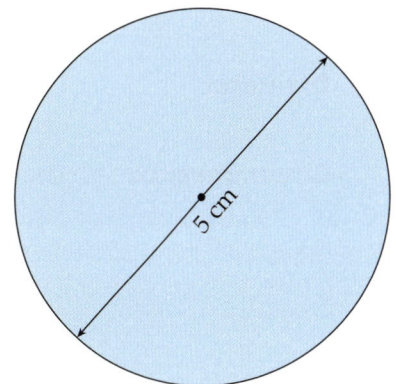

Check out

You should now be able to...

✓ Recognise and name common 3D shapes.	3	1
✓ Construct simple nets of 3D shapes.	4	2, 3
✓ Use 2D representations to visualise 3D shapes.	4	4
✓ Use a protractor to measure and draw angles.	5	5
✓ Use a ruler and protractor to construct a triangle.	5	5
✓ Know the parts of a circle.	4	6

Language	Meaning	Example
Vertex	The point on a 3D shape at which two or more edges meet (commonly known as the corner). The plural is vertices.	A cube has eight vertices
Net	The 2D shape that makes a 3D shape when it is folded.	Examples of nets on page 222
Construct	To draw a line, angle or shape accurately.	Page 230 shows you how to construct a triangle
Radius	The distance from the centre to the edge of a circle.	See page 232 for an illustration
Diameter	The distance across a circle through the centre. The diameter is twice the radius.	
Circumference	The distance around the edge of a circle.	

1

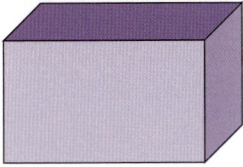

a What is this 3D shape called?
b How many faces does it have?
c How many edges does it have?
d How many vertices does it have?

2 a Which of these nets will fold to make a cube?

A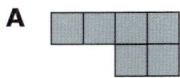

B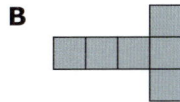

C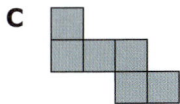

b Draw a differently shaped net that will fold to make a cube.

3

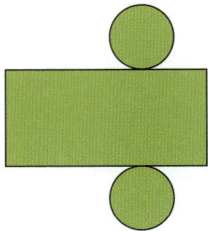

Which 3D shape is this a net of?

4 a Draw this cone from the top.
b Draw the cone from the side.

5 a Draw these triangles.

i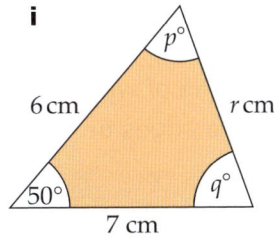

ii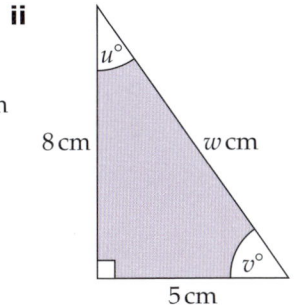

iii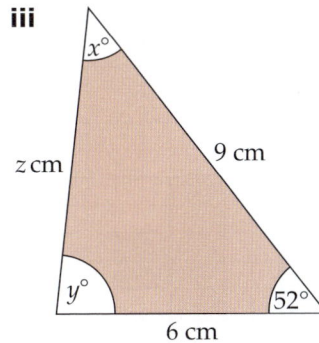

b On your drawings, measure the angles p, q, u, v, x and y.
c on your drawings, measure the sides r, w and z.

6

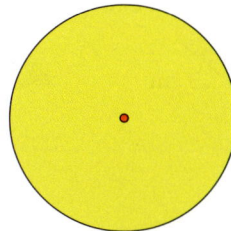

a For this circle, measure
  i the radius
  ii the diameter.
b Draw a circle with twice the radius.

What next?

Score		
	0 – 2	Your knowledge of this topic is still developing. To improve look at Formative test: 1A-12; MyMaths: 1078, 1081, 1090, 1098 and 1106
	3 – 5	You are gaining a secure knowledge of this topic. To improve look at InvisiPen: 321, 325, 326 and 371
	6	You have mastered this topic. Well done, you are ready to progress!

12a

1   Suggest possible 3D shapes from these descriptions.

   a   Six square faces

   b   Two faces, one of which is circular

   c   One face, no edges or vertices

12b

2   Which two nets will fold to make a cube?

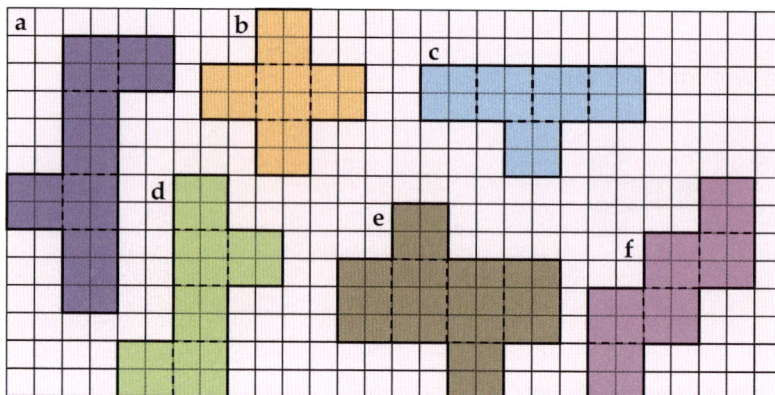

12c

3   Draw a net of each of these solids. Draw your nets accurately.

   a   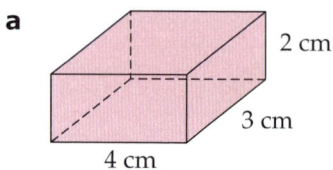   2 cm   3 cm   4 cm

   b   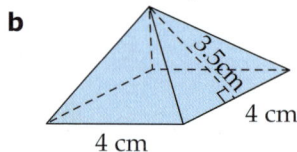   3.5 cm   4 cm   4 cm

   c   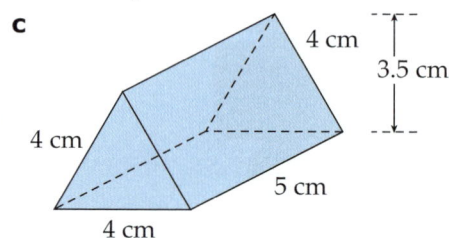   4 cm   3.5 cm   4 cm   5 cm   4 cm

12d

4   Draw the view from the top and side for each of these shapes.

   a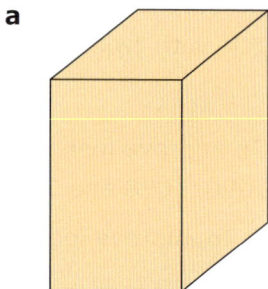

   b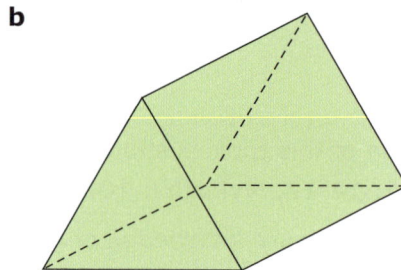

   c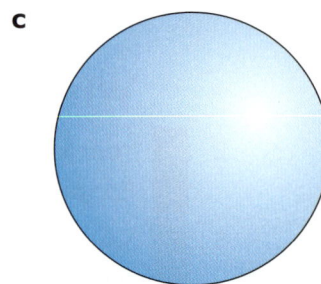

5 Measure these angles accurately using a protractor.

a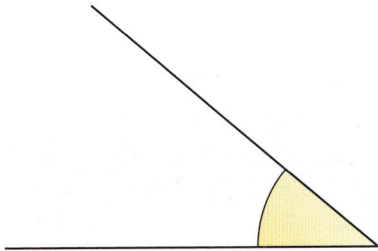

b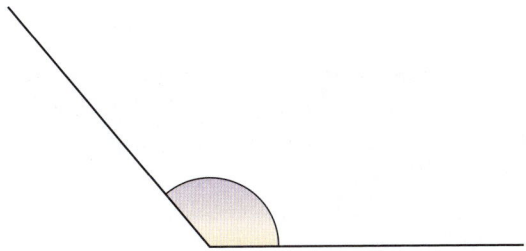

c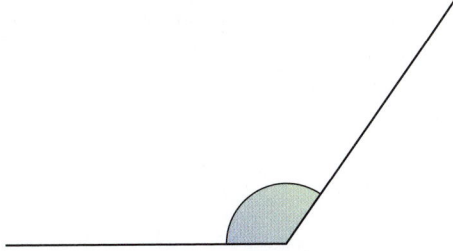

d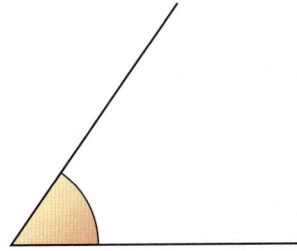

6 Draw these angles using a protractor.

   a 60°   **b** 140°   **c** 90°   **d** 45°   **e** 125°   **f** 75°

7 Draw these triangles accurately.

a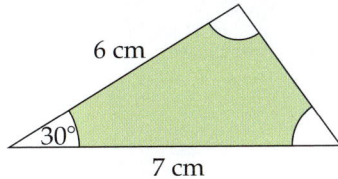

b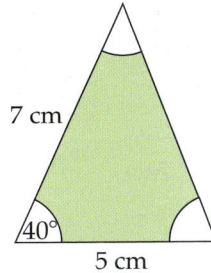

c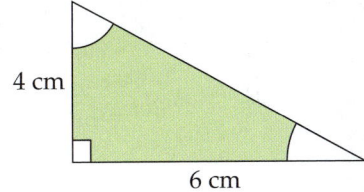

8 For each circle measure **i** the radius **ii** the diameter.

a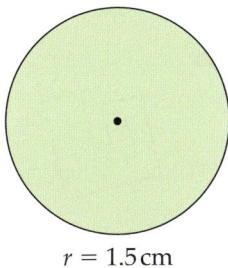

b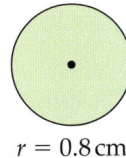

c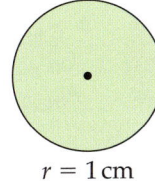

9 Draw circles with these measurements.

   a radius 4 cm   **b** radius 5.5 cm   **c** diameter 9 cm

Labyrinths and mazes have been used for a variety of purposes for thousands of years and have some interesting mathematical properties.

Labyrinths

A labyrinth is a maze with a single route that twists and turns but has no dead ends or junctions where you have to choose which way to go. When you follow the path of a labyrinth, it always takes you to the centre.

A coin from Knossos, Crete. About 280 BC

Task 1

Trace the route through the labyrinth. Do you travel along every part before reaching the centre?

Task 2

Follow these stages to draw a Cretan labyrinth. You might want to use squared paper.

a Start with this shape

b Join the bottom middle dot to the dot on its left

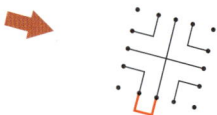

c Join the next free dot on the right to the next free dot on the left

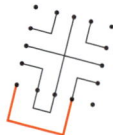

d Join the next free dot on the right to the next free dot on the left

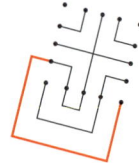

e Continue in the same way, always joining the next free dot on the right to the next free dot on the left. Always draw the lines around the bottom of the labyrinth.

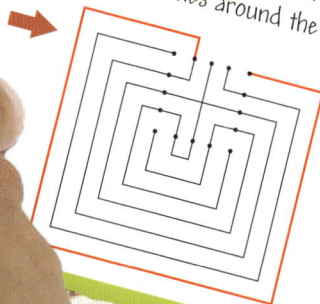

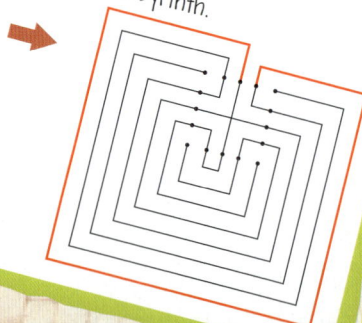

Task 3

Now try drawing a curved labyrinth in a similar way.

Mazes

A maze is more complicated than a labyrinth. It has dead ends and junctions where you have to choose which way to go. There may be only one correct route to the centre or to the exit, but it will be much harder to find.

With puzzle mazes, you often just have to find your way from the start to an exit.

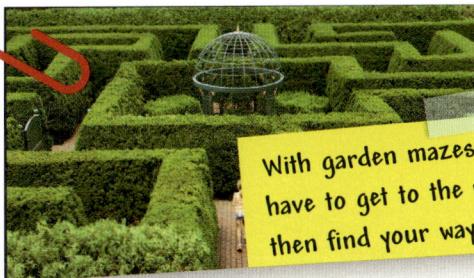

With garden mazes, you often have to get to the middle and then find your way to an exit.

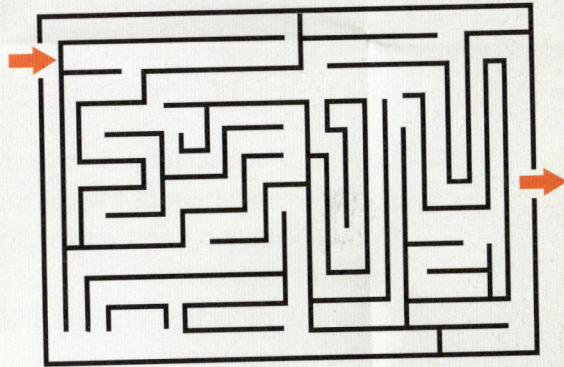

Task 4

Keep your RIGHT hand on the wall and you are bound to get out!

I thought you were meant to use your LEFT hand?

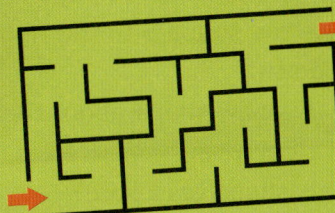

a Who is correct? Will the method work in the maze shown?
b What about the larger maze above?

Look at the way this maze is opened out:

c What happens to the walls inside the maze? How does that help explain why the hand-on-the-wall method works?

Task 5

In this maze, you have to reach the star near the centre of the maze, but keeping your hand on a wall won't get you to the star.

a Why does the method fail for this maze?
Hint: Try the hand on the wall method and keep track of the walls that you touch.

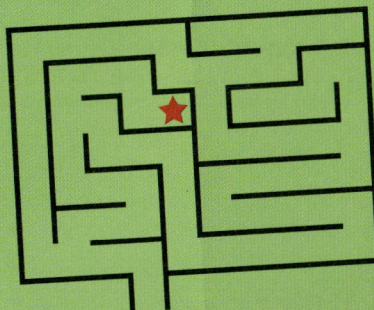

b You can add just one line to the maze to make the hand on a wall method work. Where would you add the line and why would it make the method work?

239

These questions will test you on your knowledge of the topics in chapters 9 to 12.
They give you practice in the types of questions that you may see in your GCSE exams.
There are 50 marks in this test.

1   Look at these shapes. Copy or trace them and draw the lines of symmetry.

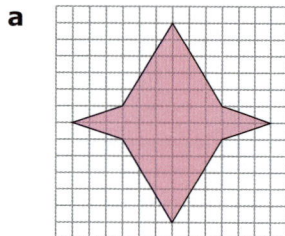

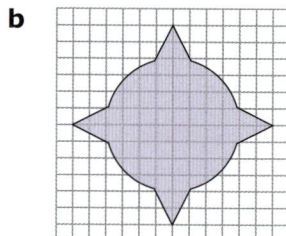

    a   b   (2 marks)

2   Look at these shapes. The dashed
line is the position of the mirror line.
Copy each shape and mirror line onto
squared paper.
Draw the reflection of each shape
in the mirror line.

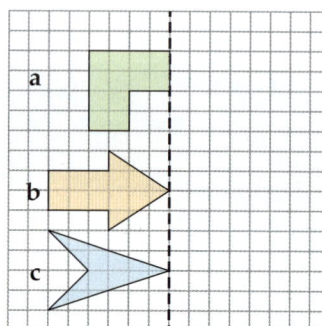

                                                                           (3 marks)

3   Copy this shape on squared paper.
    a   Translate the shape 5 to the right,
          then 5 down.   (2 marks)
    b   Rotate this new shape about the
          dot 90° clockwise.   (2 marks)
    c   Does this shape tessellate?   (1 mark)

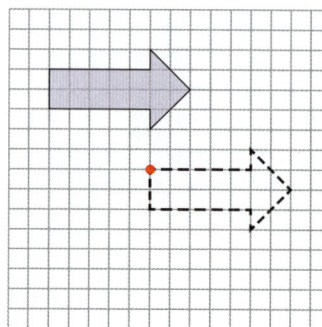

4   Work out the outputs
for this function.   (3 marks)

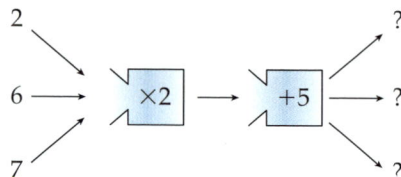

2 →   → ?
6 → ×2 → +5 → ?
7 →   → ?

5   Copy and complete this function machine.
Replace the ? mark with the correct
number and operation.

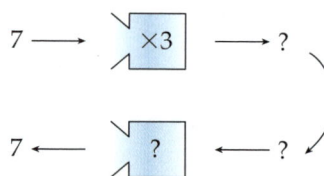

7 → ×3 → ?

7 ← ? ← ?

                                                                (3 marks)

6 Find the value that makes each equation balance.

    a $4 + y = 7$ (1 mark)   **b** $t + 18 = 23$ (1 mark)

    c $25 + n = 34$ (1 mark)   **d** $4 + 9 = 6 + m$ (1 mark)

7 Use function machines to find the value of the letter in each equation.

    a $w + 9 = 14$ (1 mark)   **b** $8 \times p = 40$ (1 mark)

    c $d - 8 = 4$ (1 mark)   **d** $f \div 5 = 6$ (1 mark)

    e $14 - g = 4$ (1 mark)

8 Fill in the missing factors for the number 12.

    The factors of 12 are ☐ , 2, ☐ , 4, ☐ , ☐   (2 marks)

9 Write down all multiples of four which are **less than** 30.   (2 marks)

10 Here is a list of some square numbers. Copy and complete the list.

    a $5^2 = 5 \times ? = 25$ (1 mark)   **b** $8^2 = ? \times ? = ?$ (1 mark)

    c $?^2 = 7 \times ? = ?$ (1 mark)   **d** $?^2 = ? \times ? = 81$ (1 mark)

11 Which numbers from this group: 75, 550, 256, 349, 642, 123

    cannot be **divided exactly** by at least one of the numbers 2, 3, 4, 5 or 10?   (2 marks)

12 Name the shapes that have these properties.

    a Circular base and top and no straight sides   (1 mark)

    b Six faces, twelve edges not all the same size and eight vertices   (1 mark)

13 Here is a cube.
Draw this as a net
on squared paper.   (2 marks)

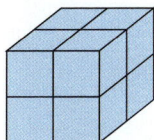

14 Here are the nets of some 3D objects. Identify the 3D objects in each case.   (3 marks)

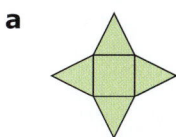

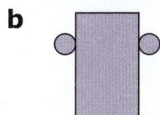

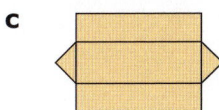

    a   **b**   **c**

15 a   Using a ruler, protractor or   (4 marks)
        compasses, draw these shapes
        to scale.

    b   What are the lengths p, q and r?   (3 marks)

    c   What size is the angle x?   (1 mark)

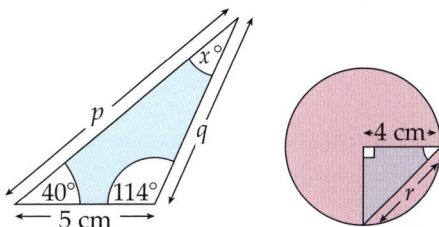

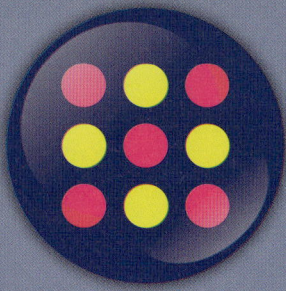

13 Sequences

Introduction

Humans are good at spotting patterns. You can see patterns all around you in the natural world – there are symmetrical patterns in snowflakes and starfish, complex spirals in shells and pineapples, and fractal-like patterns in clouds and coastlines. There are patterns in the way rivers meander, patterns in the sand as the tides ebb and flow, patterns in crystals, patterns in birdsong, and patterns in the markings of animals like zebras and leopards.

What's the point?

By following the patterns that occur in nature, we can understand natural phenomena and predict possible changes.

Objectives

By the end of this chapter, you will have learned how to …
- Find patterns in sequences of numbers.
- Describe a sequence using a rule to find the next term.
- Generate terms in a sequence using a rule.
- Use negative numbers in a sequence.

Check in

1 **a** Write all the even numbers between 19 and 29.

   b Write all the odd numbers between 10 and 20.

2 **a** Put these temperatures in order, starting with the lowest.

   5°C, 3°C, -2°C, 1°C, -9°C

   b Put these numbers in order, starting with the smallest.

   4, -3, 0, 2, -1, 1, -7

Starter problem

Here are the first three terms of a sequence made from
exactly 15 circles.

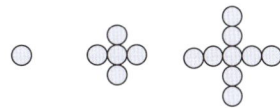

Describe the sequence in words.

Use the 15 circles to make the first three terms of a different sequence.

Describe your new sequence in words.

Can you find another sequence that uses all 15 circles?

Investigate.

Every Saturday, Ilisha counts the number of leaves on her pea plant as it grows.

Number of
leaves: 1 3 5 7 9

She writes the number of leaves as a **sequence**.

1, 3, 5, 7, 9

She shows the sequence on a number line.

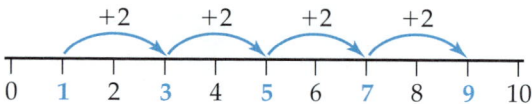

> My plant is growing two new leaves each week.

<p.14

Example

Ted is demolishing a brick wall. He removes four bricks at a time.

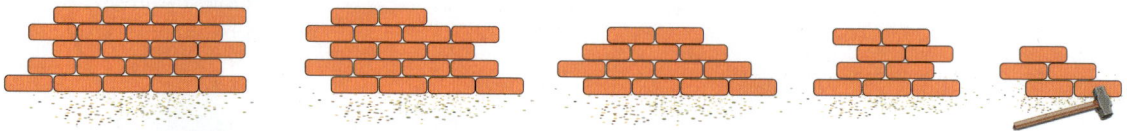

a Write the number of bricks remaining as a sequence.
b Show this sequence on a number line.
c How many bricks will be left after one more swing of Ted's hammer?

a 21, 17, 13, 9, 5   Count the bricks.

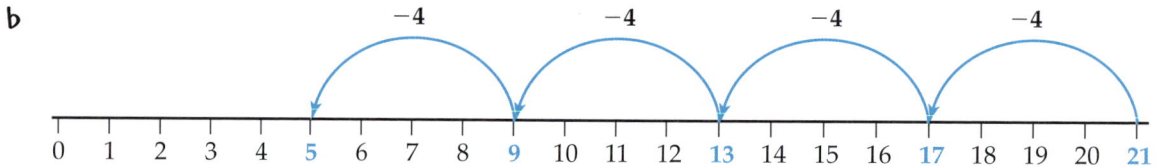

b

<p.132

c The number of bricks left will go down by 4
   5 − 4 = 1 brick left.

Exercise 13a

1 Write the missing numbers on these scarf sequences.

a

| 31 | | 33 | 34 | | 36 | | 38 |

b

| 3 | | 7 | | 11 | 13 | | 17 | 19 |

c

| 6 | | | 15 | | 21 | | 27 |

d

| 41 | | 33 | | | 21 | | 13 |

2 Write these patterns as number sequences.

a

b

c

d

3 a Write the sequence shown on each number line.

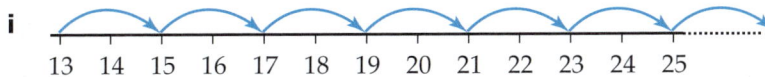

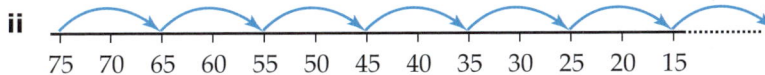

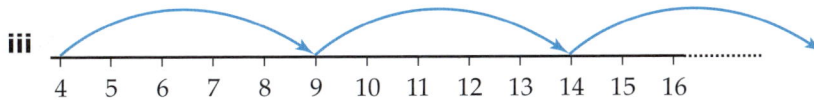

i

13 14 15 16 17 18 19 20 21 22 23 24 25

ii

75 70 65 60 55 50 45 40 35 30 25 20 15

iii

4 5 6 7 8 9 10 11 12 13 14 15 16

b What is the difference between the numbers in each sequence?

c Find the next number in each sequence.

Did you know?

▲ A sequencer is an electronic musical device that stores sequences of notes and plays them back.

Problem solving

4 Find the next two numbers in each sequence.

a 5, 8, 11, 14, ..., ...

b 7, 13, 19, 25, ..., ...

c 32, 28, 24, 20, ..., ...

d 2, 4, 8, 16, ..., ...

5 Find the number of small triangles needed to make the next two diagrams.

6 Sam has mixed up his sequence, and he has lost some numbers.
Can you write out his sequence in order and identify the missing numbers?

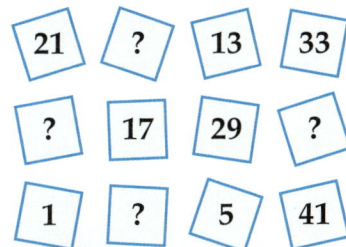

| 21 | ? | 13 | 33 |

| ? | 17 | 29 | ? |

| 1 | ? | 5 | 41 |

Harry is loading apples into a crate.

He starts with an empty crate and adds 2 apples time.

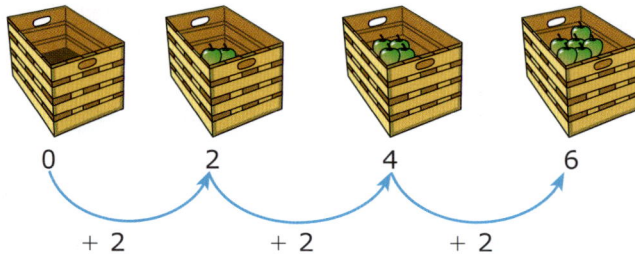

| 0 | 2 | 4 | 6 |

+ 2   + 2   + 2

Harry thinks he can do it faster!

He starts with 4 and multiplies by 2 each time.

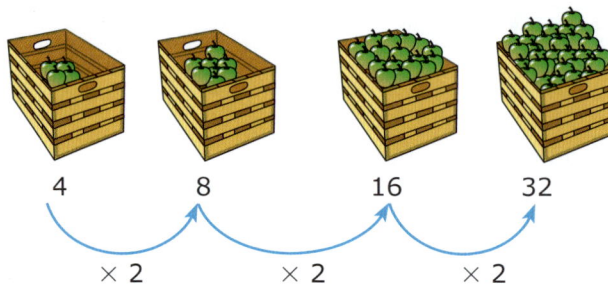

| 4 | 8 | 16 | 32 |

× 2   × 2   × 2

The **rule** tells you how to get to the next number.

⬤ To make a sequence you need a **starting number** and a **rule**.

For example, start at 10 and +2 each time.   10, 12, 14, 16

+2 +2 +2

Example

Describe these sequences.

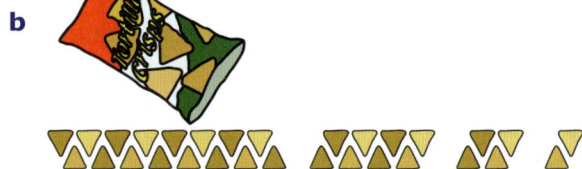

a

b

a Write down the sequence.

10, 7, 4, 1

−3   −3   −3

The rule is −3.

Start at 10 and −3.

b Write down the sequence.

16, 8, 4, 2

÷2 ÷2 ÷2

The rule is ÷2.

Start at 16 ÷ 2.

Exercise 13b

1 **a** Write each tile pattern as a number
   sequence.

   i

   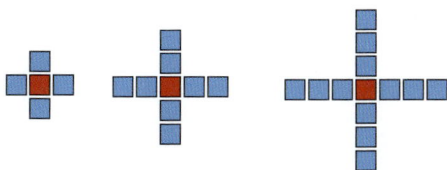

   ii

   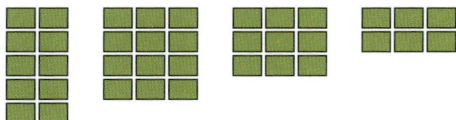

   iii

   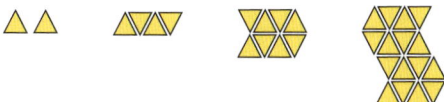

   iv

   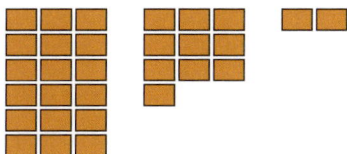

   b Describe each sequence using
   'Start at ____ and ____.'

   c Find the next two numbers in each
   sequence.

2 Match each description with a sequence.

a	Start at 100 and ÷ 2
b	Start at 1 and + 7
c	Start at 100 and × 2
d	Start at 100 and − 50
e	Start at 1 and × 3
f	Start at 1 and + 3

A	100, 50, 0, -50, -100
B	100, 50, 25, 12.5
C	100, 200, 400, 800, 1600
D	1, 3, 9, 27, 81
E	1, 4, 7, 10, 13, 16
F	1, 8, 15, 22, 29

3 Write a description for each sequence.

   a 1, 2, 4, 8 … **b** 1, 3, 9, 27 …
   c 8, 11, 14, 17 … **d** 5, 25, 125, 625 …
   e 24, 12, 6, 3 … **f** -9, -6, -3, 0 …
   g 19, 15, 11, 7 … **h** 2, 3.5, 5, 6.5 …

Problem solving

4 Ernie the explorer is crossing an old
   rope bridge. He steps on the first plank,
   then every third plank after that.
   He sees a gap ahead. The 17th plank is
   missing. Will he fall through the hole?

   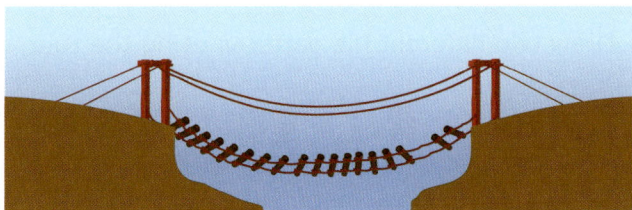

5 Write the next three terms in this sequence.
   23, 18, 13, 8, ☐, ☐, ☐
   Explain how you know that 0 cannot be a
   term in this sequence.
   What is the value of the term nearest to 0?

Did you know?

People have used
sequences of
pictures to tell a
story as far back
as the Stone Age.

Ilisha's bean plant grows two more leaves each week.
The **rule** is 'add 2 leaves'.

She wants to use
the rule to draw
the pattern.

> But where
> do I start?

WEEK 1 2 3 4   OR   WEEK 1 2 3 4

In week 1, the plant has 2 leaves.
Now Ilisha can draw the sequence.

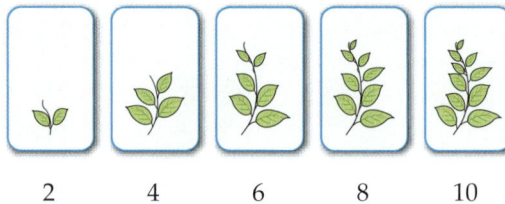

2   4   6   8   10

🔴 The numbers in a sequence are called the **terms**.

> The first term of
> a sequence is the
> starting number.

This table shows how Ilisha's bean plant grows.

Week	1	2	3	4	5
Number of leaves	2	4	6	8	10

↑ 1st term   ↑ 2nd term   ↑ 3rd term   ↑ 4th term   ↑ 5th term

Example

Draw two different tile patterns using the rule 'add 3'. Draw five terms.

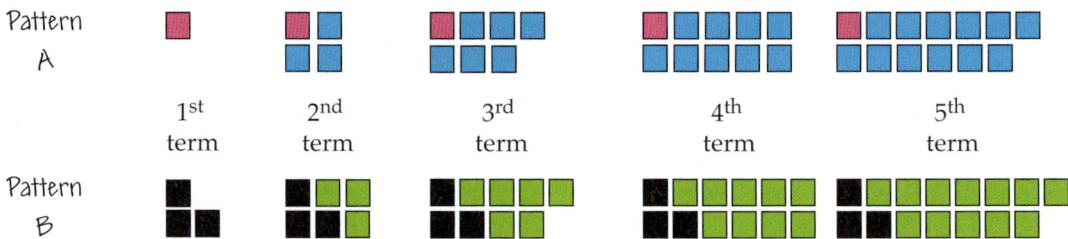

Pattern A

1st term   2nd term   3rd term   4th term   5th term

Pattern B

Example

Write the sequence
'Start at 29 and -3'.
Stop at the 4th term.

Use a number line.

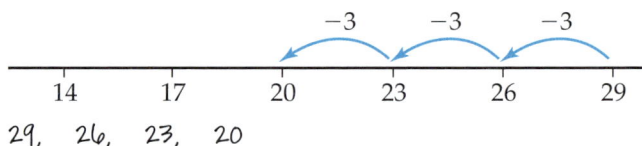

−3   −3   −3

14   17   20   23   26   29

29,   26,   23,   20

Exercise 13c

1 **a** Draw any pattern of tiles that has the rule 'add 4'.
       Draw four terms.
   b Write your pattern as a sequence of numbers.

2 This plant loses three leaves each week.

   a Draw the pattern for the next three weeks.
   b What is the first term of the sequence?
   c Describe this sequence fully in words.

3 Here is a sequence of numbers:
   95, 90, 85, 80, …
   a What is the rule?
   b What is the next term?
   c Would 24 be in this sequence? Give your reason.

4 Write the first four terms of each sequence.
   a 'Start at 6 and +4'
   b 'Start at 80 and ÷2'
   c 'Start at 2 and ×3'
   d 'Start at 25 and −6'
   e 'Start at 11 and +7'

Problem solving

5 A lift starts on the 2nd floor of a building.
   It stops every three floors.
   There are 20 floors in the building.
   Write the journey of the lift as a sequence.

6 These two lifts are in the same building.
   The building has 20 floors.
   The North lift starts at floor 1 and stops at every three floors.
   The South lift starts at floor 3 and stops at every two floors.
   a Write each lift's journey as a sequence.
   b On which floors do both lifts stop?
   c Which floors have no stop?

7 Chelsea lives in the 10th house to the left of number 113. Calculate the number of Chelsea's house.

Did you know?

The seeds of a sunflower grow in a spiral sequence pattern.

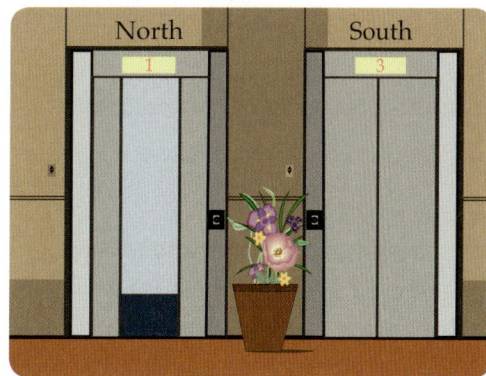

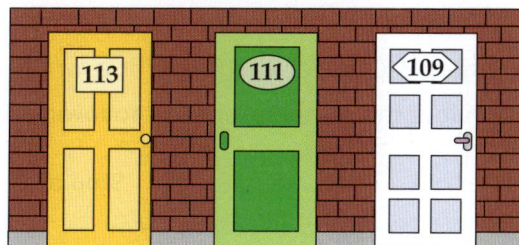

⬤ Sequences can involve negative numbers as well as positive numbers.

Tyler borrowed £12 from his dad to buy a computer game.
He owes his dad £12.
He pays him back £3 per week.

I have negative £12! How long will it take to pay Dad back?

‹ p.14

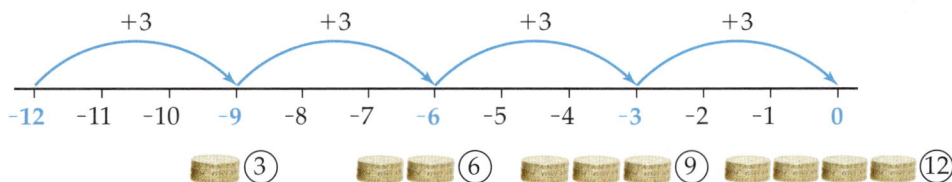

The sequence is 'start at -12 and add 3.'
It takes 4 weeks to pay his dad back.

Example

Maria owes £16 and is paying her friend back using this sequence.
   -£16, -£12, -£8, -£4
a   How much does she pay back each week?
b   How long will it take her to pay back her friend?

a   The rule is add 4.
    She pays back £4 each week.
b   4 weeks

⬤ You can find the first term of a sequence by working backwards.

Example

Write the first term of this sequence.
☐, 2, 7, 12, 17

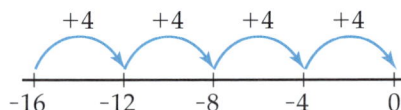

The rule is add 5.
Work backwards from the second term.
This means −5.

‹ 10b

The first term is $2 - 5 = -3$

Example

The minimum night-time temperature on Wednesday was 2°C.

It gets 3°C colder each day for a whole week!

What is the temperature the following Tuesday?

-16°C is very cold indeed!

2, −1, −4, −7, −10, −13, −16   Stop at the 7th term.
The temperature on Tuesday is −16°C.

Exercise 13d

1 Fill in the missing numbers in these scarves.

a

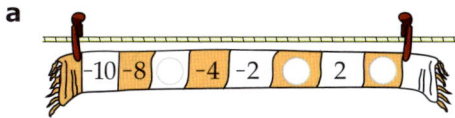

b

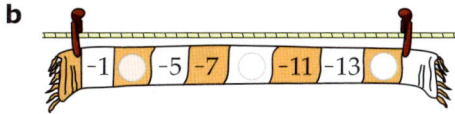

2 Sam has borrowed £15. If he pays back £5 per week how long will it take for him to pay back completely?

3 Use these number lines to help you find the missing terms. Write the rule for each sequence.

a -10, -7 ☐, ☐, ☐

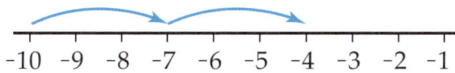

3 b -15, -12, -9, ☐, ☐

c ☐, -3, -1, 1, ☐

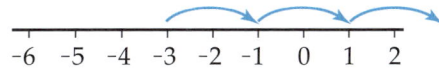

d ☐, ☐, -4, -2, 0

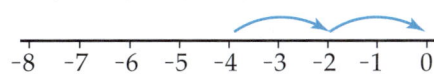

e 2, 0, -2, -4, ☐

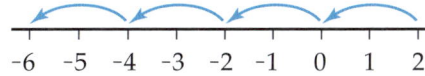

f ☐, 1, -2, -5, ☐, ☐, ☐

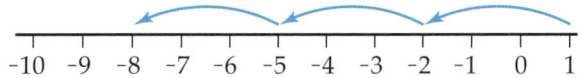

Problem solving

4 Chloe is doing an experiment.
She has cooled down a very strong salt solution and is allowing it to warm up.
She records its temperature every minute on this table.
Copy the table and fill in the missing temperatures.

Time (minutes)	0	1	2	3	4	5	6
Temperature (°C)			-2	2	6	10	

5 Sam owes money!
If he promises not to spend any more until September, when will he pay back completely?

Date		Money IN	Money OUT	Total
2 July	Pocket money	£10	/	- £55
9 July	Pocket money	£10	/	- £45
16 July	Pocket money	£10	/	- £35
23 July	Pocket money	£10	/	- £25

Check out

You should now be able to ...

Test it ➡

Questions

✓ Find patterns in sequences of numbers.	3	1, 2
✓ Describe a sequence using a rule to find the next term.	4	3, 4
✓ Generate terms in a sequence using a rule.	4	5
✓ Use negative numbers in a sequence.	4	6 – 8

Language	Meaning	Example
Sequence	A set of numbers that follow a rule.	1, 3, 5, 7, 9, ...
Rule	An operation to describe the link between two numbers that are next to each other in a sequence.	To get from 7 to 9, you apply the rule 'add 2'
Term	A number in a sequence. (The word 'term' is also used to mean part of an expression in algebra).	The second term is 3

1 Write this pattern as a number sequence.

2 Find the next two numbers in each sequence.
  a 3, 6, 9, 12, …, …
  b 5, 9, 13, 17, …, …
  c 8, 14, 20, 26, …, …
  d 3, 15, 27, 39, …, …
  e 50, 48, 46, 44, …, …
  f 60, 52, 44, 36, …, …

3 Write a description for each sequence.
  a 7, 17, 27, 37, …
  b 9, 16, 23, 30, …
  c 30, 27, 24, 21, …
  d 2, 4, 8, 16, …
  e 3, 12, 48, 192, …
  f 200, 100, 50, 25, …

4 For each sequence
  i   describe the sequence
  ii find the next two terms in the sequence.
  a

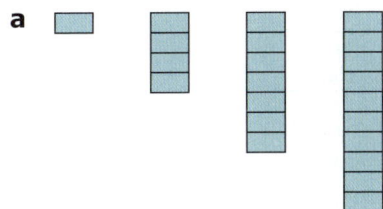

b

5 Work out the first four terms of the sequences with these descriptions.
  a *Start at 3 and +5*
  b *Start at 7 and +11*
  c *Start at 50 and -9*
  d *Start at 2 and ×5*
  e *Start at 1 and ×6*
  f *Start at 5000 and ÷10*

6 Find the missing terms of each sequence.
  a -12, -8, …, 0, …
  b -1, …, -5, -7, …
  c -18, …, -4, 3, …

7 Write a description for each sequence.
  a -17, -11, -5, 1, 7
  b -5, -8, -11, -14, -17

8 Work out the first four terms of the sequences with these descriptions.
  a *Start at 9 and -7*
  b *Start at -14 and +8*
  c *Start at -7 and -11*

What next?

Score	0 – 3		Your knowledge of this topic is still developing. To improve look at Formative test: 1A-13; MyMaths: 1173
	4 – 6		You are gaining a secure knowledge of this topic. To improve look at InvisiPen: 281
	7 – 8		You have mastered this topic. Well done, you are ready to progress!

13a

1 Write the missing terms in each sequence.

a 8, 10, ___ , 14, 16   **b** 0, ___ , 14, 21, 28

c 21, 18, 15, 12, ___   **d** 2, 4, 6, ___ , 10

e ___ , 6, 18, 54, 162   **f** 11, ___ , 17, 20, ___

g ___ , 16, 14, ___ , 10   **h** 33, ___ , 22, 17, ___

i 8, ___ , ___ , 20, 24   **j** ___ , ___ , 19, 15, 11

2 Jack is on his 'Space Hopper'. He is bouncing along a number line.

a

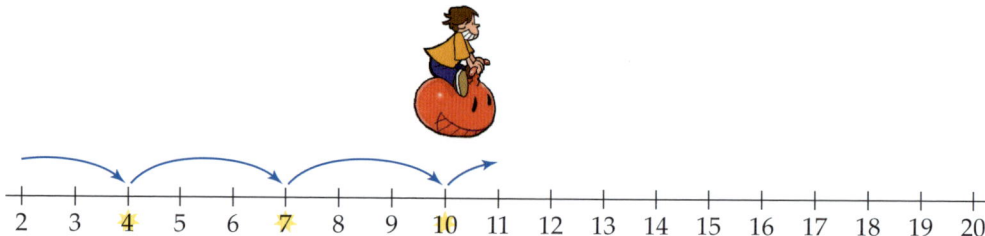

What is the next number Jack will land on? What is the rule?

b

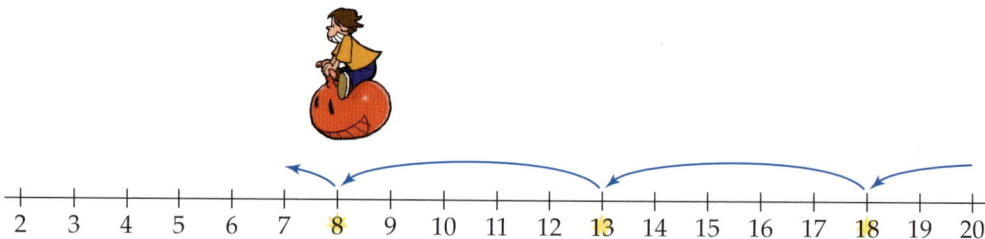

What is the next number Jack will land on? What is the rule?

3 What is the next number in each sequence?

a 2, 4, 6, 8, ___   **b** 1, 4, 7, 10, ___

c 3, 5, 7, 9, ___   **d** 2, 6, 10, 14, ___

e 5, 10, 15, 20, ___   **f** 10, 20, 30, 40, ___

g 9, 7, 5, 3, ___   **h** 15, 12, 9, 6, ___

i 20, 16, 12, 8, ___   **j** 60, 50, 40, 30, ___

13b

4 Match the sequences on the right with the statements on the left.

a	'Multiply by 3'
b	'Add 35'
c	'Divide by 4'
d	'Multiply by 5'
e	'Subtract 25'
f	'Divide by 6'

A	105, 80, 55, 30
B	45, 80, 115, 150
C	768, 192, 48, 12
D	25, 75, 225, 675
E	12, 60, 300, 1500
F	5400, 900, 150, 25

Algebra Sequences

5 Write the first four numbers in each sequence using the rule.

   a   The first number is 2. The rule is +4.

   b   The first number is 5. The rule is +3.

   c   The first number is 21. The rule is −3.

   d   The first number is 50. The rule is −10.

   e   The first number is 11. The rule is +5.

   f   The first number is 24. The rule is −4.

6 Write out the first five terms for each sequence.

   a   Start at 4. The rule is +5.   **b**   Start at 23. The rule is −3.

   c   Start at 0. The rule is +4.   **d**   Start at 21. The rule is −4.

   e   Start at 30. The rule is +2.   **f**   Start at 32. The rule is −5.

7 Copy and complete this description for each of these sequences:

> Start at _____. The rule is _____.

   a   1, 4, 7, 10, …   **b**   17, 14, 11, 8, …   **c**   9, 13, 17, 21, …

   d   80, 70, 60, 50, ….   **e**   29, 24, 19, 14, …   **f**   8, 15, 22, 29, …

8 Copy and complete these statements for each of the sequences.

> ▶ The rule is _____.
>
> ▶ The next three terms are _____, _____, _____.

   a   2, 5, 8, 11, …   **b**   2, 3, 4, 5, …

   c   20, 18, 16, 14, 12, …   **d**   5, 7, 9, 11, 13, ….

   e   2, 10, 18, 26, …   **f**   3, 6, 9, 12, 15, …

   f   30, 26, 22, 18, 14, …   **h**   20, 30, 40, 50, …

9 Use the number lines to help you find the missing terms.

   a

-22 -20 -18 -16 -14 -12 -10 -8 -6 -4 -2 0   -22, -18, -14, ☐, ☐, ☐

   b

-10 -9 -8 -7 -6 -5 -4 -3 -2 -1 0 1 2 3   ☐, -7, -4, ☐, ☐, ☐

   c

-10 -9 -8 -7 -6 -5 -4 -3 -2 -1 0 1 2 3   3, ☐, -5, ☐, ☐, ☐

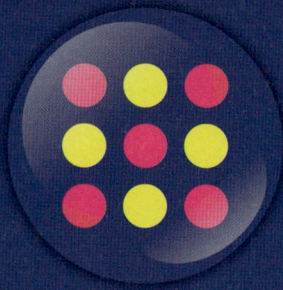

Introduction

Scott Flansburg is known as the 'human calculator'. He is in the Guinness Book of World Records for adding the same number to itself more times in 15 seconds than a person can do using a calculator. Scott uses lots of different strategies to do his calculations so quickly rather than relying on just one method.

What's the point?

Having a range of mental strategies might not turn you into the next 'human calculator' but it will help you to make important decisions about your money quickly and accurately.

Objectives

By the end of this chapter, you will have learned how to ...

- Consolidate multiplication facts up to 12×12.
- Multiply by 10 and 100.
- Multiply whole numbers using mental and written methods.
- Divide whole numbers using mental and efficient written methods.
- Use a calculator and interpret the display in different contexts, including money.

Check in

1 Copy and complete these additions and subtractions.

a
```
    3 3
  + 1 6
  _____
  □ □
```

b
```
    2 8
  − 1 2
  _____
  □ □
```

c
```
    5 6
  + 2 □
  _____
  □ 9
```

d
```
    1 6 □
  − □ 2
  _____
  □ 1 2
```

e
```
    □ 1 5
  + 3 □ 2
  _____
  9 5 □
```

Starter problem

Here is a different way to multiply 53 × 57.

The first digit is a 5. Add one to this digit to get 6.

Multiply 5 × 6 and you get **30** as your first answer.

Multiply the units digits of each number together 3 × 7 = **21** is your second answer.

Put the two answers together and you get **3021**.

Try multiplying 53 × 57 and see what you get....

Investigate.

14a Multiplication

4 people have 3 balloons each.

3 + 3 + 3 + 3 = 12

They have 12 balloons altogether.

What if 9 people have 7 balloons each?

7 + 7 + 7 + 7 + 7 + 7 + 7 + 7 + 7

9 × 7 = 63

They have 63 balloons altogether.

It's easier to use multiplication facts than to use repeated addition.

⬤ Knowing your **multiplication tables** lets you calculate faster.

Example

Fill in the numbers missing from this multiplication table.

×	1	2	3	4	5
1	1				
2	2		6		
3					15
4	4				
5		10			

1 × 2 = 2   2 × 2 = 4

×	1	2	3	4	5
1	1	2	3	4	5
2	2	4	6	8	10
3	3	6	9	12	15
4	4	8	12	16	20
5	5	10	15	20	25

Example

Jacob's bike has two wheels.

He and four friends take their bikes to the park.

How many wheels are there altogether?

There are 5 bikes.

5 × 2 = 10

There are 10 wheels altogether.

Exercise 14a

1 Fill in the numbers missing from each multiplication table.

a

×	1	2	3	4	5	6
1					5	
2						
3		6				
4						
5			15			
6						

b

×	7	8	9	10	11	12
7						
8						96
9	63			90		
10						
11					121	
12						

2 Use multiplication facts to calculate each answer.

a 2 × 4 **b** 3 × 5 **c** 7 × 2
d 8 × 4 **e** 5 × 5 **f** 3 × 7
g 1 × 9 **h** 10 × 4 **i** 6 × 3
j 9 × 9 **k** 8 × 2 **l** 8 × 7
m 4 × 5 **n** 7 × 8 **o** 4 × 7

3 Match tiles with the same value.

12 × 3		132
12 × 11		81
9 × 7		36
11 × 10		63
9 × 9		110

Problem solving

4 Each house has 10 windows.
How many windows do 8 houses have?

5 Each photo frame has 6 studs.
How many studs do you need to decorate 6 frames?

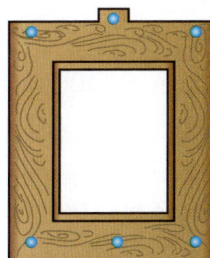

6 11 girls play for the Woodley Wolves football team.
a Each girl has one pair of boots. How many boots are there altogether?
b Each girl takes 5 practice shots at the goal. How many shots are taken in all?

MyMaths.co.uk 1367 SEARCH

14b Multiplying by 10 and 100

Luja knows how to multiply by 10 quickly. She imagines a place value table.

> To multiply 3 by 10, the 3 digit moves one place to the left.
>
> | H | T | U |
> |---|---|---|
> | | | 3 |
> | | 3 | 0 |

> Move the digits one place to the left and put a 0 in the units column.

🔴 To multiply a number by 10, move the digits one place to the left.

Example

Multiply these numbers by 10.

a 35 **b** 712 **c** 230

a

H	T	U
	3	5
3	5	0

35 × 10 = 350

b

Th	H	T	U
	7	1	2
7	1	2	0

712 × 10 = 7120

c

Th	H	T	U
	2	3	0
2	3	0	0

230 × 10 = 2300

Luja also knows how to multiply by 100.

> To multiply 4 by 100, the 4 digit moves two places to the left.
>
> | H | T | U |
> |---|---|---|
> | | | 4 |
> | 4 | 0 | 0 |

> Move the digits two places to the left and fill the gaps with two 0s.

🔴 To multiply a number by 100, move the digits two places to the left.

Example

Multiply these numbers by 100.

a 35 **b** 712 **c** 230

a

Th	H	T	U
		3	5
3	5	0	0

35 × 100 = 3500

b

T Th	Th	H	T	U
		7	1	2
7	1	2	0	0

712 × 100 = 71 200

c

T Th	Th	H	T	U
		2	3	0
2	3	0	0	0

230 × 100 = 23 000

Number Multiplying and dividing

Exercise 14b

1 Multiply these numbers by 10.

   a 3   **b** 8   **c** 7   **d** 9   **e** 16   **f** 17   **g** 19

   h 20   **i** 50   **j** 971   **k** 607   **l** 670   **m** 500   **n** 707

2 Multiply these numbers by 100.

   a 3   **b** 5   **c** 12   **d** 15   **e** 17   **f** 24   **g** 35

   h 60   **i** 90   **j** 468   **k** 506   **l** 380   **m** 700   **n** 909

3 One pipe is 10 metres long.

Two pipes joined together measure $2 \times 10m = 20m$.

Work out the total lengths of these joined-up pipes.

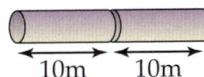

10m   10m

‹ p.38

   a   Work out 3×10 metres.

   b

   c

   d

4 The total length of 25 of the pipes from question **3** is

$25 \times 10m = 250m$

Work out the lengths of these numbers of pipes.

   a 9 pipes   **b** 11 pipes   **c** 19 pipes   **d** 23 pipes

   e 7 pipes   **f** 35 pipes   **g** 42 pipes   **h** 44 pipes

   i 20 pipes   **j** 123 pipes   **k** 240 pipes   **l** 300 pipes

Problem solving

5 A bag of cement weighs 10 kg.

   a If you need 50 kg of cement, how many bags would you buy?

   b If you need 40 kg of cement, how many bags would you buy?

   c Lisa can carry 30 kg. How many bags can Lisa carry?

   d Look at the picture.

      The top bag has split and spilled 3 kg of cement.

      What do the four bags weigh now?

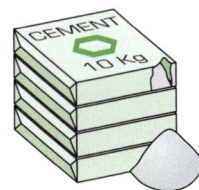

6 Ethan's glass holds 100 mℓ of water.

   a If he drinks 4 glasses in a day, how much water has he drunk?

   b If he drinks 22 glasses in a week, how much water has he drunk?

   c He drinks 15 glasses the next week. How much water is this?

   d How much is 15 glasses of water in litres?

1 litre = 1000 mℓ

14c Mental methods of multiplication

You can think of multiplication as **repeated addition**.

so 56 × 3 = 56 + 56 + 56

You might need to then work this out on paper.

However there are tricks you can use to multiply quickly in your head.

$$\begin{array}{r} 56 \\ 56 \\ +56 \\ \hline 168 \end{array}$$

Quick multiplying by 10 and 100

To **multiply** 46 by 10, move the **digits** one place left.

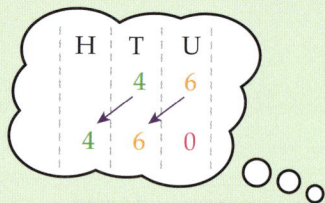

H	T	U
	4	6
4	6	0

46 × 10 = 460

To multiply 46 by 100, move the digits two places to the left.

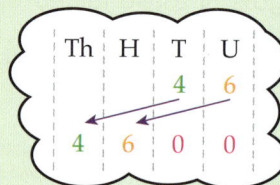

Th	H	T	U
		4	6
4	6	0	0

46 × 100 = 4600

Use zeros to fill gaps in the T and U columns.

Partitioning

Split numbers into simpler numbers.

16 × 5

Split 16 into 1 ten and 6 units.

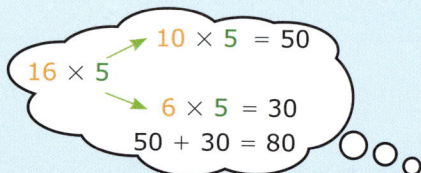

16 × 5
10 × 5 = 50
6 × 5 = 30
50 + 30 = 80

16 × 5 = 80

Doubling and halving

13 × 8

Double the first number and **halve** the second one. Repeat this three times. Make **jottings** to help.

13 × 8 = 104

13 × 8
×2   ÷2
26 × 4
×2   ÷2
52 × 2
×2   ÷2
104 × 1

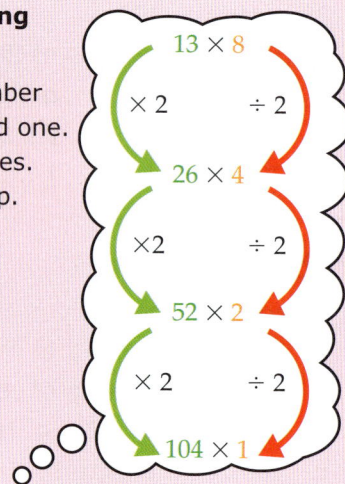

To work out 56 × 3, I'd use partitioning.
50 × 3 = 150, and
6 × 3 = 18
150 + 18 equals 168.

To work out 56 × 4, I'd use doubling and halving.
56 × 4 = 112 × 2
= 224

Exercise 14c

1 Fill in the missing numbers.

   a $2 \times \square = 8$ **b** $5 \times \square = 20$

   c $3 \times 6 = \square$ **d** $\square \times 10 = 40$

   e $7 \times 3 = \square$ **f** $\square \times 2 = 16$

   g $5 \times \square = 35$ **h** $\square \times 4 = 32$

2 Complete these multiplication problems.
Make jottings to show your working.

   a 20×5 **b** 30×6

   c 40×5 **d** 20×12

2 **e** 40×10 **f** 15×4

   g 13×3 **h** 18×4

   i 22×5 **j** 30×6

3 Use mental methods to solve these problems.

   a 35×2 **b** 39×2

   c 43×10 **d** 53×10

   e 130×4 **f** 150×4

   g 21×7 **h** 21×8

Problem solving

4 Matthew's toy crane can hold up to 12 kg.
He has a pile of 500 g weights.
How many weights can he put
on the crane before it breaks?

❮ p.38

5 Freya is at the shops and needs to do some quick multiplying.
She doesn't have a calculator.
Which method should she use for each calculation?
Use the method to find the answer.

   a 'Onions are 10p each. I need 13 onions. How much does that cost?'

   b 'Bread is £1.20 a loaf. I need 3 loaves. How much does that cost?'

   c 'Carrots come in bunches of 6. I need 14 bunches for my rabbits.
How many carrots is that?'

6 There are patterns in the 9 times table.
The digits in the answer always add up to 9.
The digits in the 10s column increase by 1 each time;
the digits in the 1s column decrease by 1 each time.

Continue the 9 times table and see what happens.

$1 \times 9 = \mathbf{9}$ $(9 = 9)$
$2 \times 9 = \mathbf{18}$ $(1 + 8 = 9)$
$3 \times 9 = \mathbf{27}$ $(2 + 7 = 9)$
$4 \times 9 = \mathbf{36}$ $(3 + 6 = 9)$
$5 \times 9 = \mathbf{45}$ $(4 + 5 = 9)$

7 Look at the 8 times table.

   a Can you find a pattern in the way the tens and
units digits change?

   b Can you explain the pattern?

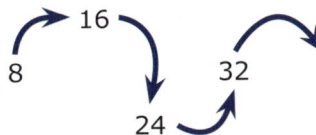

Laura and Jack are working out some harder multiplication problems.
They need to use a written method.

Laura uses **partitioning**.

Jack uses the **grid method**.

Estimate

$$235 \times 4$$

$$250 \times 4 = 1000$$

200   30   5

200×4 30×4 5×4

800 + 120 + 20 = 940

$235 \times 4 = 940$

p.134

426×6
$426 = 400 + 20 + 6$

Estimate

$$450 \times 6 = 2700$$

×	400	20	6
6	$6 \times 400 = 2400$	$6 \times 20 = 120$	$6 \times 6 = 36$

$2400 + 120 + 36 = 2556$

$426 \times 6 = 2556$

Example

a Use partitioning to solve 432×3

b Use the grid method to solve 181×6

a Estimate is $400 \times 3 = 1200$

$432 = 400 + 30 + 2$

400×3 + $30 \times 3 + 2 \times 3$

1200 + 90 + 6 = 1296

1296 is close to the estimate. ✓

b Estimate is $200 \times 5 = 1000$

$181 = 100 + 80 + 1$

×	100	80	1
6	600	480	6

$600 + 480 + 6 = 1086$

1086 is close to the estimate. ✓

🔴 You can use a standard column method to multiply any two numbers.

Luja uses a standard column method to multiply on paper.
This is how Luja works out Laura's and Jack's problems.

```
    2 3 5
  ×     4
  ─────────
    9 4 0
    ₁ ₂
```

```
    4 2 6
  ×     6
  ─────────
    2 5 5 6
    ₁ ₃
```

$235 \times 4 = 940$ $426 \times 6 = 2556$

There, that was simple!

Luja started on the right.

$4 \times 5 = 20$ She put 0 in the units column and wrote 2 as a **carry digit** in the tens column.

$4 \times 3 = 12$
$\underline{+ 2}$
14
She remembered to add the carry digit. She wrote down 4 and carried 1.

$4 \times 2 = 8$
$\underline{+ 1}$
9

Exercise 14d

Start each question by making an estimate.

End each question by checking your answer against your estimate.

1 Partition these numbers into 100s, 10s and 1s.
The first is done for you.
a 264 = 200 + 60 + 4
b 357   **c** 158
d 333   **e** 796
f 609   **g** 850
h 700   **i** 999

2 Use partitioning to answer each question.
a 23×4 **b** 43×4
c 52×3 **d** 74×5
e 126×3 **f** 236×3
g 319×5 **h** 285×6
i 4×378 **j** 5×555

3 Copy these grids and complete each multiplication.
a $32 \times 4 =$

×	30	2
4		

b $53 \times 5 =$

×	50	3
5		

3 c $27 \times 4 =$

×	20	7
4		

d $213 \times 6 =$

×	200	10	3
6			

e $251 \times 5 =$

×	200	50	1
5			

f $468 \times 4 =$

×	400	60	8
4			

4 Use the standard column method to complete these multiplications.
a 124×3 **b** 213×2
c 325×3 **d** 145×3
e 362×3 **f** 217×2
g 324×5 **h** 253×6
i 375×4 **j** 999×6

Problem solving

5 Make the largest answer you can by multiplying using these digits only once.

3   7   8   9

6 Find the missing digit.

$$
\begin{array}{r}
2\,\square\,9 \\
\times \quad\quad 5 \\
\hline
1\,3\,9\,5 \\
\hline
{\scriptstyle 3\ \ 4}
\end{array}
$$

14e Mental methods of division

● You use **division** when you **share** something.

Jack shares 12 tickets **equally** between his four friends.

$12 \div 4 = 3$

They have three tickets each.

● You can also think of division as **grouping**.

12 students get into groups of 3.

$12 \div 3 = 4$

There are four groups altogether.

$3 \times 4 = 12$
$12 \div 4 = 3$
$12 \div 3 = 4$

❮ p.192

Example

Share these beads into 5 groups.
There are 20 beads.

Share out the beads into 5 equal groups.

There are 4 beads in each group.

$20 \div 5 = 4$

● You can use a number line to help you to divide.

$28 \div 4$

$-4 \quad -4 \quad -4 \quad -4 \quad -4 \quad -4 \quad -4$

0 2 4 6 8 10 12 14 16 18 20 22 24 26 28

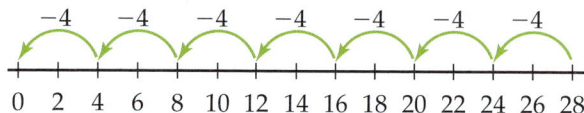

There are 7 jumps, so $28 \div 4 = 7$.

You can think of division as repeated subtraction.

Example

Divide $48 \div 12$

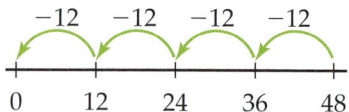

$-12 \quad -12 \quad -12 \quad -12$

0   12   24   36   48

There are four jumps of 12 in 48

$48 \div 12 = 4$

● When you divide by 10, you move the digits one place to the right.

$210 \div 10 = 21$

H	T	U
2	1	0
	2	1

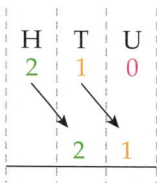

● When you divide by 100, move the digits two places to the right.

$3800 \div 100 = 38$

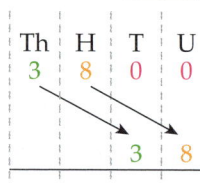

Th	H	T	U
3	8	0	0
		3	8

Number Multiplying and dividing

Exercise 14e

1 Use the multiplication grid to help with these division problems.

×	1	2	3	4	5	6	7	8	9	10	11	12
1	1	2	3	4	5	6	7	8	9	10	11	12
2	2	4	6	8	10	12	14	16	18	20	22	24
3	3	6	9	12	15	18	21	24	27	30	33	36
4	4	8	12	16	20	24	28	32	36	40	44	48
5	5	10	15	20	25	30	35	40	45	50	55	60
6	6	12	18	24	30	36	42	48	54	60	66	72
7	7	14	21	28	35	42	49	56	63	70	77	84
8	8	16	24	32	40	48	56	64	72	80	88	96
9	9	18	27	36	45	54	63	72	81	90	99	108
10	10	20	30	40	50	60	70	80	90	100	110	120
11	11	22	33	44	55	66	77	88	99	110	121	132
12	12	24	36	48	60	72	84	96	108	120	132	144

a 28 ÷ 7 **b** 24 ÷ 8
c 45 ÷ 5 **d** 32 ÷ 8
e 72 ÷ 9 **f** 54 ÷ 6
g 42 ÷ 6 **h** 63 ÷ 7

2 Complete these division problems.
a 80 ÷ 10 **b** 100 ÷ 10
c 120 ÷ 10 **d** 390 ÷ 10
e 25 ÷ 10 **f** 48 ÷ 10
g 1500 ÷ 100 **h** 2000 ÷ 100

3 Use number lines to help you with these divisions.
a 12 ÷ 4 **b** 16 ÷ 8
c 28 ÷ 7 **d** 35 ÷ 5
e 27 ÷ 9 **f** 66 ÷ 11
g 39 ÷ 13 **h** 45 ÷ 15

Did you know?

The Earth gets 100 tons heavier every day due to falling space dust.

Problem solving

4 Starting with 3, follow the numbers that 3 will divide into exactly.
Which letter do you reach? Repeat this for 7, 6 and 5.

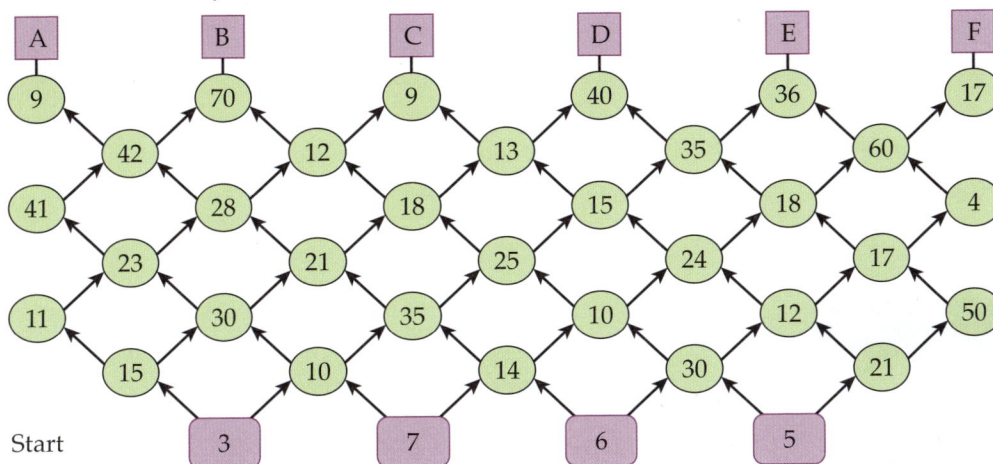

p.212

5 Tanya has five boxes containing cups.
Each box contains a different number of cups.
She wants the same number of cups in each box.
How many should she have in each box?

12 cups, 7 cups, 9 cups, 14 cups, 3 cups

MyMaths.co.uk 1228, 1392 SEARCH

‹ p.212 Whole numbers do not always divide exactly.

Betty shares 14 cakes onto three plates.
She has two cakes left over.

As a division, this is 14 ÷ 3 = 4 r 2

'r' stands for **remainder**.

🔴 You must look at the question to decide how to deal with any reminder.

Example

Anna and Josh have baked 23 cakes.
They want to pack them in boxes.
Each box holds six cakes.
How many boxes do they need?

‹ 16 23 ÷ 6 = 3 r 5
There are five cakes left over – these need a box too!
They need 3 + 1 = 4 boxes.

Example

A necklace needs three beads.
Maggie has 70 beads.
How many necklaces can she make?

To work out 70 ÷ 3
split it into easier numbers.

$$70 ÷ 3 = 60 ÷ 3 + 10 ÷ 3$$
$$= 20 + 3 \text{ r } 1$$
$$= 23 \text{ r } 1$$

Maggie can make 23 necklaces from 70 beads.
There is one bead left over.

Exercise 14f

1 Answer these division problems. Give a remainder.

   a 8 ÷ 3   **b** 11 ÷ 5   **c** 10 ÷ 4   **d** 19 ÷ 4   **e** 28 ÷ 5   **f** 23 ÷ 3
   g 36 ÷ 10   **h** 21 ÷ 6   **i** 32 ÷ 7   **j** 50 ÷ 9   **k** 38 ÷ 11   **l** 65 ÷ 12

Problem solving

2 A carpenter needs to cut each rod into three equal lengths.
   When she has finished how long will the marked lengths be?

   a 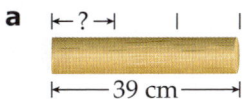 **b**  **c**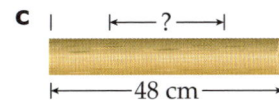

   d  **e**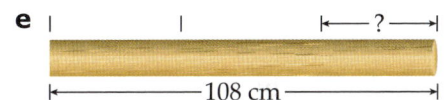

3 Answer these division problems by sharing equally.

   17 apples

   5 bags

   a How many apples are placed in each bag?
   b How many are left over?

   32 sweets

   3 boxes

   c How many sweets are placed in each box?
   d How many are left over?

   23 pound coins

   4 friends

   e How many coins does each person get?
   f How many are left over?

4 Eggs are packed in boxes of six.
   How many boxes do you need to pack 138 eggs?

5 Pete is making necklaces. He uses five beads on each necklace.
   How many necklaces can he make if he has

   a 35 beads   **b** 85 beads   **c** 125 beads?

6 **a** It costs £2 for an ice-cream.
       Joe has £13.
       How many ice creams can he buy?

   b Ayesha earns £4 per hour on her paper round.
       She wants to buy a bag for £33.
       How many hours does she need to work?

MyMaths.co.uk   🔍 1391, 1392   **SEARCH**

14g Written methods of division

> For some division problems you can use a number line.

Hey, this is just repeated subtraction!

Example

Use subtraction on a number line to solve $27 \div 5$.

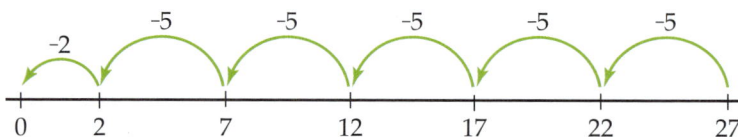

There are five jumps of 5 in 27 and a **remainder** of 2.

$27 \div 5 = 5 \text{ r } 2$

> For divisions involving large numbers it is best to use a standard written method.

Example

Find $196 \div 6$.

Use repeated subtraction.
$10 \times 6 = 60$, start by subtracting groups of 60.

```
 6)196
  -60    ⟵  6 × 10
  136
  -60    ⟵  6 × 10
   76
  -60    ⟵  6 × 10
   16
  -12    ⟵  6 × 2
    4          32
```

There are 32 groups of 6 in 196 with a remainder of 4.

$196 \div 6 = 36 \text{ r } 4$

Use a standard written method.

```
      32 r 4
  6)196
   -18↓      6 × 30
    16
   -12       6 × 2
     4
```

$196 \div 6 = 32 \text{ r } 4$

The standard method is quite like repeated subtraction.

Yes, but it is usually faster.

Exercise 14g

1 Using your knowledge of the times tables, answer these division problems.

   a $12 \div 2$ **b** $9 \div 3$

   c $12 \div 4$ **d** $20 \div 5$

   e $16 \div 2$ **f** $24 \div 6$

   g $18 \div 9$ **h** $28 \div 4$

   i $21 \div 7$ **j** $48 \div 6$

2 Use a number line or repeated subtraction to answer these.

   a $35 \div 4$ **b** $43 \div 5$

   c $45 \div 6$ **d** $66 \div 10$

   e $53 \div 7$ **f** $67 \div 8$

3 Divide these numbers using the standard method.

   a $132 \div 3$ **b** $124 \div 4$

   c $176 \div 4$ **d** $130 \div 5$

   e $186 \div 6$ **f** $132 \div 4$

   g $255 \div 5$ **h** $288 \div 9$

4 Use the standard method to solve these divisions.
The first has been done for you.

a
$$
\begin{array}{r}
24 \\
4\overline{)98} \\
-8 \\
\hline
18 \\
-16 \\
\hline
2
\end{array}
$$

> $4\overline{)98}$ means $98 \div 4$

$98 \div 4 = 24 \text{ r } 2$

   b $5\overline{)75}$ **c** $3\overline{)96}$

   d $6\overline{)84}$ **e** $5\overline{)225}$

   f $4\overline{)98}$ **g** $5\overline{)123}$

   h $6\overline{)374}$ **i** $8\overline{)544}$

   j $10\overline{)285}$ **k** $11\overline{)342}$

   l $12\overline{)508}$ **m** $4\overline{)1793}$

   n $6\overline{)3883}$ **o** $3\overline{)2073}$

   p $11\overline{)6845}$ **q** $5\overline{)63217}$

Problem solving

5 Liam is having a party.
He needs 134 balloons to make a balloon arch. They are sold in packs of 6.
How many packs does he need?

6 Mia has £78.
She wants to buy 6 T-shirts at £12 each.
Does she have enough money?

7 Some sweets are shared equally between five jars.

   a If there are 40 sweets altogether in five jars, how many sweets are there in one jar?

   b If there are 80 sweets altogether in five jars, how many sweets are there in one jar?

   c If there are 160 sweets altogether in five jars, how many sweets are there in one jar?

14h Calculator skills

Calculators help you to do difficult calculations quickly and to check your answers.

‹ p.130

Example

Solve 3450 + 1458 using a calculator.

Estimate first   3450 is close to 3500.   3500
                        1458 is close to 1500.   + 1500
                                                       5000

3 **4** **5** **0** **+** **1** **4** **5** **8** **=**

3450 + 1458
                    4908

3450 + 1458 = 4908

You need to think carefully about the question to work out the right answer from your calculator display.

‹ p.12
‹ p.16

Three shirts cost £50 in a sale.
How much does one shirt cost?

50 ÷ 3 ➡ **5** **0** **÷** **3** **=** ➡

50 ÷ 3
            16.66667

£50 for 3

For an amount of money, you need to **round** to 2 decimal places (dp).

Look at the third decimal place.   16.666 ➡ 16.67   6 rounds up

One shirt costs £16.67.

Example

Use your calculator to find each answer. Give your answers to 2 dp.
a   £7.30 ÷ 8   b   £50.85 ÷ 12

a   Estimate £8 ÷ 8 = £1

7 **.** **3** **÷** **8** **=**

Look at the third decimal place.
7.3 ÷ 8 = 0.91②5   You don't need to type the zero for pence.
        = 0.91 (2 dp)   2 rounds down so the 1 doesn't change.
£7.30 ÷ 8 = £0.91

b   Estimate £50 ÷ 10 = £5

5 **0** **.** **8** **5** **÷** **1** **2** **=**

50.85 ÷ 12 = 4.23⑦5   7 rounds up and changes the 3 to 4.
          = 4.24 (2 dp)
£50.85 ÷ 12 = £4.24

Exercise 14h

1 Use your calculator to solve these problems. Estimate first.

  a 1207 + 1345   1207 is close to _____.

                          1345 is close to _____.

  b 3459 − 3214

  c 1234 + 5678

  d 3405 − 3201

2 Use a calculator to do these decimal problems.

Enter **3** **.** **4** for 3.4

  a 3.4 + 2.6   **b** 5.8 + 6.3

  c 4.3 + 2.4   **d** 14.3 + 18.7

  e 6.5 − 4.8   **f** 9.0 − 6.6

  g 16.8 − 9.8   **h** 30.5 − 18.4

3 Use your calculator to find the new temperatures. **‹ p.14**

For **b** enter **(−)** **6** **+** **1** **3** **=**

  a Start at 4°C and rise by 9 degrees.

  b Start at -6°C and rise by 13 degrees.

  c Start at 2°C and fall by 7 degrees.

  d Start at -12°C and rise by 7 degrees.

  e Start at -3°C and fall by 9 degrees.

4 Round these calculator answers to 2 decimal places (2 dp).

  a 0.143   **b** 0.639

  c 6.129   **d** 2.032

  e 1.375   **f** 4.2384

5 Use your calculator to answer these division problems.

Round your answers to 2 dp.

The first has been worked through for you.

  a £3.27 ÷ 4

  ➡ **3** **.** **2** **7** **÷** **4** **=** 3.27÷4 0.8175

  ➡ Rounded to 2 dp = £0.82

  b £7.53 ÷ 9   **c** £3.79 ÷ 3

  d £16.54 ÷ 8   **e** £0.79 ÷ 4

  f £21.57 ÷ 14   **g** £573.29 ÷ 17

6 Use your calculator to answer these money problems.

  a £2.26 + £3.54   **b** £8.47 − £2.07

  c £2.20 × 4   **d** £6.80 ÷ 4

  e £0.79 + £15.11 **f** £9.47 − £8.07

  g £4.60 × 6.50   **h** £16 ÷ 2.5

Problem solving

7 Use a calculator to answer these problems.

  a Josh and his two friends earn £40, cleaning windows. Can the money be shared out **exactly** between the three of them?

  b Tara opens her money box and finds:

      eleven 1p coins, six 2p coins, three 5p coins, seven 10p coins, four 20p coins, nine 50p coins and three £1 coins.

      How much has she in total?

Did you know?

Until 2006, one million Turkish Lira was worth about 40p, so almost everybody in Turkey was a millionaire!

Check out

You should now be able to ...

Test it ➡

Questions

✓ Consolidate multiplication facts up to 12 × 12.	3	1, 2
✓ Multiply by 10 and 100.	4	3, 4
✓ Multiply whole numbers using mental and written methods.	4	5, 6
✓ Divide whole numbers using mental and efficient written methods.	4	7 – 10
✓ Use a calculator and interpret the display in different contexts, including money.	4	11

Language	Meaning	Example
Multiplication	The act of repeated addition.	$7 + 7 + 7 + 7 + 7 + 7 + 7 + 7 + 7$ can be written much more simply as 9×7
Division	The act of sharing or grouping.	Jade shares £12 equally between her four friends. $12 \div 4 = 3$ They get £3 each.
Partitioning	Splitting a number into smaller parts. It is a method usually used to make calculations simpler.	$153 \times 2 = 150 \times 2 + 3 \times 2$ $= 300 + 6$ $= 306$
Doubling and halving	A method for multiplying two numbers.	$7 \times 8 = 14 \times 4$ $= 28 \times 2$ $= 56$
Remainder	The amount left over when one number is divided by another (often denoted by r or rem).	$47 \div 3 = 15 \text{ r } 2$

1 Each child has 9 grapes. How many grapes do 7 children have?

2 Calculate
   a 5×8 **b** 4×6
   c 6×7 **d** 9×11

3 Multiply each number by 10
   a 8   **b** 21
   c 174   **d** 360

4 A water carrier can hold 10 litres of water. How many carriers will by needed to carry
   a 30 litres
   b 100 litres of water?

5 Complete these multiplication problems.
   a 30×5 **b** 7×40
   c 12×4 **d** 6×15

6 Use a column method to complete each multiplication.
   a 27×5 **b** 359×6
   c 98×7 **d** 663×4

7 Complete these division problems.
   a $450 \div 10$ **b** $64 \div 10$
   c $15 \div 3$ **d** $21 \div 7$
   e $54 \div 9$ **f** $32 \div 4$

8 Answer these division problems giving your answers with a remainder.
   a $13 \div 5$ **b** $21 \div 2$
   c $59 \div 6$ **d** $238 \div 4$

9 Use a written method to work out these divisions. Give your answers with a remainder.
   a $37 \div 3$ **b** $65 \div 4$
   c $69 \div 8$ **d** $80 \div 9$

10 a A taxi can carry 5 people. How many taxis are needed for 26 people?
   b A kilt is made from 7 m of tartan. Hector has 40 m of material. How many kilts can he make?
   c A recipe for a cake uses six drops of vanilla essence. Jolie plans to make 24 cakes. Her bottle of vanilla essence says it contains 150 drops. Will she have enough to make all the cakes?

11 Use a calculator or a written method to calculate these money problems.
   a £5.78 + £18.92
   b £14.99 − £2.45
   c £8.47 × 5.5
   d £12.75 ÷ 4

What next?

Score		
0 – 4		Your knowledge of this topic is still developing. To improve look at Formative test: 1A-14; MyMaths: 1014, 1021, 1023, 1024, 1027, 1041, 1228, 1367, 1391 and 1392
5 – 9		You are gaining a secure knowledge of this topic. To improve look at InvisiPen: 114, 122, 123, 126, 127, 129 and 135
10 – 11		You have mastered this topic. Well done, you are ready to progress!

14a

1 Work out:

    a 7×6 **b** 6×8 **c** 4×9 **d** 6×9

    e 5×6 **f** 9×8 **g** 10×7 **h** 11×4

2 Complete these multiplication grids.

a

×	3	8	2	7	5	11
4					20	
7			14			
10						
3						
8	24					
9						

b

×	2	4	8	10	9	12
6	12					
3			24			
5		20				
7						
8						
4						

14b

3 Connor has a pencil that is 10 cm long.

He uses his pencil to measure his desk and his classroom.

His table is 6 'pencils' wide, 12 'pencils' long and 7 'pencils' tall.

What are these lengths in centimetres?

What are they in metres?

His classroom is 85 'pencils' wide.

What is this in metres?

4 A woodpecker is excavating a hole in a tree for his nest.

Each day he removes 100 g of wood.

    a How much wood will be removed in a week?

    b How much wood will be removed in 30 days?

         Give your answer in kilograms.

14c

5 To multiply a number by 8, you can double it three times over.

for example, 14×8 ⟶ $14 \times 2 = 28$

                              $\times 2 = 56$

                              $\times 2 = 112$

Use doubling to work out these multiplications.

    a 13×8 **b** 15×8 **c** 16×8

    d 20×8 **e** 21×8 **f** 71×8

6 Use partitioning to work out these multiplications.

    a 18×5 **b** 22×6 **c** 54×7

    d 4×36 **e** 15×9 **f** 11×37

7 Use a standard written method to work out these multiplications.

    a 156×3 **b** 247×2 **c** 321×3

    d 482×4 **e** 359×4 **f** 567×5

    g 426×7 **h** 861×8 **i** 345×9

    j 4116×5 **k** 6307×4 **l** 2643×7

8 Work out these divisions in your head.

    a $70 \div 10$ **b** $90 \div 10$ **c** $110 \div 10$

    d $500 \div 100$ **e** $24 \div 6$ **f** $77 \div 7$

    g $124 \div 4$ **h** $132 \div 6$ **i** $84 \div 12$

    j $88 \div 11$ **k** $639 \div 3$ **l** $248 \div 8$

9 A big dipper holds eight passengers.
Sixty-eight people are waiting to travel on the big dipper.
How many trips will be needed so that everyone has a ride?

10 Use a standard written method to work out these divisions.

    a $453 \div 3$ **b** $621 \div 3$ **c** $744 \div 4$

    d $856 \div 4$ **e** $765 \div 5$ **f** $873 \div 9$

    g $637 \div 7$ **h** $4496 \div 8$ **i** $2548 \div 7$

    j $2190 \div 6$ **k** $3168 \div 9$ **l** $14500 \div 4$

11 Use your calculator to work out these problems.

    a $5.2 + 3.1$ **b** $7.8 + 2.9$ **c** $16.1 - 5.7$

    d £7.76 $\div$ 8   **e** £10.29 $\div$ 7   **f** £1.20 $\times$ 8

12 a Six friends win £20 in a raffle. They agree to share the money equally. How much money do they get each?

    b On Monday the temperature is -5°C.

       i The temperature falls 3°C on Tuesday. What is the temperature on Tuesday?

      ii The next Monday the temperature has risen 13°C. What is the temperature now?

Have you ever thought about how many things you have around the house that use electricity? Have you considered how much electricity the various things use? As energy costs rise, more and more people are keeping an eye on how they use their electricity.

Electricity usage in a typical household

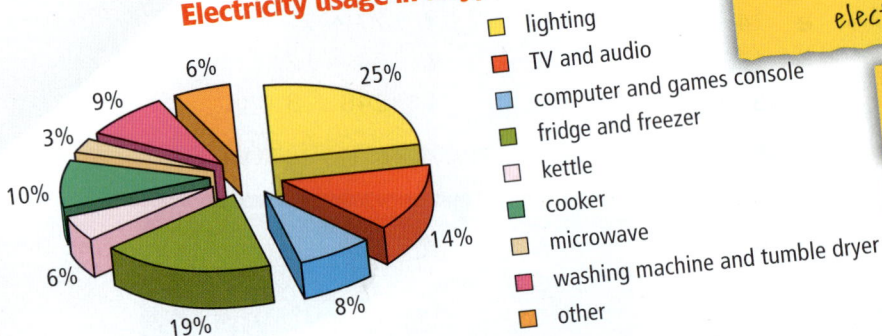

- lighting 25%
- TV and audio 14%
- computer and games console 8%
- fridge and freezer 19%
- kettle 6%
- cooker 10%
- microwave 3%
- washing machine and tumble dryer 9%
- other 6%

Task 1:

a i What uses the most electricity?
   ii Is that what you expected?
   iii What fraction of the total electricity does it use?

b What uses the least electricity?

c Where do you think that savings in the use of electricity could most easily be made?

Switch off to save money

Consumers are wasting up to £200 a year on electricity bills by leaving appliances on standby rather than switching them off, according to recent research.

A typical microwave oven uses more electricity to run its clock than it does to cook food! Although cooking the food uses much more power than running the clock, most microwave ovens

8.45

are in standby mode for at least 99% of the time.

```
200 × 6 = 1200
7 × 18 = 126
1200 + 126 = 1326
```

Task 2
This table shows you the electrical energy used by different household appliances.

Item	power used when on (W)	hours in use per day	power used on standby (W)	hours on standby per day	energy used per day (Wh)
Television	200	6	7	18	1326
Satellite TV	30	5	13	19	
DVD player	12	1	7	23	600
Main light	100	6	—	0	
Microwave oven	700	0.1	5	23.9	
Desktop computer	125	4	15	20	
Laptop computer	29	4	2	20	

a Copy the table.
   Complete the final column by using the method shown for the television.
b i Which item uses the most electricity each day?
   ii Which uses the least?
c What would happen if the items that are left on standby were turned off instead? Would the same items use the most and least electricity per day?

Here is some data on three fridges.

Fridge A £99.99

Fresh food storage
❄ volume 86 litres

Freezer compartment
❄ volume 10 litres

Energy efficiency
❄ class 'A'

Energy consumption
❄ 139 kWh per year

Fridge B £179.99

Fresh food storage
❄ volume 245 litres

Freezer compartment
❄ none

Energy efficiency
❄ class 'A'

Energy consumption
❄ 164 kWh per year

Fridge C £299.99

Fresh food storage
❄ volume 122 litres

Freezer compartment
❄ volume 18 litres

Energy efficiency
❄ class 'A'

Energy consumption
❄ 234 kWh per year

Electricity costs 15p per kWh

Task 3

a Look at the energy consumption figures for each fridge. Work out the annual cost of running each fridge. Give your answer in pounds and pence.

b Which fridge has the most space for fresh food?

c Which fridge would you choose and why?

Task 4

The average annual electricity usage per household in the UK is 3300 kWh (kilowatt hours).

a If electricity costs 15p per kWh, how much would a typical household pay for their electricity per year?

b How much would this work out as per month?

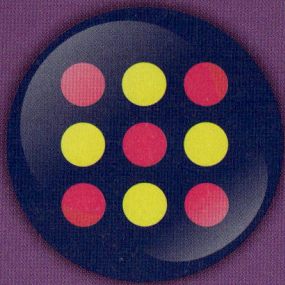

15 Ratio and proportion

Introduction

When you ride a bike, the seat, handlebars and pedals are positioned so that you can reach all of them at the same time. The designers make sure that the different parts of a child's bike are in proportion to the size of the 'average' child. This process of fitting technology to the human body is called ergonomics.

What's the point?

If designers didn't understand proportion, people wouldn't be able to ride bikes or drive cars – they wouldn't be able to reach the pedals!

Objectives

By the end of this chapter, you will have learned how to …
- Write and use ratios and proportions.
- Solve simple problems involving ratio and proportion.
- Solve arithmetic problems in context.
- Construct and interpret scale drawings.

Check in

1   What fraction of these beads is red? Write your answer in its simplest form.

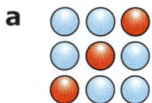

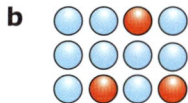

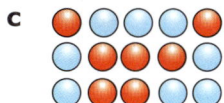

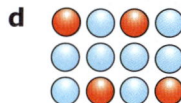

   a **b** **c** **d**

2   Calculate

   a $8 + 7 + 11 + 4$ **b** $67 - 48$ **c** 128×6 **d** $132 \div 6$

3   Write these quantities using the units shown in brackets.

   a 3 m (cm)   **b** 250 cm (m)   **c** 1.5 kg (g)   **d** 2000 g (kg)

Starter problem

Leonardo da Vinci thought that your head (measured from your forehead to your chin) was exactly one tenth of your height.

Is this true?

Investigate the lengths of different body parts to see if any of them are in proportion to each other.

Laura is making a necklace. She uses a pattern of two red beads to one yellow bead.

The **ratio** of red to yellow is 2 to 1
or 2 : 1

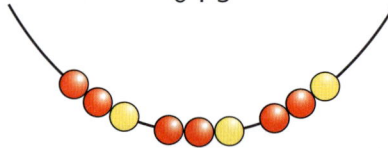

Laura keeps going …

4 red beads and 2 yellow beads
4 : 2

6 red beads and 3 yellow beads
6 : 3

Compare this...

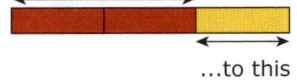

⬤ A ratio lets you compare different parts of a whole.

...to this

Laura has finished her necklace.

There are 12 beads in total:
eight red beads and four yellow beads.

The **proportion** of yellow beads
is 4 out of 12.

The proportion of red beads
is 8 out of 12.

❮ p.66
$\frac{4}{12}$ or $\frac{1}{3}$

$\frac{8}{12}$ or $\frac{2}{3}$

⬤ A proportion tells you what part of a **whole** something is.
▶ You can write a proportion as a fraction, a decimal or a percentage.

Compare this...

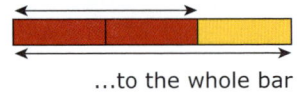

...to the whole bar

Example

a What is the ratio of blue beads to green beads?
b What proportion of the beads are green?

a There are 2 blue beads and 4 green beads.
The ratio of blue beads to green beads is 2 : 4 or 1 : 2

2 : 4
÷ 2   ÷ 2
1 : 2

❮ p.68

b There are 4 green beads out of 6 total beads.
The proportion is 4 out of 6, which is $\frac{4}{6}$ or $\frac{2}{3}$.

Ratios are like fractions. You should simplify them.

Exercise 15a

1 For each of these drawings, give
   i the number of apples
   ii the number of oranges
   iii the ratio of apples to oranges
   iv the proportion of apples
   v the proportion of oranges.

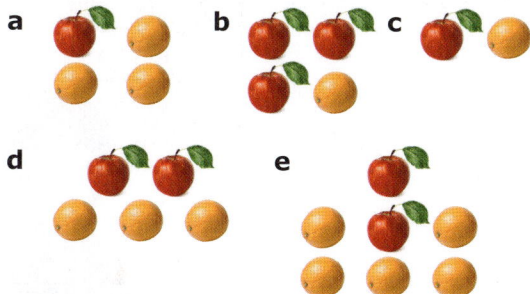

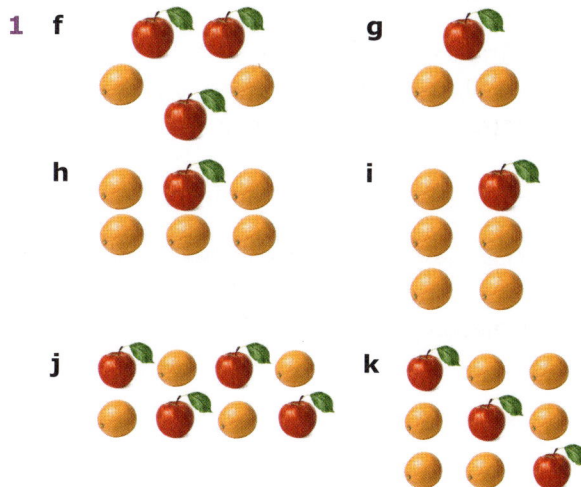

a   **b**   **c**

d   **e**

1 **f**   **g**

h   **i**

j   **k**

Problem solving

2 Aidan is making a necklace. The ratio of red beads to yellow beads is 1 : 4. He has 12 yellow beads and 4 red beads. Can he make his necklace and use up all his beads?

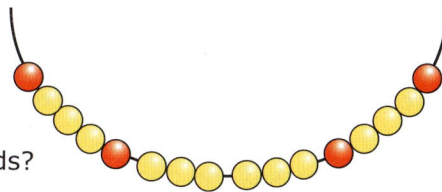

3 Micah is mixing red and yellow paint to make orange.
   To make orange, he mixes 3 tins of yellow to 1 tin of red.
   a What is the ratio of red paint to yellow paint?
   b Micah has two tins of red paint. How many tins of yellow paint will he use to mix orange?

4 Micah now makes green paint.
   For each tin of yellow paint he uses two tins of blue paint.
   a What is the ratio of yellow paint to blue paint?
   b Micah has three tins of yellow paint. How many tins of blue paint will he use to mix green?
   c As a fraction, what proportion of the paint is yellow?

5 Here are 20 sweets.
   Give your answers as a fraction.
   a What proportion of the sweet wrappers are red?
   b What proportion of the sweet wrappers are purple?
   c What proportion of the sweet wrappers are yellow?
   Can you simplify any of your answers?

MyMaths.co.uk   1052   SEARCH   283

Alec is making a necklace.
He uses two blue beads for every three red beads.
This is a **ratio** of 2 : 3

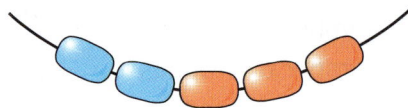

His necklace has 15 beads in total.

The **proportion** of **blue** beads is 6 out of 15.

The proportion of **red** beads is 9 out of 15.

$$\frac{6}{15} = \frac{2}{5}$$ ÷3

$$\frac{9}{15} = \frac{3}{5}$$ ÷3

> You can simplify a ratio, or a proportion just like a fraction.

Knowing about ratio and proportion helps you to solve problems involving quantities that are mixed together.

Example

a   Alec makes the necklace longer. What colour is the 20th bead?

b   In a 25-bead necklace, how many red beads are there?

?

c   How many blue beads are there in a 25-bead necklace?

a   Write out the pattern.

B B R R R   B B R R R   B B R R R   B B R R (R)
  5 beads   5 beads   5 beads   5 beads

The 20th bead will be red.

b   For each group of five beads, three are red.
25 beads make five groups.
5 lots of 3 red beads = 15 beads.
5 × 3 = 15
There will be 15 red beads in a necklace of 25 beads.

c   5 lots of 2 blue beads = 10 beads
5 × 2 = 10
There will be 10 blue beads.

Blue beads	Red beads	Number of beads
2	3	5
4	6	10
6	9	15
8	12	20
10	(15)	25

Check: 15 + 10 = 25

Exercise 15b

1 Sarah threads beads onto a string.

She records the number and colour of beads in a table.

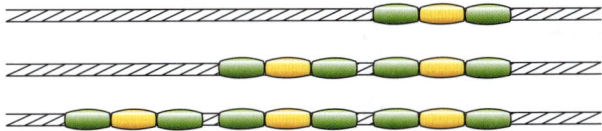

Yellow	Green	Total number
1	2	3
2	4	6
3	6	9

   a What is the ratio of yellow beads to green beads?

   b Copy and continue the table by adding three more rows.

   c What colour will the 15th bead be?

   d As a simple fraction, what proportion are green beads?

2 Sarah makes a string of 30 beads

   in the same pattern as question **1**.

   a How many are yellow?

   b How many are green?

3 This is a recipe for salad dressing

   a Rose mixes up the dressing.
      How many parts does she put
      together to make the total?

   b What proportion of the dressing is oil?

   c What proportion of the dressing is vinegar?

> 6 parts oil
> 2 parts vinegar
> 1 part lemon juice
> 1 part chopped herbs

Did you know?

You can increase or decrease the quantities in a recipe but you must keep the ingredients in the original proportions.

4 This is a recipe for short crust pastry

   a As a simple fraction, what proportion of the pastry is flour?

   b As a simple fraction, what proportion of the pastry is water?

   c Max needs to make a large amount of pastry.
      He starts with 40 parts flour.
      List how many parts butter, water and sugar he will add.

> 8 parts flour
> 5 parts butter
> 2 parts water
> 1 part sugar

Problem solving

5 This is part of a stained glass window in the village hall.

   a What is the ratio of colours,
      blue to **red** to **yellow**?
      ? : ? : ?

   b As a simple fraction, what proportion of the whole
      pattern is blue?

6 Hannah and Joe's; mum gives them £20 to spend.
   They share it in the ratio 3 : 1.
   How much do they each get?

Clara's top tips for solving a problem!

- Read and understand the problem ✓
- Decide which operations (+, −, ×, ÷) and which numbers to use ✓
- Write a sum and work out the answer ✓
- Relate your answer to the problem and check it is sensible. ✓

Example

In a bag of sweets there are nine toffee sweets, five fruit cream sweets and 13 hazelnut sweets.

a **How many** sweets are there in one bag?

p.130 −137

b If all the hazelnut sweets are **removed**, how many sweets are left?

c If **each** bag costs £1.20, how much will six bags cost?

p.258 −273

d If three friends **share** a bag of sweets, how many sweets does each person have?

I understand the problem.

I'll use addition to solve this.
$9 + 5 + 13 = 27$

This is a subtraction problem.
$27 − 13 = 14$

This is a multiplication problem.
$6 × £1.20 = £7.20$ – don't forget the £ sign and the decimal point!

This is a division problem.
$27 ÷ 3 = 9.$

a $9 + 5 + 13 = 27$ There are 27 sweets in each bag.
b $27 − 13 = 14$ There are 14 sweets left.
c $6 × 1.2 = 7.2$ Six bags would cost £7.20.
d $27 ÷ 3 = 9$ They would each have nine sweets.

Be careful with money problems – check you have written your answer correctly.

You should take your time reading the question before you start to calculate.

Exercise 15c

Problem solving

1 Shiva is standing in a swimming pool.
The water is 125 cm deep.
Shiva is 158 cm tall.
How many centimetres of Shiva's body are
above the surface?

2 After their holiday Laura had £228 and $164 in her purse.
Roy had £108 and $88 in his wallet.
  a How many dollars ($) did they have between them?
  b How many pounds (£) did they have between them?

3 Pears cost £1.55 a kilogram.
Apples cost 98p a kilogram.
Oranges are 35p each.
Charlotte buys 2 kg of pears and four oranges.
How much does she pay altogether?

‹ p.38

4 Here are some ingredients for spaghetti bolognese.
Brenda only has 200 g of mince.
  a How much spaghetti does she need?
  b How many tins of tomatoes does she need?

spaghetti bolognese
600 g mince
3 tins tomatoes
900 g spaghetti

5 The adult price for entry into a cinema is £6.00.
Children are half-price. Forty people visit the cinema
and half of this number are children.
  a How much money does the cinema take that day for
  child visitors?
  b How much money does the cinema take that day for
  adult visitors?

6 What operation sign and number is missing from each circle?
Choose from the red list
of numbers and operation
signs to make sense of
this 'number chain'.

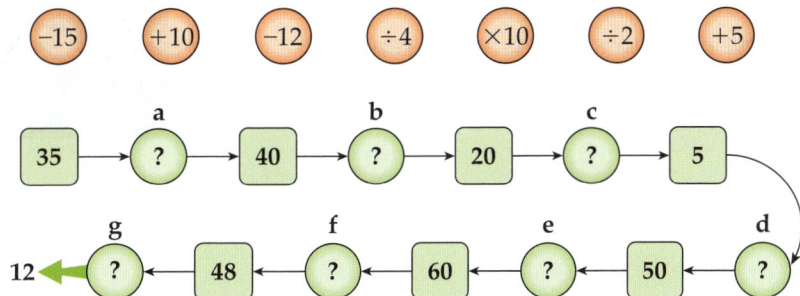

−15   +10   −12   ÷4   ×10   ÷2   +5

35 → a ? → 40 → b ? → 20 → c ? → 5

12 ← g ? ← 48 ← f ? ← 60 ← e ? ← 50 ← d ?

Bill is a gardener. He is working out what vegetables to plant in his raised bed next year.

He draws a plan to help him.
He uses a scale drawing, otherwise the plan would be the same size as his garden!

He uses 1 cm to represent 1 m.

> A scale shows you how a length in real life is represented on a plan.

You can write a scale as a ratio.

1 cm : 1 m
1 : 100

< p.38

Example

Bill wants to plant a row of beans that is 1 m wide and 5 m long. What size rectangle should he draw on his plan?

The scale is 1 cm : 1 m or 1 : 100.
1 cm on the drawing represents 1 m in real life.
The rectangle will be 1 cm wide and 5 cm long.

1 cm
5 cm

Example

On Bill's plan, the drawing of the potato bed is 3 cm long and 2.5 cm wide.
How big is the potato bed in real life?

The potato bed is 3 m by 2.5 m in real life.

2.5 cm
3 cm

Exercise 15d

1   Here is Bill's plan of his raised bed garden.
    The scale is 1 cm : 1 m.

   a   How long is the garden in metres?
   b   How wide is the garden?
   c   How wide is the carrot bed?
   d   How long are the rows of peas?
   e   How wide is the compost heap?

2   Write the length and width of each rectangle in real life.

   a   Scale 1 cm : 2 m   **b**   Scale 1 cm : 3 m   **c**   Scale 1 cm : 2 m

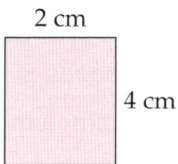
2 cm
4 cm

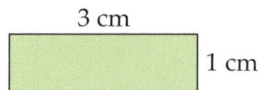
3 cm
1 cm

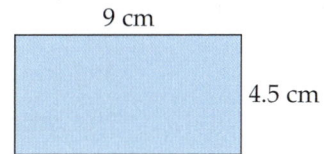
9 cm
4.5 cm

3   Mei-Ling has drawn a sketch of a shape.
    Make an *accurate* scale drawing.
    Use a scale of 1 cm : 1 m.

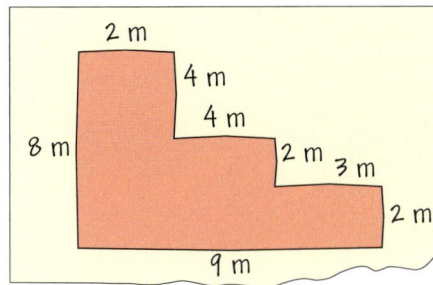
2 m
4 m
4 m
8 m
2 m
3 m
2 m
9 m

Problem solving

4   Mya is reorganising her bedroom.
    Here is the list of furniture she wants.

    Bed   – 2 m by 1.5 m
    Chest of drawers   – 1 m by 1 m
    Wardrobe   – 1 m by 1.5 m
    Chair   – 0.5 m by 0.5 m
    Sofa   – 2 m by 1 m

    Her mum says it won't fit!
    Is she right? Make a scale drawing to find out.

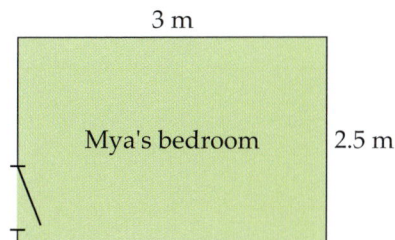
3 m
Mya's bedroom
2.5 m

15 MySummary

Check out

You should now be able to ...

Test it ➡

Questions

✓ Write and use ratios and proportions.	4	1
✓ Solve simple problems involving ratio and proportion.	5	2
✓ Solve arithmetic problems in context.	5	3, 4
✓ Construct and interpret scale drawings.	5	5

Language	Meaning	Example
Ratio	A comparison between one part or quantity and another part or quantity.	There is one gold bead for every three red beads. The ratio of gold to red beads is $1:3$
Proportion	A comparison between one part and the whole.	Three out of four beads are red. The proportion of red beads is $\frac{3}{4}$.
Scale	The ratio between the size of an object and its portrayal on a diagram.	A plan has a scale of $1\,cm:1\,m$ or $1:100$ $1\,cm$ on the plan represents $1\,m$ in real life.

1   In each drawing
   i   write the ratio of squares to triangles
   ii write the proportion of squares.

   a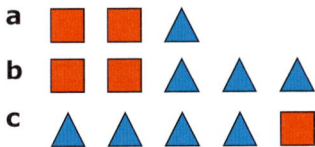
   b
   c

2   A necklace is made using 4 yellow beads
   to every 1 green bead.

   a   What is the ratio of green beads to
       yellow beads?
   b   How many yellow beads will be
       needed if there are 3 green beads?
   c   How many green beads will be
       needed if there are 8 yellow beads?

3   The cost of a ticket to a basketball match
   is £20 for an adult. Children's tickets are
   half-price. What is the cost of
   a   two adult tickets and a child ticket
   b   4 adult tickets and three child tickets
   c   10 adult tickets
   d   30 child tickets and 5 adult tickets?

4   Peaches cost £2.50 for a pack of four and
   plums cost 60p each. What is the cost of
   a   5 plums

4   b   3 packs of peaches
   c   1 pack of peaches and 3 plums
   d   8 peaches
   e   16 peaches and 10 plums?

5   Write the length and width of each
   rectangle in real life
   a   scale 1 cm : 1 m

   b   scale 1 cm : 3 m

   c   scale 1 cm : 4 m

6   A garden is a 10 m by 4 m rectangle. Draw
   a scale drawing of the garden using a
   scale of 1 cm : 2 m

What next?

Score			
	0 – 2		Your knowledge of this topic is still developing. To improve look at Formative test: 1A-15; MyMaths: 1037, 1052, 1117 and 1393
	3 – 5		You are gaining a secure knowledge of this topic. To improve look at InvisiPen: 191, 192 and 195
	6		You have mastered this topic. Well done, you are ready to progress!

15a

1 Express each of these ratios in its simplest form.
   a 14 : 16   b 3 : 9   c 10 : 15   d 5 : 25   e 24 : 40   f 27 : 36

2 Coloured tiles are used to make a pattern.
   a What is the ratio of yellow tiles to blue tiles?

   b Write down the proportion of blue tiles as a fraction in its simplest form.

3 Coloured tiles are used to make another pattern.
   a What is the ratio of red tiles to green tiles?

   b As a fraction, what proportion of the finished tiling is red?
   c As a fraction, what proportion of the finished tiling is green?

15b

4 Jo is making concrete using this mixture.
   a What is the ratio of sand to cement?
   b What proportion of the concrete is
      i cement   ii sand?
   c Jo has 12 units of sand to make concrete with.
      i   How much gravel is required?
      ii   How much water is required?
      iii How much concrete will be made?

Gravel	5 parts
Cement	2 parts
Sand	4 parts
Water	1 part

5 a Three sisters, Jean, Rita and Barbara, live in the same street. They decide
      to take their families to see their brother George. Their cars use petrol at
      different rates. During the journey Jean's car consumed 10 litres of petrol, Rita's
      consumed 12 litres and Barbara's consumed 14 litres. Express the figures as a
      ratio in its simplest form.
   b The three sisters decide to take their families to see their other brother Tony,
      who lives further away than George. If Jean's car uses up 15 litres of petrol for
      this journey, how much is used up by
      i   Rita's car
      ii Barbara's car?

6 The school is organizing a trip to the theatre.

Childrens tickets cost £4.00, adult tickets cost £8.00.

There must be one teacher for every eight students on the trip.

The school is going to take 48 students.

  a How much do the students' tickets cost?

  b How many teachers need to go on the trip?

  c What is the total cost of the trip?

7 Here is a recipe for pancakes.

Sam has 5 eggs.

  a How much milk is required?

  Give your answer in litres.

  b How much flour is required?

  Give your answer in Kilograms.

Milk	300 ml
Eggs	1
Plain flour	100 g
Salt	pinch

8 Apples are sold for £1.22 per kilogram.

Oranges are sold in bags of four £1.40.

Lemons cost 32 p each.

What is the cost of

  a 5 lemons

  b 3 kg of apples

  c 4 bags of oranges

  d 2 kg of apples and 3 lemons

  e 5 kg of apples and 2 bags of oranges

  f 12 oranges and 10 lemons?

9 This is a scale drawing of Sam's garden. The scale is 1 cm : 2 m.

  a How wide is the garden?

  b How long is the greenhouse?

  c How wide is the patio?

  d How wide is the flower bed?

  e How long is the flower bed?

10 Sam wants to add a pond to the drawing. The pond is to be rectangular with dimensions 3 m by 2 m.

What size rectangle should be drawn on Sam's scale drawing?

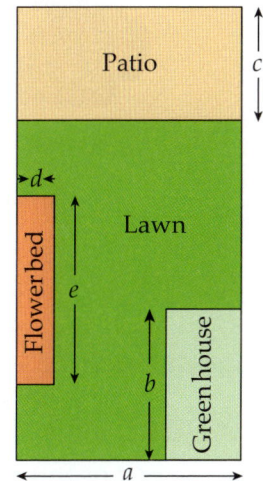

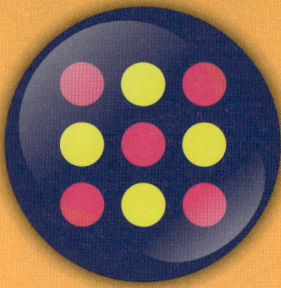

16 Probability

Introduction

Human beings seem fascinated with games. As soon as babies interact with their parents they start to play peek-a-boo, and as toddlers taking their first tumbling steps they begin to play hide and seek. The love affair with games continues into sports, board and card games and in modern times the ubiquitous computer game. Games have such a strong appeal because they not only entertain and amuse but also help you develop strategic thinking.

What's the point?

Most games are based upon a mixture of skill and chance. Understanding probability helps you make better decisions in games that involve chance.

Objectives

By the end of this chapter, you will have learned how to …
- Use the vocabulary and ideas of probability, drawing on experience.
- Understand and use the probability scale from 0 to 1.
- Sort objects using a Venn diagram.

Check in

1 This pie chart shows the amount of time Clare spent on her homework on Thursday.

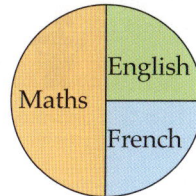

a What fraction of her time did Clare spend on English?

b Clare spent a total of 40 minutes on her homework on Thursday. How long did she spend on mathematics?

2 Copy and complete this table.

Decimal	Percentage	Fraction
0.1	10%	
0.5		$\frac{1}{2}$
		$\frac{1}{4}$

Starter problem

For this game you will need a dice.

The sheep (S) needs to get home before the wolf (W) catches her.

When you roll the dice, a 1 or 2 moves the sheep one square in any direction; a 3, 4, 5 or 6 moves the wolf one square in any direction.

Is the game fair?

Investigate.

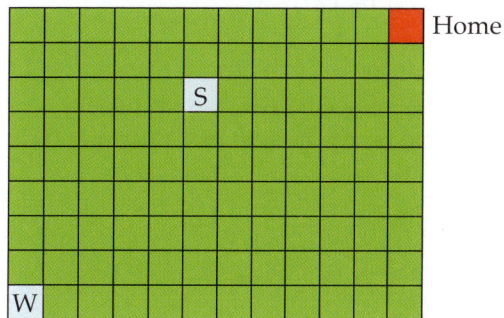

How likely is something to happen?

Some things are...

certain

The sun sets today

This will definitely happen.

impossible

It rains cats and dogs

This will definitely not happen.

uncertain

United win the cup

This may or may not happen.

Example

Give an example of something that is

a certain   b impossible   c uncertain.

a The day after Tuesday will be Wednesday.
b Teaching a hamster to play chess.
c Whether or not it will rain in Manchester tomorrow.

You'll be able to think of other examples.

● **Probability** is about how **likely** events are.

Example

Penny and Tim can't agree.

It is certain to snow here on Christmas Day this year!

No, it is uncertain.

Who is correct?

It is uncertain – Tim is correct.
However, somewhere in the UK usually
has snow on the ground on Christmas Day.

Did you know?

In May 2013 it snowed in many parts of the UK. This was unlikely but it did happen!

Exercise 16a

1 Use one of these probability words to describe each event.

Impossible Unlikely Likely Certain Uncertain

Can you give a reason why?

a It will snow in the Sahara desert next Christmas day.

b The sun will rise tomorrow.

c You can teach a worm to play the violin.

d If you flap your arms fast enough, you will fly.

e You will sleep tonight.

f A flipped coin will land on heads.

g You will get a 7 when you roll a dice.

h It will rain tomorrow.

i You will suffer arthritis at some point in your life.

2 Karen places tokens labelled 1 to 100 in a bag and picks one out without looking. Use a probability word to describe

a picking a token with an even number on it.

b picking a token with 105 on it.

c picking a token with 34 on it.

d picking a token with a number less than 90 on it.

3 Think about the events which happen to you.

a Give an example of something which is
   i certain
   ii uncertain
   iii impossible.

b Are some events more certain than others?

Problem solving

4 Insurance companies work with probability. The greater the chance of disaster means the greater the amount you pay for insurance.
Describe the probability of disaster in these situations using words.

a

b

c

5 Put these events in order from most likely to happen to least likely to happen.

a The price of petrol will increase this year.

b If you toss a regular six-sided dice it will show an even number.

c Oxford or Cambridge will win the boat race.

d You will get 100% in your next maths test.

e It will not rain in January.

○ You can describe the **probability** of an event using words.

An even chance means something is equally likely to happen as not to happen.

It is *certain* that the sun will rise tomorrow.
It is *very unlikely* that you will win the lottery.

○ You can show a scale of probabilities like this.

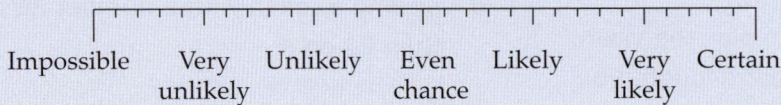

Impossible   Very   Unlikely   Even   Likely   Very   Certain
unlikely   chance   likely

Example

Describe the probability of each event and mark it on the scale.
a   It will snow in July in Hawaii.
b   You will flip a coin and get Heads.
c   You are in a maths class.

a   This is almost impossible, but could happen!
b   There is an even chance this would happen.
c   This is almost certainly the case!

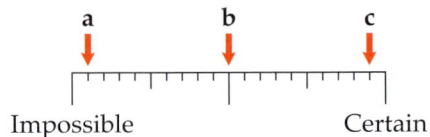

a   b   c

Impossible   Certain

You can use probability to help you work out your chances of something happening in real-life situations.

Example

Daniel has ten biscuits in a bag. Two are chocolate, eight are plain.
Daniel sticks his hand in the bag and pulls out a biscuit without looking.
How likely is it that he will choose
a   a chocolate biscuit
b   a plain biscuit
c   a fruit biscuit?

a   Unlikely – there are only two.
b   Likely – there are eight to pick from.
c   Impossible – there are no fruit biscuits for him to choose.

Exercise 16b

1 Match each event with the probability that it will happen.

Impossible   Very unlikely   Even chance

Very likely   Certain

a   You will watch TV tonight.
b   It will be dark tonight.
c   It will rain tomorrow.
d   You will earn £1 million today.
e   A sheep will win a horse race.

2 Sam rolls an ordinary six-sided dice. Explain how likely he is to get a score that is
a   less than 4
b   an odd number
c   a multiple of 3
d   exactly 5.

3 Dave spins an ordinary coin six times. Explain in words how likely these results are.

a   The coin lands on heads all six times.
b   The coin lands on heads three times and tails three times.
c   The coin lands on tails eight times.

4 Carla places raffle tickets numbered 1 to 60 in a bag, and picks one out without looking.
Give an example of an outcome that is
a   certain
b   impossible
c   very likely (but not certain)
d   very unlikely (but not impossible).

Problem solving

5 Put this list of events in order of probability, with the **most likely** events at the top of the list and the **least likely** ones at the bottom.
Explain your answers.
a   You will go swimming during the next week.
b   You will use a computer in the next 24 hours.
c   You will use a telephone within the next week.
d   You will fly in a plane within the next week.
e   You will have an English lesson tomorrow.

6 How likely are these events?
a   You roll a regular six-sided dice.
   i   You score an odd number.
   ii   You score a factor of 6.
   iii You score a multiple of 3.
b   You toss two coins.
   i   You get two heads.
   ii   You get two tails.
   iii You get a head and a tail.

MyMaths.co.uk Q 1209 SEARCH

You can use numbers to describe probabilities.

> ● The **probability scale** uses values between 0 and 1.
> ▶ A **certain** event has probability 1 (100%).
> ▶ An **impossible** event has probability 0 (0%).
> ▶ An **even chance** event has probability $\frac{1}{2}$ (0.5 or 50%).

Probabilities can be given as fractions, decimals or percentages.

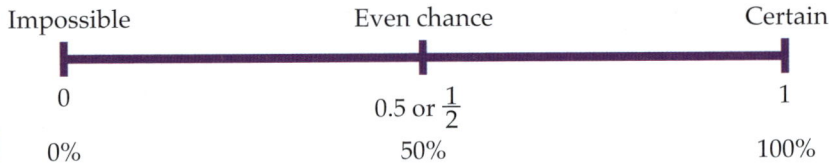

Impossible	Even chance	Certain
0	0.5 or $\frac{1}{2}$	1
0%	50%	100%

< p.80

Example

What is the probability of each event?
a You can balance a pencil upright on its point.
b You get an odd score when you roll an ordinary dice.
c You will eat something this week.

a This is almost impossible. The probability is close to 0 (0%).
b This has an even chance. The probability is $\frac{1}{2}$ (0.5 or 50%).
c This is almost certain. The probability is close to 1 (100%).

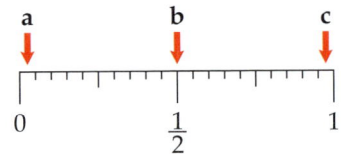

Example

Tyler is almost certain that he will have pasta for tea.
What could this be as a number?

'Almost certain' means a probability very close to 1.
If could be $\frac{95}{100}$ (0.95 or 95%) or higher.

I'm 100% sure that we've reached the end of the page!

Example

Eddie has 12 coloured marbles in a bag: 6 red, 4 blue and 2 white.
She picks out one marble at random. What is the probability that it is
a red   b blue   c white
d green   e red *or* blue   f *not* blue

a There are 6 red marbles and 12 to chose from.
   Probability is $\frac{6}{12} = \frac{1}{2}$

b Probability is $\frac{4}{12} = \frac{1}{3}$

c Probability is $\frac{2}{12} = \frac{1}{6}$

d There are *no* green marbles.
   Probability is $\frac{0}{12} = 0$

e Probability is $\frac{6+4}{12} = \frac{10}{12} = \frac{5}{6}$

f Red and white marbles are *not* blue.
   Probability is $\frac{6+2}{12} = \frac{8}{12} = \frac{2}{3}$

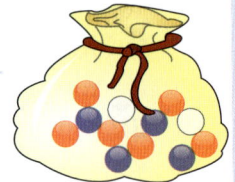

Exercise 16c

1 Match up the purple probability cards with the correct yellow description cards.

0.1	1%	100%

65%	0	0.5

Impossible	Quite likely	An even chance

Certain	Unlikely	Very unlikely

2 A weather forecast says,
'there is a 30% chance of rain tomorrow'.
What does this mean?

3 A game at a school fair has a poster saying, 'every entry wins a prize'.
What is the probability of winning the game?
Explain your answer.

4 Sophie has 10 marbles in a bag.
She picks one out.
What is the probability that it is

a blue
b red
c black

Hint: Use the number line to help you.

$$0 \quad \frac{1}{10} \quad \frac{2}{10} \quad \frac{3}{10} \quad \frac{4}{10} \quad \frac{1}{2} \quad \frac{6}{10} \quad \frac{7}{10} \quad \frac{8}{10} \quad \frac{9}{10} \quad 1$$

d green
e red *or* black
f red *or* blue
g red, blue *or* black?

Problem solving

5 Tom and Zachary are playing a board game.
Tom's dice lands on 6 for 39 rolls out of 100.
Zachary says it's not fair.
Is he correct?

6 Carry out an experiment.
a Take two coins and toss them both.
In a tally chart record whether you got two heads, two tails or one head and one tail. Repeat your experiment 40 times.
b Show your results in a bar chart.
c Explain whether or not your results are what you expected.

2 heads	1 head 1 tail	2 tails
II	IIII I	IIII

‹ p.146
‹ p.152

Riley has six shapes that he wants to sort into categories.
There are lots of ways that he can group the shapes.

Example

> A **set** is a collection of **objects**.

Sort Riley's shapes into these sets

a   the set of triangles   b   the set of green shapes.

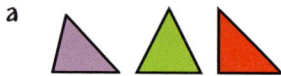

a   b

The objects in a set could be anything – numbers, words, letters, shapes...

> A Venn diagram uses circles to sort objects into sets.

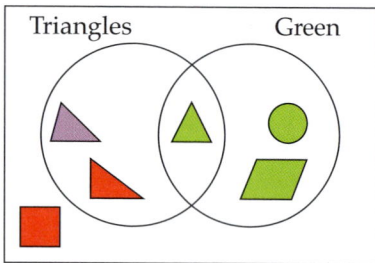

Triangles   Green

The green triangle is in both sets, so it goes in the overlap.

The red square goes outside the circles because it is not green or a triangle.

> You can draw Venn diagrams with numbers to show how many objects are each set.

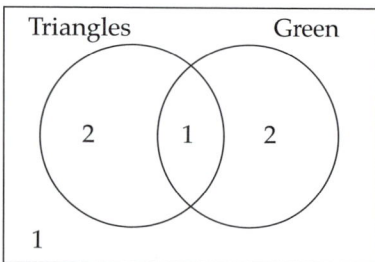

> You can describe the regions of a Venn diagram in words.

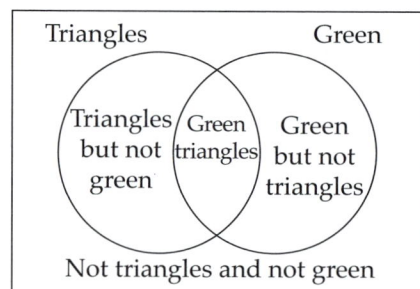

Triangles   Green

2   1   2

1

Triangles   Green

| Triangles but not green | Green triangles | Green but not triangles |

Not triangles and not green

There is 1 object, the red square, which is not a triangle and not green.

There are 2 objects, the green circle and the green rhombus, which are green but not triangles.

Exercise 16d

1 **a** Sort the numbers

1 2 3 4 5 6 7 8 9

into each Venn diagram.

b Write descriptions for each part of the Venn diagram.

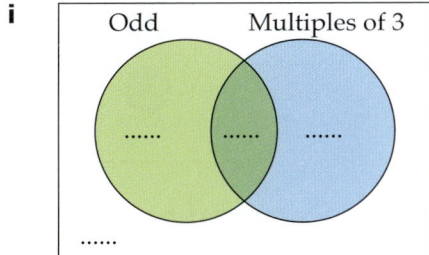

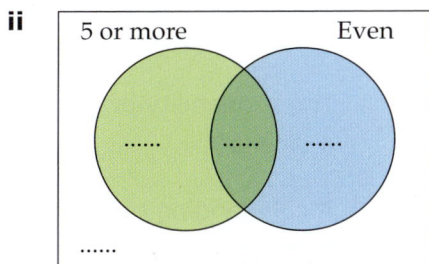

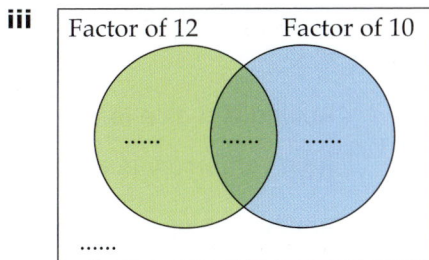

i

Odd   Multiples of 3

....

......

ii

5 or more   Even

....

......

iii

Factor of 12   Factor of 10

....

......

2 Complete the Venn diagram. Use numbers to show how many objects are in each set.

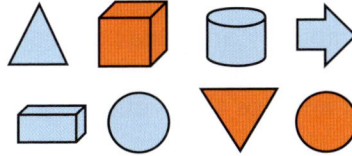

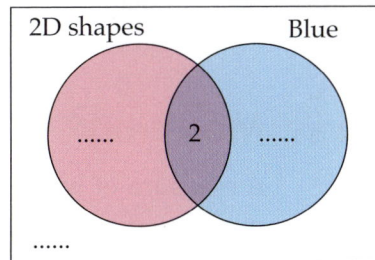

2D shapes   Blue

......   2   ......

......

3 Max asks 30 students at his school if they have a cat or a dog.

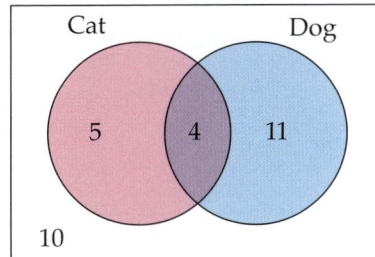

Cat   Dog

5   4   11

10

How many students have

a a cat but not a dog?

b a dog and a cat?

c a dog?

Problem solving

4 Match each group of objects to the correct Venn diagram.

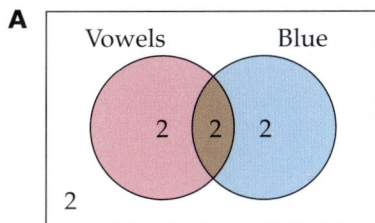

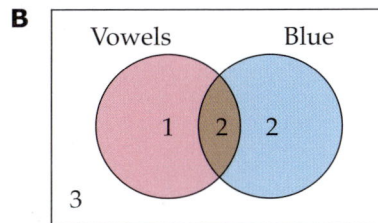

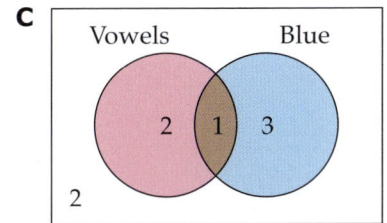

A

Vowels   Blue

2   2   2

2

B

Vowels   Blue

1   2   2

3

C

Vowels   Blue

2   1   3

2

1 A C E H
I M S T

2 A B I L
O P R T

3 A C E F
I N U Z

MyMaths.co.uk

1235   SEARCH

Check out

You should now be able to ...

Test it ➡

Questions

✓	Use the vocabulary and ideas of probability, drawing on experience.	4	1, 2
✓	Understand and use the probability scale from 0 to 1.	5	3
✓	Sort objects using a Venn diagram.	4	4

Language	Meaning	Example
Probability	A measure of how likely an outcome is to occur. It is described using words (certain, very likely, unlikely, ...) or numbers (50%, 0.85, $\frac{1}{4}$, ...).	The probability of it raining tomorrow is very unlikely. The probability of rolling a 6 on a dice is $\frac{1}{6}$.
Even chance	The probability for an event which is as likely to happen as not happen.	A coin landing heads up or a coin landing tails up.
Event	An activity.	The weather tomorrow is the event. Rolling the dice is the event.
Outcome	A result of an activity.	Rain tomorrow is an outcome. Rolling a 6 is an outcome.
Venn diagram	A diagram that sorts objects into sets.	

1 Describe the probability of these outcomes in words.

    a You will get an odd number when you roll a dice.

    b You will see a pig flying.

    c You will eat some food today.

    d It will rain in Newcastle on a randomly picked day in April.

2 The 26 letters of the alphabet are written on cards and put in a bag. One card is chosen at random. Describe the probability that it shows

    a the letter A

    b a consonant

    c the number 3.

3 Describe these probabilities using any of these words.

| Impossible | Very unlikely | Unlikely |
| Even chance | Likely | Very likely | Certain |

    a 0   **b** 0.2

    c 0.5   **d** 0.8

    e 1%   **f** 99%

    g 30%   **h** 100%

4 A group of students listed their hobbies. The Venn diagram shows how many said "listening to music" and "playing sport".

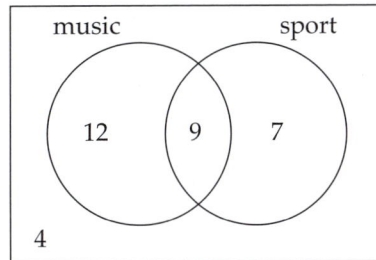

How many students

    a listen to music and play sport

    b play sport

    c listen to music

    d neither listen to music nor play sport?

5 Here is a collection of shapes.

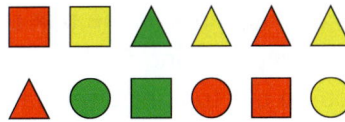

Copy the Venn diagram and sort the shapes into it.

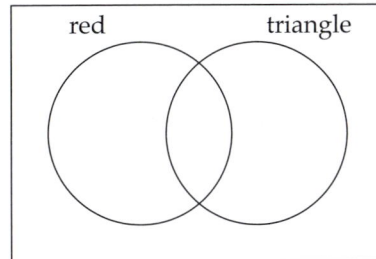

What next?

Score		
	0 – 2	Your knowledge of this topic is still developing. To improve look at Formative test: 1A-16; MyMaths: 1209 and 1235
	3 – 4	You are gaining a secure knowledge of this topic. To improve look at InvisiPen: 451 and 471
	5	You have mastered this topic. Well done, you are ready to progress!

16a

1 Read each statement and choose a word from the list that describes the chance of it happening.

> Certain
> Likely
> Unlikely Impossible
> Equal chance

a You will drink something before midnight.

b An elephant will become Prime Minister.

c The next person you phone will be a girl.

d You are looking at this book.

e You will walk on the sun tomorrow.

f You will find treasure in the park.

g It will snow in August.

h You will learn to drive a car at some time in your life.

2 Use one of the words in the box to classify each of these events.

> Certain
> Likely
> Unlikely
> Impossible
> Uncertain

a If you keep running for long enough you will tire out.
b If you go out tonight after dark you will see a full moon.
c If you go out on a very cold morning you will see ice.
d If you arrive at a level crossing and the gate is closed, a train is coming.
e The year 2076 will be a leap year.
f The year 2077 will be a leap year.

16b

3 If you are also able to choose from this list, can you give a better description for the events in question 2?

> Almost impossible
> Quite unlikely
> Even chance
> Very likely
> Almost certain

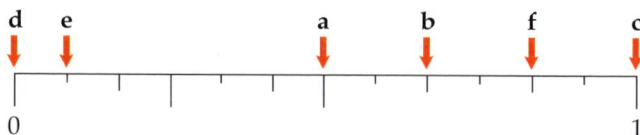

4 Use words to describe the probability of the points shown on this probability scale.

d e   a   b   f   c

0   1

5 Which statement best describes your chances of picking a red cube?

a		b		c	
	A good chance No chance Certain		Impossible Unlikely Certain		Certain Impossible Unlikely
d		**e**		**f**	
	Likely Unlikely Equal chance		Equal chance Unlikely Impossible		Unlikely No chance Equal chance

6 The dominoes shown here are shuffled and placed upside down on a table.

If one is then picked up, find the probability that it will have

a 7 dots **b** an odd number of dots

c an even number of dots **d** a five on it

e a four on it **f** a four *or* a five on it.

7 The Venn diagram shows the numbers 1–10 organised into even numbers and multiples of 3.

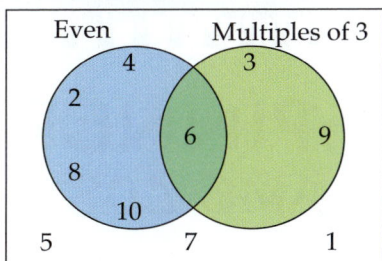

a Write down the numbers that are multiples of 3 but not even.

b Write down the numbers that are even but not multiples of 3.

c Write down the numbers that are neither multiples of 3 not even.

d Copy the Venn diagram and expand it to include all the whole numbers up to 20.

A school is holding a fair to raise money. They need to make sure that they make a profit.

Task 1

a What is your chance of winning if you have the red card?

b What is your chance of losing if you have the blue card?

c Is the stall holder right to say "A prize every game"? Do you think it is misleading?

SPIN IT TO WIN IT!

To play the game, pay 50p and choose a coloured card.

The spinner will spin when all 5 colours have been bought. The person with the colour the spinner stops at wins a prize!

a prize every game!

50p per go!

Task 2

Look at the notebook page entitled 'SPINNER GAME COSTS.' The total cost of prizes has been smudged out.

a Find the total cost of prizes for this game.

b How many games need to be played before the stall makes any profit?

Task 3

a Could the stall run out of the more expensive prizes before it makes a profit?

b Suggest how the stallholder could make the game fairer.

SPINNER GAME COSTS

3 cuddly toys @ £3.00 each
5 boxes of chocolates @ £2.20 each
10 key rings @ 20p each
10 cans of drink @ 25p each

Total cost of prizes:

308

Task 4

The tombola is filled with 100 tickets numbered from 1 to 100.

a Find the probability that the first person to buy a ticket wins a prize.

b Find the probability that the first person to buy a ticket does not win a prize.

c Find the probability that the first person to buy a ticket wins the watch.

d **(Challenge)** What is the largest profit that could be made from this game? How likely is that to happen?

Task 5 (Challenge)

Bethan is running a drinks stall.

She has bought 5 bottles of squash and 6 packs of cups.

Each bottle costs £1.80 and can make 30 cups of squash.

The packs of cups cost £2.20 each and there are 24 cups in a pack.

How much will Bethan need to charge per cup to ensure she makes a profit before she runs out of squash or cups?

50p per go

TOMBOLA
All tickets ending in 0 or 5 win a prize!

65

40

15

100

65

These questions will test you on your knowledge of the topics in chapters 13 to 16.
They give you practice in the types of questions that you may see in your GCSE exams.
There are 70 marks in total.

1 For these sequences
  a find the next two numbers in each sequence (3 marks)
  b say what is the difference between the numbers in each sequence. (3 marks)
  i 24, 20, 16, 12, …   **ii** 4, 6, 8, 10, …   **iii** 4, 9, 14, 19, …

2 Write a description for each sequence using 'start at …. and …. each time'.
  a 32, 16, 8, 4, … (2 marks)   **b** -11, -7, -3, 1, … (2 marks)
  c 17, 26, 35, 44, … (2 marks)   **d** 3, -1, -5, -9, … (2 marks)

3 Here is a description for a sequence 'start at -3 and +7 each time'.
  a Use this description to find the first three terms. (3 marks)
  b Write down the first five terms of a sequence if the description is
    'start at -4 and +7 each time'. (3 marks)

4 Use multiplication or division facts to calculate each answer.
  a 9 × 7 (1 mark)   **b** 8 × 5 (1 mark)
  c 32 ÷ 4 (1 mark)   **d** 81 ÷ 9 (1 mark)

5 Use multiplication facts to calculate each answer.
  a 62 × 10 (1 mark)   **b** 57 × 100 (1 mark)
  c 17 × 100 (1 mark)   **d** 23 × 10 (1 mark)

6 Use a number line and repeated subtraction to calculate each answer.
  a 47 ÷ 5 (1 mark)   **b** 96 ÷ 6 (1 mark)
  c 63 ÷ 4 (1 mark)   **d** 29 ÷ 7 (1 mark)

7 Use your calculator to answer these problems.
  a £4.07 ÷ 5 (1 mark)   **b** £9.64 × 6 (1 mark)
  c £9.87 − £4.51 (1 mark)

8 Mortar is being made by adding 1 part cement to 5 parts sand.
  a Write this as a ratio of cement to sand. (2 marks)
  b If 2 kg of cement is used how much sand is needed. (1 mark)
  c If 3 kg of cement is used how much mortar would you make. (2 marks)

9 To make 10 blueberry muffins you need 200 g of flour, 100 g of butter and 80 g of blueberries.

    a What is the ratio of flour to butter to blueberries?   (2 marks)

    b How much of each ingredient will you need to make

      i 30 muffins   **ii** 15 muffins?   (4 marks)

10 Using the recipe in question **9**, flour costs 97 p per 100 g, butter £1.30 per 200 g and blueberries £2.00 per 80 g.

    a How much does it cost for 200 g of flour?   (1 mark)

    b How much does it cost for 100 g of butter?   (1 mark)

    c How much does it costs to make 10 muffins?   (2 marks)

11 Describe the likelihood of these events using the list of words below.

impossible   unlikely   even chance   likely   certain

    a It will rain tomorrow.   (1 mark)

    b Obtaining a Head when you toss a coin.   (1 mark)

    c The sun will rise tomorrow.   (1 mark)

12 An ordinary six-sided dice is thrown.

Describe in words how likely it is to get a score

    a exactly one   (1 mark)

    b an odd number   (1 mark)

    c more than four.   (1 mark)

13 a For the dice thrown in question **12**, mark on the probability scale using the letters *a*, *b* and *c* the probability of these events occurring.   (3 marks)

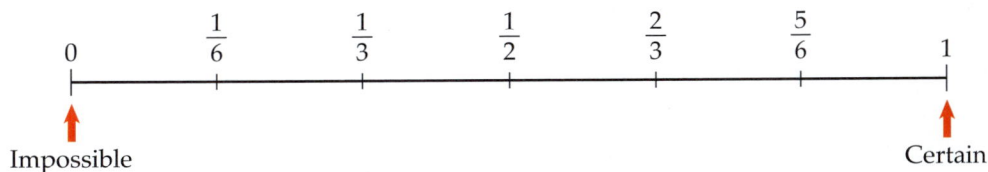

$$0 \quad \frac{1}{6} \quad \frac{1}{3} \quad \frac{1}{2} \quad \frac{2}{3} \quad \frac{5}{6} \quad 1$$

Impossible   Certain

    b Calculate each one of the events as a fraction.   (3 marks)

    c Write these probabilities as a percentage.   (3 marks)

14 In a sixth form 27 students study physics, 22 students study mathematics and 14 students study both subjects.

    a How many students do not study both subjects?   (2 marks)

    b Draw a Venn diagram to summarise this information.   (3 marks)

17 Everyday maths

In this chapter you will meet the students and teachers of Swinley School. The head teacher, Ms Beckford, has decided that Year 7 is to organise a swimming gala for the school. There is a lot to do, a surprising amount of which will need your mathematical skills – just like real life!

Solving real life problems often requires you to think for yourself and to use several areas of mathematics at once. If you are to be successful you will need to practice your basic skills.

Fluency – Do you know how to do arithmetic and basic algebra?

Reasoning – Can you work out what maths to use and show your workings mathematically?

Problem solving – Can you apply your skills to solving a problem?

Fluency

Fluency in arithmetic is vital in ensuring you manage your money effectively.

Every time you use a checkout you rely on the person who programmed the till having done so correctly. How do you know that you get the correct change?

Similarly, calculators can perform lots of amazing tasks, and can be a real help when working out hard sums. However their maths ability is only as good as the person who programmed them!

Reasoning

Working out the most efficient way of doing things often involves mathematical reasoning.

An example would be the most efficient way to lay out a pattern on a piece of cloth.

Similar problems have to be solved when arranging files on a hard drive so as to minimise wasted space or packing oranges in a box so as to reduce the need for packaging.

Problem solving

People use maths to solve problems in their daily working lives – not just mathematicians!

Distribution centres face a difficult task in planning the best routes, loads and timetables. To guide them, they collect data on fuel costs, journey times, stock shortages, and so on. By carefully analysing this data they can monitor and improve their performance.

17a The swimming gala

Ms Beckford, the head teacher, decides Year 7 students are going to have a swimming gala. She tells the Year Group in assembly.

Fantastic!

Oh no

The year 7 swimming gala is in two weeks.

Disaster

Help

The first task for the head teacher is to check the school swimming pool.

This pool is a health and safety hazzard... Clean it up!

10 m

2 m

25 m

1 Using the diagram above
   a how wide is the swimming pool
   b how long is the swimming pool
   c how deep is the water in the pool?

Christos the Site Manager is called. His first job is to paint a red line around the edge of the swimming pool – this will mark the perimeter of the pool.

2 How many metres is the perimeter of the swimming pool?

The diving pool is a rectangle that measures 6 metres by 5 metres.

3 What is the perimeter of the diving pool?

Christos has to clean the tiles on the swimming pool wall. The end wall is 10 metres wide and 2 metres high.

4 How many metre squares is the area of the end wall?

The diving competition must take place.

I have a plan.

The diving platform is dangerous and cannot be used. Ms Beckford does not want to cancel the diving competition.

Mr Nutweed, the Technology teacher, says that a diving platform can be constructed using scaffolding poles.

Mr Nutweed produces this design.

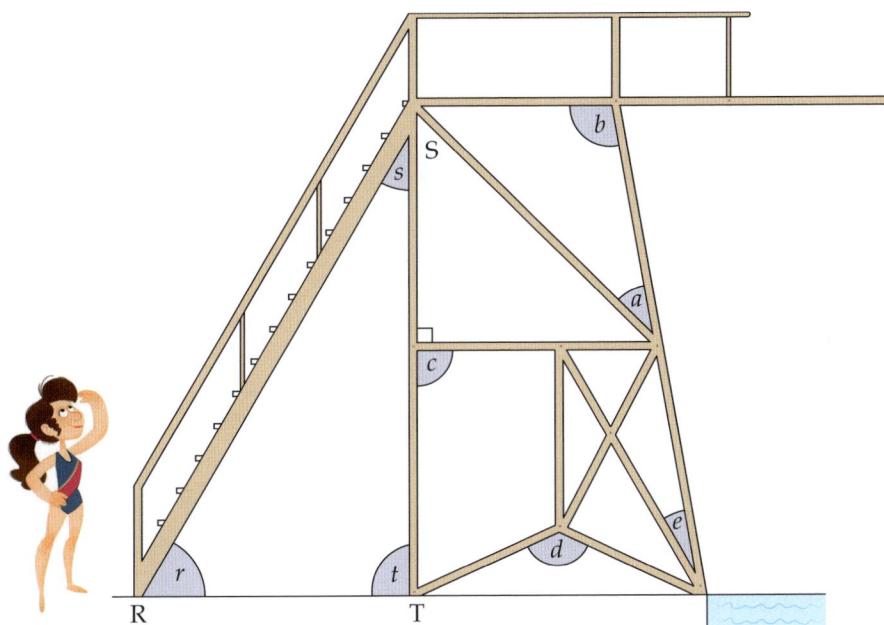

5 Ellen stands beside Mr Nutweed's diving platform. She is 1 metre and 50 centimetres tall. Use her height to estimate the total height of the diving platform.

6 How many triangles can you see in the drawing?

7 Decide if the following angles are: an *acute* angle, a *right* angle or an *obtuse* angle?

Angle *a* is ......   Angle *b* is ......   Angle *c* is ......

Angle *d* is ......   Angle *e* is ......

8 **a** RST is a triangle. Use a protractor to measure the angles of the triangle.

Angle *r* = _____°   Angle *s* = _____°   Angle *t* = _____°

b Add the three angles together.
What is the total?

MyMaths.co.uk

For safety, diving pools have to be very deep at one end.

Length

Shallow wall

Floor

?

1 a Use your ruler to measure the deepest part of the pool.
   The scale is 1 cm : 1 m.

   b Now find **i**   how long the pool floor is
             ii   the length of the pool
            iii   the depth of the shallow wall.

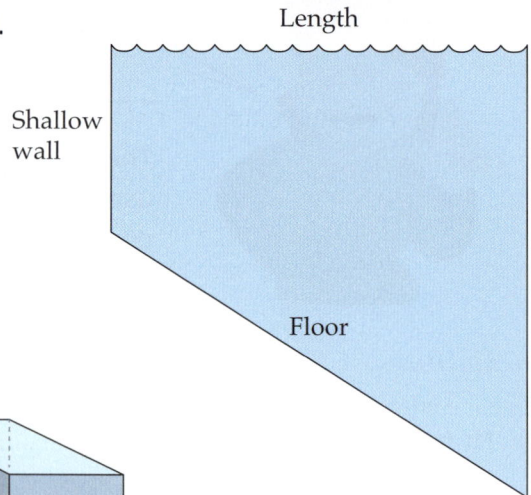

2 What is the name of the shape of this side wall view?

3 The 3D shape of the pool looks like this. Which of these nets could fold to make the pool shape?

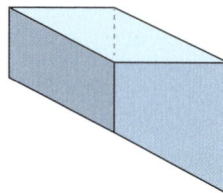

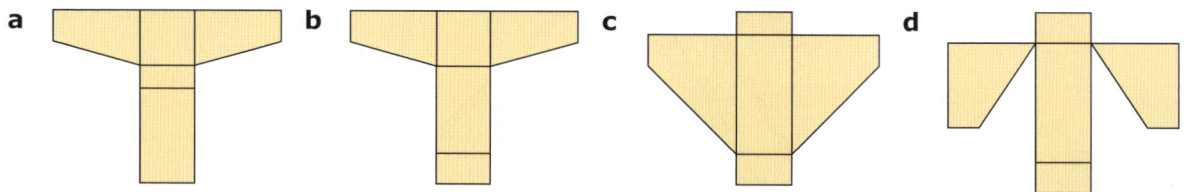

a   **b**   **c**   **d**

Lizzie offers to re-paint the empty pool.

Her friend Dennis plays a trick on her.
He has swapped the lids from the paint tins.

Ms Beckford told Lizzie to paint the pool blue.

4 a What is the probability that Lizzie will open the tin of blue paint?
   Write your answer as a fraction.

   b Whoops! Lizzie didn't pick blue.
   What was the probability of this happening?

5 Dennis thinks that she has more chance of opening the can of green paint because it is his favourite colour. Why is Dennis wrong?

It takes Lizzie 20 minutes to paint $\frac{1}{5}$ of the pool.

6 How many minutes will it take altogether?

7 Ms Beckford has allowed Lizzie 1 hour and 30 minutes to do the job. Will Lizzie finish in time?

There are four classes in Year 7.
Each class sells tickets for the gala.

Ms Beckford drew this tally chart showing the number of tickets shown by each class. She forgot to fill in the totals.

Class	Tally	Total
7A	﹢﹢﹢﹢ ﹢﹢﹢﹢ ﹢﹢﹢﹢ ﹢﹢﹢﹢ ﹢﹢﹢﹢ ﹢﹢﹢﹢	
7B	﹢﹢﹢﹢ ﹢﹢﹢﹢ ﹢﹢﹢﹢ ﹢﹢﹢﹢ ﹢﹢﹢﹢ II	
7C	﹢﹢﹢﹢ ﹢﹢﹢﹢ ﹢﹢﹢﹢ III	
7D	﹢﹢﹢﹢ ﹢﹢﹢﹢ ﹢﹢﹢﹢ ﹢﹢﹢﹢ ﹢﹢﹢﹢	

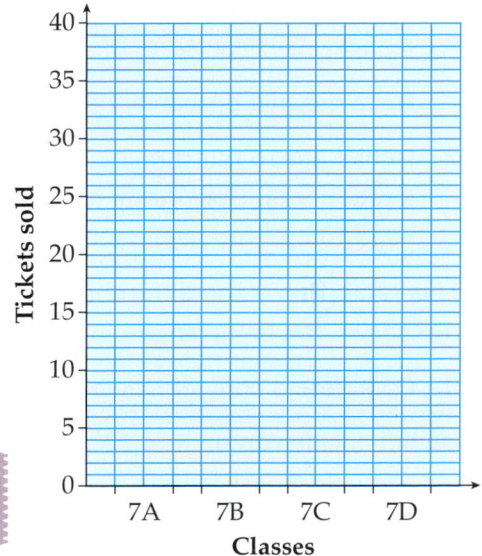

8 Help Ms Beckford by completing the **Total** column.

9 She wants to show the numbers of tickets sold by each class, in the school newsletter.
Draw a bar chart like this to show the results.

10 Use the chart to find the missing words in these sentences for the newsletter.

a Well done Year 7. They sold a total of .... tickets.

b Class 7 ... sold the most tickets, selling ...... tickets altogether.

c The range of sales is ......

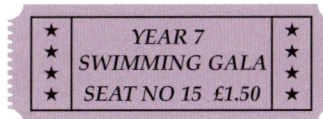

★ YEAR 7 ★
★ SWIMMING GALA ★
★ SEAT NO 15 £1.50 ★

Tickets cost £1.50 each.

11 Joel's job is to count and keep the money from ticket sales. Here is his record.
Complete Joel's record sheet.

12 Use the table to complete this line from the newsletter.

Year 7 collected a total of £......

Class	Tickets sold	Total
7A	30	30 × £1.50 = £45
7B		
7C	18	18 × £1.50 = ?
7D		
	Total	

13 Joel tells Ms Beckford that Year 7 have sold a half of the total number of seats.
How many seats are there altogether?

14 The rest of the tickets can be bought 'on the door'.
Tickets sold on the door will cost £2.50 each.
How much more money can be made?

15 All tickets for the gala were sold in the end.
Complete this line of the newsletter for Ms Beckford.

The total of money raised by the gala was £......

Joel pays the money into the school fund and the last sentence of the newsletter says

Thanks to our swimming gala, we now have £2350

16 How much money was there in the school fund *before* the swimming gala?

My Maths.co.uk

Daniel is setting out the 160 chairs needed for the crowd.

1 The chairs come in four colours. ■ ■ ■ ■
There are equal numbers of each colour.

   a Complete a copy of this sentence.

> The chance of sitting in a blue chair
> is .... out of ....

   b Write this probability as a fraction.

2 Daniel has to put the chairs into two equal sized blocks. How many chairs will he need to put into each block?

This table shows the different ways in which the chairs can be arranged in a block.

3 Complete a copy of Daniel's table for him.

Number of chairs in a row	Number of rows	Total
8	10	8 × 10 = 80
		= 80
		= 80
		= 80

Daniel decides on an 8 × 10 arrangement for each block.

Here is part of his arrangement.
It shows rows A to H and columns 1 to 10.

4 How many more chairs are needed to finish this block?

5 **a** Daniel's brother Joel, is sat in seat (1, G). What is the colour of his chair?

   b His sister Jessie is sat beside Joel. What is her seat number?

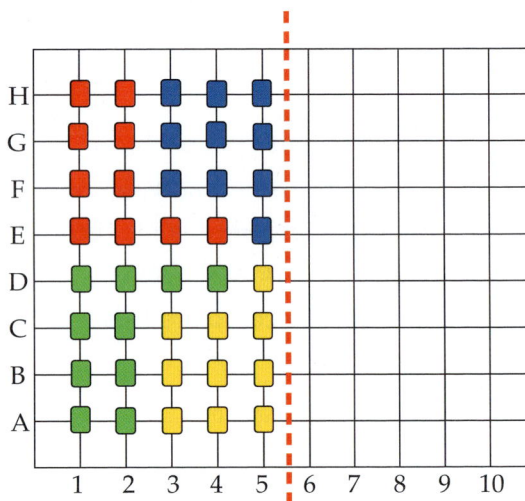

6 Melanie's seat number is (2, C).
She wants to swap her place to sit in a blue chair.
What is the seat number of the nearest blue chair?

7 Daniel wants the colours of chairs to be symmetrical in the dotted line drawn on his plan. Which of these arrangements will complete the plan so that it is symmetrical?

A   B   C   D

   6 7 8 9 10   6 7 8 9 10   6 7 8 9 10   6 7 8 9 10

The pool is 25 metres long.
Students are about to finish the
25 metre sprint.

8 How far does each swimmer have to
swim to finish?

9 At this point in the race, how far is
the swimmer in Lane 1 ahead of the
swimmer in Lane 2?

10 David swims 5 lengths of the pool
in training.
How many metres is this?

Each swimmer has been timed. Here are
the results.

7A – Ahmed   27.7 seconds
7B – Jack   28.0 seconds
7C – Rio   25.6 seconds
7D – Ryan   27.0 seconds

11 a Who came first?
   b Who came third?

The swimming lanes are divided by
ropes, suspended on floats.

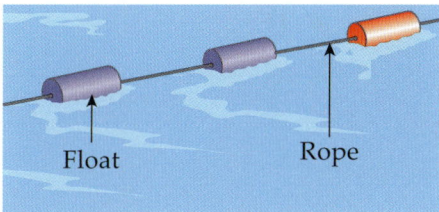

Float   Rope

There are 16 floats on each lane rope.
4 of the floats are red (2 red floats at each end).
2 green floats mark the half-way point.
The other floats are blue.

12 In total how many of the floats in the pool are
   a blue?   **b** red?   **c** green?

13 How many metres of rope are used to mark out the lanes?

14 a What proportion of the floats are green?
   b What is the ratio of green to red to blue floats?

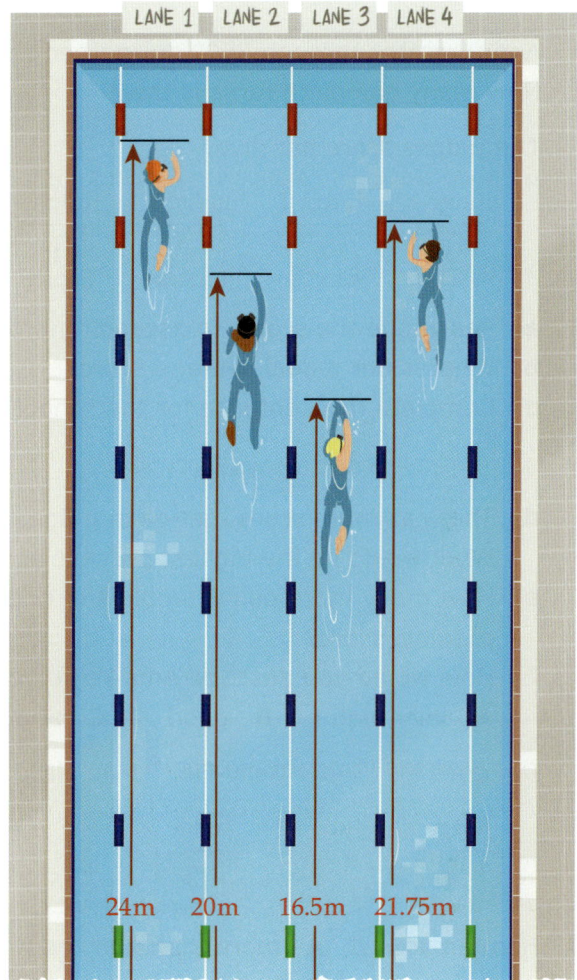

LANE 1   LANE 2   LANE 3   LANE 4

24m   20m   16.5m   21.75m

1   Amira rotates through 360° during her dive.
How many complete turns is this?

The judges score her dive.

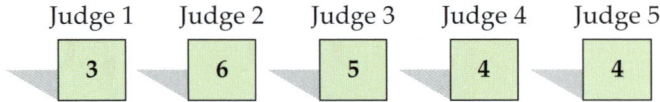

Judge 1	Judge 2	Judge 3	Judge 4	Judge 5
3	6	5	4	4

2   **a**   Rearrange the scores in ascending order.

  b   What is her modal average score?

  c   Complete this sentence for the school newsletter.

   Amira's median average score was ......

  d   The maximum score that each judge can give is 6.
     What would be the highest possible score that can be achieved?

  e   How many more points would she need to reach the maximum
     possible score?

  f   How would you describe Amira's score? Say why.

     A   very high   **B**   good   **C**   about average   **D**   low

Ian does his 'Super Belly-Flop' dive. Here are his scores.

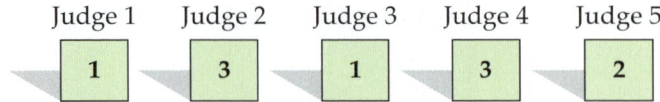

Judge 1	Judge 2	Judge 3	Judge 4	Judge 5
1	3	1	3	2

3   Has Ian scored   **A**   more than half the maximum points

            B   half the maximum points

            C   less than half the maximum points?

4   In Team 7C, Karl scores the points below. His total was 24.
What score did Judge 5 give him?

Judge 1	Judge 2	Judge 3	Judge 4	Judge 5
6	2	5	5	?

5   Alisha is in Team 7C.

  a   What is her score so far?

   Team 7A is Mr Leeson's
   class. They are not doing
   very well, so he starts
   cheating! He gives
   Alisha a score of -4.

3	5	3	6	
Ms Morris	Mrs Wild	Mr Storm	Mr Ford	

3	5	3	6	-4
Ms Morris	Mrs Wild	Mr Storm	Mr Ford	Mr Leeson

  b   When we include
   Mr. Leeson's score, what is Alisha's new total?

In the Pool Café, Carol the manager checks the tea and coffee machine.

6 Copy and complete the sentences about the readings on the dials.

    a The pressure is ………… bars.   **d** The hot water temperature is …………… °C.

    b The electricity reading is ………… volts.   **e** The hot milk temperature is ………… °C.

    c There are ………… litres of water in the machine.

All food items in the Pool Café are marked with a symbol that tells the price.

$a = 30p$ $b = 40p$ $c = 50p$ $d = 60p$ $e = 85p$

cake   tea   crisps   coffee   sandwich

apple   pie   soup   cola   roll

An order for a cup of tea and a cake will be expressed like this………

$b + a =$
$40p + 30p =$

7 Using the symbols, write expressions for the cost of items shown in these pictures.

    a   **b**   **c**

8 How much do these bills come to, using these expressions. The first one is done for you.

    a $c + e$ **b** $a + c$ **c** $c + b$ **d** $d + b + a$

        $= 50 + 85 = 135p$ or £1.35   **e** $a + e + b$ **f** $a + a + d$ **g** $b + e + b$

17e The invitation event

Students of all ages can enter the event but it would be *unfair* for a Year 11 student to race a year 7 pupil.

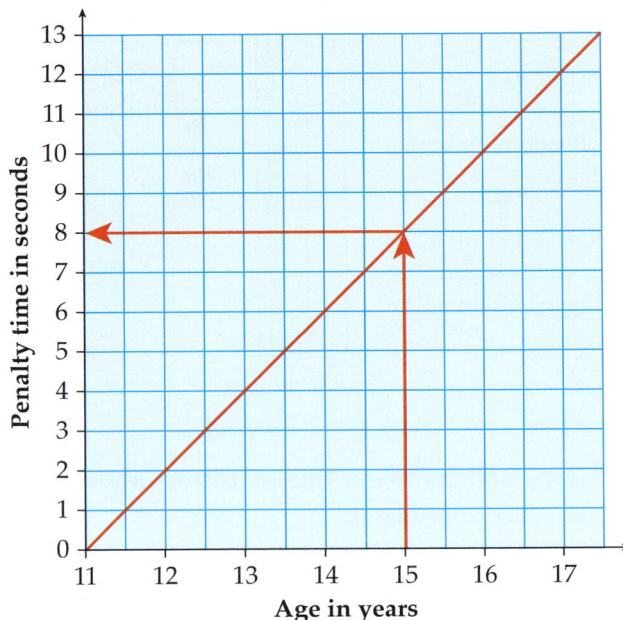

Its not fair.

So older pupils get a *time penalty*.
The older the student, the bigger the time penalty added to their time.

Using the graph, a 15 year old student will have 8 seconds added to their time.

1 What are the final times, including the time penalties, for these swimmers?

   a Connor (aged 12) finished in 31 seconds.

   b Grace (aged 14) finished in 25 seconds.

   c Iman (aged 13) finished in 29 seconds.

   d Rio (aged 17) finished in 20 seconds.

   e Eric (aged $13\frac{1}{2}$) finished in 27 seconds.

2 After adding the penalty times, who came 1st, 2nd, 3rd, 4th and last?

While the final results are calculated, the Parents versus Teachers Relay takes place!

The teachers line up for a photograph.
Using the clues, work out how old the teachers are!

91 years
51 years   56 years   96 years

Mr Adams   Ms Brown   Mrs Court   Mr Dean

The combined ages of pairs of teachers are shown above their heads.
The total age of the teachers is 147 years.
Mr Adams is 27 years old.

3 How old is

   a Ms Brown   **b** Mrs Court   **c** Mr Dean?

Imran records the scores for the events.

The winners have the most points.

	Team	Crawl		Backstroke		Breaststroke		Diving	Totals
		25 m	50 m	25 m	50 m	25 m	50 m		
		Points		Points		Points		Points	
Boys	7A	3	2	4	1	1	4	1	
	7B	2	1	3	3	4	1	4	18
	7C	4	3	4	2	2	3	2	
	7D	1	1	2	4	3	2	3	
Girls	7A	1	2	4	4	1	3	3	
	7B	2	4	1	3	3	2	4	
	7C	3	1	3	2	2	4	1	
	7D	4	3	2	1	4	1	2	17

4 Complete Imran's table to find the total points for each class, for both boys and girls.

5 Ms Beckford writes this in her newsletter. Use the table above to check to see if she is correct.

   a In the Boys' Crawl, Team 7C were best and Team 7D came last.

   b The Girls' Backstroke events were won by Team 7A.

   c The Girl's Diving event was won by Team 7C.

   d The boys overall winners were Team 7C.

   e The overall winners in the girls' competition were Team 7A.

6 a The Dolphin Trophy was awarded to the team (boys and girls together), who came first. Who won the trophy?

   b Which teams in came 2nd, 3rd and 4th positions?

Year 7 swimmers

7 The 'Wooden Spoon' was awarded to the team who never had a first position. Who won this award?

8 This bar graph shows the points scored by the boys and girls for each team. Use your table to complete the bar graph.

Graph of boys' and girls' points scored

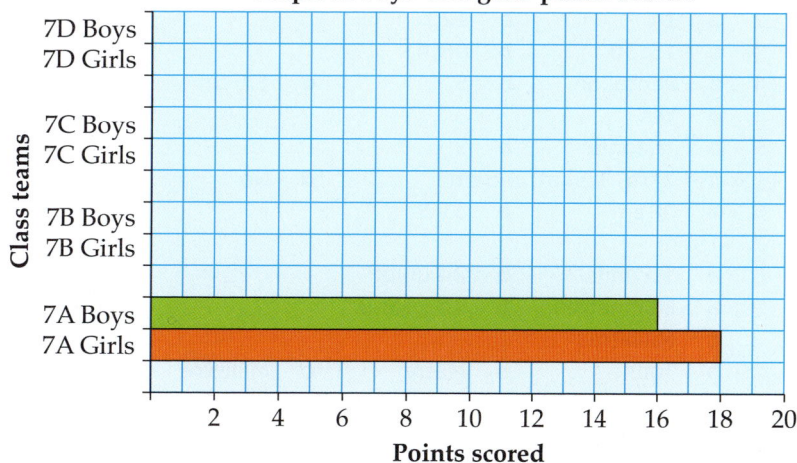

(Class teams: 7D Boys, 7D Girls, 7C Boys, 7C Girls, 7B Boys, 7B Girls, 7A Boys, 7A Girls; Points scored axis: 2, 4, 6, 8, 10, 12, 14, 16, 18, 20)

Ms Beckford has invited an Olympic swimmer to present the trophy.

He competed in the Tokyo Olympics of 1964! He was 26 years old when he competed.

9 How old is the Olympian now?

MyMaths.co.uk

Check in 1

1 **a** 4, 5, 6, 7, 8   **b** 10, 11, 12, 13, 14, 15
2 **a** 7 + 3 = 10   **b** 5 + 9 = 14
   c 8 + 4 = 12   **d** 4 + 6 = 10
3 Level 0

MyReview 1

1 **a** 6 hundreds, 600
   b 6 units, 6   **c** 6 tenths, 0.6
   d 6 tens, 60
2 88, 208, 280, 802, 820
3 **a** 91.6   **b** 418.1   **c** 70.4
   d 8052.5
4 **a** >   **b** <   **c** >
   d <
5 25p
6 **a** 84p   **b** 324p = £3.24
7 **a** -6 °C   **b** -5 °C   **c** 0 °C
   d -9 °C
8 **a** 4470   **b** 4500   **c** 4000
9 **a** 135 cm   **b** 165 cm
10 **a** 3   **b** 36   **c** 7
   d 2   **e** 33   **f** 8
   g 36   **h** 4

Check in 2

1 **a** 12:15   **b** 4:45   **c** 10:10
2 Length: metre, millimetre, kilometre, centimetre
   Weight: gramme, tonne, kilogram
   Time: second, day, year, hour, century, week

MyReview 2

1 **a** 3.2 cm   **b** 4.7 cm
2 **a** 14   **b** 120
3 **a** 15:30   **b** 06:45
4 **a** Pentagon   **b** 5   **c** 1.5 cm
   d Yes
5 **a** Triangle   **b** 3
   c 2 cm, 1.5 cm, 2.5 cm   **d** No
6 **a** 28 cm   **b** 31 cm
7 18 cm
8 **a** 10 units^2 **b** 24 units^2
9 **a** Millimetres   **b** Kilograms
   c Millilitres
10 **a** Tonne   **b** Metre   **c** Millilitre
   d Millimetre

Check in 3

1 **a** 17   **b** 24   **c** 4
2 **a** 2   **b** 7   **c** 5

d 4   **e** 3   **f** 6
g 8   **h** 1
3 Michael   11 + 4 = 15
   Billy   6 + 4 = 10
   Kevin x + 4

MyReview 3

1 $n - 2$
2 $2m$
3 **a** 120   **b** $15p$ **c** $15q + r$
4 $25 - d$
5 **a** $2a$ **b** $7b$ **c** $20c$
6 **a** $2f$ **b** $16g$ **c** $5h$
   d $5i$
7 **a** 9   **b** 2   **c** 15
   d 25
8 **a** 6   **b** 16   **c** 48
   d 3   **e** 8   **f** -8
9 **a** Number of spoons = 2 × number of people
   b $s = 2p$ **c** 24
10 **a** $W = L + 2$ **b** 9

Check in 4

1 **a** $\dfrac{6}{12} = \dfrac{1}{2}$ **b** $\dfrac{2}{8} = \dfrac{1}{4}$ **c** $\dfrac{6}{9} = \dfrac{2}{3}$

MyReview 4

1 **a** $\dfrac{2}{3}$ **b** $\dfrac{5}{9}$
2 **a** $1\dfrac{1}{2}$ **b** $2\dfrac{1}{3}$ **c** $3\dfrac{3}{4}$
3 **a** $\dfrac{8}{3}$ **b** $\dfrac{5}{4}$ **c** $\dfrac{15}{2}$
4 **a** $\dfrac{1}{3}$ **b** $\dfrac{5}{20}$ **c** $\dfrac{1}{2}$
   d $\dfrac{1}{4}$
5 **a** 5   **b** 4   **c** 10
   d 6
6 **a** 16   **b** 12   **c** 6
7 **a** 4   **b** 8   **c** 12
   d 20   **e** 24   **f** 10
8 **a** 6   **b** 18   **c** 24
   d 30   **e** 42   **f** 60
9 **a** **i** $\dfrac{1}{10}$ **ii** 0.1
   b **i** $\dfrac{1}{5}$ **ii** 0.2
   c **i** $\dfrac{2}{25}$ **ii** 0.08
   d **i** $\dfrac{1}{2}$ **ii** 0.5

Check in 5

1. **a** 120   **b** 30   **c** 145
   d 90   **e** 160   **f** 230
   g 175   **h** 180
2. **a** 55   **b** 68   **c** 87
   d 100   **e** 114   **f** 126

MyReview 5

1. **a** 45°   **b** 140°
2. **a** 150°, obtuse
   b 45°, acute
   c 90°, right-angle
   d 300° reflex
3. **a** 40°   **b** 75°
4. **a** 140°   **b** 20°
5. **a** 240°   **b** 165°
6. **a** 53°   **b** 68°
7. **a** $a = 54°$, scalene
   b $b = 45°$, right-angled and isosceles
   c $c = d = e = 60°$, equilateral
   d $f = 80°$, $e = 20°$, isosceles
8. North

Check in 6

1. **a, b**

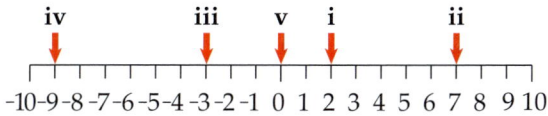

   -10 -9 -8 -7 -6 -5 -4 -3 -2 -1 0 1 2 3 4 5 6 7 8 9 10

2. **a** 4   **b** 7   **c** 2.5
   d 7.5

MyReview 6

1. A (6, 3)   B (2, 5)   C (0, 3)
   D (4, 1)
2. E (2, -1)   F (-3, 4)   G (-2, 0)
   H (-4, -2)
3.

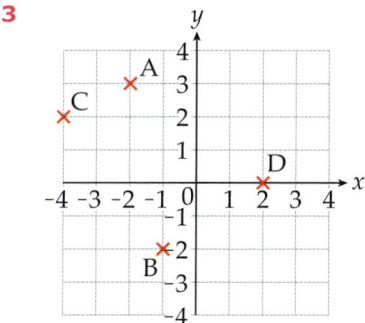

4. Graph **c**
5. **a** 7 cm   **b** day 3

Check in 7

1. **a** 3   **b** 8   **c** 5
   d 9   **e** 7
2. **a** 11   **b** 90   **c** 24
   d 260
3. **a** 5   **b** 20   **c** 12
   d 35

MyReview 7

1. **a** 80   **b** 95   **c** 50
   d 78   **e** 7   **f** 30
   g 35   **h** 69   **i** 82
   j 120   **k** 379   **l** 189
2. **a** 41   **b** 47   **c** 20
   d 35   **e** 55   **f** 35
   g 38   **h** 61   **i** 128
   j 196
3. **a** 78   **b** 987   **c** 41
   d 411
4. **a** 92   **b** 1053   **c** 18
   d 119
5. **a** 169   **b** 114   **c** 1245
   d 506
6. **a** 334p = £3.34 **b** 166p = £1.66

Check in 8

1. **a** iii   **b** ii
2. **a** $\frac{1}{2}$ **b** $\frac{1}{4}$ **c** $\frac{1}{8}$
   d $\frac{1}{8}$

MyReview 8

1. Possible questions include
   How often do you come to the cinema in a year:
   1 / 2 – 12 / 13 – 48 / more?
   What is your favourite type of film:
   comedy / thriller / horror / other?
   What age group are you in:
   0 – 10 / 11 – 18 / 18 – 30 / older?
   How many miles have you travelled to get to the cinema:
   0 – 1 / 2 – 5 / 6 – 20 / further?

2.

Shape	Frequency
Square	6
Circle	3
Triangle	5

3. **a** Saturday   **b** 3.5 hours

4 a 10   **b** 50

   c 4 people

   d

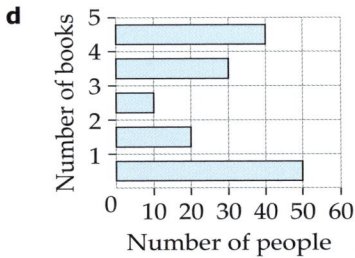

5 a Packed lunch **b** $\frac{1}{2}$

6 a 3   **b** 14 and 16 **c** 28

   d No mode

7 a i 4   **ii** 4

   b i 15.5   **ii** 7

   c i 27   **ii** 5

   d i 5   **ii** 4

Check in 9

1 a Clockwise 90° **b** Anticlockwise 90°

   c Clockwise or anticlockwise 180°

2 a (1, 1), (1, 4), (3, 1)

   b (1, 1), (1, 3) (5, 3) (5, 1)

   c (2, 1), (2, 5), (4, 4), (4, 0)

MyReview 9

1 a 1   **b** 2   **c** 3

   d 5

2 a   **b**

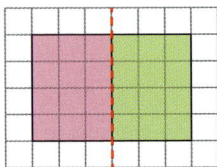   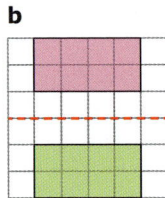

   c   **d**

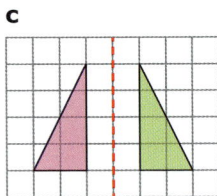   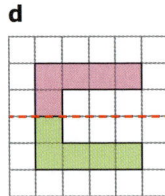

   e   **f**

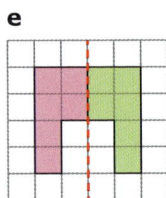   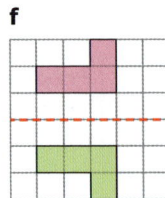

3 a 6 right, 3 down

   b 6 left, 3 up

   c 2 right, 4 down

   d 2 left, 4 up

   e 4 left, 1 down

   f 4 right, 1 up

4

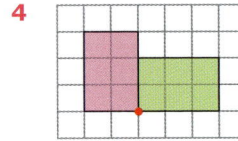

5

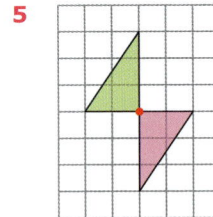

6 For example

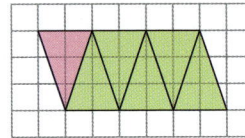

Check in 10

1 a 22   **b** 12   **c** 31

   d 15   **e** 36   **f** 9

   g 24   **h** 8

3 a $p + 5$ **b** $k - 100\,\text{cm}$

MyReview 10

1 a 12   **b** 7   **c** 36

   d 4

2 a $\times 11$ **b** $\div 10$ **c** -5

   d $+ 12$

3 a -7   **b** $+ 9$ **c** $\div 4$

   d $\times 3$

4 a 6   **b** 18   **c** 14

   d 12   **e** 16   **f** 50

5 a 4   **b** 5   **c** 9

   d 7   **e** 0   **f** 11

6 12 kg

7 a 6   **b** 35   **c** 11

   d 32

Check in 11

1 a 10   **b** 70   **c** 7

   d 5   **e** 9   **f** 10

2 a Even   **b** Odd   **c** Even

   d Odd   **e** Odd   **f** Odd

MyReview 11

1 **a** 1, 2, 4
   b 1, 2, 3, 6
   c 1, 2, 4, 5, 10, 20
   d 1, 5, 25
   e 1, 2, 13, 26
   f 1, 2, 3, 5, 6, 10, 15, 30
   g 1, 2, 3, 4, 6, 9, 12, 18, 36
   h 1, 2, 4, 11, 22, 44
2 **a** 1, 2, 3, 4, 6, 12
   b 1, 3, 5, 15   **c** 1, 3
3 **a** 3, 6, 9, 12, 15, 18, 21, 24, 27, 30, 33, 36, 39, 42, 45
   b 5, 10, 15, 20, 25, 30, 35, 40, 45, 50
   c 15, 30, 45
4 7, 14, 21, 28, 35, 42, 49, 56, 63, 70
5 1, 2, 5 and 10
6 **a** 110, 120, 130
   b 220, 230, 240, 250, 260
   c 510, 520, 530, 540
   d 1020, 1030, 1040, 1050, 1060, 1070, 1080
7 **a** 88   **b** 146   **c** 1002
   d 1010
8 **a** 72   **b** 240   **c** 160
   d 444
9 **a** 87   **b** 363   **c** 588
   d 675
10 **a** 240 or 270   **b** 420 or 440
   c 315, 330 or 345
11 **a** 25   **b** 49   **c** 1
   d 121

Check in 12

1 Accept within 10° of exact values.
   a 25°   **b** 130°   **c** 300°
2 Check student's work for circle with 10 cm diameter.

MyReview 12

1 **a** Cuboid   **b** 6   **c** 12
   d 8
2 **a** B and C
   b There are 9 other possible nets.

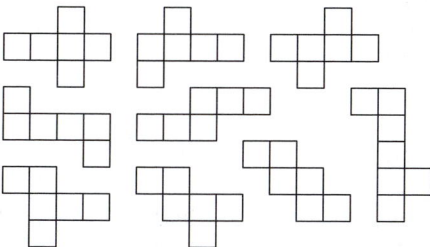

3 Cylinder
4 **a**   **b**

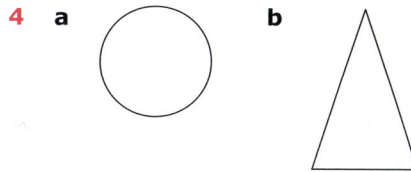

5 **a** Accurate drawings will have the following measurements correct.
   b **i** $p = 74°$, $p = 56°$
     ii $u = 32°$, $v = 58°$
     iii $x = 42°$, $y = 86°$
   b **i** $r = 5.6$ **ii** $w = 9.4$ **iii** $z = 7.1$
6 **a** **i** 1.5 cm   **ii** 3 cm
   b Check accuracy of circle, diameter 6 cm.

Check in 13

1 **a** 20, 22, 24, 26, 28
   b 11, 13, 15, 17, 19
2 **a** -9 °C, -2 °C, 1 °C, 3 °C, 5 °C
   b -7 , -3 , -1 , 0 , 1 , 2 , 4

MyReview 13

1 2, 4, 6, …
2 **a** 15, 18   **b** 21, 25   **c** 32, 38
   d 51, 63   **e** 42, 40   **f** 28, 20
3 **a** Start at 7 and add 10
   b Start at 9 and add 7
   c Start at 30 and subtract 3
   d Start at 2 and double / multiply by 2
   e Start at 3 and multiply by 4
   f Start at 200 and halve / divide by 2
4 **a** **i** Start at 1 and add 3
     ii 13, 16
   b **i** Start at 26 and add subtract 3
     ii 14, 11
5 **a** 3, 8, 13, 18
   b 7, 18, 29, 40
   c 50, 41, 32, 23
   d 2, 10, 50, 250
   e 1, 6, 36, 216
   f 5000, 500, 50, 5
6 **a** -12, -8, -4, 0, 4
   b -1, -3, -5, -7, -9
   c -18, -11, -4, 3, 10
7 **a** Start with -17 and add 6
   b Start with -5 and subtract 3
8 **a** 9, 2, -5, -12   **b** -14, -6, 2, 10
   c -7, -18, -29, -40

Check in 14

1
  a   33 + 16 = 49
  b   28 − 12 = 16
  c   56 + 23 = 79
  d   164 − 52 = 112
  e   615 + 342 = 957

MyReview 14

1   63

2   **a** 40   **b** 24   **c** 42
    d 99

3   **a** 80   **b** 210   **c** 174
    d 36 000

4   **a** 3   **b** 10

5   **a** 150   **b** 280   **c** 48
    d 90

6   **a** 135   **b** 2154   **c** 686
    d 2652

7   **a** 45   **b** 6.4   **c** 5
    d 3   **e** 6   **f** 8

8   **a** 2 r 3   **b** 10 r 1   **c** 9 r 4
    d 59 r 2

9   **a** 12 r 1   **b** 16 r 1   **c** 8 r 5
    d 8 r 8

10 **a** 6   **b** 5
    c Yes (144 < 150)

11 **a** £24.70   **b** £12.54   **c** £46.59
    d £3.19

Check in 15

1   **a** $\frac{3}{9} = \frac{1}{3}$ **b** $\frac{3}{12} = \frac{1}{4}$ **c** $\frac{7}{15}$
    d $\frac{4}{12} = \frac{1}{3}$

2   **a** 30   **b** 19   **c** 768
    d 22

3   **a** 300 cm   **b** 2.5 m   **c** 1500 g
    d 2 kg

MyReview 15

1   **a** **i** 2 : 1   **ii** $\frac{2}{3}$
    b **i** 2 : 3   **ii** $\frac{2}{5}$
    c **i** 1 : 4   **ii** $\frac{1}{5}$

2   **a** 1 : 4   **b** 12   **c** 2

---

3   **a** £50   **b** £110   **c** £200
    d £400

4   **a** £3   **b** £7.50   **c** £4.30
    d £5   **e** £16

5   **a** 4 m by 2 m   **b** 3 m by 15 m
    c 14 m by 16 m

6   Rectangle drawn 5 cm by 2 cm

Check in 16

1   **a** $\frac{1}{4}$ **b** 20 mins

2

Decimal	Percentage	Fraction
0.1	10%	$\frac{1}{10}$
0.5	50%	$\frac{1}{2}$
0.25	25%	$\frac{1}{4}$

MyReview 16

1   **a** Even chance   **b** Impossible
    c Certain   **d** Likely

2   **a** Unlikely   **b** Likely
    c Impossible

3   **a** Impossible   **b** Unlikely
    c Even chance   **d** Likely
    e Very unlikely   **f** Very likely
    g Unlikely   **h** Certain

4   **a** 9   **b** 16   **c** 21
    d 4

5

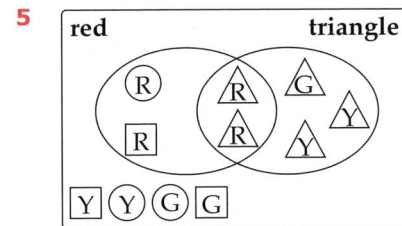

or

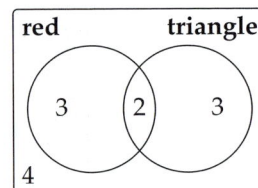

Index